CAMBRIDGE AIR SURVEYS

II

MEDIEVAL ENGLAND
AN AERIAL SURVEY

TO
F. R. SALTER (1887–1967)
IN GRATEFUL THANKS FOR HELP
AND ENCOURAGEMENT

MEDIEVAL ENGLAND
AN AERIAL SURVEY

M. W. BERESFORD
PROFESSOR OF ECONOMIC HISTORY IN THE
UNIVERSITY OF LEEDS

J. K. S. St JOSEPH
PROFESSOR OF AERIAL PHOTOGRAPHIC STUDIES IN THE
UNIVERSITY OF CAMBRIDGE

CAMBRIDGE UNIVERSITY PRESS

CAMBRIDGE

LONDON · NEW YORK · MELBOURNE

Published by the Syndics of the Cambridge University Press
The Pitt Building, Trumpington Street, Cambridge CB2 1RP
Bentley House, 200 Euston Road, London NW1 2DB
32 East 57th Street, New York, NY 10022, USA
296 Beaconsfield Parade, Middle Park, Melbourne 3206, Australia

First published 1958
Second edition 1979

Set, printed and bound in Great Britain by
Fakenham Press Limited, Fakenham, Norfolk

Library of Congress cataloguing in publication data

Beresford, Maurice Warwick, 1920–
Medieval England : an aerial survey.

(Cambridge air surveys; 2)
Includes bibliographies and index.
1. England – Historical geography.   2. Photography in
archaeology – England.   I. St Joseph, John Kenneth
Sinclair, joint author.   II. Title.   III. Series.
DA610.B4   1979   942   77-90200
ISBN 0 521 21961 2   8002

PREFACE TO THE SECOND EDITION

The revisions in this second edition fall into several categories. Firstly, those arising from the availability of more and better photographs, taken from new angles or in different seasons: some of these have been substituted for illustrations in the first edition. Whenever necessary, the commentaries have been revised to take account of the changed direction of view and of any additional features now revealed. Secondly, since 1958 photography of a far wider range of sites has been undertaken: some of these illustrate the themes of the book more adequately than those chosen for the first edition. Thirdly, the discarding of a few subjects has enabled us to add new topics that may appropriately be displayed in aerial photographs. In the commentaries on the remaining photographs we have corrected errors that have come to our attention, and have added new references to documentary sources or to published work, where relevant to the photograph.

We hope that these adjustments are in the best traditions of improving husbandry: to fashion new tools; to take in new ground; to adopt new approaches; but in general to maintain a pace of change that gives little comfort to those seeking 'revolutions' in the affairs of the field.

Our book was designed to set a treatment of specific examples within a general account of changes and survivals in the medieval landscape, but not to offer anything like a textbook of medieval economic history. In the twenty years since our text was completed in 1957 no large-scale textbook of medieval economic history has appeared, although a good deal about England can be learned from *The Cambridge Economic History of Europe* (I, 2nd revised edition, 1966, II, 1952, and III, 1963). Volume IV of *The Agrarian History of England and Wales* (1967) now provides an authoritative treatment of the transition from the medieval period, volume II has dealt with the Roman and Anglo-Saxon periods, and other medieval volumes are projected. Yet the medieval landscape rather than the medieval economy formed our central theme and, since the chronology and causation of change that we adopted is not dissimilar to that of these *Histories*, we have made no attempt to re-write our own linking commentary nor given references to these *Histories* in our footnotes, as we might had we been writing for the first time in 1977.

Work in landscape history itself has not lacked progress in the last twenty years, and the air photograph as a tool of study has assisted this progress of scholarship, whether in the hands of economic historians, historical geographers, fieldworkers, or archaeologists. When our first manuscript was completed, it may be noted, the periodical *Medieval Archaeology* was unborn and, although *The Making of the English Landscape* was published, Professor Hoskins had yet to write *Local History in England* and *Fieldwork in Local History*. We have assumed that any serious reader will have constant reference to these works as well as to the issues of *The Local Historian*, although again we would no doubt have made frequent reference to them had we been preparing a totally new book. At the local level, there have been valuable studies of non-Midland field-systems, particularly by Dr Alan Baker,[1] and of the totality of a local landscape in the recent *Dorset, Cambridgeshire* and

[1] A. R. H. Baker, 'Field-systems in the Vale of Holmesdale', *Ag.Hist.Rev.* XIV (1966) 1–24 and articles cited there.

Northamptonshire volumes of the Royal Commission on Historic Monuments. If we have not made extensive reference to these it is because Dr Baker's Kentish field-systems do not readily yield themselves to the aerial camera, while the Royal Commission volumes have themselves brought many aerial photographs to public view. Since 1957 one of us has published a long book on medieval town-scapes and been jointly responsible for a survey of village studies. With these available, we have not felt the need to revise or to elaborate those parts of the first edition embodying ideas that were developed in later books except where opinions expressed in 1957 seem to us untenable in 1977.

CAMBRIDGE   M. W. BERESFORD
June 1977   J. K. S. ST JOSEPH

PREFACE TO THE FIRST EDITION

The varied pattern of the English landscape with its towns and villages is a subject that lends itself particularly well to air photography. It seemed to the General Editors of the *Cambridge Air Surveys* that a representative series of photographs illustrating some of the many different aspects of settlement history would be very suitable for inclusion in the series. In 1951 Mr M. W. Beresford, then lecturer in Economic History at Leeds University, was invited to collaborate in such a book. A choice was made of photographs already available, and subjects that would make the collection more fully representative were proposed for future photography. Sometimes interesting photographs prompted search for documents; often well-documented sites led to suggestions for further photographs; and in this way the number of photographs grew rapidly. They proved valuable not only for presenting large towns and villages in a single comprehensive view which could be subjected to historical analysis, but as a means of research in historical topography.

The photographs have been chosen to illustrate a wide range of towns and villages, their communications, industries and agriculture. Many alternative sites might have been included and the selection has been limited, not for any lack of photographs (in the first draft of the book twice as many illustrations were chosen) but by the need to consider what could be presented in a volume of reasonable size. It only became apparent as the work proceeded, how much of the history of English villages is written in their plans. In the countryside, traces of medieval industry, of agriculture, quarrying, and of defences – whether the vast earthworks of castles or the small moats of fortified farmhouses – are clearly incised upon the surface of the land.

The preparation of this book fell into two parts. Mr Beresford undertook the primary documentation of the photographs chosen as illustrations, and this often involved search amongst records in public collections and in private hands. The planning of the necessary flights, the identification of the sites to be photographed, and the actual photography itself, are the work of the present writer. The text has been the subject of much consultation between the authors and is presented as the joint work of both. The photographs, all of which have been taken during the last few years in the course of special flights, have been chosen from the Cambridge University Collection of Aerial Photographs, where the original material may be consulted. While future flights will yield many further records of the kind with which this book is concerned, the photographs now available in the University Collection are numerous enough to provide widely representative illustrations of the subject. Photographs from the very extensive collections maintained by the Air Ministry have also been consulted by the authors, whenever it was thought that they might help in elucidating some special point.

The editors are indebted to the Air Ministry for permission to reproduce the air photographs which are Crown copyright. The authors wish to express thanks to the following for their kindness in giving information or providing maps or documents for study: the Rev. C. J. Collis, Rector of Whitechurch; Sir Edmund Craster, All Souls College, Oxford; Mr F. G. Emmison and Miss Hilda Grieve of the Essex Record Office; Dr E. J.

Fisher; the Rev. J. W. H. Faulkner, Rector of Cublington; Dr W. O. Hassall, Bodleian Library, Oxford; Mr P. I. King of the Northamptonshire Record Office; the Lord Leconfield; Mr R. B. Pugh and Mr P. M. Tillott of the Victoria County History Committee; the Rev. H. E. Ruddy, Rector of Braunston; Mr R. A. Skelton of the British Museum Map Room; the Earl Spencer; Mrs J. Varley of the Lincolnshire Archives Committee. Clive Semple and Clifford Farrar, friends and former students of Mr Beresford, enabled him to visit by car many of the places described in this book. Other assistance is acknowledged in the footnotes. The line-drawings in the text have been prepared at the University Press from original sketches by Dr K. J. Allison.

CAMBRIDGE   J. K. S. ST JOSEPH
May 1957

CONTENTS

MAPS AND PLANS

ACKNOWLEDGEMENTS

We are grateful to the following for permission to reproduce early plans:

The Shakespeare Birthplace Trust (fig. 5B, Ilmington, 1778); the Librarian of All Souls College, Oxford (7B, Padbury, 1591); the Lord Monson and Lincolnshire Archives Committee (8A, Broxholme, c. 1600); Public Record Office, London (14B, Carburton, 1615, 61B, Old Bolingbroke, 1718 and 66B, Old Byland, 1598); Sir Richard Hyde-Parker (26A, Long Melford, 1580); Trustees of the British Museum (28B, Aldborough, 1709); the Editor of *V.C.H. Huntingdonshire* (32B, Great Gidding, 1541); the Librarian, Cambridge University Library (32C, Great Gidding, 1858 and 73B, St Ives, 1808); the Rev. C. J. Collis (40B, Milton Abbas, 1771); Buckinghamshire Record Office (41A, Boarstall, 1444); Cambridgeshire Record Office (43B, Chippenham, 1712); Corporation of Chester (78A, Chester, c. 1580); the Lord Salisbury (79B, Berwick-upon-Tweed, c. 1575); Essex Record Office (96A, Chelmsford, 1591).

We are also grateful to the following for the use of maps and plans upon which figures are based:

Lord Leconfield (fig. 1B, Nun Monkton, 1607); Trustees of the British Library (2B, Toddington, 1581 and 3A, Leighton Bromswold, 1680); Northamptonshire Archives Committee (20B, Holdenby, 1580 and 1587); Jervaulx Abbey Estate Office (39B, East Witton, 1627); Nottinghamshire Record Office (42B, Ogle, 1632); Miss Hilda Grieve (96C, Chelmsford, reconstruction of Domesday topography); G. R. Walshaw, Esq., Colesbourne (111A, Marsh Chapel, 1595); the Librarian of All Souls College Oxford (117B, Padbury, 1591).

Figs. 2B, 32A, 80B, 111A, 117B and C are reproduced from the first edition of this book, for which they were prepared. Figs. 1B, 3A, 20B, 39B, 42B, 96C, 103B, 104B and 119 were drawn by B. M. Thomason. The assistance of Mr N. B. Clayton in editing and in 'seeing' the material through the press is much appreciated.

ABBREVIATIONS USED IN THE SOURCES AND FOOTNOTES

Add. Ch.	Additional Charters, B.L.
Add. MSS.	Additional Manuscripts, B.L.
Ag. Hist. Rev.	*Agricultural History Review*
Amat. Hist.	*Amateur Historian*
Ant. Jnl	*Antiquaries' Journal*
Arch. Aeliana	*Archaeologia Aeliana*
Arch. Cant.	*Archaeologia Cantiana*
Arch. Jnl	*Archaeological Journal*
Beds. Hist. Rec. Soc.	*Publications of the Bedfordshire Historical Record Society*
B.L.	British Library
Br. Arch. Reports	*British Archaeological Reports*
Bucks. Rec. Soc.	*Publications of the Buckinghamshire Record Society*
C.	followed by a number: classes of documents in the P.R.O.
Cal. Ch. Rolls	*Calendar of Charter Rolls*
Cal. Cl. Rolls	*Calendar of Close Rolls*
Cal. Misc. Inq.	*Calendar of Miscellaneous Inquisitions*
Cal. Pat. Rolls	*Calendar of Patent Rolls*
Cal. Rot. Cart.	*Calendar Rotuli Cartarum* (Record Commission, 1837)
Cal. S.P.D.	*Calendar of State Papers, Domestic*
Camden Soc.	*Camden Society Publications*
Derbys. Arch. Jnl	*Derbyshire Archaeological Journal*
D.L.	followed by a number: classes of documents in the P.R.O.
Dugdale Soc.	*Publications of the Dugdale Society*
E.	followed by a number: classes of documents in the P.R.O.
Econ. Hist. Rev.	*Economic History Review*
Eng. Hist. Rev.	*English History Review*
Feudal Aids	*Feudal Aids and Analogous Documents*
Geog. Jnl	*Geographical Journal*
Hist. MSS. Comm.	*Reports* of the Historical Manuscripts Commission
Inq. A.Q.D.	Inquisitions *ad quod damnum*: P.R.O., C. 143
Jnl Brit. Arch. Assoc.	*Journal of the British Archaeological Association*
Jnl Derbys. Arch. and Nat. Hist. Soc.	*Journal of the Derbyshire Archaeological and Natural History Society*
Lincs. Rec. Soc.	*Publications of the Lincolnshire Records Society*
L.R.	followed by a number: classes of documents in the P.R.O.
M.A.	Ministers' Accounts: P.R.O.
Med. Arch.	*Medieval Archaeology*

M.P.C. ⎫	
M.P.D. ⎪	
M.P.E. ⎬	classes of maps in the P.R.O.
M.P.F. ⎪	
M.R. ⎭	
Northants Rec. Soc.	*Publications of the Northamptonshire Record Society*
O.S.	Ordnance Survey
Parly Survey	Parliamentary Surveys: P.R.O.
P.N.	followed by *county name*: county volumes of the Place Name Society
P.R.O.	Public Record Office, London
Proc. Dorset Nat. Hist. and Ant. Field Club	*Proceedings of the Dorset Natural History and Antiquarian Field Club* [afterwards as below]
Proc. Dorset Nat. Hist. and Arch. Soc.	*Proceedings of the Dorset Natural History and Archaeological Society*
Proc. Geol. Assoc.	*Proceedings of the Geologists' Association*
Proc. Suff. Inst. Arch.	*Proceedings of the Suffolk Institute of Archaeology*
R.C.H.M.	followed by *county name*: Royal Commission on Historical Monuments, *Inventories* of the counties of England and Wales
Rot. Hund.	*Rotuli Hundredorum* (Record Commission, 1812–18)
Rot. Parl.	*Rotuli Parliamentorum* (1771–83)
S.C.	Special Collections: documents at the P.R.O.
S.P.	State Papers, Domestic: P.R.O.
Surtees Soc.	*Publications of the Surtees Society*
Trans. Beds. Arch. Soc.	*Transactions of the Bedfordshire Archaeological Society*
Trans. Birm. Arch. Soc.	*Transactions of the Birmingham and Warwickshire Archaeological Society*
Trans. Caerns. Hist. Soc.	*Transactions of the Caernarvonshire Historical Society*
Trans. Cumb. and West. Arch. Soc.	*Transactions of the Cumberland and Westmorland Archaeological and Antiquarian Society*
Trans. Devon Assoc.	*Report and Transactions of the Devonshire Association for the Advancement of Science, Literature and Art*
Trans. E.R. Ant. Soc.	*Transactions of the East Riding Antiquarian Society*
Trans. Hist. Soc. Lancs. and Chesh.	*Transactions of the Historic Society of Lancashire and Cheshire*
Trans. Inst. Brit. Geog.	*Transactions of the Institute of British Geographers*
Trans. Leics. Arch. Soc.	*Transactions of the Leicestershire Archaeological Society*
Trans. Shrop. Arch. Soc.	*Transactions of the Shropshire Archaeological Society*
Trans. Thoroton Soc.	*Transactions of the Thoroton Society*
U.L.C.	University Library, Cambridge
Wilts. Arch. and Nat. Hist. Mag.	*Wiltshire Archaeological and Natural History Magazine*
Wilts. Arch. and Nat. Hist. Soc. Rec. Branch	*Wiltshire Archaeological and Natural History Society Records Branch*
Yorks. Arch. Jnl	*Yorkshire Archaeological Journal*
Yorks. Arch. Soc. Rec. Ser.	*Yorkshire Archaeological Society Records Series*
V.C.H.	*Victoria County History*

STANDARD WORKS OF REFERENCE

Baker, *Northants.* Baker, G., *The History and Antiquities of the County of North-ampton* (1822–30)

Blomefield, *Norfolk* Blomefield, F., *An essay towards a Topographical History of the County of Norfolk,* I, II and III (pp. 1–677) (1739–45); by C. Parkin, III (pp. 678 to end), IV and V (1769–75)

Bridges, *Northants.* Bridges, J., *The History and Antiquities of Northamptonshire,* compiled from the manuscript collections of J. Bridges by the Rev. P. Whalley (1791)

Camden W. Camden, *Britannia* ... first published in Latin 1586, with subsequent editions to 1639. First English translation 1610; an edition with additions and improvements was published 1695 and 'enlarged with the latest discoveries' by R. Gough in 1789 (both with subsequent editions).

Dugdale, *Monasticon* Dugdale, W., *Monasticon Anglicanum,* edited by Caley, Ellis and Bandinel (1817–30; also the edition of 1846)

Dugdale, *Warwicks.* Dugdale, W., *The Antiquities of Warwickshire* (the whole revised, augmented and continued by W. Thomas, 1730)

Extenta Manerii *Extenta Manerii* in *Statutes of the Realm,* I. 242–3. The document itself is of uncertain date but was collected under 4 Edw. I, i.e. 1275

Hodgson, *Northumb.* Hodgson, J., *A History of Northumberland* (parts published 1827–40, 1820–35; complete edition 1858)

Hutchins, *Dorset* Hutchins, J., *The History and Antiquities of the County of Dorset* (3rd edn, corrected, augmented and improved by Shipp and Hodson, 1861–74)

Lysons, *Magna Britannia* Lysons, D. and S., *Magna Britannia* being a concise topographical account of the several counties of Great Britain (1806–22); Beds., Berks., Bucks., Cambs., Cheshire, Cornwall, Cumberland, Derby and Devonshire only

Nichols, *Leics.* Nichols, J., *The History and Antiquities of the County of Leicester* (1795–1811)

Norden, *Surveior's Dialogue* Norden J., *The Surveior's Dialogue* (1607)

Northumberland County History *The History of Northumberland,* published by the Northumberland County History Committee, 15 vols. (1893–1940)

Thoroton, *Notts.* *Thoroton's History of Nottinghamshire* edited and enlarged by J. Throsby (1796; this being a new edition of Thoroton, R., *The Antiquities of Nottinghamshire* (1677))

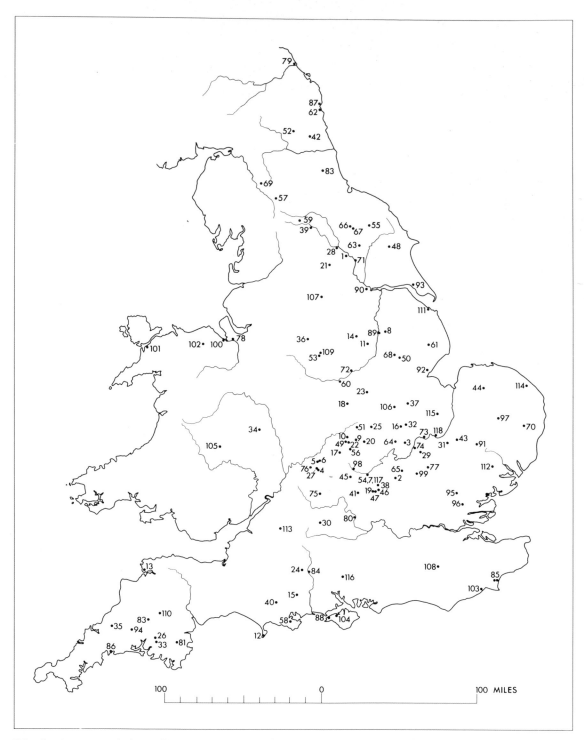

Distribution map of places illustrated in this book.

PART ONE

INTRODUCTION

1

AIMS AND LIMITATIONS

We poore Countrymen doe not thinke it good to have our Lands plotted out, and me thinks indeed it is to very small purpose: for is not the field itselfe a goodly Map for the Lord to looke upon, better than painted paper?

THE FARMER IN NORDEN'S *Surveior's Dialogue,* 15

This book has been conceived as a work of observation, illustration, comment and suggestion. Its source is the English landscape viewed from the air, and it selects what can be seen from that point of vantage to illustrate the visible remains of human activity in a certain period in history. The chronological limits set are broadly those of the 'Middle Ages', a period which lingers into what political histories would call 'early modern', and for some of the topics the limit is only set by the sweep of industrialisation which Blake deplored. The building of Satanic Mills in England's green and pleasant land is a separate subject, with its own archaeology and much scope for the camera.

The observation which was necessary to assemble illustrations is the joint work of the authors. Sometimes interesting photographs suggested profitable research among documents which might explain them; sometimes documents suggested profitable photographs. Some of the topics illustrated are well known to historians, and the only novelty lies in the clarity and comprehensiveness which air photographs can give. Still other topics, it is believed, receive a fresh contribution when the subject-matter is seen from the air. The function of the air photograph is not always that of making new discoveries, but of clarifying what is but partly visible on the ground. This book is intended to suggest how the documentary and the pictorial tools of research can work in alliance, and indeed for many subjects in medieval history *must* work in alliance. Wherever possible, analysis of a photograph has been supported by examining whatever documents could be found, and where two or three equally useful alternative places had been photographed, the one chosen for publication has been the best documented.

Archaeological inquiry, which examines the physical remains of a civilisation, is the common and accepted technique for all periods in English history up to the Norman Conquest: the paucity of documents has driven students willy-nilly to archaeology. When documents do become available spades and field observation have usually been set aside, and the written word has become the principal historical evidence. This is quite proper, and in many medieval studies is the only way to proceed. The archaeology of government, taxation, diplomacy or church organisation is likely to pay poorer dividends than an equal amount of time spent in archives. An air photograph may show Fountains Abbey or its granges but nothing of the bustling activity when the wool-clip left for Italy; it can show the Pilgrim's Way but no company of pilgrims; it can show a manorial mill but nothing of the legal ties which linked its owner to its peasant users. But in certain medieval studies, particularly those of economic activity, physical remains may compensate for the absence of a written record.

This collection of photographs shares one virtue with all pictorial illustration. By making explicit and actual some such general term as 'saltings', 'road system', and 'open fields', it gives reality to the abstract. The features to be studied are set in their proper physical environment so that the influence of geography, geology or the vegetational background is made more explicit. The work of man in determining or limiting some of these environmental controls is also brought into prominence. Physical features of the present day are seen alongside medieval remains for comparison of sizes. How did the open-field 'furlong' compare with a modern hedged field? How large was medieval Chester? How wide were the field-roads of a pre-Macadam age? Questions of this kind can be answered at a view.

Air photographs have other advantages over those taken at ground level: comprehensiveness and elucidation. An air photograph comprehends in a glance, and records permanently, a broad sweep of countryside. On the ground the range of vision is limited by such barriers as a hedge, a dip in the ground or a belt of trees. Extensive earthworks are seldom visible in their entirety from any one point on the ground, so that an observer cannot take in their whole character except from a map. From the air, earthworks can be viewed comprehensively, and the relation of the several parts to the whole becomes apparent.

The aerial camera is able to record small irregularities in the surface and 'crop-marks', and to render them lucid by virtue of being seen at a distance. Their relationship to other features, either invisible on the ground or, if seen, taken only at their individual worth, becomes apparent. Distance lends elucidation as well as enchantment to the view. The more prominent physical remains of the Middle Ages can be measured and drawn on maps. In a map, however, each feature is conventionalised and the reader must interpret the symbols and make his own mental image. Nor may a map convey the texture of a landscape. A wire fence or a beech hedge is represented by the same hair-line; the cottage of Cotswold stone and the brick house of Cambridgeshire are both represented by the same black rectangle.

Ephemeral but important details like crops and vegetation are not recorded on maps. Since human activity is the subject to be illustrated it can be of great advantage to record the work of men's hands in other terms than symbols. Even so the air photograph, not possessing all the attributes of maps, is their ally and not their rival.

For the purpose of this book oblique photographs seemed preferable to vertical views despite the difficulty of making a straightforward comparison with maps. The vertical air photograph presents certain difficulties of interpretation to the layman's eye. The vertical views that have been included show how many adjustments have to be made by those who have to recognise a building from its roofs without any glimpse of the elevation. In oblique photographs a house is seen as a house, and although a circle is seen as an ellipse the act of interpretation called for here is one which the mind performs daily and without effort.

In this book the power of air photographs to comprehend detail as a unity will appear best in the discussion of settlement shapes. The relationship of house to house and street to street cannot be grasped without going away from house and street and looking at the village as a whole. The older the town, and the narrower the streets, the more difficult it becomes for a traveller on foot to comprehend the plan; even a methodical tour of the streets, lanes and alleys of an old town with their many bends and turns gives only a confused sense of its form. The air photograph improves on the church tower as an observation-point because it includes the church tower in its view, and there is no danger of failing, like one of G. K. Chesterton's characters, to see any church in the village because one is standing on its tower.

The earthworks and crop-marks recording man's activities in the Middle Ages are no less characteristic than those of prehistoric times. Until recently, professional archaeologists have paid comparatively little attention to the earthworks of medieval England. The reason for this is partly the very small number of professional archaeologists in this country; not only have they been so busy with prehistory as to exclude history, but some might claim that the complacency of medieval historians has misled them.

Medieval archaeology has also suffered from the conservatism of settlement in the last thousand years. When the prehistorian excavates the sites of early settlements he may often count on a fairly lonely situation, with only agricultural land to disturb, and little interference by later settlers depositing their own remains. It is the misfortune of medieval archaeology that successive generations have quarrelled so seldom with the original choice of site. Any medieval village which has become a town has covered the sites of cottages and crofts with houses and shops; there has been rebuilding: the density of modern settlement and the high values of urban land have not offered much room for those who would excavate. Only the accident of a bomb or a by-pass sometimes reveals the village beneath the town.

The village which has not expanded into a town has been all the more conservative in its siting. As will be seen, the evidence of the earliest maps (from the sixteenth century) suggests that the general direction of streets and the relative position of the house-and-garden units have not changed much in the last four hundred years, whatever the changes in earlier centuries; but the ideal site for illustration is one where later, modifying influences have been weak. The village or town abandoned before the Great Rebuilding of the period 1540–1640; the medieval port choked by silt; the borough which wilted soon after its first plantation; the market-town 'fossilised' by a diversion of routes: these make the best material.

A preoccupation with decay may seem to haunt some of the illustrations. It does not come from a romantic delight in ruins or an interpretation of the Middle Ages which gives a high place to broken columns and fallen masonry. From some points of view the photograph of a decayed medieval borough with its grassy burgage tenements (as may been seen at Newtown, Isle of Wight, fig. 104) is a better illustration than a famous city like Norwich where medieval features have been overlaid or surrounded by buildings of the last two centuries. The shrunken and deserted villages suit better some purposes of exposition than the village which was rebuilt in brick in the nineteenth century; the abandoned medieval roads may be better for the present purpose than those which are now modern highways.

Had ill fortune descended only on the inefficient, the ill-conceived, the ill-planned, or the ill-adjusted, the collection would be heavily weighted with antiquarians' pieces, weaklings and invalids, but, as medieval men were well aware, Fortune and Misfortune were indiscriminate visitors.

Where the modern overlies the medieval, the modern feature has been included in the descriptive commentary. It is inevitable that photographs will show post-medieval economic change, and this has not been ignored. On the other hand an attempt has been made to exclude photographs in which the focus of interest is something wholly the product of the years after 1650. At the other extreme, occasional trespass has been made into the Dark Ages, and some features described as 'medieval' will have existed before the Norman Conquest or whatever point is taken as the beginning of 'medieval'. For this the excuse lies in part in the 'darkness' of the Dark Ages.

It will be noticed that the human activity which is illustrated is principally economic. Another volume in this series has been devoted to monastic buildings, and while other religious and secular buildings of government and war may appear in the photographs, interest has here been focused on the influence of the building in determining who lived nearby and where they should live. The choice is not governed by any belief that medieval man was exclusively an economic creature but because it is the visible and tangible remnant of his existence which a camera records. Any major modification of the landscape is made for reasons which conventionally fall within 'economic history'. Thus this volume is concerned with buildings on which medieval man spent time and money; with fields created and maintained for the sale of their produce; with the face of nature scarred by the search for raw materials. Even where a building was to be used for spiritual purposes or the prestige and glory of the temporal monarch, money or labour had to be spent upon it. Conversely, the photographs often suggest the scale of expense and effort required for some formidable feats of construction. The energies of the medieval peasant in cottage-building have left few remains; none of the produce of the tax-paying villeins survives as a monument to his perennial labour: but churches, castles, and abbeys are evidence of more than the labours of the masons who built them. They represent work financed (in money terms) by the gifts, tithes and taxes of the faithful and liegemen, and (in real terms) by diverting some of the product of labour from towns, villages and fields to these other ends.

A word may be in place about the limitations of this book. By no means every variety of village and town topography has been illustrated nor, indeed, could the wide range of village and town histories be exhaustively gathered into 'types' with much profit. It was not always possible to be flying in a given part of the country on a clear day in the right season and at an hour when sunlight and shadows could be used to best advantage. Other villages of interest have been omitted when there was no information from documents to support the visual evidence.

The map on p. xviii shows the distribution of sites illustrated in this book, and it will be seen that except for one topic the distribution is confined to England. The conquest of Wales in the thirteenth century gave an English king an unparalleled opportunity to build fortified towns which would also attract merchants as settlers, and Edward I's place in the history of European town-building is such that his Welsh towns cannot be passed over. The settlement history of Wales, Scotland and Ireland presents special problems to a historian who will concern himself with such matters.

The distribution map may suggest that the western counties have not been as thoroughly treated. This is partly a question of distance and accessibility; there are also climatic obstacles to air photography of sites among the hills. The really unrepresented type of English village is that which is not compact but a wide scatter of single houses; the width of the scatter means that a photograph which takes in all the relevant area would have to be on a very small scale. 'Nucleated' villages would have had to have been reproduced at twice the page size of this book if all important details were to emerge. When the area to be photographed is even wider, much significant detail would inevitably be lost.

5

The arrangement of text and plates in this volume differs from that adopted in the first volume of *Cambridge Air Surveys*. Here, the *Introduction* takes the form of a commentary on various remains of the 'medieval' landscape as they appear today when viewed from the air. Divided into sections according to subject-matter, it runs continuously through the book. The commentary on each photograph is intended to elucidate certain features and to set the particular view in its historical context. In this way, each photograph and commentary make a self-contained whole and references are given to relevant documents and printed sources. As has been written: 'The reconstruction of historical topography is not antiquarian, for the topography is a human creation, or rather a creation of men struggling with and using natural resources. When documents are silent, then landscape helps, and one dare use no stronger word.'

The aim of this book is well summarised in these words.

2

OLD MAPS AND NEW PHOTOGRAPHS

Take with you the mappe of England set out
in faire colours, one of the biggest sort I
meane, to make shew of your countrey ....
RICHARD HAKLUYT'S *Advice*, 1580 (*Principal
Navigations* III. 271)

As far as possible, photographs have been
chosen that illustrate features of the English rural
and urban landscape assignable to the period
between the Anglo-Saxon settlement and the
end of the reign of Elizabeth I. No phrase exactly
defines this interval, but it had its own unity: it
was the pre-cartographic period. Its start is
marked by the arrival of settlers whose choice of
habitat and forms of livelihood were to domi-
nate the rural landscape for more than a thousand
years. Its end came at the time when property-
holders had at their command surveyors skilled
in the accurate recording of the landscape. In the
dissolution of the medieval forms of land-
holding and land-use the landlords found the
'plot' (or plan) an invaluable record of existing
property-rights and a basis from which to project changes. This dissolution, in which the
familiar features of the modern countryside
spread across the English plains, forms the subject of a later chapter. Once the making of large-
scale maps had become common, only the
imperfect survival of such maps and plans stands
between the modern student and the study of the
seventeenth- or eighteenth-century towns and
countryside.[1]

The main object of this book is to supplement
surviving maps and documents: hence the pre
cartographic period demands the greater part of
the available space. The use of the word
'medieval' in the title is the least clumsy way of
defining briefly the period involved: strictly, it is
'medieval and Tudor', with some topics pursued
beyond 1603 and some cut short even before
1485 (or whenever the Middle Ages may conventionally be said to have ended). The history

of landscape features does not fit easily into the
periods of political history.

In the earliest Anglo-Saxon documents there
were instances where verbal descriptions of
property were set down and attested. Domesday
Book itself was a valiant attempt to reduce a
kingdom to parchment. The standardised form
of the manorial survey set out in the 'Statute'
Extenta Manerii (*c.* 1275) shows what were considered the essential questions to ask and the
essential facts to record. Rentals of the thirteenth
century, such as those taken for Edward I's new
towns, often have sufficient detail to serve as the
basis for a map. Both the *Extenta Manerii* and the
methodical inquiries of the surveyors' handbooks of Shakespeare's England have been
constantly used in planning this book and inter-
preting the visible remains shown in air photographs. Phrases from the two interrogatories
have been freely used at the head of chapters.
When asking questions about past landscapes it
is appropriate to begin with those which contemporaries asked.[2]

A useful bridge between the known and the
unknown, the certain and the interpretative, is
made by setting a selection of sixteenth- and
seventeenth-century plans alongside photographs of the same areas. The comparison
indicates the types of remains to be expected
elsewhere and permits an estimate of the degree
of change after 1600 which might confuse inter-
pretations of the modern landscape in historical
terms.

Between the accession of Elizabeth and the
death of Charles I, English landowners and public officials had by their patronage greatly
augmented the experience and skill of surveyors
engaged to draw up large-scale plans. It was an
age in which land was frequently changing
hands, and in a litigious age, with land-hungry

[1] E. Lynam, *British Maps and Mapmakers* (1944); G. H.
Fowler, *Records of Bedfordshire, Quarto Series* (1928–36);
J. L. G. Mowat, *Sixteen Old Maps of Oxfordshire* (1888); F. G.
Emmison, ed., *Catalogue of Maps in the Essex Record Office*
(1947).

[2] E. G. R. Taylor, 'The Surveyor', *Econ. Hist. Rev.* XVII
(1947) 121–33; H. C. Darby, 'The agrarian contribution to
surveying', *Geog. Jnl* LXXXII (1933) 529–35; C. R. Straton,
transcr. *Survey of the lands of William, first Earl of Pembroke*
(Roxburgh Club, 1909) I, introduction; E. Kerridge, ed.,
'Surveys of the manors of Philip, first Earl of Pembroke and
Montgomery, 1631–2', *Wilts. Arch. and Nat. Hist. Soc.
Records Branch* IX (1953) introduction, vii–xiv.

7

men abroad in the countryside, it was an additional security when a title was questioned if a map were available showing boundaries, areas and tenants' names.[3]

Maps were not only made for litigants on the defensive. Some were commissioned because men wished to change the face of the countryside pictured upon them. The farmer's hostility to the surveyor's profession in Norden's *Dialogue* derived from a suspicion that a visit from a surveyor meant that the lord would soon be making changes: an increase of rent, or perhaps a complete reorganisation of the estate with an enclosure of the common fields and a division of the commons. A surveyor's visit might presage some radical change in agricultural land-use or be followed by prospectors digging for minerals. One of the oldest Northumbrian open-field maps [4] is a large-scale plan of a few adjacent furlongs with the principal interest not in the strips but in the little coal-pits scattered over them, one here, one there, very like the twelfth-century iron-pits protruding from the strips in the photograph of Bentley Grange (fig. 107).

It is in the sixteenth century also that the cities of England begin their long series of large-scale street plans designed to be engraved and printed for as many as might be tempted to buy them and that the county atlases began to place small sketch-maps of the more important towns in the margins of their pages. It is from maps like Speed's Flint or Chester that the gap between the medieval town and the early nineteenth-century town of the first edition of the Ordnance Survey maps can be bridged. And the same century saw the descriptions written by John Leland and William Camden as they travelled across a landscape in the process of transformation. From this time onwards the roads of England were never free from the inquiring traveller with a notebook, sometimes the great antiquary, sometimes the credulous, gossiping diarist.

The photographs in this book show the remains, not only of the medieval landscape, but of changes already in progress when the first large-scale plans were being drawn. Our task would have been well nigh impossible had subsequent transformations been radical enough to erase all the principal features of the medieval landscape and distort the principal medieval forms of village plan. Fortunately, urban expansion apart, the principal changes have been in the fields, and air photographs are particularly suited to detecting and illustrating what successive changes have affected a given area of soil. Old methods of ploughing showing beneath the new, old field-boundaries revealed among the modern hedges, and old road systems supplanted by new alignments often leave traces in the form of earthworks, or marks in the soil and the vegetation, traces which are quickly detected from the air.

It would be beyond the power of air photographs to record equally radical change within a village. Where building has succeeded building on the same site, or one macadamised road overlies another, the air photograph cannot trace them. The closely planted enclosed plot of a back-garden is too small to show soil-marks and too heterogeneous in its cropping to yield significant crop-effects. All the evidence points, however, to very few radical changes in the internal lay-out of most villages in the last five centuries. To suggest that the average village shows extreme conservatism in the alignment of its houses and streets is not to ignore that the individual cottage is unlikely to be medieval. It is piecemeal rebuilding which has done so much to preserve the street and garden plan of the later Middle Ages. Yet with this conservatism in plan there has been an almost complete disappearance of the medieval cottage. Shortly after the end of the Middle Ages came the building revolution.[5] In part, this extensive rebuilding of small domestic houses was the product of new techniques and building-materials which offered cheaper and more comfortable houses; in part, it was the expression of increased wealth from agriculture coming to the husbandmen and yeomen. Medieval cottages of wattle and daub which survived this period of rebuilding might, with patching and alteration, still be found in the late nineteenth century, but by the mid-twentieth they are zealously sought as the curios of the architectural historian. Villages described as 'picturesque' or 'old English' usually have sixteenth-century buildings.

But a village is more than single houses: it is a complex of buildings in a setting. It is this setting, made up of streets and crofts, which weathered the Great Rebuilding and the spread of Victorian brick. Conservatism shows itself very markedly in the permanence of street-lines and the boundary-lines between crofts, though

[3] E. Lynam, 'English maps and map makers of the sixteenth century', *Geog. Jnl,* CXVI (1950) 7–28; Sir George Fordham, 'Some surveys and maps', *ibid.* LXXI (1928), 50; U.L.C. MSS. Mm. 3. 15; Norden, *Surveior's Dialogue.*

[4] J. U. Nef, *The Rise of the British Coal Industry* I (1932) 307, from E. 134/41 Eliz., Easter 19 (1598).

[5] W. G. Hoskins, 'The rebuilding of rural England, 1570–1640', *Past and Present,* no. 4 (1953); M. W. Barley, 'Rural housing in England', in J. Thirsk, ed., *The Agrarian History of England and Wales* IV (1967) 696–766.

the position of the house within the croft was often changed at rebuilding. In a modern village a frontage of garden gates or house doors facing the street is very usual. Sixteenth-century plans show that this was not the rule at earlier times: cottages might be built end-on to the street; they might stand some distance back within their croft, with their neighbour's house at a different distance from the street.

Yet to alter the boundary of a croft in any direction would have meant an encroachment. The economic value of an enclosed area like the croft at the back of a house was high and neighbours would not allow the bounds to move. In the croft grew the garden crops and into it the animals could be driven for wintering. The objections to an extension of the crofts at either end would come from an even larger body of neighbours, for at one end of the crofts were the common fields and at the other end the street or green.[6] If it was difficult to move the boundaries of crofts it was even more difficult to make any major alterations in the street plan. An open thoroughfare might pass from being an alley to a street, and the spread of houses might turn a footpath into an alley, but there were strong barriers of property-rights and custom to thwart great changes. The really radical reconstructions, like the removal or destruction of a village, come only when there is a sole proprietor in law or a sole arbiter *de facto*, or when there is an intervention as serious as the wholesale fire which struck Blandford Forum in 1731.

In the town, and particularly in the village-turned-town, the crofts were too valuable to be left as a garden or an animal-run when house-room became precious, goods needed storage, and craftsmen required working-space. The narrow crofts then appear as open yards with stables, outbuildings, storerooms and workshops. But they still show as long, narrow units of property in many of the borough and town photographs, nowhere more clearly than at Chipping Campden (fig. 76), Corfe (fig. 58) and Warkworth (fig. 62). It was easy to adapt the street frontage of a market-town to serve the tastes of an eighteenth-century grocer or a twentieth-century multiple store, but however changed the façade appears, the influence of the former crofts has been hard to disguise.

Another feature of the house-and-croft plan has commonly survived: this is the back-lane running at the far end of the croft, making a circuit of the whole built-up area. By this lane animals could be brought in and out of the croft without passing the houses or coming through the village street; equipment could be taken along it from the sheds to the fields. In the village which has grown into a market-town this back-lane often appears quite unchanged in position, running parallel to the main street behind the inns, shops and houses. It now provides access to garages and to the goods-entrances of stores, or leads to the bicycle-park and the side-entrance for the cheap seats at a cinema.

Other obstacles to radical changes in a village plan existed besides property rights or custom. There were important buildings which would not move, and as long as they were focal points in village life the need remained for streets to give access from one focal point to another. A church is the most obvious example, another is a castle, another a monastic house. If the village had a much-used market-place, the road system would be centred upon it, and there would be no thought of altering the system. Streets and lanes which led to windmills and watermills would also be unlikely to change their position. The best point to take advantage of wind and water would not be chosen casually, and, the choice once made, there would be little occasion to change.

Outside the village centre itself, the road system of the fields was tied to the needs and routines of the fields; only at the dissolution of the medieval landscape did the need arise for wholesale new tracks between new hedges. Until then, the ploughs and oxen went to the furrows along traditional paths; the animals were driven the same way to the pastures; the way to the market-town lay the way it had always lain.

In the following pages some of the earliest surviving large-scale village plans have been set alongside air photographs of the same villages today. The number of occasions on which this can be done is small, not because other and different examples might be fatal to an argument, but because there are so few early maps drawn on a scale large enough to show a village other than pictorially.

---

[6] Excavations at Wharram Percy (Yorks. E. R.) carried out since 1954 show that the ruins of the latest medieval houses, which form the earthworks of the deserted village, conceal layers of older structures frequently rebuilt, not always on the same alignment. Similar eccentricity of axis was found in Dr Axel Steensberg's excavation of Danish peasant houses, and now that excavations elsewhere show the same it must induce caution, for the house plans revealed by air photographs may be no older than the generation prior to the desertion of the site. See also pp. 129–32 below.

Fig. 1A. Nun Monkton; vertical photograph, October 1972. Scale 1:4000.

1. NUN MONKTON
Yorkshire, West Riding

For the first of these comparisons the village of Nun Monkton has been chosen (fig. 1A): it lies at the junction of the River Nidd with the Ouse, seven miles north-west of York. Between the two rivers there is a long, isolated neck of land occupied by Nun Monkton parish. The lane which serves this village, though a cul-de-sac, bore much traffic before the time of railways. Goods were brought up the Ouse to an unloading-point at Nun Monkton and then taken inland on pack-saddles and carts. The riverside is now deserted, but a small toll-house survives from the days when tolls were levied upon river traffic.

There are three extant surveys of the village. The priory lands, the demesne estate, were surveyed at the Dissolution. This written description (c. 1538) is not much more than a rental. Thirty-three tenements in Monkton town were paying rent to the lord. The second survey in 1567 comprises all the houses and fields and not merely those of the demesne, and the third survey, a map of 1607, is among the muniments at Petworth House, Sussex. This accurate and beautifully coloured map does not photograph well and a line-drawing (fig. 1B) has been prepared from it.

West from the scite of the saide late monasterye is the towne of Nun Monkton sceated; whereof the sowthe rowe of the same butteth upon the comon towardes the northe and the comon Field called the Towne field on the sowthe. Begin at the easte ende therof and goe westwarde, and there first. . . .

These instructions of 1567 fix our starting point at the apex of the green and at the head of the south row.

The green is the 'comon towardes the northe', and the 'comon Field' lies below the crofts or gardens of the cottages. The lines of the former strips belonging to *Barthoram Garthes Furlong*

10

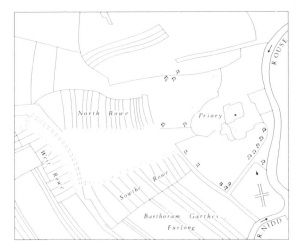

Fig. 1B. Nun Monkton in 1607.

appear in the fields below the cottages. The Ouse is the broad river to the right; its confluence with the much narrower channel of the Nidd lies east of the village. The sole remnant of the priory of Benedictine nuns which lay on the banks of the Ouse is the parish church, of which the long narrow roof can be seen among the trees. The large building adjoining it is the present 'priory', the successor to the manor house built by the post-Dissolution owners. The village lay with the apex of the green at the gate of the nunnery.

Of the cottages already mentioned, the surveyor of 1567 listed thirteen in *Sowthe Rowe* which, it will be seen, is the same number as in the map made forty years later. There are now only ten separate buildings along the Row, two of which are churches and a third a public house, but the width of some of the crofts shows where adjacent holdings have been thrown together when the house at the front decayed. In *West Rowe* thirteen buildings appear in 1567 and 1607. Consolidation has reduced these to six, so that the northern half of the former frontage is incomplete. On the third side of the triangle, *North Rowe*, more has survived. The survey reckoned seventeen houses here, one of which had the distinction of being 'covered wyth slate', the others presumably being thatched. Nearly all this frontage is now occupied with buildings.

The surveyors did not end with the village houses: like the map-maker they passed out into the fields ... 'to the towne there are belongynge three fields, the one of them is knowen and called bye the name of the Towne Fielde, the second the Middel Fielde and the three [*sic*] is called the West Fielde.'

The fields behind the crofts of *Sowthe Rowe* lay chiefly in the *Towne Fielde* and remained 'open'

until the parliamentary enclosure of 1767. The fields to northwest of the village were already enclosed in 1607, and those behind *North Rowe* were virtually enclosed, with only four open-field strips marked on the map. '... the Towne Fielde lyeth, the river of Nidd on the sowthe, the common on the northe, the Middel Fielde weste and the scite of the manor on the easte ...'

Nun Monkton has been fortunate in preserving its Tudor building-plan with no more alteration than a change of building-materials and building-fashion, and the loss of a few cottages along the frontage of the green with the addition of some modern houses along a field-lane.

The green, the *comon* of the surveys, is particularly well preserved from encroachments. This must be partly due to its having been an estate or 'squire's village' since the Dissolution; before the Dissolution the priory was at the end of the green to keep a watchful eye on the village.

It is possible to assess the size of the village even two centuries earlier than the Dissolution, for in 1379 forty-six married couples and twenty-one other persons paid the poll tax. The frontage must then have had slightly more cottages in its array than at the Dissolution, for only forty-three houses are named in the sixteenth-century surveys and in the map of 1607. The village's tax-quota of 1334 is also high for this part of Yorkshire, being twenty-one shillings. It was not a purely agricultural village; among the craftsmen who paid more than the ordinary husbandman's groat in 1379 were three male weavers, one woman weaver, two tailors, a wright and smith.

Sources

1334: E. 179/206/75; 1379: E. 179/206/49; 1539 survey: E. 315/401; 1567 survey: B. L. Harl. MSS. 4781; 1607 map: Petworth House, Sussex, used by kind permission of Lord Leconfield; refusal to allow encroachments: Percy MSS. (Letters and Papers), Alnwick Castle, IX, 59 (1606).

2. TODDINGTON   Bedfordshire

The village of Toddington (fig. 2A) lying on a hill-top on the Dunstable–Ampthill road, seven miles north-west of Luton, stands at the nodal point of six roads. It has had the right to a market and a fair since 1218. In 1671 when hearths were counted for taxing, Toddington was as large as Ampthill or Dunstable. In 1334 it was paying well above the average for a Bedfordshire village. Here there have been none of the sub-

Fig. 2A. Toddington; looking NE, June 1962.

tractions from the street frontage so marked at Monkton. The problem is one of addition: has the growth of population since 1581 so distorted the appearance of Toddington that it would no longer be possible to discern the main features of its Tudor plan, were there no contemporary map?

The Tudor lay-out has been preserved in the magnificent large-scale survey in twenty sheets made by Ralph Agas in 1581, from which fig. 2B is derived. The medieval castle (1) was only a little hillock by the time of Agas' map. The principal building on his map is the parish church at the apex of the green, here seen from the south. This green is formed by the junction of two main streets which have not diverged from the lines which Agas plotted. The central green (2), the market-place, is unaltered in size. The white house (3) in front of the church is the survivor of a row of three in 1581 and the empty corner-plot at its right hand had a dwelling-house upon it when Agas and a jury perambulated the green.

A very small cottage which stood in front of the white house has now disappeared but there is a new encroachment (4) since Agas' day at the right-hand side of the green. The village may-pole also has gone. At the site of the market-cross on Agas' map now stands a memorial at the head of the open triangle of grass. For the rest, the frontage of houses along the converging roads corresponds to the tiled roofs of 1581,

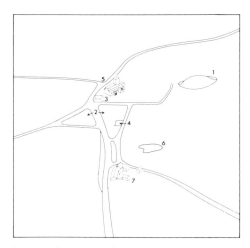

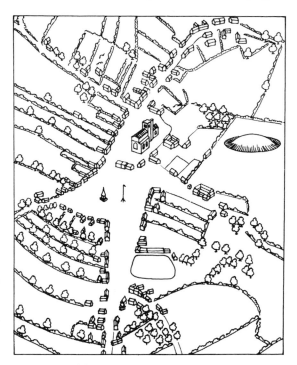

Fig. 2B. Toddington in 1581, after Agas.

Key to figs. 2A and 2B.

1. Mound and ditch 2. Market-place
3. Compare building in this position on the map of
   1581, fig. 2B
4. Encroachment since 1581
5. Compare the projecting corner and narrowing of
   the road here with the corresponding points on
   the map of 1581, fig. 2B
6. Pond in 1581, 'The common water'
7. Inn and inn-yard

however un-Tudor the modern buildings appear. It will be noticed that the white corner-house (5) to the left of the church, projects into the street just as did the house on this site in 1581; the village pond (6) is still there, a little neater and more ornamental than the 'common water' near which Agas sketched two water-carriers, pannier to shoulders, a detail too small to be included in our drawing. The position of the inn (7) with its large yard, just below the pond, is unchanged. The broadening of the modern road near the bottom right-hand corner and the bottle-neck above the church are also seen to be due to the permanence of a building-line already well established in 1581.

The expansion of Toddington to a population of over 2000 has produced ribbon-development along the roads leading to it, so that cottages and houses appear where Agas saw only hedges, but the fundamentals of the plan are unaltered.

Sources

V.C.H. Beds. III (1912) 438; Agas' map: B.L. Add. MSS. 38065; for Agas himself see E. G. R. Taylor in *Econ. Hist. Rev.* XVII (1947) 121–33; survey of 1333: C. 135/35/33; 1332 tax: E. 179/71/13.

It might be argued that comparisons with Tudor maps do not take us far enough back in time. What if the Tudor village plans represent a lay-out of streets only a century or so old when the surveyors measured them? It has already been suggested that the immobility and importance of certain medieval buildings in the village make it unlikely that any radical change in plan can have taken place. A village like Earl's Barton centred on a church with a pre-Conquest tower must have had its principal building in that central position for five centuries at least when Tudor surveyors passed by.

Is air-survey capable of detecting occasions when a radical change in site or a very considerable shrinkage has taken place? If it is, then villages without signs of shrinkage or movement may more confidently be assumed not to have experienced such changes. Later sections of this book are particularly devoted to the visible remains left behind when the streets, houses and crofts of a village decay, but two examples are brought forward to this point in order to illustrate the present argument.

3. LEIGHTON BROMSWOLD
Huntingdonshire

The first of these is Leighton Bromswold, eight miles west-north-west of Huntingdon. The present village contains about forty houses lying along both sides of a single main street, at the south-east end of which stand the church and the

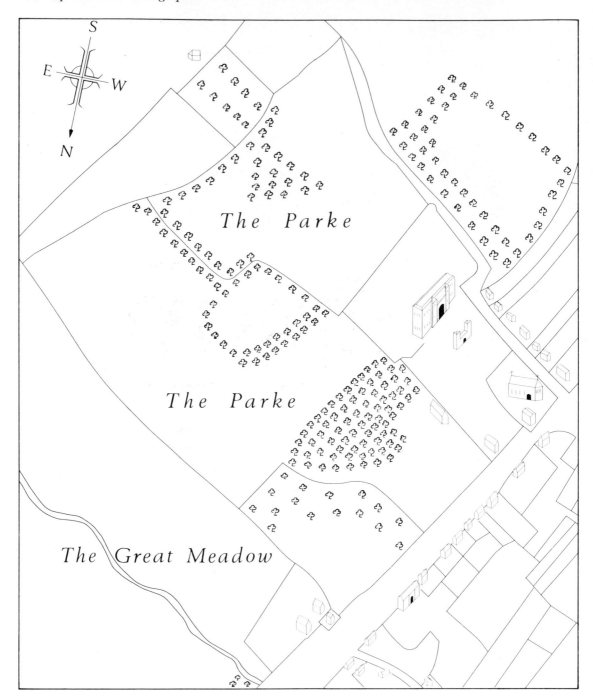

Fig. 3A. Leighton Bromswold in 1680, after Norton.

manor house. The village was surveyed in 1680 by Thomas Norton, and his plan has been published in the *Victoria County History*. It was originally intended to treat Leighton in this book in the same way as Nun Monkton, that is, by an examination of the village plan to discover what differences, if any, time had brought to it since 1680. This examination showed that for the most part Leighton resembled the other village, since its long main street and green leading north-west from the castle and church were substantially unchanged; the modern houses stand where the seventeenth-century houses stood, apart from some rebuilding of farmhouses and the absorption of two crofts into one.

Fig. 3C of our first edition had in its foreground the irregular earthworks south of the rectilinear castle earthwork. In the photograph

Fig. 3B. Leighton Bromswold; looking S, May 1962.

now reproduced as fig. 3B a low sun illuminates the church tower, throws long shadows from the trees and hedgerows, and helps to emphasise these earthworks which are still under grass (top centre). It also shows, in a very light tone, ploughed-out features in a field farther south-east (top left) that formed part of the *Parke* of 1680. But its principal interest lies in the demonstration that the village once extended considerably beyond the present built-up area. Between the lines of trees in the foreground a grass field with grazing cattle has several shallow hollows or boundary-ditches, as well as one or two house-platforms near the road. On the farther side of the road, within the *Parke* of the 1680 plan, a large area that was under grass when photographed in 1945, was ploughed in 1953. Although the earthworks were levelled, material turned up at each ploughing gives rise to light-toned lines in the bare soil.

The boldest of these can be equated with subdivisions of the *Parke* in the 1680 plan; the three isolated trees near a pond (foreground, left) are survivors from one of the hedge-lines. There are,

as well, a number of isolated patches of light-coloured soil, and wider bands extending towards the church; these may mark the site of former houses, hollow-ways or streets.

Between the pond and the road in the left foreground are other soil-marks. These seem to correspond in position to houses shown on the 1680 plan along this road; and across the road the earthworks already mentioned correspond to yet more houses. Thus we have an area outside modern Leighton where houses have disappeared since 1680, and a further area within the *Parke* where it seems likely that houses had already disappeared by that date. There are no documents which reveal whether these houses and streets were displaced by the castle and its park, nor indeed whether the village of Leighton once covered this area in addition to its present site, or whether its present site is a migration from an earlier settlement shown in this photograph. The existence of houses here as late as 1680 would give some support to the second of these possibilities.

In any event, displacement, shrinkage or

Fig. 4. Lower Ditchford; looking E, December 1968. Low earthworks mark the site of this deserted village set amongst its fields in ridge-and-furrow.

migration, the number of households concerned gives the operation a scale which would make it most interesting to have further information. Leighton's tax record shows that it was a very substantial village in the early fourteenth century: in 1327, eighty households paid tax at a time when by no means every household in an English village was wealthy enough to fall within the taxable range. In 1279, the Hundred Rolls recorded sixty-three villeins and at least ten other households here. There was a fair from 1211.

Even if the history of Leighton is not fully elucidated, the examination shows that radical changes in the plan of a village are unlikely to escape the aerial camera. Thus, a village with no such signs of change can reasonably be considered to have conformed to its present plan for at least the five centuries between Domesday Book and the coming of the first large-scale surveys. Whether such a village site could claim to be the direct successor in plan of the 'original' settlement will be discussed in a later chapter.

Sources

V.C.H. Hunts. III (1936) 86; map of 1680 from B.L. Add. MSS. 18030B; tax of 1327: E. 179/122/4; 1279 survey: *Rot. Hund.* II. 616; R.A.F. vertical air photograph, C.P.E. U.K. 1925/3322; part of the 'village' earthworks sketched in R.C.H.M. *Huntingdonshire* (1926) 181; *P.N. Hunts.* (1969) 231 and 245.

4. LOWER DITCHFORD Gloucestershire

At Ditchford, eleven miles south of Stratford-on-Avon, there has been no overbuilding to confuse the issue, and the earthworks of a former village lie completely undisturbed. The buildings in the foreground are those of Ditchford Mill. A stream is marked by a curved line of willows extending from the mill diagonally across the photograph (fig. 4). The fields within the photograph, now mostly pasture, fall into three categories. Those forming a broad belt beside the stream preserve the smooth surface of old meadows. In contrast, fields in the background and on the right have been fashioned into ridges and furrows characteristic of medieval ploughlands, which can be seen to halt at the meadow edge. More will be said of these earthworks in chapter 3. The large field at the centre of the photograph is of different appearance again, being divided by hollows into a number of small island-like platforms of slightly higher ground.

These mounds and hollows mark the site of the village of Lower Ditchford, a hamlet in the large parish of Blockley which once formed a detached island of Worcestershire in Gloucestershire. The administrative geography at this tangled meeting-place of shires has never been simple. There were three villages of Ditchford, named after the ford where the *Dic* (dyke) of the Fosse Way crosses a small brook. In 1491 John Rous, a priest of Warwick, noted that 'Tres Ditchford' had all tumbled down in his lifetime. There was a church of St Giles at one of the Ditchfords, one and a half miles north-east of Stretton on Fosse, and this lost its parish status in 1642, being joined to Stretton and thus falling into Warwickshire. The two other Ditchfords, represented now by the farm of Upper Ditchford and by this site, remained in Blockley. This is an instance where three settlements with a common name, and probably a common origin, have been pulled by the force of manorial overlordship into two different counties.

It may seem surprising that the earthworks of Lower Ditchford appear so clearly, and yet that there are so few signs of cottages or other buildings. The lines of the streets, the hollow-ways, have been worn deep by the continued passage of men, animals and carts from village to fields and back. The village was abandoned in the last quarter of the fifteenth century when the fields were turned over to sheep, and the site of the village has remained as pasture ever since. The streets gathered a shroud of blown and washed humus, quickly colonised by grass. This covering of grass has preserved the old differences of level between houses, gardens and streets. The boundary ditches between the crofts have produced the narrower depressions which break up the grass platforms as into a web. The houses, probably of timber, wattle and daub, have rotted away and there are no substantial foundations such as the camera may record in those deserted villages where stone was used for building (fig. 50).

It will be noticed that the present hedges have been thrown indifferently across meadow, house, street, and former arable as the convenience of the grazier dictated. The large field on the left is typical of an early enclosed pasture (*Grounds*) in the Midland counties. These hedges represent boundaries set in the fifteenth century: the changed farming conditions of the last two hundred years have caused some of the large pastures to be subdivided. The plough has returned to some of these fields since 1939 although not totally eliminating the marks of the medieval division into strips. The line of an abandoned railway completes the archaeology of economic change.

Sources

V.C.H. Worcs. III (1913) 268–9; Rous: B. L. Cot. Vesp. A. XII, fols. 73–4; *P.N. Worcs.* (1927) 98; Dugdale, *Warwicks.* 597; Worcs. Rec. Office Eccles/2/92007–8; C. 133/255/6; C. 136/25/12; in a survey of 1299 Middle Ditchford had 21 customary tenants: M. Hollings, ed., *The Red Book of Worcester* (Worcestershire Historical Society, 1934–50) 302–4; National Grid ref. SP226367.

PART TWO

THE FIELDS AND VILLAGES

3

THE FIELDS

I. INTRODUCTORY

A Mannor in substance is of Lands, Wood,
Meddow Pasture and Arable: it is compounded
of demeisns and services of long continuance. .
. . You are to present the names of all your
common Fields and how many furlongs are in
every Field and their names and the common
meddows and their names. . . .

NORDEN, *Surveior's Dialogue,* 39 and 98

There are good historical reasons for con-
sidering the village fields before the villages.
Villages were created in waves of colonisation;
the impetus for each was the acquisition of fertile
land. Where field-land proved productive and
easily augmented, villages grew and multiplied:
where the field-land was unproductive villages
remained small and widely scattered.

The size and frequency of villages and also the
character of each was influenced by the uses to
which the fields were put. On easily reclaimed,
good quality arable land there sprang up villages
where arable farming was the principal daily
concern; villages where the social, legal and
economic ties between villager and villager (and
between villagers and their lord) were based on
the assumption that most men's lives were
centred in the fields.

As will be seen in chapters 5 and 6, colonisation and reclamation imposed no single village shape and no uniform village position.[1] Yet,
within all this variety of local shape and character
exhibited by English villages, there are two
widespread features: the compact or 'nucleated'
collections of houses, and the siting of a village
in the midst of its fields.

Two necessities of farming life seem to have
been important in holding the communities of
colonists together in compact groups. The first
was defence: in numbers lay safety from such
enemies as other men, wild animals and the
return of scrub to the cleared land. The second

arose from the size and scarcity of the plough and
the ploughteam. In circumstances of very
limited capital resources and a hand-to-mouth
existence, a plough was not likely to be within
the means of single families. For the working of
the plough, numbers were equally important.
While cultivated land was still scarce, the claims
of animals for grassland came second to the
claims of the settlers themselves for arable produce. Each autumn there was a great slaughter of
animals that could not be kept through the
winter. Only a community of some size could
afford to keep the oxen that made up the
plough-yoke, and could effect economies in the
use of man-power to permit works of maintenance on fences and ditches.

The physical appearance of the open-field
landscape is so different from that of today that a
glance at a pre-enclosure map is enough to show
a farmer ignorant of history that his fields were
once managed in a very different way. The
important features of the old landscape were the
strips, the furlongs, the fields and the balks.
These appear in the oldest surviving documents
and field-maps, and have left their trace large on
the landscape even till today. In section II of this
chapter some photographs of the modern landscape are set side by side with maps of the same
area drawn before the open fields were destroyed. First, however, it must be suggested
how the open-field landscape was created in the
centuries-long process of tree clearance (or
'assarting') which did not reach completion even
in easily worked soils until the thirteenth century, when there is abundant evidence of new
land still being taken into the fields. The Statute
of Merton in 1236 attempted to protect the rights
of those landowners whose grazing-rights were
being diminished by this nibbling at grassland
and woodland. In less easily worked soils there
was land which did not see the plough before the
seventeenth and eighteenth centuries.

With the land-hunger of the thirteenth century there was considerable agitation for the
restriction or abolition of the privileges of the

---

[1] For dispersed colonisation see B. K. Roberts, 'Medieval
colonisation in the Forest of Arden', *Ag. Hist. Rev.* XVI (1968)
101–13, and M. W. Beresford, 'Dispersed and group settlement in medieval Cornwall', *ibid.* XII (1964) 13–27.

'forest', the areas where the law set limitations on cultivation in order to preserve the land for hunting. The owners of pasture rights were not alone in feeling the effects of invasion by the plough.

There is an indignant protest by the forest-loving chronicler of Pipewell Abbey (Northants.) who was writing soon after 1320: his examples of destroyed woodland are all taken from the years 1315–22. He asks himself one question: why is the forest being denuded of trees on all sides? and he sets out an elaborate ninefold answer. The first culprits were the hearths which used up the oaks as fuel, then the grants of timber for windmill sails: 'How many windmill sails they gave in different abbots' times no one knows, except God to whom all things are known!' The worst grievance was the process of assarting.

It is well known that the furlong of arable called Coleshawe by East Grange once had a wood on it, as indeed the foundation charter shows. Now it is all arable, the monks having permitted the men of Barford to assart it and bring it under cultivation (*assartare et in agriculturam terram redigere*).[2]

It is a curious irony that within two hundred years the arable fields of Barford were converted to pasture and the 'men of Barford' were no more; and, in the present century, ironstone-workings in turn are removing the pastures.

Elsewhere, monastic houses viewed the assarting with more enthusiasm. There were other Cistercian houses not far from Pipewell where colonisation was actively organised by the monastery. Others benefited indirectly by the advance of the plough. At Ormsby, in the North Riding, the nuns of Spaldington were granted a piece of land at a time when the fields could not have extended to the parish boundary: the grantor promised (*c.* 1154–89) 'if it so happens that the bounds of the tilled land be extended further than they are at present, then the nuns' (holding) will be increased in area as much as will the others in the village.'[3]

A noticeable feature of the expansion of cultivated land in England between the Norman Conquest and the early fourteenth century was that it took place principally from old-established centres. There were indeed new villages being founded in areas where the forests were still dense, the heaths wide and the marshes undrained, and some of these will be considered

in chapter 5. Yet, compared with the total number of villages already in existence, the number of new villages was small. Estimates of the expansion of population in the old, well-settled counties such as the Midlands and East Anglia put the increase between 1086 and 1377 as threefold. Most of these mouths must have been fed from new fields which had been added to the old villages.

Thus, the most recently created blocks of arable land shown on Elizabethan maps need not then have been more than three hundred years old: while the oldest cleared land, that near the village, might have been in use for as much as a thousand years before it was first mapped.

It was this centuries-long piecemeal reclamation which gave the open-field landscape its patchwork of furlongs. The *furlongs* (or *flatts* in some parts of the country) were the groups of strips such as may be seen on sixteenth-century maps. Each furlong had its name and, if written descriptions of villagers' holdings were compiled, the scattered strips which made up a man's holding were located by their position in the named furlongs.

The furlong was not a unit of length as it is today. 'Furlong' was used as a descriptive noun well before it came to mean 220 yards, as was 'foot' before it acquired the meaning of a length of twelve inches. The furlongs can be regarded as the successive increments of land brought into the fields. Those nearest the village will be the oldest of the arable, the nucleus on which the first generations of settlers were fed. When more mouths needed to be fed, this would be insufficient. A new parcel of ground would then be cleared of trees and taken in.

There was no particular reason why the first additional ground to have been carved out of forest should be that adjacent to the earliest fields, though clearance would proceed most naturally outwards from a centre.[4] As successive increments were cleared away, the blocks of arable would sooner or later become continuous but still not necessarily encircling the village houses, for convenience might keep the arable all on one side of the village in the optimum position for drainage, soil, sun and shelter. As population and the demand for new land increased, less and less choice of position was possible. Natural factors limited the ground available: a stream might lie in the way of expansion in one direction, an outcrop of poor soil or a wet patch

[2] Dugdale, *Monasticon* (ed. 1846) v. 434; M. W. Beresford, *The Lost Villages of England* (1954) 75, 206, 292 and 366.
[3] F. M. Stenton, ed., *Transcriptions of . . . Charters (of) Gilbertine Houses. Lincs. Rec. Soc.* XVII (1922), 62.

[4] An attempt to identify the build-up of the first furlongs and fields by colonisation has been made by E. A. Pocock, 'The first fields in an Oxfordshire parish', *Ag. Hist. Rev.* XVI (1968) 85–100.

of marsh in another. Such considerations as these, together with changes in slope, explain why the furlongs are not of equal size nor all aligned in the same direction.

Mr Bishop has shown how northern villages in the twelfth and thirteenth centuries were marrying newly cleared land to an older core of open-field land.[5] Such assimilation of the new to the old was not experienced everywhere. Some of the land which was not cleared until late in the Middle Ages went, on reclamation, straight into a hedged field individually owned, so that some Elizabethan maps show villages with a large inner block of open-field furlongs but an outer ring of hedged fields. This double landscape was quite compatible with the maintenance of open-field farming. The furlong which has been described was not the equivalent of a modern field. It had no permanent fence or hedge separating it from adjacent furlongs. It was occupied not by one man but by many. The token of the presence and claims of many occupants was the *selion*, the subdivision of the furlong into the long, narrow strips, which were basic units of medieval fields. As a synonym for 'selion' the word 'strip' seems to be a modern, economic historians' term which, having the advantage of being self-explanatory, is commonly used.

The fact that the division into selions was associated with a scattered pattern of ownership and occupation suggests that it represents an allocation of newly cleared land to the families who had assisted in the clearing and ploughing: a reward to those who had contributed an ox to the ploughteam or their labour to that clearance and digging which had just succeeded in creating arable land out of scrub or forest. The assumption that agricultural effort will be mutual is implicit in many other practices of open-field husbandry.

Open-field maps of the late sixteenth century show a pattern of land ownership and tenancy in which something of the medieval complexity had been simplified in the interest of convenience and economical working. In the fifteenth century, peasant bargains and landlord concessions had enabled some villagers to make exchanges and sales so as to bring together the scattered strips of a holding. Not many men succeeded in bringing all their land into two or three large parcels, but almost everyone had moved in this direction.

Yet the system was stubborn. To change it, as would-be enclosers found, needed the agreement of almost everyone else in the fields. Quite apart from the natural conservatism of the countryside, there were arguments in its favour. It ensured a rough justice in possessing both good and bad land. Yet its tenacity sprang first from its practical origin. As long as land continued to be added to the fields by the efforts of groups of men and not individuals, then the practical problem of sharing the rewards of effort always remained. To give one man a whole furlong and to tell others that they would get a furlong in due course when more clearing could be undertaken was out of the question. The next new furlong might not come for years, and meanwhile men were land-hungry. The furlong was divided, and each man took his selion, a long, narrow strip, often shaped with the 'aratral curve', a reversed $\int$.[6]

Both voluntary and involuntary changes of ownership modified this simple pattern, but there are clear signs that it once existed. As might be expected, the evidence is clearest for the glebe land whose ownership had remained unchanged for so many years, being made up of the original endowment of the parish church together with the gifts of the faithful in succeeding generations. When glebe strips were surveyed even as late as the eighteenth century it was sometimes found that they still occupied a standard position in each furlong all over the field-land. At Langtoft, East Riding, the glebe strips were the 11th, 12th, 26th, 27th, 30th and 31st in each furlong. At Great Givendale, East Riding, in 1684 the parson's strip was always the end one in a furlong, with that of the lord of the manor next to it.[7] Regularity of this type cannot be accidental or due to a late readjustment. It can only be explained as the result of successive allocations of newly cleared land. The unit-holding consisted, at any given moment, of the sum of strips attached to a village house. A new occupant would take over the holding and, if any fresh clearings were made in his lifetime and he shared in the work, he would pass on to his successors a few more strips than he originally had.

In 1964 Dr Joan Thirsk challenged some of the accepted orthodoxies and argued for a thirteenth-century date for the maturity of common-field topography. Her article also emphasised the widespread occurrence of field-systems of a non-classical type, such as appear in section IV of this chapter. Regular positioning of

[5] T. A. M. Bishop, 'Assarting and the growth of the open fields', *Econ. Hist. Rev.* VI (1935) 13.

[6] S. R. Eyre, 'The curving plough strip', *Ag. Hist. Rev.* III (1955) 80–94.

[7] M. W. Beresford, 'Glebe terriers and open field Yorkshire', *Yorks. Arch. Jnl* XXXVII (1950) 337; see also *Coucher Book of Selby Abbey. Yorks. Arch. Soc. Rec. Ser.* XIII (1893) 42.

an owner's selions within furlongs, which we have treated as a survival of original distributions, she assigns to wholesale reallocations by seigneurs, probably in the thirteenth century. The occasion would be on rearranging something like an infield–outfield system into 'mature' open fields of the classical type. Since it is now known that seigneurs could lay out towns on common heaths, make burgages from selions, and replan the inhabited area of a village, an operation of this magnitude is not perhaps so startling as it would once have seemed.

There is still the difficulty that Dr Thirsk has been unable to cite any document specifically mentioning a reallocation within the fields of an English village such as that from Isarhofen in Germany, 'when the abbot of the monastery owning the village ordered a fresh apportionment of holdings on the grounds that war and the desertion of farms had caused such confusion that no one knew the boundaries of his land.'[8] But the type of event that set off this reapportionment at Isarhofen was not part of normal English agrarian history,[9] and the other continental evidence of reapportionment rests on equal distribution of tenants' holdings through the fields.

Since Dr Thirsk's article was not accompanied by maps, it is impossible to say with any certainty whether the redistribution of ownership she alleges also involved a complete redesign of selion size, selion numbers, selion directions, furlong grouping and, therefore, of the position of balks and access roads.[10] Such a topographical revolution as this would mean that patterns of selions and furlongs of the kind so often recorded on air photographs and old plans[11] may take us no further back than the thirteenth century; the pattern we see could then tell us nothing of the initial process of colonisation.

If the suggested reallocation were indeed one of topography as well as of ownership, the practical difficulties still seem to us to be enormous. In a typical 1000-acre parish there would have been 4000 or so selions: the difficulties that modern farmers have in attempting to eradicate surviving ridges and furrows by transverse or staggered ploughing suggest how formidable the medieval ploughman would have found it if he was directed to redesign the axes and boundaries of established furlongs. It should be noted however that several of our new photographs show ridge-and-furrow (or equivalent soil- and crop-marks) within later crofts. Assimilation of selions to new crofts must always have occurred as the built-up area of a village increased.

The 'standard' length and width of strips (220 yards and five and a half yards) would give an area of only a quarter of an acre, a rood. This may puzzle those who have been brought up to believe in the 'acre-strip'. When examined, the evidence for strips of one acre is tenuous. It is easy to see how the idea arose. Medieval and Tudor surveys often used the word 'acre' as the equivalent of the Latin 'selion'. In this sense 'acre' was descriptive and not meant as a measurement of area. This use of 'acre' appears most clearly in such statements as 'X holds three acres in such-and-such a furlong, being three roods', and the apparent paradox that three acres could be three quarters-of-an-acre is resolved. If the strips shown on open-field maps are measured (and there are thousands of strips available), it is found that the commonest size is between one-quarter and one-third of an acre. This point has more than antiquarian interest. It helps to explain why the physical remains of the open-field strips which are illustrated in the next section were for so long unrecognised for what they were. As long as plots an acre in area were being sought it is not surprising no examples were found, and the candidature of ridge-and-furrow could not be seriously considered.

The length of 220 yards may represent a common optimum distance for which an ox-team would pull. A short run involves frequent turns and is wasteful of effort; but the oxen will not pull long distances without tiring: the fur-

---

[8] Joan Thirsk, 'The common fields', *Past and Present* 29(1964) 9–10, see also the remarks in the Preface to the 3rd edn of C. S. and C. S. Orwin, *The Open Fields* (1967) viii–xv and references cited there; for another view see J. Z. Titow, *English Rural Society* (1969) 20–3 with references cited there.

[9] One would look for examples at the time of the civil war of Stephen and Mathilda; Ulceby, Lincs. (*c.* 1163–76) was still a temporary sheep ranch until men could return to recolonise its fields, C. T. Clay, ed. *Yorkshire Deeds* VIII. *Yorks. Arch. Soc. Rec. Ser.* CII (1940); T. A. M. Bishop's post-Conquest recolonisations, referred to by Dr Thirsk and ourselves, above, would also be relevant in a search for overlapping and redesigned furlongs. But it should be noted that they lay in the North Riding, not East, *pace* Dr Thirsk ('Common fields' pp. 15 and 25).

[10] Reallocations of *furlongs* to different fields and the subdivision of the field-area into two, three or four miniature three-field systems are all known from post-medieval examples, but again without evidence that selion and furlong axes were disturbed – these were cropping and ownership reallocations: I. Beckwith, 'The remodelling of a commonfield system', *Ag. Hist. Rev.* XV (1967) 108–12 (Corringham, Lincs.); R. A. Butlin, 'Enclosure and improvement in Northumberland in the sixteenth century', *Arch. Aeliana,* 4th ser. XLV (1967) 149–60.

[11] The earliest surviving plan which shows selions is that of Boarstall (Bucks.), made in 1444. It is reproduced as fig. 41A, p. 110 below.

long length (which would vary with the heaviness of the soil) represents the best compromise. The common width of about five and a half yards may also be a compromise. If the strip is ploughed by making a journey first up and then down its length, and continuing in the same manner, there is a period when the plough is idle. It reaches the end of the run and is lifted while the oxen cross the headland and turn ready for their pull in the other direction. As more land is ploughed, the distance over which the oxen cross with the ploughshare idle will increase. The medieval ploughman and ploughteam seem to have found about five and a half yards a convenient width. The modern ploughman finds his convenient width four or five times as great.

It was at one time thought that the strips had narrow grass-covered boundaries known as 'balks'. They were banished by Dr and Mrs Orwin but reprieved for certain parts of the country by Colonel Drew, while in a more recent article Dr Kerridge has a nineteen-line footnote with a convincing list of manuscripts where balks are located 'between neighbour and neighbour'.[12] The visible evidence of former strips offered in the next section of this chapter has not revealed the remains of a distinctive boundary other than the furrow. Only one survey is known to us which specifically marks balks between strips.[13]

Written surveys frequently use the word 'balk' in locating strips, but the 'balk' to which they refer was often not a grass boundary between strips but the grass access-way between furlongs. This is what the Elizabethan maps in the All Souls' College muniments meant by 'balks'. The 'balks' at Laxton ran between furlongs and not between strips. Many of the photographs show these balks or access-ways. Centuries of ploughing have sometimes lowered the general level of the surrounding soil, so that the balks remain as grassy banks above the level of the fields. In the open-field system of farming the word *field* was reserved for the largest unit of all, the great division of the arable territory of a village into the two, three or four portions by which the annual rotation of fallow progressed. The field, often described by a locational name such as *North*, *Mill* or *Hill*, was a geographically compact area. The furlongs which comprised it lay in the same quarter of the parish, and one field might be separated from the next by some permanent boundary – a road, a thick fringe of scrub, a stream, a piece of meadow. These bounds are not particularly distinctive today, and it is unlikely that the boundaries of the fields of a village could be reconstructed simply from physical remains.

In the last centuries of open-field farming the use to which the land was put was much modified. Whole furlongs of grassland appeared among the arable furlongs; portions of the open fields by-passed the fallow rotation altogether, and other portions moved in long-period rotations of grass and arable.[14] Yet these and other modifications make very little difference to the physical remains of the open fields with which this book is primarily concerned. A strip of land ploughed for centuries retains the shape imposed upon it by the plough, not seriously modified even if the land is given over to different agricultural uses.

II. THE STRIPS AND FURLONGS

... how many fields are there of the demesnes, and how many acres are in every field, and what is every acre worth?

EXTENTA MANERII

The characteristic physical features of medieval strips and furlongs have now been described and explained. Before passing on to the non-arable fields and to other medieval field-systems, it is necessary to inquire what surviving visible remains there are of these former units of cultivation.

Some words of John Norden may be set at the head of the investigation.[15]

Because we saw not the earth's former deformities, we dreame it was then, as now it is, from the beginning ... Our forefathers left unto us that faire and fruitfull, free from bryers bushes and thornes whereof

[12] C. S. and C. S. Orwin, *The Open Fields* (1938) 46–7, but see their version in the 1967 edition, 43–51, and Dr Thirsk's remarks in the Preface, xi; C. D. Drew, 'Open arable fields at Portland', *Antiquity* XXII (1948) 79–82; E. Kerridge, 'A reconsideration of some former husbandry practices', *Ag. Hist. Rev.* III (1955) 32–40; but see H. A. Beecham, 'A review of balks', *ibid.* IV (1956) 22–44; Mrs H. M. Spufford (*née* Clark), 'Selion size and soil type', *ibid.* VIII (1960) 91–8; H. P. R.

Finberg, 'The open field in Devonshire' *Antiquity* XXIII (1949) 180–2.
[13] Survey of Woolley (Yorks.) by Arthur Scot (1749), Wentworth Woolley MSS., Brotherton Library, Leeds.
[14] The fullest account of permitted variations in open-field cropping is in M. A. Havinden, 'Agricultural progress in open-field Oxfordshire', *Ag. Hist. Rev.* IX (1961) 73–83.
[15] Norden, *Surveior's Dialogue*, 184.

Fig. 5A. Ilmington. Fields NE of the village, looking WSW, May 1957. The medieval furlongs in ridge-and-furrow are crossed by the hedges of existing fields laid out at the enclosure in 1778.

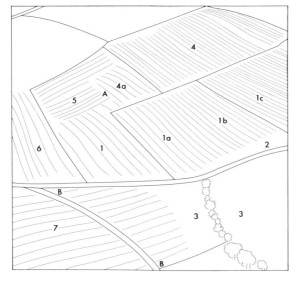

Key to figs. 5A and 5B.
The numbers 1–7 refer to the open-field divisions named in the map of 1778 (fig. 5B) according to the key below. The numbers in brackets after the names are those given to the furlongs by the surveyor of 1778.

1. Drift Way Furlong (69)
1a. Drift Way Furlong (68)
1b. Drift Way Furlong (67)
1c. Drift Way Furlong (66)
2. Grass (70)
3. Rod Meadow (90)
4. Middle Furlong (61)
4a. Middle Furlong (60)
5. End of Windmill Hill (59)
6. Shoe Furlong (72)
7. Furlong Shooting to Rod Meadow (83)

A and B–B refer to features commented upon in the text.

Fig. 5B. Map of part of Ilmington parish at the time of enclosure with the surveyor's sketch for new roads and hedges. The road junction (right) lies just outside fig. 5A.

they found it full ... And this field wherein now we are may be an instance, for you see by the ancient ridges or lands though now overgrowne with bushes, it hath been arable land ...,

The surviving feature most easily linked with the medieval fields is that which caught Norden's eye, the 'ancient ridges or lands', that is, ridge-and-furrow.

In many English counties 'ridge-and-furrow' appears as wave-like undulations in the surface of the fields. The ridge-and-furrow is seen most clearly in the pastures of the grassy shires where the plough has been banished for four or five hundred years. In dry seasons the humped back of the former ridges is accentuated by parched

grass while the furrows remain green. The extent of ridge-and-furrow surviving in relief has been much reduced by the great increase in arable in recent years, but bands of different colouring in the soil or crop are proof of its former presence.

If each unit, from furrow to furrow, marks a single strip of the open fields it should not be difficult to see whether the pattern of ridge-and-furrow on the ground corresponds with the pattern of strips as they appear in the pre-enclosure maps. Since, as has been seen, the 'grain'[16] (or direction of the long axis of the

[16] The term 'grain' was aptly invoked by Dr W. R. Mead, 'Ridge and furrow in Bucks', Geog. Jnl CXX (1954) 34–42.

strips) often changed from furlong to furlong, the furlongs should also be outlined by the changes in direction of the ridge-and-furrow.

How did the strips obtain this high-backed conformation? It would seem that the strips were ploughed as separate units, one ploughman meeting his neighbour at the boundary furrow. Such ploughing, repeated year after year, century after century, built up ridges to a height of a foot or two, as may sometimes still be seen. The ridges would be highest in heavy soil which retained the form imposed upon it by ploughing.

If the lighter soils were ever ploughed into ridges they would more easily be levelled by weathering or deliberate ploughing-out in recent years. The chalklands have very few signs of ridge-and-furrow, although these areas include villages with open fields. Ridge-and-furrow is rare in East Anglia, but can be found all over the Midland plain, in the Welsh border counties and the eastern coastal plain of Yorkshire, Durham and Northumberland. Some of the clearest ridge-and-furrow in the country occurs on the lower slopes of the Cheviots in villages which went over to grass in the fifteenth century. It is rare in areas of late-surviving woodland, such as Essex, the Chilterns, the Forest of Arden and the Weald.

Ridge-and-furrow which is demonstrably older than existing hedges, and which has the 'aratral curve' and the frequent changes of direction characteristic of 'furlongs', can be accepted as the physical remains of medieval strips. The absence of ridge-and-furrow, on the other hand, is inconclusive: in the lighter soils a field now level may once have lain in strips that have been obliterated by subsequent ploughing (see figs. 8, 14, 15), or it may never have had strips. Apart from the truism that the ridges nearest the village are likely to be the oldest, it is only possible to date ridge-and-furrow when other earthworks or disturbances of known age have interfered with it. In fig. 107 closely spaced spoil-heaps from medieval iron-workings can be seen overlying the ridges, so that there the ploughing must be older than the heaps. Documentary sources show that these fields were turned over to mining by the monks of Byland early in the thirteenth century. Structures of known date such as mottes, moats, windmills or chapels can sometimes be seen to override ridges in the same way (fig. 23, and p. 64 below, n. 22).

The commonest of such overlying features is, of course, the hedge. As will be seen in chapter 6, the arrival of the hedge was spread over at least five hundred years; but there has been much progress in recent years in dating the pre-parliamentary enclosure of parishes, and it is not usually difficult to establish by eye whether the ridges in fields of any particular area are overlaid by a system of hedges.

In dating ridge-and-furrow particular interest attaches to photographs of abandoned and migrated villages. Here, the plough is usually known to have retreated before 1550, and the ridge-and-furrow surrounding the crofts can be seen to be older than any existing field boundary. Corroboration of its antiquity is provided by disused roadways spreading out from the village which are demonstrably integral with the blocks of ridge-and-furrow among which they run. The old road system is co-existent with the ridges.

Over the country as a whole, not all the visible ridge-and-furrow will have been simultaneously under cultivation. The ridge-and-furrow on marginal land in Northumberland need not have been colonised at the same time as the East Anglian breckland. The time of maximum encroachment upon these particular marginal areas cannot fall later than the early fourteenth century; there is good evidence for thousands of acres having never seen the plough since.

5. ILMINGTON — Warwickshire

The village of Ilmington lies on the slopes of the Cotswolds, nine miles south of Stratford-on-Avon. The more level ground north of the village, towards Crimscote (fig. 6), still remained 'open field' until parliamentary enclosure in 1778. The open fields were surveyed for the enclosure; the map made at the time is preserved at Stratford.

Comparison of the photograph (fig. 5A) and the eighteenth-century survey of the same area will show which of the hedges seen today were the creation of parliamentary enclosure, conceived as firm ink lines ruled across the map (fig. 5B). The areas within these lines were marked with the names of their new owners. Thus, the two rectangular fields above the lane on the right of the photograph were to go to Mr Thomas Salmon to be settled, according to the legend on the map, on his eldest son Samuel and on his second son Thomas. In the L-shaped field on the left of these, a triple change of direction is shown by the ridges (A in the key). Near the lane they run in one way; in the middle of the field some run one way and some another; at the farther end all run parallel. The portion of the 1778 map reproduced shows that this field, which was to go after enclosure to Mr William Slatter, was made up of parts of three furlongs. One of these was *Drift Way Furlong*, the whole area marked 1, 1a and 1b on the key. The last seven strips of this furlong lie within Slatter's new field; and seven ridges may be counted within it. It is also clear both from the map of 1778 and from the modern photograph that the left-hand hedge is set atop an eighth strip, not part of *Drift Way Furlong* but the first of the next furlong, *Shoe Furlong* (6). At right angles to the 'grain' of *Drift Way Furlong*, but still within Slatter's new field, were the six short strips of *End of Windmill Hill* (5), and six corresponding ridges parallel to the lane can be counted.

The surveyor of 1778 identified the owner of each strip by his initials, placed in the middle of the strip. Where a proprietor had two or more adjacent strips these were shown undivided, and the number of strips included was indicated by a figure placed in front of the initials. Thus under the two 'l's of the boldly written *William* (4a) there were three strips belonging to *DS*, one to *BP* next to them, and then two to *JL* farther to the right. The widths were respectively 161, forty-six and a half and ninety-five 'links' of just under eight inches. These particular strips were very short; the surveyor's practice in the case of normal, longer strips was to measure the width at each end to allow for variations and to put the two measurements on either side of the initials. Thus the next strip to the right after *2JL*, belonging to *RW*, was forty-seven links wide at the upper end and forty-three links at the lower.

In the right foreground there is a field where ridge-and-furrow tails off into level ground, while there are no signs of ridge-and-furrow in the semi-circular field, to the right. Reference to the map of 1778 shows that this field was *Rod Meadow* (3), in permanent grass, and never part of the village arable. 'Grass' is also written in the belt of land (2), above the lane. The two dotted lines on the map at right angles to the strips mark a balk against which the ridge-and-furrow is seen to end on the photograph. However, the proprietorial dotted lines continue over this 'grass', as they do in the furlong numbered 7 on the key, and it would seem that each strip-owner had a share in the meadow as if it were divided among the proprietors by each staking out a continuation of his strip. This was an alternative method to a practice of staking strips of meadow and then allocating by lot ('Lot Meadow'). In either case, the non-arable use is indicated by the absence of ridge-and-furrow. The curving double hedge (B–B) crossing the ridges in the foreground marks the former track of the Stratford-on-Avon and Shipston-on-Stour horse-tramway.

Sources

1778 map: Stratford-on-Avon, Birthplace Library MSS; *V.C.H. Warwicks.* v (1949) 98–103; *Econ. Hist. Rev.* 2nd ser. 1 (1948) 44–5; assistance from Miss M. Cox, Mr Peter Ransom and Dr Levi Fox is acknowledged with thanks.

6. CRIMSCOTE Warwickshire

There is no better example of the variety of local enclosure experiences than Whitchurch in Warwickshire (four and a half miles south-east of Stratford-on-Avon), and its two hamlets, Wimpstone and Crimscote. Each had a separate set of open fields but there the resemblance ends. The open fields of Whitchurch were finally enclosed for sheep pasture between 1498 and 1548 by Sir Edward Belknap, sometime General Surveyor of Crown lands to Henry VII, an active south Warwickshire enclosing landlord who possessed more royal pardons for depopulation than any man in the country. Yet the open fields of Wimpstone and Crimscote were among the last to disappear from the English landscape. When the Tithe Award was drawn up in 1842 every acre of Crimscote was unenclosed and the map which accompanies the Award is an open-field map in every particular.

Why should Crimscote remain immune from enclosure when Whitchurch afforded such an example of the profitability of enclosure so early? The answer seems to lie in a mixture of geography and biography. The Belknaps sold Crimscote in 1500 and the later lords of Crimscote were not able to enclose by consent so long as they had six freeholders well dug in, with good legal titles.

The delayed enclosure may also have arisen from the poor quality of the arable, giving little hope that even an enclosure would be a profitable improvement. In 1938 there were extensive areas where the land was reverting to scrub. During the second world war this land was brought back under the plough, but despite tractor-ploughing the high-backed ridges have remained imprinted in the heavy, wet clayland. The photograph (fig. 6) looks south-west towards Crimscote Field Farm.

On the north (right) of the modern road, the ridges have been ploughed out on the higher ground, and now appear only as crop-marks (furlong cxv in 1842). The modern fence does not, however, coincide with the edge of the medieval furlong, and for a space of a few yards the ridges remain bold and unploughed with little mounds to mark the end of the plough-turn

Fig. 6. Crimscote. Medieval open fields, looking SW towards Crimscote Field Farm, May 1953.

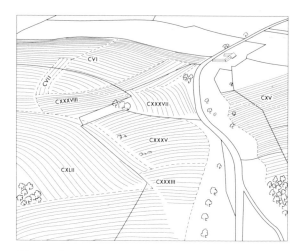

Key to fig. 6.

The details of the open-field strips and the furlong-numbers are taken from the Tithe Award of 1842.

where soil has been deposited. There are even signs that on occasion the plough came farther down the slope before turning, leaving fainter ridges. These extensions to the strips may date from years of land-hunger.

The key, based upon the Tithe Award of 1842, shows the boundaries of the furlongs so that other comparisons of ridge-and-furrow with strips can be made. The furlongs have been given the numbers they bear in the Tithe Award. Near the centre of the left-hand margin is the area shown in an air photograph published by C. S. and C. S. Orwin in 1938 where there is a complicated junction of furlongs. Only a few trees now remain from the scrub shown in that photograph and cross-ploughing has almost obliterated the pattern of ridges which intersected at that point, but the Tithe Award map shows that each of the ridges in the Orwins' photograph was a medieval strip.

Sources

Tithe Award: Warwicks. County Council Record

Office; enclosure of Whitchurch: I. S. Leadam, *Domesday of Inclosures* (1897) 426, 478 and 659; ground and air photographs of Crimscote before 1939: C. S. and C. S. Orwin, *The Open Fields* (3rd edn 1967) plates 11*a* and *b*; sale of 1500: *Warwickshire Feet of Fines* III, *Dugdale Soc.* XVIII (1943) no. 2774; National Grid Ref. SP 230470.

7. PADBURY   Buckinghamshire

The open fields of Padbury, two and a half miles south-east of Buckingham, survived until 1796. The photograph (fig. 7A) shows an area north of the village, which lies among the trees in the background. The foreground is shared by four fields with parallel hedges, and at parliamentary enclosure these fields were assigned to a proprietor who built Grange Farm (left foreground) to replace an old farmstead in the village. A map of the parish in 1591 was drawn by Thomas Clerke and Thomas Langdon for All Souls College, Oxford: part of it is reproduced in fig. 7B, and the details of the medieval fields included in the key are based upon it.

Comparison of the photograph and the map shows that the hedged lane on the right of the photograph follows part of the course of the field-way named *Stighegate* (9) in 1591. On the right of this lane there is a portion of a grass field where two different alignments of ridge-and-furrow can be seen, one parallel to the lane and the other at right angles to it and continuing beyond a hedge into an arable field. These two sets of ridges delineate *Greate Whitelandes* (10) and *Greate Bamrache* (11) furlongs.

In 1591 a second track, *Whadden Waye* (3), ran out from the village approximately where an unfenced track now crosses the first large field (top left). A single tree beside this track stands next the junction of the great *Whadden Waye Furlonge* (1) with the small group of strips of *Tho. Spratley* (2), the rectangle near the margin of the photograph and to the left of the tree. The ridges of *Whadden Waye Furlonge* continue past the hedge and come down to the clumps of trees in the middle field of the photograph. Here, between the two groups of trees, was a block of strips (4a) not named in 1591; and on the right of these, the strips of *Stighegate Furlonge* (8) extend towards the lane and the unridged meadowland near the stream where no strips were marked in 1591. This area was then named *Cockmore Myers* (5) and no doubt its wetness inhibited the plough. It would have served to augment the small supply of grassland in medieval Padbury. In the immediate foreground above the level of the *Myers* another furlong began.

In this photograph, therefore, two landscapes can be seen superimposed: a landscape of open-field furlongs and a landscape of enclosed and hedged fields, and the Elizabethan map proves that the pattern of ridge-and-furrow is that of the pre-enclosure strips. Had there been no map, the antiquity of the ridge-and-furrow could have been deduced from the stubborn way in which the ploughing-ridges ignore existing hedges. The exact correspondences with the map of 1591 make the deduction a certainty.

Several other All Souls' maps delineate open-field holdings. The set of plans for Weston Pinkney, six miles north of Brackley, comprises a plan of the whole parish, including the nearby hamlet of Milthorpe, together with a number of enlarged sections at such a scale that the cartographer had room to write for each furlong the names of owner or tenant on every strip. The area of each strip belonging to the college in 1593 was also measured.

Sources

Hovenden Maps, All Souls College, Oxford: a photograph of Weston and parts of the relevant map were published in *Country Life* CV (1949) 472–3.

8. BROXHOLME   Lincolnshire

The final comparison of open-field map and air photograph concerns the village and fields of Broxholme, four miles north-north-west of Lincoln on the eastern bank of the River Till. Since the village and fields were surveyed in the early seventeenth century the whole appearance of both has radically changed. As well as the usual enclosure of the fields the village has been reduced to a small group of houses. On the large scale Ordnance Map a curious scatter of *W*'s marks the wells of the vanished houses.

Internal evidence establishes that the map (fig. 8A) was drawn between 1593 and 1610. It shows a village with a small network of streets near the church at the north end, and a long extension of the built-up area southwards along a single frontage. Two of the three open fields abutted the village. *The Mill feylde* is named in a scroll at the bottom, and a similar scroll bears the words *The Northe feylde* at the top. On the left of the map are three closes recently taken from Mill Field and made up partly of open-field strips, their former lines sketched in, and partly of riverside grassland coloured green on the original map. Behind the houses on the right there was also grassland. The furlongs which were still open when the map was drawn were left white but with dotted lines to indicate strips. Each house in the village had the usual croft.

Fig. 7A. Padbury. Fields NE of the village, looking SW, May 1953. Most of the ground within the photograph lay in Padbury Hedge Field in 1591. Grange Farm, bottom left, was built after the enclosure of 1796.

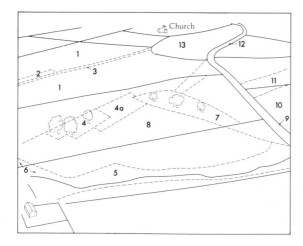

Key to figs. 7A and 7B.

1. Whadden Waye Furlonge
2. 'Tho. Spratley'
3. Whadden Waye
4. No detail given on 1591 map
4a. Block of strips, unnamed in 1591
5. Cockmore Myers
6. Cockemore small waye
7. 'Tho. Harris'
8. Stighegate Furlonge
9. Stighegate Waye
10. Greate Whitelandes
11. Greate Bamrache
12. St Katherines Waye
13. Churchyard Furlonge

Fig. 7B. Padbury Hedge Field in 1591; map by Clerke and Langdon.

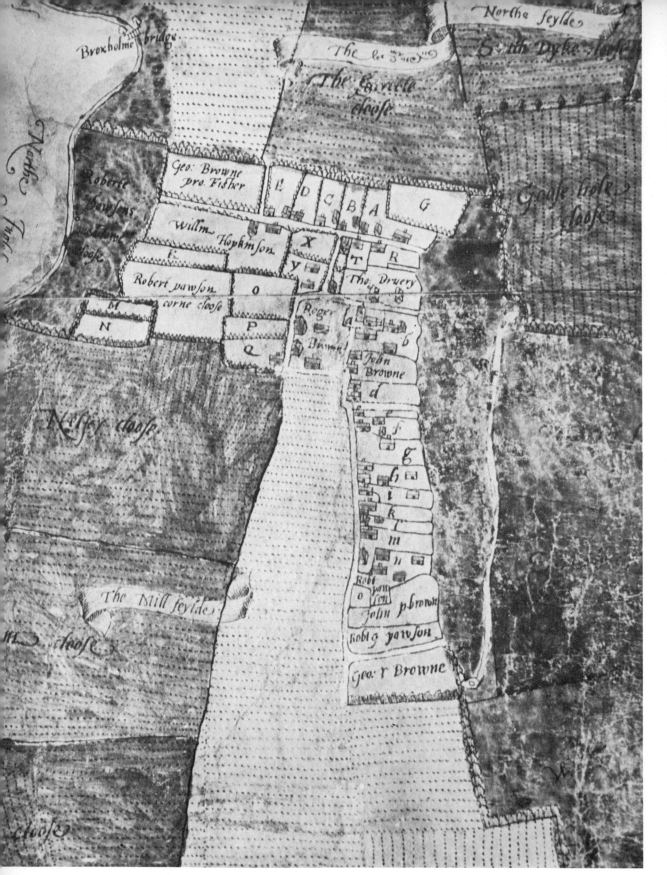

Fig. 8A. Broxholme; map of about 1600.

34

Fig. 8B. Broxholme; looking NNE, April 1953. The main street of the medieval village and the boundaries of cottage gardens are seen in the centre of the photograph. The ridge-and-furrow compares closely with the open-field strips of *c.* 1600 in fig. 8A.

The same area is represented in fig. 8B, looking almost due north, the lower edge of the photograph coinciding with that of the map. The meander in the River Till at the top left-hand corner of the photograph can be seen in the same position on fig. 8A and, indeed, all the essential features of the Jacobean map can be identified on the air photograph. At the bottom of the photograph modern ploughing has levelled the ridge-and-furrow, but soil-marks reveal its former course. In the grass field farther north, which extends to the whole width of the figure, the ridges are undisturbed, all of them running in an 'across' direction. Comparison with the Jacobean map will show that the ridging follows the pattern of the furlongs.

Another set of strips has been 'fossilised' in the top left-hand quarter of the photograph. On the left of the modern road there is a small group of 'up-and-down' ridges surrounded by ridges at right angles. Reference to the map shows that these correspond to the intrusion of a north–south furlong just above the *close* of *Nelsey cloose*, then a recently enclosed part of *Mill feylde*.

The modern road in this quarter can also be seen to cut through the line of ridges, proving that they antedate it. The map shows that there was no road at that point in the early seventeenth century. The village street then lay farther to the right, on the eastern edge of the furlongs of *Mill feylde*. It is now seen as a long hollow-way cut into the grass at the eastern edge of the ridges on the right of the modern road.

The crofts of the houses along this former street are marked by their boundary ditches. Half-way up the street, two modern buildings and their orchards survive in the medieval position. Beyond them are more empty crofts. There has been further depopulation in the streets surrounding the church, which can be seen among the trees, although this part of the village is too far from the camera for any detailed comparisons. On the right of the crofts is the level surface of the old grassland.

No documents have been found to date the decay of the fifty-four buildings marked on the old map, but such a wholesale depopulation coupled with the bodily shift westwards of the main street suggests a single and deliberate act rather than a long period of house-by-house decay. In Domesday Book there were ten teams of oxen recorded as ploughing at Broxholme; there were the church and twenty-six households, about four times as many as are seen on the photograph. Eighty-four persons over the age of sixteen paid the poll tax of 1377. The modern population is probably less than that of 1377. If it is remembered that in 1377 the countryside had not recovered from the Black Death of 1349 and the succeeding plagues, there is good reason to think that the population of Broxholme is now well below that of 1300.

Sources

Map: Lincolnshire Archives Committee, *Monson* 17/1; 1086: *The Lincs. Domesday. Lincs. Rec. Soc.* XIX (1924) 96; 1377: E. 179/237/75.

The evidence that ridges are found where open-field strips were once ploughed does not rest only on comparisons such as those made here. There is a good deal of documentary and literary evidence, published elsewhere, that both in the Middle Ages and in the sixteenth and seventeenth centuries 'ridges' were equated with strips. The word 'ridge' was commonly used in

written surveys to describe a strip; and, on occasions, witnesses in courts of law, attempting to prove that certain land had been part of the open-field arable, drew attention to the ridges and furrows which could be seen upon it. A classical instance is the surveyor of the depopulated Whatborough whose map was made for an All Souls' law-suit in 1586. He used the evidence of local witnesses to show the position of the former strips and furlongs which cover more than half his map. When he came to the enclosed parkland he added 'theise grounds doe appeare to have bene arrable' and in the next close 'theise groundes doe likewise lie ridge and forrow'.

The identity of ridge-and-furrow with strips has been argued here at some length,[17] principally because the identity was challenged in a sceptical article by Dr E. Kerridge published in 1951. With a wealth of quotation from farming writers he was able to show that post-enclosure farming practice continued to employ ridges (which, of course, the hedged fields had willy-nilly inherited). He also showed that modern ploughing could throw up ridges; but it must be pointed out that these are not the size of medieval strips and that the 'hedge-test' would also make it impossible for anyone to take these for medieval strips. He showed that ploughing of new intakes during the Napoleonic Wars produced ridges: in areas where it can be proved that land was first ploughed during this wartime boom this is a necessary caution which must be endorsed. He also emphasised, as has been emphasised here, that there were many parts of England where open-field husbandry did not throw the strips up into ridges.

But to Dr Kerridge, comparison of the kind made here is only 'an approximate coincidence'. He concludes that

it merely proves something that might well have been assumed, to wit, that the lie of the land has remained the same throughout the ages. As long as the lie of the land remains the same, then ninety-nine ploughmen of a hundred will plough their ridges in the same direction, the tractor ploughman of today just as the medieval husbandman.

Dr Kerridge has overlooked the fact that existing ridge-and-furrow has identity of length,

[17] For the discussion of ridge-and-furrow see M. W. Beresford, 'Ridge and furrow and the open fields', *Econ. Hist. Rev.* 2nd ser. II (1948) 34–45; E. Kerridge, 'Ridge and furrow and agrarian history', *ibid.* IV (1951) 14–36; and 'A reconsideration of some former husbandry practices', *Ag. Hist. Rev.* III (1955) 32–40; see also an agreed note by M. W. Beresford and W. R. Mead in *Geog. Jnl* CXXI (1955) 125–6; J. C. Jackson, 'The ridge and furrow controversy', *Amat. Hist.* V (1961) 41–53.

breadth and position with medieval strips, as a comparison of contemporary maps with air photographs has shown: not merely that the ridges and furlongs run the same way as the strips.[18] It will only be when these precise, and far from approximate, comparisons can be discredited that those who argue the identity of strips and ridges will be thrown on the defensive. A footnote to Dr Kerridge's 1951 article promised such a complementary contribution, based on field work from the late Professor J. D. Chambers. But this did not appear.

There are always dangers in urging a general identity, such as that of ridges with strips: it is an identity which needs cautious handling, possibly more cautious than at its first formulation. But there is no danger that we shall monopolise incaution. Two quotations from Dr Kerridge will suffice. 'Suppose that the Yorkshire Wolds were found gathered into ridge and furrow.... Field-work would not disclose that the Wolds were mostly sheep-walk until about 1770.' In fact, parts of the Wolds *can* be found gathered into ridge-and-furrow (as Mr Alan Harris has shown) so that Dr Kerridge's challenge can be met. The medieval villages of the Wolds had, of course, arable fields and the idea that they were 'mostly sheep-walk' makes no sense. The Wolds maintained a multi-field system in their villages, combining corn-growing with pasture. The wholesale sheepwalks from which the agricultural improvers of the 1770s rescued the Wolds were no older than the fifteenth and sixteenth centuries when so much of the medieval arable was going down to grass, many villages being depopulated in the process and most others shrinking in population. Because Dr Kerridge finds them a sheepwalk in the agricultural writers of the 1770s he must not assume that agrarian history begins only in 1540. The Wolds have had a succession of land-uses: corn-and-grass in the Middle Ages, largely grass in Tudor and Stuart times, and then back to corn with the improvements of such pioneers as the Sykes of Sledmere. Ridges on the edge of a depopulated Wolds village will be seen in fig. 48, and, at Whin Wold, on the hills above South Cave, Mr Harris has shown that the existence of ridges and furrows in the grass was taken in a lawsuit of 1773 as proof that the land there had

once been arable, although in grass from time beyond which no one could recall.[19] Nearly two hundred years earlier the surveyor who drew the map of Whatborough for All Souls had made the same deduction.

The second quotation from Dr Kerridge needs no comment. The italics alone are ours. 'Most of the ridge and furrow to be seen in the English countryside today is *the result of fairly recent ploughing, not so much medieval as nineteenth century, and mostly in enclosures.*'

The choice of illustrations now moves from the known to the unknown, from those villages which have surviving open-field maps to that much greater number which lacks maps. In their fields, is the appearance of ridge-and-furrow congruous with the argument of the previous pages and with comparisons of maps with ridges which have been carried out elsewhere?

9. near WATFORD   Northamptonshire

This photograph shows the effect of different agricultural treatments on the survival of ridge-and-furrow in these fields, which lie to the east of the Watford Gap service area on the M1 motorway. Only one-fifth of the area of Watford parish remained unenclosed after 1644 and the straight hedge-lines and rectangular shapes of the fields in this part of the parish clearly place them in the period of enclosure by Act of Parliament (p. 134 below). Much of this land has never been ploughed since enclosure and well-preserved ridge-and-furrow belonging to a number of different furlongs of the open fields of Watford parish is picked out by the low sun of a mid-winter afternoon. However, in the dark-toned field across the centre of the photograph, and in the lighter fields towards the upper left-hand corner, which are currently ploughed, the ridges have been levelled and at best can now be traced only as soil-marks. Two fields in the immediate foreground of the photograph with closely set, narrow lines of crop, probably roots, likewise no longer show ridge-and-furrow. The way in which the existing hedgerows over-ride the ridge-and-furrow seen here leaves no doubt that it belongs to a system of agriculture earlier than the present fields.

Many of the ridges are not quite straight but have gently sinuous shapes with reversed ∫-bends; seen, for example, in the right foreground. At a number of points, particularly in the distance of this photograph, rows of low

[18] Other published air photographs of medieval strip surviving as ridge-and-furrow: O. G. S. Crawford, *Luftbild und Vorgeschichte* (1938) 55; L. D. Stamp, *Man and the Land* (1944) pl. 3; *V.C.H. Leics.* II (1954) 159 and 192; C. S. and C. S. Orwin, *The Open Fields* (1967) pls. 4, 11 and 28; M. W. Beresford, *The Lost Villages of England* (1954) pls. 2, 3, 6, 12, 15.

[19] A. Harris, 'Pre-enclosure agricultural systems in E.R. Yorks.' (M.A. thesis, Univ. London, 1951–2), 62–6.

Fig. 9. Watford. Ridge-and-furrow in fields near the M1, looking W, December 1968.

mounds are seen where soil has accumulated at the ends of the plough-runs. A curvy double row of these humps shows where the ploughing pattern has been interrupted at a track or 'access way' which is evidently subsequent to the laying out of this furlong. Most of these strips, some broad, some narrow, exactly correspond on the other side of this 'way', indicating that the strips were originally continuous. No such humps appear at their near ends. The impression conveyed by this photograph is that there has been encroachment by the first ridge of the adjoining furlong.

In a number of different furlongs groups of ridges notably narrower than the majority may be seen: like the broad ridges, these, too, are mounded up at their ends, so they certainly reflect the same process of medieval ploughing. The amalgamation of ridges to form broader strips of varying widths has been noted at Ilmington (p. 29 above), but the significance of these regular groups of narrow ridges requires further investigation.

38

Sources

Bridges, *Northants*. I. 585; Northamptonshire ridge-and-furrow is discussed in R.C.H.M. *Northamptonshire* I (1975) esp. xlii–xliv, and III (forthcoming); National Grid ref. SP 601688.

10. ONLEY   Northamptonshire

At Ilmington and at Watford we have noted that the strips in medieval furlongs may vary in width, and we concluded from the evidence of the Ilmington enclosure map of 1778, that farmers who owned two or more adjacent strips might throw them together so that they could be ploughed as one, or perhaps, as the ridge-and-furrow at Watford suggested, a strip of 'normal' width might be subdivided for some purpose. Here at Onley, in the parish of Barby, two different styles of ridging can be seen preserved in grass fields which contain the earthworks of a deserted village. The deep hollow-ways, croft boundaries and level house-platforms are typical of sites on the Mid-

Fig. 10. Onley Grounds looking W, January 1969. Ridges of different widths surround and partly over-ride the deserted village of Onley.

land clay, of which Ditchford has been illustrated as an example (fig. 4).

Two areas in this photograph are ridged in narrow, mathematically straight and closely set strips in marked contrast to the broad, slightly sinuous and well-mounded selions. The distribution is notable; the two types of ridging are never to be found intermingled as they are at Ilmington and Watford. Here, two separate parcels of land have been worked into narrow ridging which nowhere seems to encroach on the balks, or on the 'cow-commons' of access ways between furlongs. However, the most striking feature at Onley is the narrow ridging in the field beyond the stream of which the course is marked by a line of bushes. These ridges are clearly seen there to be superimposed upon the earthworks of village crofts. Some of the crofts on the near side of the stream also bear faint traces of ridging, which may be slight possibly because ploughing here was not maintained. The nearest crofts appear quite unridged.

May it be that this sequence records successive stages of desertion of the village? The regularity and straightness of these small ridges suggests that they are of no great antiquity, but yet the work of farmers who had cause to respect the old land boundaries. This question would be clarified if the purpose of the work were known. Strips of such dimensions seem to be awkwardly narrow and close-set to be worked regularly as arable. An explanation in terms of a scheme to improve pasture on wet clay land for the furtherance of sheep-raising seems more likely. The change from early medieval arable to sheep-farming might, indeed, have been the initial cause of the abandonment of the village.

Sources

K. J. Allison *et al.*, *The Deserted Villages of Northamptonshire* (1966) 44; Bridges, *Northants.* I. 24; a full account of the earthworks, with a plan, will be found in R.C.H.M. *Northants.* III (forthcoming); National Grid ref. SP 512705.

Other photographs in this book include, incidentally, ridge-and-furrow in all stages of preservation and in many different counties. It will occasionally be possible to refer to open-field maps corresponding to these photographs, although the formal comparisons are now concluded. Ample material is available to show whether there is any truth in the equation of ridge-and-furrow with medieval strips, and what are the limitations to the equation.

If precise comparisons can indeed be made, a village with no open-field map and no documents to suggest where the open fields lay may recover the plan of its open fields by careful examination of ridge-and-furrow to see whether this has the medieval characteristics that have been illustrated. The mere fact that a theory, if correct, would remedy a deficiency of pre-enclosure maps makes caution necessary. A theory may be accepted because it is useful rather than because it is true. The numerous comparisons that can be made between air photographs and early maps leave little doubt that the ridge-and-furrow still visible today does preserve many of the details of medieval fields, and it may confidently be asserted that, in villages for which early maps are lacking, the proposition will not run counter to documentary evidence. If documents are absent, the evidence of ridge-and-furrow may be called in to assist investigations into the character and progress of local medieval agriculture.

III. SURVIVING OPEN FIELDS

11. LAXTON — Nottinghamshire

Laxton stands three miles from the Great North Road, a little to the south-west of Tuxford. Each year the village has its visitors anxious to see open-field farming still in operation. There is much for them to see: but in an important particular they are not looking at an undisturbed medieval landscape. Laxton has, indeed, managed without enclosure, so that great open and unhedged fields can be seen outside the limit of the crofts. But the village has not escaped consolidation of holdings.

The landscape in fig. 11 may look very like an open-field map; but it lacks strips. Between 1906 and 1909 a wholesale exchange of strips took place to give each farmer a more compact holding. The patchwork of light and shade on the photograph is one of holdings and cropping and not of furlongs.

The nature of this reorganisation was put succinctly by Professor J. D. Chambers, in 1928:

the strips themselves are unexpectedly large, owing to the fact that some twenty years ago the Lord of the Manor, Earl Manvers, having bought up all the freeholders' property in the open fields, decided to consolidate the scattered strips in each field and redistribute them on a more convenient plan. The result is that farmers who formerly had 40 or 50 scattered strips of an average size of half an acre, may now have only half a dozen of about 4 or 5 acres in size....

It is not surprising that the concept of a standard medieval strip of an acre or more persists so long when the best-known survival shows visitors these large strips, not more than seventy years old. The well-known film of Laxton, *Medieval Village*, does not emphasise the disappearance of the medieval strip into the larger modern holding. The publication of the map of the fields made in 1635 has made it possible to see the position and alignment of the strips while they still had their original medieval size.

Air photographs show the old divisions underlying the new. The boundary furrows which were in use for so many centuries before the reorganisation still appear as crop-marks. Their nature can be confirmed by comparisons with the map of 1635. On some of the steeper slopes the old strips still survive unconsolidated, marked out as small terraced lynchets. In fields now grass, the pattern of strips and furlongs is identical with the ridge-and-furrow; in the arable fields after ploughing and just before harvest the rise and fall of the old ridges can be seen from ground level, breaking up the five- or six-acre allotments, and often running counter to the shallow lines of the wider ridges of modern ploughing or to the lines of sowing.

The South Field of Laxton comprised just over 500 acres, and almost all of it is included in fig. 11. The stream at the foot was the boundary between South and East Fields. The meadow between the road and the stream lay in the latter field: it was *Laxton Long Meddow* (1) which the map of 1635 shows extending between the stream and the road for nearly a mile.

The South Field is divided into three by the two roughly parallel tracks, which extend from side to side across the photograph. The farther of these follows the line of *The Sike* (2), the artery of unploughed grassland through which ran Ellen Tree Brook in 1635. The lower track was *Rigg Gate* (3), now a little broader than in 1635 by a process described by Professor Chambers: 'at the same time [i.e. 1906–9] Earl Manvers rearranged and improved the grass roads so as to

Fig. 11. Laxton; South Field, looking S, July 1949.

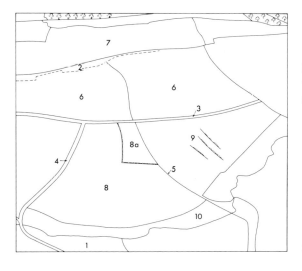

Key to fig. 11.

The details of the medieval fields are taken from the survey of 1635.

1. Laxton Long Meddow
2. The Sike
3. Rigg Gate
4. }
5. } Tracks each on the line of a 'common balke'
6. Long Lands
7. The Furlong which leadeth up the Stubbing Side
8. Middle Bank Hill
8a. Middle Furlong
9. Middle Banche (sic) Landes
10. Common or waste ground in South Field

enable the plough-turning to take place on uncultivated ground.' The slight **S**-curve in some of the strips shows where the medieval ploughmen had begun to prepare for the turn at the end of the furrow. At the right of the photograph there are signs of Earl Manvers' work: for a few yards the marks of former strips continue into what is now the road, *Rigg Gate* (3).

Two modern tracks (4 and 5) leave *Rigg Gate* and come down the photograph to cross the stream. The left-hand one (4) follows the line of a *common balke* (no. 1021 in the terrier accompanying the 1635 map). The other (5) continues beyond *Rigg Gate* up to *The Sike*, on the site of balk 1533 in the terrier. It divides the great furlong of *Long Lands* (6) with more than one hundred strips within it. Beyond *The Sike*, stretching to the edge of the distant woodland, was another block of arable strips, *The Furlong which leadeth up the Stubbing Side* (7).

One modern holding in the centre of the photograph (8*a*) has been hedged in, and a few scattered trees have grown up elsewhere on the banks of the two balks or tracks. In the block of strips (9) there are three short lengths of bushes which look at first sight like the skeleton of old hedges. In fact, they also are bushes lodged on unploughed ground. The slope of the hill, together with continuous ploughing along the line of the strips, have produced a slight terracing; between the terrace of one strip and the next is a steep low bank of earth on which scrub is growing. Similar lynchets occur in other parts of Laxton Fields, and the 6-inch Ordnance Map marks them as banks.

The photograph shows three stages of agricultural technique: the hedged fields represent a stage further than the consolidation of the holdings in 1909; the unhedged allotments are the logical conclusion of the piecemeal and occasional consolidation of strips which the 1635 terrier shows in progress. The medieval strips are no longer the units of ownership nor of cultivation, but (as the camera shows) they have not been wholly obliterated, for they constitute the ridge-and-furrow which makes the corrugations in each of the allotments in the modern patchwork.

Sources

C. S. and C. S. Orwin, *The Open Fields* (1938) *passim*, including map and terrier of 1635 from Bodleian MSS. C17/48/9 [the map was omitted from the 3rd edn (1967)]; J. D. Chambers, 'The open fields of Laxton', *Trans. Thoroton Soc.* XXXII (1928) 102–25; *Laxton: the Last English Open Field Village* (H.M.S.O. 1964).

12. ISLE OF PORTLAND   Dorset

Colonel C. D. Drew added the Isle of Portland to the living museums of open-field farming. Like Laxton, it is a living museum-piece with the strips still in cultivation, but encroachment of houses and quarries has severely reduced the area of the island under crops. The strips ('lawns') have recently been scheduled as an Ancient Monument.

The portion of the island here illustrated (fig. 12) lies towards the southern tip, looking south-west along the road to the Coastguard Station at Portland Bill. Most of the strips were in cultivation when the photograph was taken.

As Colonel Drew has pointed out, *between* the Portland strips there are balks of grass and these can be clearly seen in the photograph. The strips, which are up to 300 yards long, are mostly curved and vary in width from ten to seventy yards. These strips show the intimate connection between balks of this type and lynchets. Very little of the island is flat. In the area covered by the photograph the land slopes down from a height of 150 feet on the right to the coast where quarrying is in progress. In adjusting themselves to the slopes, some of the strips have taken on the slightly terraced appearance well illustrated by Colonel Drew's ground photographs in *Antiquity*. 'The growth of lynchets is still in progress.' Something of this terracing can be seen in fig. 12 in three fields to the right of the road.

Enclosure of strips has taken place piecemeal. Several such fields appear centre right and centre left where, in the fields bounded by stone walls, all trace of strips has now been erased. A map of the open fields of Portland, made in 1745 by the Keeper of the Quarries, shows that nearly the whole of the plateau was then under open fields, with unenclosed common on the lower ground at Chesil and Fortunewell. The fields are marked only in a generalised and conventional way, distinguished from the commons. The area in the photograph then lay in the *South Field*, but if the furlong divisions of the map were taken literally they could not be matched with the open-field furlongs of Portland as they appear today. But a note on the margin of the map sums up its imperfections: 'This plan when compared with that of 1800 will appear to be only an Eye Draught or Sketch of the Island, and what are here called the King's Lands will appear to be but a loose and very imperfect Sketch of them, both as to their situation and Boundaries.' Of the 825 acres of open fields shown on the Tithe Map of 1842, about 150 acres survive today.

Fig. 12. Isle of Portland. Open fields in cultivation, looking SSW, December 1965.

Sources

Colonel C. D. Drew, *Antiquity* XXII (1948) 79–81; map of 1745: M.P.E. 356; survey of 1608: L.R. 2/214; survey of 1650: E. 317/Dorset 12. A detailed account of the strip-fields of Portland with a diagram, will be found in R.C.H.M. *Dorset* II, *South-East*, pt 2 (1970) 258–9. The fields shown in fig. 12 lie at SY 686696.

13. BRAUNTON GREAT FIELD
Devonshire

The existence of an unenclosed arable field at Braunton, five miles north-west of Barnstaple, has been known to historians at least since Phear's *Notes* of 1889, while H. L. Gray, J. A. Venn and the Orwins devoted attention to it. Until the late Professor H. P. R. Finberg examined the documentary evidence the Braunton Great Field was usually explained as a comparatively modern feature, resulting from the reclamation of land in the Taw estuary and its division among the inhabitants of Braunton to supplement their upland holdings. Professor Finberg was able to demonstrate that dispersed arable strips in this very quarter of the village fields could be documented as early as 1324 and

Fig. 13. Braunton. Open fields in cultivation, looking NE, July 1953.

went on to show 'fossilised' strips in the long, narrow hedged fields in the other quarters of the parish. An example of such early enclosure can be seen in the bottom left-hand corner of the photograph (fig. 13), with tree-lined hedges.

The strips in Braunton Field have undergone, like those at Laxton, a certain measure of consolidation in recent years. There are now only twenty proprietors to share the scattered strips, and two owners have only one strip each. Nevertheless a considerable degree of intermixed holdings still prevails, as the differences of colour in the photograph indicate. The dividing line between strip and strip is here a narrow grass balk about one foot wide, the *landsherd* (Old English *landscearu*, boundary; cf. *lawndshed* for the balks in the Isle of Portland). Where adjacent strips have been consolidated under one owner only the outer boundary-balk has been left in grass. The varying widths of the holdings visible on the photograph have arisen from varying degrees of consolidation, but sufficient single

strips survive (e.g. bottom right) to indicate their original size.

The photograph, taken from the south-west, looks across *Gallowell, Lower, Middle* and *Higher Thorn Furlongs* towards the village which is on slightly higher ground. In the foreground is marshland with dried-out curving channels showing faintly in the grass. At the right-hand margin are the furlongs of *Pitlands* and *Longlands*. The lane, now partly hedged, which comes into the photograph from the left margin is Greenaway Lane, the *westegrenewaye* of 1324.

Sources

H. P. R. Finberg, 'The open field in Devon', in W. G. Hoskins and H. P. R. Finberg, *Devonshire Studies* (1952) 265–88, with plans; J. Phear, Notes in *Trans. Devon. Assoc.* XXI (1889) 202; J. A. Venn, *Foundations of Agricultural Economics* (1923) 14 and photographs. According to W. G. Hoskins, *Devon* (1954) 347, there are now only twelve proprietors in the Great Field. 'Within living memory' there were eighty-five.

IV. OTHER FIELD SYSTEMS

In the description of open-field topography more uniformity has been suggested than would be found in modern textbook discussions of medieval farming. These, based on documentary sources, make it less necessary to emphasise here the very important local variations which modify the simple picture of open-field topography already described. In particular, the nature of the photographic evidence prevents illustration of some of the interesting variants revealed on the lighter soils, especially in Norfolk and Wiltshire; the absence of visible ridge-and-furrow and the paucity of soil- and crop-marks do not mean that open-field farming was not practised in these counties. It thus happens that the minor units and divisions of the open-field landscape are marked most clearly just in those parts of England, the Midlands and the coastal plains of the north-east, where open-field husbandry was organised in its simplest forms, with arable fields occupying a large proportion of the parish and their cultivation the prime occupation of the villagers.

Elsewhere in England, and on differing terrain, there were incentives and disincentives operating to produce very different forms of husbandry. The area of field-land in proportion to grass, orchards or woodland might be considerably lower than in the Midlands. A complementary and enduring sheep-and-corn husbandry developed in the later Middle Ages on the chalk wolds in contrast to farming practice elsewhere. The importance of sheep in manuring and treading firm the light chalk soils has not always been noted by the historian.

Yet these differences do not lend themselves easily to visual illustration from the air. They can be well studied in such maps as those of Elizabethan Norfolk, preserved at Holkham, or in the surveys commissioned by the Earls of Pembroke for their Wiltshire estates, and there has been much discussion in print of the whole topic of regional variations both in medieval and Tudor farming. Where the visual evidence does not permit a thorough reconstruction of medieval topography it should not be overlooked as a partial contribution to the elucidation of these variant field-systems, but, for the reasons given above, even partial evidence is not easily forthcoming. The small space given here to the subject is, therefore, no measure of its importance.

It will also be clear that air photographs will have nothing to reveal about the important modifications in tenurial relationships which accompanied the variations in open-field husbandry from region to region. This is a matter for investigation in documents. One photograph only is included in this section as an illustration of a variant of the 'normal' open-field village. (Other villages where variants might be expected will be found in figs. 33–36, and 69.)

14. CARBURTON   Nottinghamshire

The plan drawn in 1615, reproduced as fig. 14B, reveals an infield–outfield husbandry. The characteristics of this system have been noted in other parts of the British Isles, usually where the area of land available for tillage was large in proportion to the area which the village wished to keep under the plough. A core of land near the village was kept in permanent occupation, having strips and furlongs like an ordinary open field. It formed the 'infield'. The 'outfield' lay beyond it, taking in all the rest of the township except what was permanent woodland or otherwise unploughable. The outfield played the role of a reserve on which the community drew intermittently. A piece of it would be taken up, cropped for a run of years and then turned back to pasture. Another piece would be taken up, and, in time, it too would pass back to grass. At any one moment the fraction of outfield under the plough would not have been large. The interval of time before a given piece of the outfield was turned back to grass was not fixed; nor was the interval certain between turning back to grass and receiving the plough again.

In a sense even the normal open-field routine was a special case of the infield–outfield system. A fallow field may be regarded as that part of the outfield which was being rested: or an outfield can be looked upon as a process of very lavish and long-drawn-out fallowing.

Such a relationship of a small infield to a large outfield would only have been tolerated where the soils were unrewarding to the sower. By care and heavy manuring, a small area of infield was kept in good heart, but the outfield could only be persuaded to produce a crop if it had long resting periods. The infield–outfield villages were not many miles distant from more densely settled country. In periods of land-hunger, such as the thirteenth century, claimants came to occupy some outfields more intensively but in a significant number of other places, Carburton being one, the outfield remained intact. Wherever settlement did not take in the outfields the villagers' traditional assessment of the low fer-

Fig. 14A. Carburton; looking SW, October 1969.

tility of the land seems to have been soundly based.

Evidence from Devon underlines this point. When the pressure of population on land began to increase in the thirteenth century, areas of outfield were available for settlement, for the older villages were quite widely spaced, with abundant land between them. This intervening land was lightly cropped: not because it was poor land, but because there was so much of it and so few claimants. When claimants became numerous the new settlers absorbed it and the outfield shrank.

Some writers have been attracted by the suggestion that all open fields may have arisen in a similar way: earlier settlers making only occasional use of their outfield; later settlers being forced to bring it under more continuous cultivation until at last a piece of land was rested only once every two or three years.

At Carburton in the forest area of Nottinghamshire, there is no doubt that the limiting factor was the quality of the soil. The topography of the infield–outfield is recorded in a survey made in 1615 when Sir Charles Cavendish was at law with the Crown. The village of twenty-one houses and crofts may be seen in the upper half of the map, but the scale is not such as to enable every strip to be shown, though the cartographer has indicated which were the common fields.

Immediately below the village, the map shows *Church Feilde* as a common field of 175 acres, cut in two by a road. On its left flank two enclosed fields (of nine and five acres) have been taken from it. Alongside the stream, below and to the right of *Church Feilde* are two other common fields shaded dark: they are *Tenter Feilde* and *Water Breck Feilde*. Above the village, on the far side of the stream, is a group of fifteen closes with very suggestive shapes. Even if one of them were not named *Pardon Flat* (i.e. Furlong) their shape would suggest a set of enclosed strips. From its name, the *Oulde Feilde* (to the left of *Church Feilde*), may be included in this core of common fields, the 'infield' area.

Near the bottom of the map a long, irregular-shaped wedge of land, again shaded dark, is

46

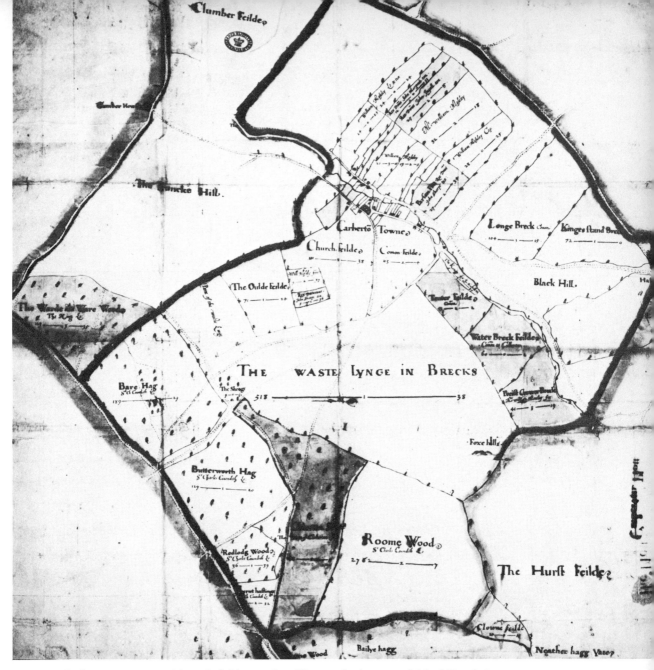

Fig. 14B. Carburton in 1615 with an infield near the village and a large outfield of 'Brecks'.

titled 'Carberton Sarts The towne of Carberton, free'. When the map was made, the upper part of this field was tree-covered, but the lower half seems to have been open land, perhaps heath or grass. The word 'Sarts' is the same as 'assarts', the familiar medieval word for land recently cleared of trees and brought into the cultivated village fields. But by 1615 the process was here in reverse: trees were returning.

A third area of land stood in an intermediate position between forest and field. This 'outfield', the Brecks, was common land, available when required for tillage but not a permanent part of the ploughlands. The largest area of breckland, 518 acres, lies prominently across the centre of the map as 'The waste Lynge in Brecks' but other brecks are marked.

A comparison of the map and the air photograph (fig. 14A) should evoke mild surprise. The air photograph has an orientation different from the map. It looks at the village from the northeast; north is towards the left-hand margin of the plan. The small enclosures are now thrown into one large field with no signs of hedges. The common fields have been enclosed. The road in the right foreground follows much

47

the same line as the road which divided *Church Feilde* into two in 1615.

Of Carburton village very little remains. The church and churchyard survive to be seen in the left foreground together with five other buildings: in 1615, there were twenty-one houses. The stream has been forced into a straight channel, the millpond filled in. In 1797 when Throsby wrote, the village was already 'about three or four houses only', so that this depopulation would seem to have been caused by a seventeenth-century emparking. Clumber Park, Thoresby Park and Welbeck Park adjoin. If the conifers are extended they will smother even the memory of a village. They have already increased in extent since the last revision of the 1-inch Ordnance Survey map.

Virtually nothing of the village or of its fields can be reconstructed from a photograph such as this. The surface reveals no traces of ancient agriculture, while the post-enclosure land-use, whether arable, grass or conifers, has effectively supplanted the boundaries and characteristics of the outfield. No visual distinction remains between an infield and an outfield when each has been superseded. Air photographs can assist historical inquiries in villages and fields only when there are visible remains, but such evidence does not exist everywhere, any more than does documentary evidence. Fortunately the two types of deficiency do not always coincide.

Sources

Plan of 1615: S.P. 14/83/80; see also Thoroton, *Notts.* III. 346; for infield–outfield references in other parts of England see M. W. Beresford, 'Lot acres', *Econ. Hist. Rev.* XIII (1943) 74–9; W. G. Hoskins, *Devon* (1954) 38–80; W. G. Hoskins and H. P. R. Finberg, *Devonshire Studies* (1952) 289–323. There will no doubt be detailed discussion of the early history of these systems in the medieval volumes of *The Agrarian History of England and Wales*. Meanwhile they are considered by several of the authors in A. R. H. Baker and R. A. Butlin, eds. *Studies of Field Systems in the British Isles* (1973).

4
THE FABRIC OF THE VILLAGE

If he will say that he can truly delineate a Mannor with all the members, as every street, highway, lane, river, hedge, ditch, close and field in forme with true curvings, angles, lengths and breadths ... I will say he is a rare man and more to be admired for his selfe-vaine opinion than for his skill.

NORDEN, *Surveior's Dialogue,* 128

It is the greatest error to suppose that history must needs be something written down; for it may just as well be something built up.
EILEEN POWER, *Medieval People* (Penguin ed.), 161

Air photographs record not only the present appearance of fields but stages of their history so far as this is preserved as earthworks or marks in the soil and crops. In villages, on the other hand, the streets and buildings now in use are the main visible feature. Occasionally, shrinkage or depopulation of a village will leave characteristic earthworks and other marks. The aspects of village history earlier than 1600 which air photographs can illuminate are principally those which have left traces in the village plan in the relationship of church, manor, cottages, green and streets. The historical significance of these topographical relationships is discussed in later chapters, and the selection of photographs which follows deals with single features within a village.

The history of some of these, such as the church and manor house, is well known, and the air photograph contributes little that is novel in their interpretation so that they are here considered but briefly and with particular reference to unusual circumstances in which they may occur.

I. THE CHURCH

Of medieval buildings the church most commonly survives and in many villages it is the oldest building. Its early foundation and its importance as a centre of congregation gave it particular influence in determining the subsequent position of streets and houses as the village population grew. The same factors brought the market-place of a town or village close to the churchyard, as the illustrations in chapter 8 show. Almost every modern village of any size has its church, although some of these are post-medieval foundations. Churches of various architectural periods and various sizes will therefore be seen in the majority of the photographs in chapters 2, 4, 5, 7, 8 and 9, but apart from seeing them unmasked by surrounding buildings it is unlikely that architectural historians will find the aerial view-point more instructive than one from the ground.

The aerial camera occasionally records a church in an unusual or isolated situation when historical curiosity may legitimately be awakened. The usual assumption of one church to a village is upset by a village with two parish churches, and the photograph (fig. 16) of the Aldwincles shows this duplication. The isolated church still used for services is a common sight in East Anglia and the Marcher counties of the west, and is associated with scattered settlement. The isolated, disused or ruined church demands an historical explanation, being the result of a decay of population rather than a decay of piety. Several such churches (or their sites) will be found in the photographs of the depopulated villages (chapter 6) alongside the earthworks of the former streets and houses of the parishioners. In the photograph of Knowlton there is a ruined church deserted at the supplanting of a medieval village but itself set within the abandoned earthworks of an earlier culture.

15. KNOWLTON   Dorset

The church and churchyard at Knowlton stand within a remarkable circular mound and ditch. The village whose inhabitants once worshipped

Fig. 15. Knowlton with the ruined church inside a prehistoric earthwork; looking SSW, December 1965.

here lay nine miles north-east of Blandford Forum, near Cranborne Chase, in a countryside scarred with the earthworks of settlers centuries older than the Anglo-Saxons. A few miles to the east, the woods and heaths of West Hampshire begin, but Knowlton stood in open country where Anglo-Saxon villages cluster along the valleys.

The alignment of their parish boundaries often suggests that the Anglo-Saxons were conscious of topographical features surviving from an earlier age. They incorporated the standing stones and barrows into their folk myths. Being prominent and easily identified landmarks, some prehistoric earthworks were taken as the gathering points for the popular assemblies of the Hundred, the administrative subdivisions of the counties. The 'rings' at Knowlton were used for this purpose, and this prehistoric ritual enclosure was also chosen as the site of a Christian church, possibly because of its earlier pagan associations. The photograph (fig. 15) shows the church from the north-east; its tower and roofless nave and chancel stand in the centre of an earthwork,

now a grassy enclave within an arable field. Eighteenth-century antiquaries and the surveyors for the first Ordnance Survey map noted a number of other earthen circles in the neighbourhood of the church. Now the only survivors are a large round barrow under the clump of trees to the left of the church and the remains of a large earthen circle enclosing the farm at the top of the photograph, which can be traced by the curved line of trees and, in the fields beyond the road, as a faint earthwork. The white marks in the two fields near the church are scattered heaps of fodder put out for cattle.

Another casualty is the village of Knowlton itself. The church was built as a chapelry to Horton, two miles to the south, but the village for which the chapel was provided is reduced to a single farm. The county historian, Hutchins, noted the depopulation, but attempts to date it have not been successful.

The church was in a state of neglect in the late seventeenth century, but a lawsuit in 1571 seems to indicate that Knowlton still had church-wardens at that date. At the height of its

Fig. 16. Aldwincle All Saints (foreground) and Aldwincle St Peter; looking WNW, April 1953.

medieval prosperity the village had a fair. No remains of the village can be detected round the church, and indeed, the site has recently been shown to lie beside the stream in the foreground of this view.

Besides the records of the Hundred court which met at Knowlton, there are three surveys of land within the village fields. The first is an early sixteenth-century strip-by-strip, furlong-by-furlong survey of *Knowlton Fielde*. Some furlongs of open-field arable were near the church. There was a 'furlong yt lyȝth next to the chyrche lanshcr'; 'next to the chyrche lyȝeth ii ac. i rd. to Jhon. Parrkers place att myll'; and 'in the northe syde off the churche ys yr a close y callyd ffrances crofte, and in ye crofte next to ye chyrche lyȝeth iii ac. to Robyn Gybbys place'.

This is all very different from the large fields of the photograph. The barrows were also used as landmarks and names in this survey. One furlong of strips was called 'the furlong att Venellys barrow' while 'the Battyd londe yt lyȝth by twyne iii [*sic*] barrowys'. A second survey is a short view of 'Knolton medowe', and the

51

third is dated March 14th, 18 Henry VIII [1527]. It is 'a view of Sir William ffelotts lond' and a duplicate contemporary copy is preserved with it. Apart from the demesne lands, eight tenants are named. The 'yerabullonde' (arable land) lay in three Fields: 'Knowlton Field', 'Middle Field' and 'The West Field lying upon Knowlton Mede'.

Sources

Hutchins, *Dorset* III. 150; surveys of 1527 etc.: Wollaton MSS. (Univ. of Nottingham Library), 6/174/29–30 and 34 with 5/164/1; 1571: E. 178/699; T. H. B. Baker, 'Knowlton Church', *Proc. Dorset Nat. Hist. and Ant. Field Club* XVII (1896) 135–40; H. Allcroft, *Earthwork of England* (1908) 564–6; S. and C. M. Piggott, 'Stone and earth circles in Dorset', *Antiquity* XIII (1939) 152–4, pl. II and fig. 9; R.C.H.M. *Dorset* V (1975) 113 and plan; National Grid ref. SU 024103.

16. THE ALDWINCLES
Northamptonshire

The origin of the double parish in manorial provision is clearly demonstrated by the twin churches of Aldwincle, both of which stand beside the street of this small village near the River Nene, two miles below Thrapston. The poll-tax collectors of 1377 recorded 174 villagers over the age of sixteen, and the tax paid in 1334 (73s. 4d.) was not particularly large for that part of the county. It was not the size of the community which called for two churches to serve the villagers. This is no overcrowded town parish crying out to be divided. Today there are only just over a hundred houses in the two parishes together.

In the village there were two manors, one belonging to the family who took their name from the village, the Aldwincles. They presented to the living of All Saints.[1] The church with a tower, the present fabric of which is mainly late thirteenth century, stands at the south-east end of the village in the foreground of the photograph (fig. 16) between the rectory and the manor house.

The second manor is associated with the church of St Peter whose spire can be seen on the right of the village street five hundred yards away from that of All Saints. St Peter's incorporates twelfth-century work, and in the first quarter of the twelfth century a priest was named among a list of the tenants of Peterborough abbey here; this manor had been the abbey's property since at least the reign of Edward the Confessor. What more natural than that the abbey should wish to provide a church for its tenants and the lord a church for his? No doubt other lords[2] and other religious houses in similar situations would have liked to make similar provision but lacked the means.[3]

Despite the two manors and the two parishes, the tax-collectors of the Exchequer took a simpler view of Aldwincle. In the collections of the clerical tax, there were naturally two units to be assessed; but in all the lay subsidies of which records remain there was only one sum assessed and collected from Aldwincle. The two parishes were united in 1879.

Sources

V.C.H. Northants. III (1930) 164–9; taxes 1334: E. 179/155/109; poll tax 1377: E. 179/155/28.

II. MANORS AND PARKS

What saie youe to oure buildinges that we have heare in Inglond of late daies, farre more excessive then at anie time heretofore?
The Discourse of the Commonweal (1549)

Only a small proportion of the manor houses seen incidentally in the photographs of villages (chapters 2–7) incorporate substantial medieval

architecture. Prosperous owners in all periods have rebuilt or extended their homes in contemporary styles or in romantic evocations of the past. As timber was replaced by stone and brick, the chances of survival increased, and the number of Tudor and Stuart manors that exist today is greater than the number from the previous centuries. Their owners built in durable

---

[1] For a church divided between six patrons, each representing a Domesday manor, see F. M. Stenton, *Lincs. Rec. Soc.* XIX (1924) xxii and 30 (Brocklesby, Lincs.).

[2] For the provision of churches by communities and not by lords, see F. M. Stenton, *Documents Illustrative of . . . the Danelaw* (1920) LXX and no. 465 (Hothorpe, Northants.); also Hedon, p. 220 below.

[3] Possible connections between local prosperity and the

foundation, rebuilding, extension and decay of parish churches are worth further local investigation: see W. G. Hoskins and H. P. R. Finberg, *Devonshire Studies* (1952) 233–46. The role of credit is important: the rebuilding of Eye steeple in 1470 was only partly paid for at the time (*Hist. MSS. Comm.* X (4) 531); compare also the Friar in the *Summoner's Tale*: 'and forty pound is owing still for stone'.

Fig. 17. Wormleighton. The existing village, the deserted medieval village and the moat; looking NW, May 1953.

materials in a style which was not incommodious for the needs and tastes of the next four hundred years.[4]

If the owner of a manor house wished to rebuild on a different site he found fewer obstacles than did the patron of a church. If room was needed for more outbuildings or for ornamental gardens the manor house could be rebuilt in parkland away from the original site in the village. These migrations have sometimes left the old manor sites vacant and visible from the air.[5]

[4] The published volumes of the *V.C.H.* and the *Inventories* of the Royal Commission on Historical Monuments provide the most comprehensive short descriptions of individual manor houses. Occasionally, such medieval documents as building-accounts or surveys provide semi-architectural descriptions of pre-Tudor building: e.g. those in *Cal. Misc. Inq.* II, no. 143 and III, no. 1013.

[5] Castles were sometimes abandoned in favour of adjacent manor sites in parkland: the de Bohuns left Midhurst Castle in 1280 for Cowdray, *V.C.H. Sussex* IV (1953) 74.

17. WORMLEIGHTON   Warwickshire

At the turn of the sixteenth century the manor of Wormleighton belonged to William Cope, Cofferer to Henry VII. Although he was not resident there, the farming was not neglected and, after the fashion of neighbouring estates, arable fields were converted to pasture to the extent of 240 acres, with the effect of putting sixty villagers out of employment. In 1499, twenty-one messuages had been depopulated. In 1506, John Spencer, a grazier from the nearby parish of Hodnell, purchased the estate and subsequently came to live there; in so doing he was the first resident owner since the death of Sir John Peche in 1386. He found the manor house to be in a dilapidated state. As he described in testimony before the Court of Exchequer in 1519, it was 'a sory thatched hows'. This he replaced with 'a mannor place newe buylded'. The new house of

53

brick, part of which survives today, was built on the hilltop near the church.

Fig. 17 looks from the village, of which church and houses lie among trees at the bottom of the photograph, down a slope towards the Coventry–Oxford canal seen in the distance, following a contour course around the hill. The construction of the canal in 1777 destroyed one side and a corner of a rectangular moat, the remains of which are still visible. The ditch and bank of upcast earth outside it are interrupted for an entrance causeway in the middle of the long north-east side. This may be the site of the old manor house which John Spencer declined to maintain. In feudal assessments occupied manor houses were often recorded as 'worth nothing beyond the cost of repair'. A decayed building would seem a paltry asset to a man of Spencer's wealth, who paid £1900 for this estate and who also owned extensive lands in the parishes round about.

The rest of the hillside is seen to be covered with earthworks which represent house-platforms and crofts bordering a hollow-way, a former street of the village. The line of the street was also followed by a stream having its source near the church. As may be seen from the photograph the upper part of this street was later converted to form four elongated fishponds fed by the overflow from a much larger, rectangular reservoir, two sides of which were retained by an earthen dam, now crowned by a hedge.

Two detailed plans of Wormleighton survive, from 1634 and 1734, when the grass field in fig. 17 was named *The Old Town*, embodying the folk-memory of houses that had once existed in the township before the depopulation.

These deserted crofts may have constituted the original settlement, recorded in a charter of 956, and later abandoned in favour of the hilltop, alongside the church. Alternatively, they may have been a secondary extension of a settlement originally established on the hilltop but abandoned in a subsequent decrease in population. In the absence of documentary record, only excavation can reveal the true sequence, and confirm the period of the manor earthworks.

Sources

1279: E.164/15, ff. 77–8; 1517 inquiry: I.S. Leadam, *The Domesday of Inclosures* (1897) 403–4 with Exchequer hearings in E.163/10/7, E.159/298 Mich., mm.17d, 18d, and E.368/292 Easter m.30r; pleadings: Leadam, *op.cit.*, 485–9 and C.43/28/8 m.11; plans of 1634 by Richard Norwood and 1734 by John Reynolds, in muniments at Althorp Park seen by courtesy of Earl Spencer. There is a full account of the history of the village in H. Thorpe, 'The lord and the landscape', *Trans. Birm. Arch. Soc.* LXXX (1965) 38–77, with air photographs and plans.

The homestead moat is now known to be a common earthwork in counties where water is readily obtained to fill moats, and where clay is available to help hold the water. Moats, on the analogy of castles, were once taken as a form of military defence; but many moats offer little hindrance to attack while the buildings within them are rarely fortified, which suggests they were not intended to be defensive. The smaller moats, indeed, are hardly larger than the ditches that our photographs show forming boundaries between village crofts, and many are smaller than the circumference banks of villages (see figs. 4, 42A, 46–51A, 52). In 1962 Mr F. V. Emery estimated that there were between 3000 and 4000 moated sites in England[6] but in Yorkshire alone a survey published by Mrs Le Patourel in 1972 recorded over 330 examples.[7] She noted how rarely they were found within the corridor in the North Riding plain along which marauders were most likely to come, and how frequently in the less-troubled southern and eastern parts of the county.

In Warwickshire Dr B. K. Roberts associated moats with late colonisation of woodland by free occupiers.[8] About one-sixth of Yorkshire examples could fall into this class, particularly where marshland was being reclaimed, but in Yorkshire 63 per cent of all moats were in or adjoined old-established villages. The village of Scredington, Lincolnshire, has five moats, a number which matches the subdivisions of the village into manors already noted in Domesday Book.[9] The most plausible explanation of the chronology and distribution of known moats makes them a passing seigniorial fashion among ranks of society well below the contemporary builders of castles. Neither distribution nor chronology seems to fit the hypothesis of a raised platform against a rising water-table in time of climatic deterioration.

[6] F. V. Emery, 'Moated settlements in England', *Geography* XLVII (1962) 378.

[7] Jean Le Patourel, 'Moated sites of Yorkshire: a survey and its implications', *Château Gaillard* V (1972), 121–32, and *The Moated Sites of Yorkshire*, Society for Medieval Archaeology Monograph no. 5 (1973). There is now a 'Moated Sites Research Group' organising local researches and publishing an annual *Report*, the first number of which (1973) contained a list of over 3000 sites.

[8] B. K. Roberts, 'Moated sites in Midland England', *Trans. Birm. Arch. Soc.* LXXX (1965) 27.

[9] M. W. Barley, *Lincolnshire and the Fens* (1952) 98.

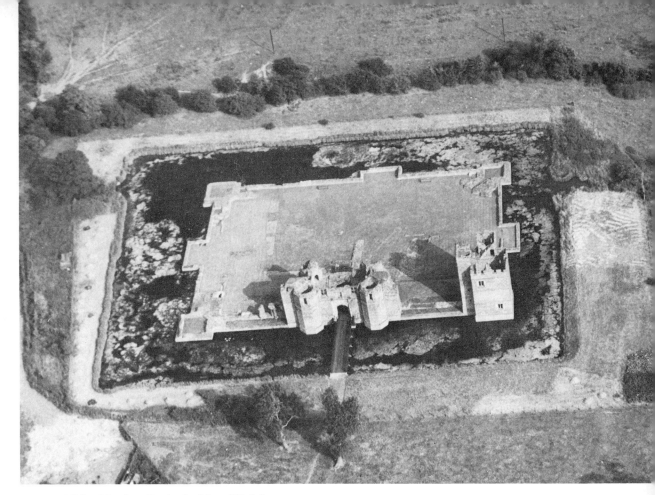

Fig. 18. Kirby Muxloe Castle; looking SE, July 1945.

An important archaeological feature of manor sites in general, whether moated or not, is that the choice of site does not seem to go back to the earliest period of a village; in many excavated examples remains of peasant houses, of croft boundaries and even of roadways have been found below the manor house platform, and cut through where the moats were dug.[10] Structural details of buried buildings at a moated site have seldom been identified from the air. Even in authenticated cases the building within a moated area may have been reconstructed or re-aligned. Nor does the absence of water mean that a moat was always dry. The piping of spring-water and the laying of field drains may easily rob a moat of its water supply. On grassy platforms and moated islands there is often very little to see of the ground-plan of a medieval manor even where no modern building has replaced it. Nor is there often more than a suggestion of the appurtenances listed in documentary surveys of

manor houses: the garden, the orchard, the dovecot and such outbuildings as barns, granaries, ox-houses, stables and dairies.

18. KIRBY MUXLOE   Leicestershire

In the autumn of 1480 the gardeners at Lord Hastings' manor house at Kirby Muxloe, four miles west of Leicester, were set to unaccustomed work. They were joined by other labourers, some of them Welsh. Their task was to excavate the wide moat designed to surround the new manor house. To create the great rectangular pool shown in the photograph (fig. 18) many hundred cubic yards of soil had to be removed and the nearby stream dammed and diverted. An older manor house at Kirby (revealed by excavations in 1911–12) was partly incorporated in the new building, but the much more ambitious scale of the new moated house took in former orchards and gardens from which the labourers had to remove trees: oaks, ashes and elms. By the spring of 1481 eleven ditchers were working four days a week on the moat, and carts were converging on the spot with

[10] E.g. D. G. Hurst and J. G. Hurst, 'Excavation of two moated sites', Jnl Brit. Arch. Assoc. 3rd ser. xxx (1967) 48–86; J. G. Hurst, 'Northolt' Med. Arch. v (1961) 211–99 and vi–vii (1962–3), 309–10.

raw materials for the building. The waggons which bought the materials were made locally. Freestone was brought from the monastic quarry at Alton Hill, eleven miles to the north-east. Lime came from Barrow upon Soar, nine miles distant. Wood, straw, sand and clay for brick-making were found on the estate. The lead for the roofs came down the Derwent from Wirksworth.

The type of manor house which Lord Hastings was building bore a superficial resemblance to the solid castles of the Middle Ages. Defence needs had to be considered: Bosworth Field was still five years ahead. The house had its gun-ports, to be seen in the gatehouse and west tower, but it was only proof against moderate assault. In its construction careful attention was given to decoration and display. The house was set back from the village with an open approach across which its proportions could be admired; brick, then a comparative novelty, was used for building-material, and courses of brickwork were made into patterned decorations culminating in an heraldic design over the main gate. Within a few years Thomas Grey was to build his house in Bradgate Park four miles away, again in brick but completely unfortified. The manor at Kirby was to be primarily a country gentleman's house and not a fortress: the same principle is seen in the new castle built at Ashby-de-la-Zouch, also by Lord Hastings. He could well afford such lavish constructions: he had extensive grants of forfeited Lancastrian estates; he drew revenues from the offices of Chamberlain and Master of the Mint; he was a pensioner of the King of France; and he married a daughter of the Earl of Salisbury, a widow of Lord Harrington.

With the work well in hand and free-masons, rough-masons, carpenters and bricklayers busy side by side, the news came of the King's death and the accession of Richard III. In June 1483, Lord Hastings was executed and the work came to a standstill. After a pause it was resumed, but the pace was slower and the scale was reduced. When the building-accounts end in December 1484 just under a thousand pounds had been spent and 1 342 500 bricks laid.

The best preserved part of the house is the great gate-tower seen in the photograph from the west. The plan has the symmetry of Bodiam Castle, with four strong corner towers and a smaller tower at the mid-point of each of the shorter sides. In the middle of the longer side, opposite the gatehouse, another small tower is placed asymmetrically. At the beginning of the present century the moat was silted up and the buildings overgrown, but the medieval appearance was regained by excavations and partial restoration carried out in 1911–13.

Sources

Professor Hamilton Thompson edited the building-accounts with an introduction and commentary in *Trans. Leics. Arch. Soc.* XI (1919) 193–345, also 87 and 109; C. R. Peers, *Official Guide* (H.M.S.O. 1917).

19. QUARRENDON   Buckinghamshire

The site of the manor which once stood within the moats at Quarrendon, two miles north-west of Aylesbury, is now as grassy as that of Wormleighton although it was in use longer. Sir Henry Lee entertained Queen Elizabeth here in 1592 for two days.

The view (fig. 19) is to the west. A massive bank forty feet wide with inner and outer moats can be seen forming two sides and half the third side of a large rectangle. The moats were fed from the River Thame that meanders across a meadow in the distance, and the outflow leaves the photograph, centre left. This manor together with the ruined parish church of St Peter, which may be distinguished to the north of the moats amid the shadows of tall trees, lay at the southern edge of Quarrendon village. The site of the village, now deserted, forms the subject of fig. 47. Regular services at St Peter's ceased in the eighteenth century, and an engraving in Lipscomb's county *History* of 1837 shows the building already in decay. The water-meadows beside the stream give place to open-field selions on either side of the moats. Beyond the river are earthworks of yet another deserted medieval settlement; this also lies within Quarrendon parish and, since there is no documentary reference to a separate community, it must be supposed that *Quarrendon* was also the name of the other settlement, though whether the two sites were contemporary cannot now be determined.

Quarrendon church and manor house, like the earthworks at Wormleighton, stand within an unusually large grass field which has the appearance of old pasture rather than of manorial parkland. However, such parkland was easily converted to the wholly utilitarian landscape of the grazier. Sixteenth-century plans often show within the same park-pale animals awaiting the butcher and deer awaiting the chase, and Quarrendon lay next to Aylesbury which will always have offered an active market.

Sources

R.C.H.M. *Buckinghamshire* I (1912) 273; the site lies at SP 801158.

Fig. 19. Quarrendon. The site of the manor house, looking WNW, December 1965.

20. HOLDENBY   Northamptonshire

A lord of the manor of the sixteenth century who wished to have a park alongside his house had to reckon with the nature and former use of the ground. Imparking was easiest where, as at Wormleighton, the village had already decayed along with arable cultivation, and the grassland was in his sole ownership or tenancy. There are many examples of parks that include the earthworks of a depopulated village and the ridge-and-furrow of long-abandoned arable. There were also some other parts of England where, even in the sixteenth century, heath and woodland were still so abundant that parks could be made without intrusion into cultivated land or without displacement of villagers, very much as Norman magnates could have taken

land into the chase or into parkland of a new castle.[11] But even with heathland, rights of commoning probably existed: in 1571 a list of Norfolk grievances presented to the Queen complained of the gentlemen who had enlarged parks by gathering together their own lands and 'made gret Inclosers not only upon ther owne londes but upon the commens'.[12]

Normally, however, parks created in the later Middle Ages and in early modern times involved the acquisition of rights over cultivated field-land, meadow, and pasture before a pale could be built to define the bounds of a new park. This was occasionally done by expropriation but more frequently by reallocation of land which gave freeholders compensatory grants of land elsewhere. Village houses could still be moved to create a private pleasaunce; one sign that there

[11] A good example of an early park is the embanked circuit of Devizes, Wiltshire, which is probably contemporary with the building of the town and castle by the Norman bishop of Salisbury; for others, see O. G. S. Crawford, *Archaeology in the Field* (1953) 190. The medieval parks of Dorset have been studied in detail by L. M. Cantor and J. D. Wilson in *Proc. Dorset Nat. Hist. and Arch. Soc.* LXXXIII (1962) 147 and sub-

sequent volumes. For another county gazetteer, see J. M. Steane, 'The medieval parks of Northants.', *Northants. Past and Present* V (1975) 211–34. For a survey of ridge-and-furrow within a medieval deer park at Oundle, Northants, see Christopher Taylor, *Fieldwork in Medieval Archaeology* (1974) 56.

[12] E. 163/16/14.

Fig. 20A. Holdenby; looking NW, November 1967.

has been some rearrangement of this sort is a village church set well inside parkland without neighbouring village houses.

In 1591 John Norden submitted to Lord Burghley a model survey and map of Northamptonshire, and in it Holdenby House was described as 'pleasantlie contrived, mountinge on a hill environed with most ample and lardge fields and goodly pastures, manie young groves newly planted ... fisheponds well replenished and a parke of fallow deare with a large warren of conyes not farr from the House'. The 'pleasant contriving' had been carried out during the occupation of Sir Christopher Hatton whose family seat this was. The pleasaunces which surrounded the gentleman's house excited Norden's admiration: 'with what industrye and toyle of man the garden hath been raised levelled and formed out of a most craggy and unprofitable grounde. The state of the same house is such and so beautiful that it may well delight a Prince.'

Thanks to two estate plans which have survived, the process by which the medieval manor house and village fields gave way to the mansion and parkland can be shown. The sketch-map (fig. 20B) shows the principal changes between the two plans, one of 1580 and the other of 1587. Although only two arches, set like gigantic croquet hoops, remain from the base court of the Elizabethan house (top right), other parts are incorporated within the present house which is seen in fig. 20A from the south-east.

The small village lies outside the park, to the north-east. The church of the medieval village now stands isolated in the park below a series of terraces which mask Norden's 'crags'. In 1580 the 'scite' of the medieval manor house was indicated immediately below the church where there is still a level platform of grass. Groups of trees to the right mark the fishponds (see fig. 20A). The terraces were used as gardens, one of the two 'rosaries' of 1580 becoming a bowling alley by 1587. The ridge-and-furrow in the foreground belonged to the furlongs of *Wood Feelde* until the imparking in 1587.

Between 1580 and 1587 the house and gardens had been matched by an extensive park in which the cartographer placed leaping deer and sitting rabbits. Around it he drew the circuit of the pale which separated the deer from the remainder of

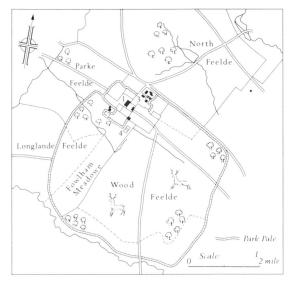

Fig. 20B. Holdenby in the late sixteenth century. The broken lines indicate the bounds of the fields in 1580 included within the park pale of 1587.

1. Holdenby House.
2. Site of medieval manor.
3. Village.
4. Fishponds.

the open fields which had contributed to the park. *Wood Feelde* was entirely absorbed and the three other fields, *Longlande, Parke* and *North* contributed smaller areas. The principal meadow, *Fowlham*, was also taken into the park making 606 acres in all, more than one-third of the parish.

Sources

Bridges, *Northants*. I. 525–6; maps: Northants. Archives Committee, Finch-Hatton MSS. 272; Norden's survey of 1591: B. L. map room, original in Bibliothèque Nationale, Paris; Hatton's works and their remains will be fully described in R.C.H.M. *Northants*. III (forthcoming).

Seventeenth- and eighteenth-century imparkings or extensions of medieval parks were usually more careful of property rights than earlier enclosures of this kind. When the great park of Stowe was made, the villagers were moved to new houses at Dodford; at Wotton Underwood[13] and Castle Howard,[14] where the new park involved the removal of village houses, there are no records of local discontent

[13] For Wotton Underwood before and after emparking see the map in *Geog. Jnl* CXVII (1951) 143; the open-field map of 1649 is in the Aylesbury Museum.
[14] For Castle Howard before and after imparking see the map in *Yorks. Arch. Jnl* XXXVIII (1951) 285.

and the villagers were probably rehoused elsewhere on the estate.

Such an imparking may not leave very clear earthworks of the former villages to be seen from the air.[15] The work of the landscape gardeners was directed towards effacing all traces of streets and houses in order to achieve open vistas of parkland. The obliteration was assisted by making lakes such as those at Milton Abbas and Wotton Underwood. Extensive ranges of outbuildings and gardens form a screen through which air photography cannot penetrate.

Outside the village area the obliteration has often been less thorough. Hedges and roads have been removed from the former field-land in order to make way for avenues and vistas but the marks of old ploughing have been more difficult to eradicate: indeed there were arguments against attempting to do so. In *The Agriculture of Oxfordshire* (1813) Arthur Young recounts that 'Sir Christopher Willoughby thirty years ago ploughed down some high ridges ... but he repented of it ever since, the land has not yet recovered. He considers that the *staple* [i.e. the top-soil] is the artificial child of cultivation; and if it is buried and the subsoil brought up by levelling, it is injured for an age. He did it for ornament in forming a lawn ...'

The grassland of parks has been jealously preserved. The owner of the park made out of the fields of the depopulated village of Compton Verney directed in his will that only two indiscretions should rob his widow of her inheritance: remarriage or the ploughing up of the park. The pattern of ridge-and-furrow in many parks suggests a kinship closer to the medieval fields than to any field shape or field groupings likely to have been produced by the short-lived ploughings of the Napoleonic Wars. Where, as in Badminton Park, or at Wimpole, the marks of ridge-and-furrow sail uninterruptedly across an avenue of great trees, it is quite clear which came first. At Wotton Underwood there is a pre-enclosure map showing the very field-strips corresponding to the ridges which now appear among the avenues.

21. HAREWOOD Yorkshire, West Riding

Harewood, seven miles north of Leeds, is a classic example of a village moved for the convenience of an eighteenth-century landowner creating a new village outside the park in a

[15] As at Nuneham Courtenay, Oxon., which is plausibly suggested as the inspiration for Goldsmith's poem 'The Deserted Village': M. Batey, 'Nuneham Courtenay', *Oxoniensia* XXXIII (1968) 108–24; plans in M. W. Beresford and J. G. Hurst, *Deserted Medieval Villages* (1971) 57.

Fig. 21. Harewood. John Carr's village, seen from the NE, with the park beyond, June 1951.

decorative and formal plan. The foundation stone of Harewood House was laid in 1759, and by the time of its completion, in 1771, the two thousand acres of gardens and grounds had been laid out by Capability Brown. The existing village and the park are seen in the photograph (fig. 21) from the north-east. The medieval village of Harewood lay near the church, which has not been disturbed and remains within the park in an isolated position, completely hidden amongst the trees on the right margin of the photograph. Harewood House itself lies amongst the trees in the centre distance. To the left of this is the lake which in its present form dates from 1776.

In the thirteenth century Harewood had been a market-village on the main route down Wharfedale. Among the more prosperous taxpayers in 1379 were two butchers, a draper, a shoemaker and an inn-keeper. In 1377 the poll-taxpayers had numbered 140. By the sixteenth century the village was much decayed. One of Burghley's correspondents was a James Rither of Harewood, prone to tender advice for the reformation of morals. He attributed the impoverishment of the village to the enclosure of the

park by the father of that Judge Gascoigne whose tomb is still in the church, who 'beinge a rich freholder within that manor did buye out first all the freeholders . . . and wher ther owne howses stood, and so laying the lands to make a demayn left the tenements without ground. The Judge's posterity have sithence bought out many freholders in other partes of the mannor.' This would date the original enclosure in the first decade of the fifteenth century.

The village had recovered its prosperity by the eighteenth century when two important turnpike roads crossed here. The Leeds–Harrogate–Ripon road crosses the photograph, following the trees at the edge of the park. The York–Skipton turnpike is the road which joins this at the open space in the centre of the figure. Before the building of Harewood House this turnpike continued straight, past where the main lodge of the park now stands. It was diverted to a riverside route half a mile to the north, but some of its old bridges remain in the park.

The present village lay-out was designed by John Carr of York. The frontage of the houses is so planned as to present a widening vista with the lodge-gates in the distance. Another set of houses lines the Leeds road, and a small block, *The Square*, is set to the right of the lodge, in the trees. The first Earl Lascelles, who moved the village, hoped to augment its prosperity with a ribbon mill, but this was short lived and the nineteenth-century villagers found their principal employment in the house and estate.

Sources

John Jones, *The History of Harewood* (1859); W. A. Eden, *Town Planning Review* XIII (1929) 181–4; Rither's letter in B. L. Lans. MS. 29, fols. 51–2; poll tax in E. 179/206/36 and 49; survey of 1636: Sheffield City Library, Strafford (Wentworth) MS. 29; of 1656, 1687, 1689, *c.* 1738, 1758, 1758 with maps of *c* 1690 and 1796: Harewood MSS, Leeds City Archives.

III. TOFTS AND CROFTS

A toft is a little peece of land upon which sometimes was situate a dwelling house ... a croft is a small plot ... neere a dwelling house.
                           NORDEN, *Surveior's Dialogue*

... of Freeholders ... of Customary Tenants ... of Cottagers ... what Cottages and Curtilages they hold ...

                           EXTENTA MANERII

In a photograph of a village having some discernible topographical form the patterns which first catch the eye are those of the perimeter, at which the fields end, and of the inner network of streets. The very shape of this network, of course, may itself be influenced and even determined by the position of certain buildings. Yet the categories of buildings which might determine the alignment of streets were limited: a small company of castles, abbeys, churches and manor houses. The majority of village buildings, the peasant houses, were followers and not leaders. Yet it is they and their attendant plots of land, called crofts, which block in and emphasise the pattern of streets and alleys.[16] The houses lie along the streets, sometimes flanking them, sometimes set end-on, a little aloof as the Elizabethan cartographers drew them. Between the houses, which were seldom linked together as a single frontage, were open spaces completing the width of the long, narrow crofts at the head of which the house was commonly set. The length of the croft ran back from the house. In a simple village plan it reached as far as the edge of the fields. At the meeting place of croft

and open-field strips there was often a back-lane, a perimeter road giving access to the crofts. This was bounded on one side by a ditch and fence which kept domestic animals from straying into the arable fields, and on the other by the croft hedges which helped to keep fox and wolf from the geese and hens. Here and there, alleyways, carrying a variety of provincial names, ran between croft and croft leading from the street to the back-lane.

The crofts, sometimes so long and narrow that they look like open-field strips gathered at the back doors of houses, were individually occupied. Communal and collective rights and obligations stopped at their boundaries, and occasionally the first stages in the piecemeal enclosure of open-field strips can be seen in progress at the crofts' end: a newly hedged field made up of a small bundle of strips carefully gathered in one man's hands and then released from the communal life of the open fields by general agreement. In East Drayton, Nottinghamshire, in 1352 the crofts[17] were measured in *selions* (that is, by the very word for a single open-field strip), 'Thomas tenet quinque seliones qui vocantur croftum.' (Thomas holds five selions which are called a croft.)

The simple street pattern of Braunston (fig. 22) shows the relation of houses, crofts, street and back-lane even though the medieval houses have long been replaced by stone and brick. The crofts may also be discerned in two other types of photograph. In the one, the village-turned-town, the crofts have been too valuable to leave for vegetables and animals, and have acquired instead a crop of outhouses,

---

[16] Minor village buildings are noticed in the *Inventories* of the Royal Commission on Historical Monuments and sometimes in the parish accounts in the *V.C.H.* The admirable three-volume *Survey of Ancient Buildings* (*Beds. Hist. Rec. Soc.* 1931–6), together with J. S. Elliott's list of windmills, *ibid.* XIV (1931) 3–50, set an example which other counties have not followed.

[17] 'thos be onelye Croftes and called Croftes which have a house belded apon thiem or joyninge to thiem or be joyned to a house and inclosed from other common feldes': *Select Tithe Causes*, ed. J. S. Purvis (*Yorks. Arch. Soc. Rec. Ser.* CXIV (1949)) 50. The definition dated from 1554.

Fig. 22. Braunston; looking NE, April 1949.

stores and workshops ranged round an interior courtyard. Thus the maximum number of houses and shop-counters were able to share the limited street frontage, while the back-lane had its cobbles echoing with the noise of waggons and pack-horses, and the alleys were bridged over. This is the pattern found in two such different towns as St Ives (fig. 73) and Warkworth (fig. 62), each making the best of space, limited in the one instance by a river-bank and the edge of open fields and in the other by the neck of a great meander.

The crofts may also be seen, naked and stripped of their houses and fences, in the photographs of deserted villages in chapter 6. They survive as grassy platforms, standing a little higher than the level of the former streets and alleys, which the trampling of feet and the swirl of rains had slowly lowered during the centuries of village life. These remains are, by Norden's definition, tofts. While Norden discriminated precisely between croft and toft for the purpose of his surveys of land-use and holdings, the distinction is of less use in dis-

cussion of deserted villages today. For simplicity therefore, 'croft' will be used henceforward to refer to the house-plots of villages whether a dwelling house sometimes was situate upon them or not.

When a village has crofts regular in length and direction, flanked by others of irregular dimensions, it is usually the sign that additions have been made to an original nucleus. The photograph of Great Gidding in chapter 5 (fig. 32E) shows such a contrast, but without an early plan or a continuous run of documents one can only assume that the addition was in a medieval expansion phase. Local observation of croft widths, and of signs of former ploughing within crofts, will indicate other interesting problems to which there may be no universal solution.[18]

[18] *Coucher Book of Selby Abbey* II. *Yorks. Arch. Soc. Rec. Ser.* XIII (1893) 237; for other descriptions of croft-making by enclosing selions from the open fields: *Yorks. Assize Rolls temp. John and Henry III. Yorks. Arch. Soc. Rec. Ser.* XLIV (1911) 48 and 58.

22. BRAUNSTON   Northamptonshire

This village, seen in fig. 22 from the south-west, lies some six miles south of Rugby, along a ridge of land overlooking the Leam. Its medieval buildings lay along only one street. The church, manor, mill and rectory form the group in the foreground. The original length of the crofts is shown by the back-lane. On the right-hand side of the village the crofts are more irregular and at their lower end show signs of ploughing, now cut into by the Grand Union canal. The enclosed fields on the extreme left beyond the back-lane have their ridging overridden by hedges. Like the closes on the right they are probably the result of early and piecemeal enclosure of strips. The final enclosure took place in 1775.

The uninterrupted ridging in the foreground shows that the village houses never extended in this direction (see also fig. 49). It is unlikely that many villages occupied more than a fraction of their present street frontage in the centuries between their foundation and their enumeration in Domesday Book (1086). In that year Braunston possessed about twenty-two households. The later growth of population, as the field-area expanded, led to new crofts being set along the same street, probably encroaching on the original core of arable furlongs. The twentieth-century additions to the village houses have generally followed this tradition.

Sources

Bridges, *Northants.* 1. 26; Baker, *Northants.* 1. 266; S.C. 12/13/17; E. 179/155/28; E. 179/155/109; C. 133/118/3; C. 134/26/5; B.L. Add. Ch. 37395; a rough plan of the open fields was found among the muniments at Castle Howard but cannot now be traced.

IV. MILLS, PONDS AND WARRENS

Of Mills, and Fishings ...   EXTENTA MANERII

Adequate water supplies are essential if men, animals and crops are to survive. Springs and streams were important in determining the sites of early Anglo-Saxon settlements. The prevalence of prehistoric settlements in higher and drier positions raises other questions such as density of population and changes in the level of the water-table.

Springs, wells and ponds within the village are not prominent on air photographs. In former open-field country, particularly in clay areas, it is quite common to find small ponds among the strips and furlongs. These are not modern ponds dug to water animals out at pasture, for modern ponds lie in field corners and can often be shown to cut through the pattern of medieval ploughing. The pre-enclosure ponds were placed along the balks, the access-ways for the ploughs described above, p. 25. They were used for watering the plough-beasts, and it is likely that some of them served a double purpose, being a source of marl and clay.

The stream which provided a village with its drinking-water was also put to practical use. It is not known when the Anglo-Saxons first employed watermills or whether any Romano-British examples may have survived to be taken over. Domesday Book records a widespread distribution of watermills wherever there were suitable streams to harness. Thus, they were recorded in 256 places in Lincolnshire and in 304 places in Norfolk.[19] Some of these mill sites must already have been in use for more than two centuries. In Castle Rising, the parish boundary has a long, narrow projecting tongue, following one bank of a stream. At the end of the projection is a mill. This can only mean that at the time when the parish bounds were determined, that is, at an unknown point in the Dark Ages, the mill was important enough to cause a strip of land for a path and the millrace to be carved out of the territory of a neighbour.[20] This does not mean that a neighbour's mill was captured: the position of a mill is determined by the gradient of a stream, and the spacing of mills along streams did not necessarily follow the spacing of villages.

Tenants might only grind their corn at the manorial mill. This economic aspect of mill ownership brought mills into the Domesday survey. More than five centuries later Norden imagined this dialogue:

[19] M. T. Hodgen, 'Domesday watermills', *Antiquity* XIII (1939) 261–79.
[20] This boundary is shown on Ordnance Survey 1:50 000 map, sheet 132, TF 687254 to TF 696256; it is probable that the mill at Ditchford (sheet 151, SP 237372) was the cause of a deviation in the county boundary between Gloucestershire and Warwickshire.

Bailiff. But here is a mill. Sir, will you take note of it upon your plot?

Surveyor. In any case: for it is not the least ornament of a Mannor.[21]

These 'ornaments' of the Jacobean manor had long taken two forms. In the last quarter of the twelfth century the first documentary references appear to wind-driven mills. It is often said that the earliest reference occurs in Jocelyn de Brakelond's account of the erection of a mill at Bury St Edmunds, but the survey of the Knights Templars' estates made in 1185 locates two windmills, one of them at the now lost village of Weedley in South Cave (Yorkshire, East Riding) where a ploughed-out mound of circular shape can be seen on an air photograph.[22]

These early mills were post-mills. To keep the sails into wind the body of the mill, containing the moving parts, could be turned upon an upright post, fixed to cross-timbers sunk in the ground. The oldest existing mill in this country was built as late as the seventeenth century but a number of later mills of the 'tower' or 'smock' form were built on the sites of the older post-mills with their characteristic deep ditch. The choice of the best site for catching the wind was unlikely to be revised, once it had been made.

Windmill earthworks consist of a simple circular mound and ditch, sometimes mistaken for a prehistoric barrow. The mound was necessary to support the legs of the mill; the ditch is simply a spoil-pit from which the earth has been taken.[23] A medieval windmill site is shown in fig. 23. Bedfordshire has its own gazetteer of windmills as part of the *Survey of Ancient Buildings* published by the Bedfordshire Historical Record Society. Mr J. S. Elliott, who compiled the list, estimated that more than eighty parishes in the county had a windmill at one time or another.[24]

Windmill sites are usually recorded on the early estate plans in the spirit of Norden's surveyor, and mills and mill sites are commonly marked on Ordnance Survey maps. From these it can be seen that the ideal site for a mill was on high ground to catch the wind but yet neither too far from the village to which the flour would have to be taken, nor too far from the fields where the corn was grown. For this reason, not all mills or mill sites stand beside existing lanes. The field-ways which used to lead up to them may have been replaced at enclosure. A statute of 1284 (13 Ed. I, c. 46) protected the builder of a windmill against actions for loss of common pasture over the ground where it was built.

Over the country at large, the distribution of windmills for corn follows the grain-growing areas and the low-rainfall areas. The number in the western half of the country falls well below that in the east. They are also found as an adjunct to East Anglian fen-drainage.

23. KIRBY BELLARS · Leicestershire

The two adjacent windmill sites shown in fig. 23 lie near the village of Kirby Bellars, two and a half miles south-west of the market-town of Melton Mowbray. The mill sites were on the hill-slope above the village, at about the 350-foot contour but not at the highest point in the parish. The view is to the north and downhill; a fall of some 100 feet occurs between the hedge in the foreground and the base of the triangle of roads in the background. The hillside is prominent enough to catch the wind in the mill sails but not so steep as to bar the ploughteams from it, as the thorough cover of ridge-and-furrow demonstrates. There was unploughed grass between the ridges and the line of the lane on the left, where the ground drops to a watercourse and the ridges curve at their ends where the ploughteams turned. The furlongs of selions did not run continuously across to the right-hand edge of the photograph: although the direction of ploughing remained the same, the ploughs halted halfway at a balk that is almost parallel to the two modern lanes. In the distance this access-way, still used as a track to the buildings in the centre foreground, is worn down below field-level, then for a space it has a broader sward of unridged ground alongside it, which narrows to a well-cut modern track leading to a field gate. The light-coloured band which crosses ridge-and-furrow, balk and modern hedges, is a modern disturbance.

[21] *Surveior's Dialogue*, 132.
[22] B. A. Lees, ed., *Records of the Templars* (1935) 131; an equally early reference is also provided by a windmill belonging to Swineshead Priory, Lincs., which was built over five strips (*seliuncas*) of arable. The gift of land is dated between 1163 and 1181: *Cal. Ch. Rolls* III, 319.
[23] Windmill mounds that have been levelled may be revealed as crop-marks which show their construction-trenches: a cross which may be enclosed by a circle. In this way the sites of many lost mills have been recorded on photographs in the Cambridge Collection. Of the five mills marked on the plan of Winchelsea (fig. 103B) only one still remains, the others were discovered as parch marks in grass.
[24] J. Salmon, 'The windmill in English medieval art', *Jnl Brit. Arch. Assoc.* 3rd ser. VI (1941) 88–102; J. S. Elliott, *Beds. Hist. Rec. Soc.* XIV (1931) 3–50.

Fig. 23. Kirby Bellars. Windmill-mounds amidst ridge-and-furrow, looking N, May 1966.

On and alongside the near part of the balk where it stands higher than the ridge-and-furrow, the two windmill earthworks may be seen. They take the form of raised mounds having a characteristic appearance of a 'hot cross bun'. The two trenches were formed by the decay of the great cross-beams, formerly buried in the mound, which carried the superstructure of the mill. The farther of the two mounds is placed astride the balk just at the point where it widens, as if the windmill were designed to fit the balk without encroaching upon arable selions; the nearer of the two clearly encroaches upon a pair of ridges and furrows at the left-hand side of the balk. Neither mill is documented, and whether the one is a replacement or a complement for the other cannot now be determined. In times when grain output was increasing to meet a growing population, and new windmills supplemented old watermills, a lord might reasonably place windmills side by side for the use of the villagers whose selions lay intermixed in the furlongs nearby. It will be seen from the plan of Great Gidding (fig. 32B) in 1541 that the windmill there also lay remote from the village, amid open-field selions, but on a broad access balk which carried 'the waye from Stamford'; and a mill mound encroaching on selions is to be seen in the photograph of Padbury (fig. 54).

Watermills, on the other hand, may be found in all areas where streams can be expected to provide power for at least a few weeks in the year. Watermills were often adapted in the later Middle Ages to mechanical tasks other than grinding: the application of water-power to fulling was an important determinant of the location of the rural cloth industry; and in the sixteenth century some watermills were turned into gig-mills for 'raising' cloth. Surveys and maps make it possible to identify certain former fulling-mills (e.g. those at Byland, to mention a village illustrated in this book) but the differences between a fulling- and a cornmill are not such as may be detected from the air, and no attempt has been made to illustrate various forms of mill better distinguished from the ground. Both wind- and watermills have in modern times met serious competition from mills driven by steam or electricity but, earlier than this, areas where the arable acreage was shrinking already had their abandoned mills.

Like windmills, the sites of abandoned watermills may have characteristic earthworks. The location of these by a stream-side is seldom likely to give rise to any ambiguity when they are noticed.

24. SOUTH NEWTON   Wiltshire

The watermill at South Newton, illustrated in fig. 24, stands on the river Wylye, four and a half miles north-west of Salisbury. For a few miles above Wilton the valley bottom, never very wide, is laced with channel after channel, some of them old meanders, some millraces and some (as Dr Kerridge has shown) channels for water-meadows. The villages stand on the dry bank just above the meadows, the *Marsh* of 1563, with the field-land behind them on the sloping sides of the chalk uplands.

In the photograph South Newton, one of these riverside villages, is viewed from the south. The houses lie for the most part on the east side of the road, which alone separates them from the stream. The church is in the distance. The mill is the building in the foreground which stands between the road and the river.

The gradient of the river is such that no very long or tortuous millrace is necessary to gain a head of water behind the millwheel. The main stream can be seen falling idly over a weir, while the millrace follows the roadside for a short distance before being put to work in the mill. This mill, with its millrace, flood-gate and pond, was carefully described in a survey made for the Earl of Pembroke in 1563. Newton mill was then the manorial mill for the tenants of Newton and the neighbouring hamlets of Chilhampton and Stoford. Newton mill was almost certainly a cornmill for the produce of the open fields of the three communities. In 1315 there were thirty-eight households in South Newton. The village has clearly shrunk, but the photograph shows no signs of a former extension of the built-up area.

Sources

Survey of the Lands of William, first Earl of Pembroke, transc. C. R. Straton (Roxburghe Club, 1909) I. 24, 26, 28 and II. 537, 545; 'Order for the floating of the water-meadows at Wylye, 1632', printed from Wilton MSS. in 'Surveys of the manors of Philip, first Earl of Pembroke and Montgomery, 1631–2', ed. E. Kerridge. *Wilts. Arch. and Nat. Hist. Soc. Records Branch* IX (1953) 138–40.

The maintenance of the banks of a millpool and millrace was apportioned among the tenants in proportion to their holding, much as in some villages the upkeep of the churchyard wall devolved on the villagers proportionately. Assisting in the carriage of the millstones is often found in customals as an obligation of the tenants.[25] In villages remote from suitable stone the organisation of a supply of millstones presupposes a long-distance trade and transport capable of handling such heavy loads. Thus, every millstone upsets the concept of self-sufficient village economies.

From the mill, Norden's surveyor and bailiff passed to the meadows. The bailiff asks what advice can be offered to make the stream more profitable. The surveyor replies, 'I could wish some cost to be bestowed here in making a fish-pond, nay it would make at the least two or three, one below the other ... many times also these kindes of ponds may have sufficient fall of water for corne mils, fulling or wake mils, syth mils and mils of other kindes.'

[25] For the carriage of millstones see *Yorks. Arch. Soc. Rec. Ser.* XCIV (1937) 62, a document of 1320.

Fig. 24. South Newton; looking NNW, April 1954.

Like field-ponds, fishponds have not been seriously studied. Popular legend links them exclusively with monasteries and monastic properties, but in fact the fishpond was a useful adjunct to any village. It provided a breeding place for the fish which augmented the meat diet, and there is evidence that villagers as well as manorial households drew from them.[26]

The earthworks of fishponds are sometimes mistaken for moats, but they can be differentiated without difficulty. Fishponds were rectangular excavations beside a small stream or near a spring: they are not usually set

[26] B. K. Roberts, 'Medieval fishponds', *Amat. Hist.* VII (1966) 119–25.

in the course of large streams. Embankments were used to maintain a pool of moderate depth with a gentle flow of water through it. A large stream would break down the embankments in times of flood and sweep the fish away.

The pond was often made by building an earthen bank across the line of a watercourse. One side of this bank might be stone-faced for rigidity, while a sluice served as a safety-valve in wet weather. In normal times there would be a slight flow over the lip of the sluice. If the valley sides were not themselves sufficiently steep, two further embankments might be constructed parallel to the stream. A fourth bank at the higher end of the pond was often constructed to complete the rectangle. That earthworks should hold water today is not a necessary criterion for them to be identified as fishponds. The containing dams are often breached, and may have no more than a trickle of water flowing through the gap, or the ponds may be completely dry if modern field-drainage or piped water-supplies have led away a stream higher up its course.[27]

In their developed form, fishponds had auxiliary breeding-chambers linked to them by a maze of channels and sluices, and probably different chambers for different types of fish; these auxiliaries taken together can make up a considerable area of earthworks. Norden's surveyor, it will be remembered, advocated 'at least two or three, one below the other'. Such a chain can be seen in the abandoned village site at Wormleighton in fig. 17. Other fishponds appear in figs. 20A, 32D. From these varied illustrations of fishponds, it seems that they might occur in the very centre of the village, away in the open fields, down in the meadows, or alongside the manor house. The important determinant was simply the location of a suitable watercourse.

For more considerable streams, fishing was by fish-garths, artificial channels through which some part of the river was turned. The garths had long stakes permanently driven into their beds and trapnets were hung on these and taken away as required. The obstruction of river navigation by the various waterworks was a constant source of litigation and local dissension, but there are no surviving earthworks of this type that might easily be photographed. The rivers themselves must be the silent witnesses of their medieval potentialities for fishing and fowling.

[27] See also C. F. Hickling, 'Prior More's fishponds' *Med.*

25. HARRINGTON   Northamptonshire

The photograph (fig. 25) shows one of the most extensive groups of ornamental earthworks in the Midlands. These lie in a shallow tributary valley of the River Ise six miles west of Kettering. The view is to the southwest: the main fishpond, its containing dam now breached, occupies the foreground. Above it, also with containing banks, is a smaller chamber, possibly for breeding. Farther back, and beyond the road, the main stream, now dry, is banked for most of its course to act as a supply-channel to the system. On the left, leading down from a row of trees, are deep supply-channels, while a relief-channel for surplus water can be seen outside the right-hand bank of the two ponds.

In the background, other earthworks extend down the slope from the village street towards the ponds. They form terraces, very similar to the Elizabethan creations at Holdenby (fig. 20A), and like them were probably for ornamental gardens. There is a rectangular sunken garden or lawn at the lowest level, while indentations in the terraces indicate where paths or steps led up presumably to the manor house. This northern quarter of the parish went down early to grass (in Bridges' time there was only a shepherd living here) and the manorial rabbit warren also lay hereabouts, its memory preserved by the name Warren Hill to the west of the village. The manor belonged to the Knights Hospitallers from 1232 until the Dissolution when it passed to Lord Dysert, but no documents have yet been found to throw light on the earthworks shown here. On the analogy of Holdenby both may be Elizabethan, but only excavation could confirm this.

Sources

Bridges, *Northants.* II. 32; J. M. Steane, 'Medieval fishponds of Northamptonshire', *Northants. Past and Present* IV (1970–1) 299–309, with plan and poem.

The study of fishponds, as has been remarked, was rather neglected until recent years, their frequency as an important adjunct to villages only coming to be understood as this survey proceeded. Another 'Cinderella' of medieval economic studies is the rabbit warren.[28] The

Arch. XV (1970) 118–23.
[28] Recognition of the importance of the rabbit in the Middle Ages and after is due mainly to E. M. Veale and J. Sheail on whose publications this section is based. For reference, see 'Sources'.

Fig. 25. Harrington. The fishponds and ornamental earthworks north of the village; looking SW, May 1962.

management of breeding-units, to use a current phrase, was highly practical in an age of limited communications and seasonal production when food, to be kept at all, was most easily kept alive. Just as the stewponds gave a ready supply of fresh fish through most of the year, so the local warren, manorial or common, offered meat, and, in addition, good furs for home use or for the market.[29]

The rabbit is said to have been brought across to the British Isles by the Normans, being first established on some offshore islands, later in colonies on a limited number of private estates on the mainland. That an animal which has been notorious for much of this century as a plague to be exterminated, should have been cherished at its introduction and protected against predators, is ironic. Some of the earliest references to warrens or

coneygarths are cases of trespass. In 1268, Richard, Earl of Cornwall complained that his coneywarren at Isleworth, Middlesex, had been broken into. The earliest record confirming the existence of a coneygarth is found in the Close Rolls for 1241 when the king ordered hay to be carted from his *cuningera* at Guildford. Other records suggest the scale of production: 2000 rabbit skins were sent out of Lundy Island in 1274, 200 skins were exported from Hull on one occasion in 1305, and in 1270 the Keeper of the estates of the Archbishop of Canterbury supplied 200 rabbits to Westminster for the royal feast on St Edward's day.

By the late Middle Ages there were many warrens, widely distributed. Placenames alone suggest the widespread popularity of rabbit keeping. The word 'warren'[30] itself still occurs frequently on maps and names involving 'coney', as 'coneygarth', 'conigree' or 'coneywarren', are further indicative of the existence

[29] At Higham Ferrers (Northants.) a mound of upcast earth from one of the fishponds was used as a warren; fish and rabbits being raised in adjacent 'units'. The warren is recorded in the fifteenth century and in 1796 the six-acre field was still known as the Coney Garth. R.C.H.M. *Northants*, I (1975) 55–6, fig. 67 and plates 8 and 9.

[30] The word can also refer to a natural warren of wild rabbits, and to the much less common hare warren.

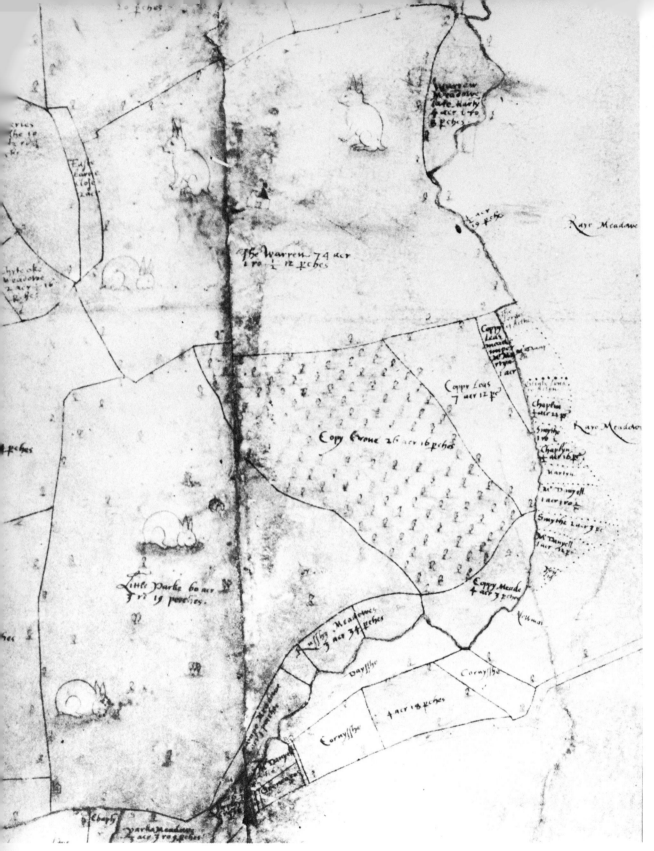

Fig. 26A. Long Melford rabbit warren; part of a map by Israell Amyce, 1580.

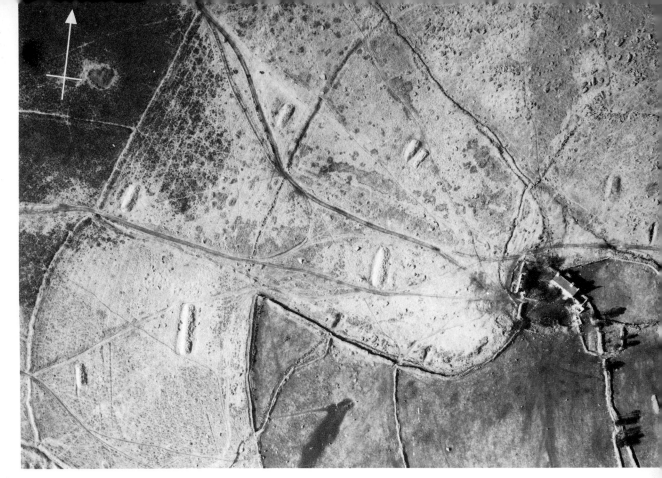

Fig. 26B. Ditsworthy Warren; vertical photograph of pillow-mounds, April 1969. Scale 1:2200.

of an enclosed, artificial warren. Warrens also appear on estate maps, being features of considerable profit to a landowner. Fig. 26A reproduces part of a sixteenth-century map of the estates at Long Melford, Suffolk, belonging to Sir William Cordell, Elizabeth's Master of the Rolls.[31] The map was drawn in 1580 by Israell Amyce, who evidently took pleasure in a careful depiction of rabbits in *The Warren* of seventy-four acres, and of two others which have strayed into *Little Parke* below. Norden instructs the surveyor to inquire whether the lord of a manor has 'any *Warren of Conies* or *Hares*, who is the Keeper of them, and what Fee hath hee by yeere, and what is the Warren of Conies worth by the yeere'.[32] There are examples in other sections of this book: at Holdenby Norden describes, in 1591, 'a large warren of conies not farr from the house' and the survey of Newlass, Yorkshire in 1539 refers to a rabbit warren there.

That the keeping of rabbits was popular is as evident as the reason for that popularity: rabbits breed with proverbial rapidity and do well on the poorest ground. In his section on land improvement, Norden suggests fishponds to exploit a water-supply (see above p. 66) and 'As for Warrens of Conies, they are not unnecessarie, and they require no rich ground to feed in, but meane pasture and craggy grounds are fittest for them.' Little is known of medieval techniques of management. Later accounts of the eighteenth and nineteenth centuries give more detail and confirm some facts of the early procedures. The profession of rabbit-keeper or warrener seems to have been soon established, and later warrens provided an official dwelling for this functionary. The quotation from Norden makes clear that he assumes there will be a keeper if there is a warren. On fig. 26A a building which might be the warrener's lodge is shown in the middle of the warren, but appears obscurely on the old drawing. Save for placenames, warrens are now located with difficulty, having left little trace on the landscape. At least this is true of medieval coneygarths, but where the ground was too rocky or too wet for rabbits to burrow, later warreners raised mounds of earth

[31] The first edition of *Medieval England* noted (p. 247) that the map of 1580 was missing. Fortunately this and another early estate map came to light a few years ago.
[32] *Surveior's Dialogue*, 107.

and stones for the animals. This was the practice recorded in more recent times, but whether it was a tradition inherited from earlier days is not known.[33] Only recently have the self-descriptive 'pillow-mounds' been identified as warren earthworks.[34] These mounds survive in uncultivated uplands (see the photograph, fig. 26B), but there are many references to suggest that they would have been constructed where necessary, by reason of water-logged ground for example, on lowland warrens. The pillow-mounds visible today have been shown by fieldwork to be post-medieval; there are some fine mounds on Dartmoor, at Huntingdon Warren, where the establishment of a new warren is recorded in 1808.

26. DITSWORTHY WARREN   Devon

To illustrate a medieval warren is not easy, and may even be impossible, since, as has been noted, investigation of pillow-mounds, the only physical remains of warrens, shows them generally to be post-medieval. Fig. 26B is a photograph of mounds which have not been excavated, whose construction is unrecorded and which, on inspection, do not declare themselves to be of recent origin. Although their age is not known there is no positive indication that they are modern and so Ditsworthy Warren may serve as an example for this section.

There have been warrens on Dartmoor near the little River Plym since the twelfth century. One at Trowlesworthy is recorded from the thirteenth century and Ditsworthy, close by, may be as old. The mounds now on the warren are probably not of that age; if the warren was worked for long the mounds would have decayed or been redesigned from time to time and thus rebuilt, perhaps on the same sites. The mounds at Ditsworthy lie on a south slope and all have their long axis down the hillside, presumably to aid drainage.

Dartmoor is the kind of marginal country where rabbit-breeding would have been of more than usual benefit as a supplement to difficult and unprofitable agriculture. Tin-mining seems to have served a similar purpose in making habitable these moors and the association of tin-mining and rabbits is recorded in the tinners' emblem: three rabbits' heads arranged in a circle.

Sources

E. M. Veale, 'The rabbit in England', *Ag. Hist. Rev.* 5 (1957) 85–90 and *The English Fur Trade in the Later Middle Ages* (1966); J. Sheail 'Historical material on a wild animal – the rabbit', *Local Historian* 9 (1970) 59–64 and *Rabbits and their History* (1971); C. D. Linehan, 'Deserted sites and rabbit warrens on Dartmoor', *Med. Arch.* x (1966) 113–14, pls. VI–VIII; Ditsworthy Warren lies at SX 583663.

---

[33] Sheail notes that there is a reference to the 'destruction' of warrens on the Isle of May in the sixteenth century. The implication of this word is that there was more structure to the warrens than just a boundary-wall.

[34] Pillow-mounds are widely distributed: the Cambridge Collection records them on Dartmoor, in the Cotswolds on Minchinhampton Common, in the uplands of Radnorshire and Brecknock, on the Long Mynd, in North Yorkshire and in Westmorland.

5

THE MULTIPLICATION OF VILLAGES

Bailiff. How then was the State of this Island
of great Britaine at the beginning when it was
first peopled?
Surveyor. A very Desert and wilderness ...
until Time taught them and Nature drew them

to find the meanes how to stock up trees
bushes bryers and thorns, and in stead therof
to plow the land to sow set and plant, to build
Cities for defence.

NORDEN, Surveior's Dialogue, 221

I. THE SITING OF VILLAGES

Before Domesday Book (1086) the progress of
settlement is recorded in documents only
sporadically, rather to be inferred from the evidence of archaeology, placenames and parish
boundaries than to be read explicitly in chronicles and charters. By the time of the Domesday
clerks the majority of English villages were
already in existence, although some of the
settlements laying claim to the title of 'vill' were
yet no more than a handful of houses. Air recon-
naissance discovers traces of settlements of all
periods. Sufficient excavation of buried sites,
revealed by crop-marks, has now been carried
out for certain of these marks to be identified,
with varying degrees of confidence, as diag-
nostic of Anglo-Saxon settlements. The distribution map of Dark Age England is now
being filled out with sites identified from the air.
These settlements, abandoned and forgotten
before the Norman Conquest, are clearly the
failures. Where the needs of the settlers continued to be met in their chosen situation the
settlement developed into an established village,
surviving, perhaps, to be visited by the Domesday clerks. But, as will be seen in later chapters,
the fortunes of any settlement, whether founded
before or after the Conquest, are by no means
constant. The origins of a long-occupied village
are to be found only by excavation, the traces of
its earliest days being hidden beneath the
medieval and modern houses. Certainly many of
our villages prove to have their beginnings in
Anglo-Saxon settlements or, perhaps, even
earlier, in Romano-British or Iron Age farming
communities. A long history of occupation is,
however, no guarantee of a successful future.
Many villages which were deserted in the fourteenth and fifteenth centuries had survived since

before Domesday, and some no doubt were of
great antiquity.[1]

Knowledge of the process of Anglo-Saxon
settlement and of its relation to the medieval
English villages of Domesday and later, though
growing, is yet limited. In this section therefore
the illustrations will record the *faits accomplis*
rather than the steps in the progress of early
settlement. They illustrate the variety of settlement pattern which had been achieved by
Domesday, and then move on to the phenomenon of the late arrivals on the rural landscape.
Since it is from surviving documents that the late
arrival of these settlements is deduced, the
photographs afford no fresh or more precise evidence for dating the later acts of colonisation:
their contribution is rather to indicate how the
whole appearance of a village such as Deeping
(fig. 37) reflects the circumstances of its creation,
so different from the villages of the plain. The air
photograph does not help to elucidate when
Wensleydale (fig. 59) was first lined with fields,
but it shows those fields in relation both to the
dale and to the surrounding moors, indicating

[1] The practice of 'total' exploration for all periods of
settlement has hardly begun in this country. For results so far
see an account by C. Bowen and B. Cunliffe of the Society of
Antiquaries Research Project 'The Evolution of the landscape', *Ant. Jnl* LIII (1973) 9–13 and B. Cunliffe, 'Chalton,
Hants.: the evolution of a landscape', *ibid.* 173–91, also
'Saxon and medieval settlement-pattern in the region of
Chalton, Hants.', *Med. Arch.* XVI (1972) 1–12; and exca-
vations reported in *Med. Arch.* XVI (1972) 13–33, 154 and XVII
(1973) 1–25, by P. V. Addyman and D. Leigh. The parish of
Wharram Percy, Yorks. is being examined by C. Hayfield in
association with J. G. Hurst's excavation of the deserted
village. Collections of papers on settlement are: 'Anglo-
Saxon settlement and landscape', ed. R. T. Rowley, *Br. Arch.
Reports* 6 (1976) and *Medieval Settlement* (1976), ed. P. M.
Sawyer.

that fields in such a neighbourhood are unlikely to have had the same history as the fields of the plains, even if there is some superficial resemblance in size and shape.

But before moving to the marginal settlements something must briefly be said of the progress of colonisation in the more 'normal' environment of the lowlands. Earlier chapters have described the expansion outwards of the cultivated fields, slowly filling in the open spaces between villages. It remains to consider how colonisation gave villagers not only fields but neighbours.[2] The general discussion will be particularised in section IV of this chapter by a short study of the three Huntingdonshire villages of Gidding.

It might be thought that the elevated position of an aerial camera would assist in recording the relation between villages and their general physical environment, particularly in connection with the choice of site. In reality, the help is somewhat limited, as the selecting of photographs for this book has shown. There seem to be two obstacles.

The first is technical: if the settlement pattern of a district is to be studied in relation to terrain and ecology, it is necessary to have a vertical or panoramic photograph covering not a single parish but a group of parishes. Such photographs have been taken, both singly and as mosaics, but there would be poor delineation of detail on any reproduction at the size permitted by the pages of this *Survey*. Merely to show an enlarged portion of part of a panorama would defeat the purpose of relating the choice of site to local conditions. There is no point in demonstrating the platitudes that villages are often sited at river-crossings, at hill-gaps and beside estuaries; and the apparent indifference in these pages to the influence of rocks, soil and drainage on the siting of villages is no measure of the significance of these factors in settlement history.

The second obstacle is historical. The most difficult of all pieces of historical reconstruction is to see the site of a village as it appeared, as virgin land, to the eyes of its first settlers. The distribution of villages can only suggest in general terms what repelled and what attracted the first generations of Anglo-Saxon invaders. Extremes of marsh and waterless chalk are avoided. An island of gravel in a clay valley will have gathered houses upon it. A line of perennial springs will attract thirsty men and animals. Sandy heaths and chalk uplands were uninviting, so that earthworks of prehistoric settlements may survive there almost untouched under a thin cover of grass.[3]

Detailed soil maps which are essential for any local work are seldom available. Moreover, centuries of human occupation have greatly modified local ecology; quite apart from long-period climatic changes, the clearing of forest and the draining of fields have yielded a water-table very different from that prevailing when settlement began. Much evidence has been lost for ever: for example, the decisions rescinded, the choices that failed, the sites abandoned after only two or three seasons' experience, the coming and going which inter-tribal warfare or native hostility would impose.

Occasionally Anglo-Saxon settlers reacted to the vestiges of early cultures which they found on the landscape: there is for example the deliberate avoidance of the line of Roman roads when siting new villages. The empty line of Watling Street, the Fosse Way and Ermine Street is much too marked to be attributed to chance. The Roman roads have not been the focal points of new settlements but the boundaries of them. If the settlers had themselves used the grass-grown roads as lines of invasion they might well have decided that it was prudent not to settle directly on a track along which others, and rivals, might come. The new settlers were a village-based people; they made a network of tracks sufficient to gain access to the fields and to such neighbouring villages as might be necessary for the elements of barter and sale. These local and parochial needs were not served by Roman roads which were only brought back into use when a more sophisticated economy was creating towns.

27. STRETTON ON FOSSE Warwickshire

This indifference to Roman roads may be seen at Stretton on Fosse, fig. 27. The village lies some four miles north-east of Moreton-in-Marsh, and nearly one-third of a mile to the west of the Fosse Way. The photograph looks obliquely across the line of the Roman road which can be traced almost to the top margin. The buildings of the village stand around two loops of streets with a road (bottom right) leading to the Fosse Way. The plan of Stretton provides a good example of the local function of medieval parish-lanes:

---

[2] A recent study of colonisation using archaeological and documentary evidence to great effect is C. C. Taylor's 'Whiteparish', *Wilts. Arch. and Nat. Hist. Mag.* LXII (1967) 79–102 and LXIII (1968) 39–45.

[3] For the determining influence of silt and peat in fenland settlement, H. C. Darby, 'Historical geography of the fenland', *Geog. Jnl* LXXX (1932) 420.

Fig. 27. Stretton on Fosse; looking NE along the Fosse Way, April 1964.

except for the road on the right the lanes give access only to the fields.

Yet the Anglo-Saxon and medieval village was not unconscious of the road which passed by its fields. The village name itself is taken directly from this distinguishing feature, and indeed doubly so: in Domesday Book it had its Anglo-Saxon name of *Stratone* (the street-township), and in 1275 the suffix *super le Fosse* is first recorded. It distinguished this village from the three other Strettons in the county, two of them (Stretton on Dunsmore and Stretton under Fosse) set back from the Fosse Way and the third, the now deserted Stretton Baskerville, set back from Watling Street.

Source

P.N. Warwicks. (1936) 119, 146, 306.

Just as roads fell into disuse, so the defended Roman towns were not all utilised by the early Anglo-Saxon settlers; some, like Silchester, went down to grass as completely as the villas and their fields. The reoccupation of Isurium as the village of Aldborough is an interesting exception. Only half the area of the old town was built upon, even at the high-water mark of medieval population, and the principal use of the walls of the Roman town was not for defence but as a quarry, just as (on a larger scale) the bricks of the Roman walls of Colchester were to be used in the Castle and St Botolph's Priory.

28. ALDBOROUGH
Yorkshire, West Riding

The vertical photograph reproduced as fig. 28A

Fig. 28A. Aldborough; vertical photograph, July 1946. Scale 1:3100.

Opposite
Fig. 28B. Aldborough in 1709; plan by Robert Smithson. True north is slightly west of the direction marked on the plan.

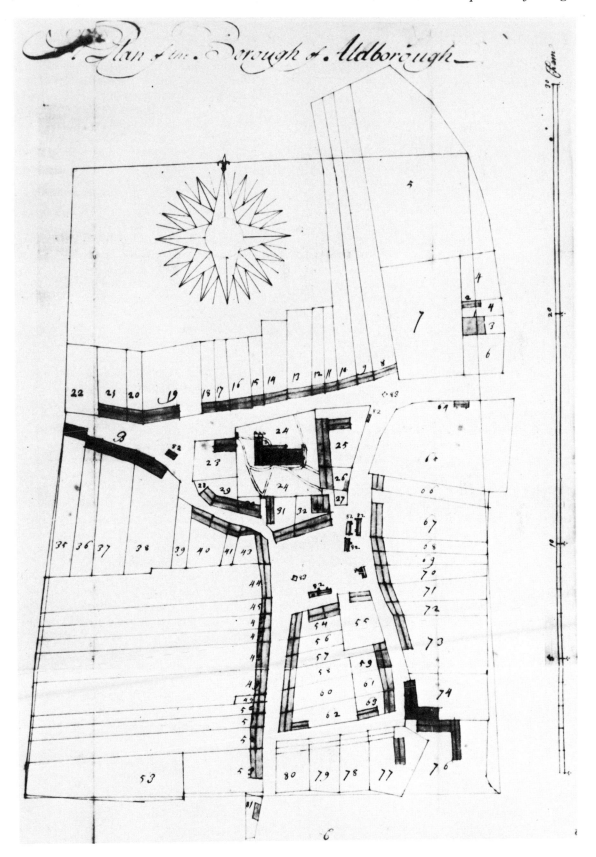

shows how the defences of the Roman town determined the direction of the streets and the limits of the house-gardens in the Anglo-Saxon and medieval village. The same area is shown in fig. 28B, part of Robert Smithson's plan of 1709. The road crossing the village from left to right runs between the west and east gates of the Roman town. A third road which leads up from the bottom of the figure enters the town at the ancient south gate. The road to the north gate is no longer in use; it was located by excavation in 1924. At the intersection of the Roman roads, the church of St Andrew now stands. To trace the walls it is best to begin at the south-west (or bottom-left) angle where their line both northwards and eastwards is marked by trees. The south-east angle and the line of the east wall can also be faintly seen. North of the east and west gates, the walls no longer exist above ground although their influence on property boundaries is apparent from the plan of 1709.

Until its disenfranchisement in 1832 Aldborough ranked as a 'rotten borough'. The Crown had sold the estate in 1628, and in 1701 it was acquired by the Duke of Newcastle. Since the vote was confined to the old burgess houses of 1553, their site and ownership were objects of more than antiquarian curiosity. Such a controversy prompted the plan of 1709. It will be seen that there were no burgess houses known in the northern half of the village, and there is no evidence that the medieval village ever occupied more than the southern half of the walled town. When Leland came here in the early sixteenth century he wrote: 'there be now Feeldes fruteful of corn in the very places wher the Howsing of the (Romaine) Town was.' In fact, the air photograph suggests that the plough did not penetrate beyond the discouragement of the wall-footings. There was no need for it to do so with nearly 2000 acres of open-field land in the parish.

A situation commanding an important river-crossing on the north–south main road gave the village early importance and at the time of Domesday Book it was in royal hands and the capital of the wapentake of *Burghshire*. The main road on which its travellers journeyed left the village by the north gate: that is, in the only direction where now there is no street. The Ure crossing to which it led was superseded early in the twelfth century by the king's new bridge half a mile farther west. This caused a diversion of the main road away from 'the old Burgh' and a new bridgehead town grew up at Borough-bridge. This market-town lay within Aldborough parish on what had previously been an outlying meadow of the village, and it was Boroughbridge, not Aldborough, which prospered by the north-bound travellers and waggons and by the river traffic at its wharves. It was Boroughbridge where the Scottish forces crossed into the West Riding in 1318, and it was the same crossing which was fatally blocked to Thomas of Lancaster in 1322. With the migration of the main road the route through the north gate of Aldborough became itself no more than a lane to the meadows, and the enclosure of 1809 saw it superseded even as a lane.

From the plan of 1709 it can be seen that burgess houses then occupied the frontages of the three main street-lines, with an irregular group of eleven houses gathered in the island around the church; five others squat on the village green. From the pattern of houses in the bottom right-hand sector it seems likely that the green had been much larger than at present. If the air photograph is compared with the plan of 1709 it will be seen that a number of burgess plots are no longer occupied, although even in 1709 there were plots (e.g. nos. 78–80) without houses.

There are more spectacular examples of Roman towns becoming (after a lapse of years) centres of local population. Sometimes the Roman defences served as a protection against new invaders: York and Chester can be seen in figs. 71 and 78. Yet there is something distinctive in this small Roman town which became a Yorkshire village, itself to be pushed into the background when it was deserted by through traffic.

Sources

Sir T. Lawson-Tancred, *Records of a Yorkshire Manor* (1937); maps and documents in the possession of Lady Lawson-Tancred; survey and plan of 1709: B. L. Stowe MSS. 883; R. G. Collingwood in *British Association Handbook* Q (Leeds, 1927).

II. THE SPACING OF VILLAGES

The existing spacing of villages must be the result of decisions made in the first centuries of colonisation followed by successive intrusions of newer settlements. As the number of late medieval settlements in the densely settled plains was not large, the distance from one village to the next is a measurement which has not changed at least since Domesday Book. At first sight, villages seem very evenly scattered over the map. This impression has been tested by measuring the distances between villages in certain areas, and the results are set out below. It would be interesting to attempt a division between mother and daughter villages, to see whether the original (or 'mother') villages were also set roughly equidistantly, but such an investigation cannot be pursued further here.

It is enough to point out that any equidistance which may be found must indicate a common local view of the desirable 'zone of tolerance'. At the time when a village was founded there could have been no conception of the ultimate extent of its fields and no possible assessment of the quality of the land which lay below still uncleared forest. The distance at which neighbours (or, for that matter, daughter settlements) came to be tolerated could not have been based on any calculation of an 'adequate' field-area when the field-area was but a tiny island in a sea of uncleared land. Yet, as an archaeologist has written of Northamptonshire villages, 'the whole has the semblance of a consciously planned and coordinated allocation of the land best suited for primary settlement ...'.[4]

In two sample areas the distance from each village church to the nearest adjacent church has been measured. The uniformity is remarkable. In the first area, that part of Northamptonshire which lies to the east of Banbury, there are fifty-three modern villages which were also recorded in Domesday Book; the average distance to the nearest village is 1.2 miles, and thirty of the fifty-three villages have their nearest neighbour between 1.0 and 1.2 miles away. In the second area, that part of Huntingdonshire lying west of the Great North Road, there are thirty-seven villages which date from at least the time of Domesday Book; the average distance from each to the nearest neighbour is here 0.95 miles, and fourteen of the thirty-seven villages lie between 0.90 and 1.00 miles apart. This is the area in which the Giddings (pp. 86–94) lie.

Such regularity could hardly be expected in a

countryside dissected by valleys with intervening uplands: the sample areas lie in undulating country without marked barriers to equal colonisation in all directions. In an area such as the neighbourhood of Salisbury, where a number of valleys converge, the villages are necessarily confined to the valleys, and the distance over the plateau to the next valley may be considerable. However, within a valley the distances between adjacent villages are not exceptional. The average distance between the twenty villages that lie in the Avon valley between Pewsey and Salisbury is 0.89 miles. The valley of the Nadder from Tisbury to Salisbury has fifteen villages, at an average distance apart of 0.9 miles; the valley of the Wylye from Warminster to Salisbury has nineteen villages, on the average 0.94 miles apart. The valleys of the Ebble and Bourne have villages as equally spaced with an average of just under a mile from one village to the next. It is obvious from these samples that where the physical conditions are uniform or nearly uniform, settlements have been tolerated at about the same distance from each other, with a strong preference, in the three districts examined, for having neighbours about a mile away.

This marked equidistance does not necessarily carry with it equality of parish area. Equality is more likely in the undulating country of the first two examples, where all the land between villages is equally capable of being cultivated and the shape of a parish tends towards a regular polygon. Here, the parishes contain between one and two thousand acres. The villages set along the narrow valleys on Salisbury Plain have large areas of downland within their parishes, thus increasing their area to three and sometimes five thousand acres, the proportion of downland being largely determined by the distance between valleys. The villagers in the Ebble valley had only about two miles to drive their sheep over the downs before they met their neighbours from the Nadder valley, while the villagers of the Avon valley between Salisbury and Upavon, on the other hand, would have had up to twice that distance before coming upon the bounds of their neighbours in the Upper Till and Bourne valleys, and their parishes are correspondingly larger.

Comparisons of this kind can only be usefully made in areas where the villages are nucleated, so that one can see without ambiguity where the original centres of settlement were, and how they lie in relation to their surroundings. In country of dispersed and hamlet settlement the abundance of available land made the question of zones of toleration an academic one. There was

[4] W. F. Grimes, *Aspects of Archaeology* (1951) 156; W. Page suggested ('Notes on the types of English villages and their distribution'. *Antiquity* I (1927) 447ff) that the parish-bounds of north Lincolnshire show settlement progressing up the valleys leading south from the Humber followed by a more regularly spaced settlement on the scarp of Lincoln Edge west of Ermine Street. This and other regularities in parish shape are illustrated in the county Reports of the Land Utilisation Survey, *The Land of Britain*, pts. 1–92 (1936–46), esp. Lincolnshire (pts. 66–7) 479 and 502; Northamptonshire (pts. 58–9) 368; good examples appear in C. D. Drew, 'The manors of the Iwerne valley', *Proc. Dorset Nat. Hist. and Arch. Soc.* LXIX (1947) 45–50; and in C. C. Taylor, *Dorset* (1970) 41–110.

no need for villagers to be concerned if another family wished to settle half a mile away when there was land enough for all and to spare. In a country of dispersed settlement single settlers were tolerated; but in a country of nucleated villages the very maintenance of arable land against the return of the forest as well as the major operations of the farming year dictated that any settlement should consist of more than one or two families. Isolated intruders would rarely occur so long as conditions militated against the economic survival of the isolated family.

The normal practice has been for villages to have elbow-room in all directions. Parishes might tend, in ideal circumstances, to be an array of hexagons but, as may be seen on Lincoln Edge and the Berkshire Downs, physical conditions usually prevented complete symmetry of shape or position.

Contiguous villages can occasionally be found. They may in some instances be an original single village which has been subdivided manorially and acquired two identities; a later shrinking of the house-frontage may have given a slight physical separation to the two parts. Villages with twin churches have something of this character. In most villages the original manorial divisions have been reflected neither in the village nor its fields, so that although in law there may have been two communities, the houses and fields are intermingled, and the eye sees only one village street and one set of fields. Elsewhere there may occur villages which are set unusually close. Where the pair has a common name it is likely that the two villages had a common origin, but in settlement history mothers and daughters do not sit quite so much on each other's doorstep as, for example, the two Gransdens illustrated in fig. 29. Each Gransden has been an independent parish as far back as records go; in Domesday Book there were separate manors. The administrative separation is more marked than in most contiguities. One village lies in Cambridgeshire and one in Huntingdonshire.

29. THE GRANSDENS
Cambridgeshire and Huntingdonshire

When the Rev. F. le Grice was inducted as vicar of Gransden in 1832 he was told that 'Great Gransden is the end of the world and Little Gransden a quarter of a mile beyond it.' Road and rail transport have broken down the isolation of the Gransdens; they lie eleven miles west of Cambridge, and they are not presented here as examples of remote villages. The pecul-

iarity of the Gransdens is that they straddle a county boundary.

In fig. 29 both villages are seen from the south. The boundary between the two parishes is marked by the lane which runs near the left-hand side of the photograph, then by a thick hedge that follows a somewhat winding course, and then, after a right-hand turn, by a straight lane that leads to the margin of the figure. The thick hedge in the centre of the photograph lies alongside the ancient churchyard wall of Great Gransden, but a recent extension of the churchyard has taken in the corner of a grass field to the right of this hedge so that funeral processions now actually pass over the parish boundary. The chancel, south aisle and tower of St Bartholomew's church at Great Gransden appear amongst the trees. The church of Little Gransden with its prominent tower stands near the road among the houses of the village, bottom right. That the village has shrunk since 1813 is indicated by empty crofts south of Little Gransden, beyond the right-hand margin of fig. 29; a plan of these has been published.

The boundary is also the boundary between Huntingdonshire on the left, and Cambridgeshire on the right. A freak of tenurial geography has thrown Great Gransden into Huntingdonshire, despite the original unity suggested by the common placename. The general lie of the county boundary makes it clear which county has annexed which village: the boundary of Huntingdonshire makes a great sweep eastwards to take in Great Gransden, just as a little farther north the boundary of Cambridgeshire swings westwards to include Eltisley and Croxton.[5]

Great Gransden took particular care about its Rogation Week ceremonies, perhaps because of the frontier position it occupied. The Rev. A. J. Edmonds, who wrote its history between 1892 and 1895, recorded grimly that a long-standing village custom ordered that the vicar should be held upside down at one point with his head in a water-hole.

The village streets of Great Gransden are spread in an irregular grid, making a rough B-shape. Little Gransden lies in an equally irregular scatter along a twisting street. In each village there is a strong contrast between the old enclosed fields near the village, with trees in their hedges, and the former field-land beyond. The open fields were not enclosed until 1843, and the number of dividing hedges is small; the absence

[5] Dr R. H. C. Davis has suggested that the 'capture' of Great Gransden by Hunts. dates from 1057 when its lord, Ælfgar of East Anglia, had his earldom transferred to that of Mercia.

Fig. 29. Great Gransden (centre) and Little Gransden (right foreground); looking NNE, June 1951.

of trees here gives an air of baldness to the land-scape.

The parish area of Great Gransden is almost twice that of its neighbour, and both the fourteenth-century taxes and the nineteenth-century households were in the same pro-portion.

Sources

V.C.H. Hunts. II (1932) 299; A. J. Edmonds, *History of Great Gransden* (1892–5); E. 179/36 and 109; E. 179/122/7 and 77; *Rot. Hund.* II. 534–5; shrinkage: R.C.H.M. *Cambridgeshire* I (1968) 167.

III. THE BOUNDS OF VILLAGES

You shall duly and diligently set downe ... all the circuit, buttes, bounds, and limits of the same ... the best experienced tenants accompany [the surveyor] for information, and some of the youth that they may learn to know the bounds in times to come.

NORDEN, *Surveior's Dialogue,* 95

To ascertain precise boundaries between parishes was as important a part of the Tudor surveyor's duties as recording precise boun-daries between properties. He was able to offer a new method of recording boundaries which had advantages over the traditional practice. From Anglo-Saxon times, as surviving charters show, men had fixed the bounds of parishes by peram-bulating the boundary, describing their journey from one landmark to the next. Oral traditions were established by the annual beating of the bounds in Rogation Week.

There were reasons why parish boundaries might be in question just at the time when sur-veyors were becoming widely employed. Agricultural improvements were destroying old landmarks: ploughland might be turned over to grass and old heath become arable. Changes in land-ownership were bringing in new proprietors who might question old traditions and call in their lawyers to expose the illogicality of village memories. Shortage of grassland would make for rivalry between villages which might otherwise have tolerated the occupation of debatable ground where a boundary wandered indeterminately. Most important of all, tithes were a live economic issue. The right to take tithes was falling into the hands of laymen who were anxious to get full return for their investment. To which parish church did a particular piece of land pay tithe?

The surveyor, perambulating the bounds, listening carefully to the words of the old men and making notes for his map, was on the bridge between the old world of reported tradition and the new world of recorded facts. The small number of Rogation Week ceremonies at the present day is not due to any abolition of parish boundaries but to the multiplication of surveys and surveyors.

A small number of charters of the Anglo-Saxon period have survived in which the delimitation of a property necessitated a careful point-to-point description of the boundaries. It has been shown by Dr Grundy that many of these boundaries can be identified with modern parish boundaries, while the very physical features by which the bounds were first located may still be visible.[6] Among the villages included in this book are some where such charters exist to witness that a pre-Conquest community took for its own use the very same ground which would now be encircled if the parish bounds were beaten on Rogation Days (e.g. Braunston, fig. 22; Wormleighton, fig. 17).

The appearance of the ground will have changed considerably since the charters were written. It is unlikely that the whole of the territory belonging to a village was then occupied by fields. The bounds commonly take broad sweeps, with only occasional right-angled turns, in a fashion suggesting that they were fixed when there was still much woodland or half-cleared scrub, across which a boundary could be agreed without having to take into account existing rights to particular patches of arable. Such boundaries could run uninterruptedly from one landmark to another, or follow the course of a stream or a watershed. Jagged boundaries, with right-angled turns, suggest that the bounds had to accommodate themselves to already existing boundaries of cultivated land.

In determining early parish boundaries in country not then intensively cultivated, it was only natural to seek landmarks which would impress themselves on the memory and could not be easily moved or simulated.[7] The descriptions of boundaries in Anglo-Saxon charters are full of pits, streams, hilltops and cliffs. The bounds of Braunston (fig. 22) described in 956 went from a *pytt* to a *beorg* (hill), from a *thorn stybb* to a *cumb* (valley), from a mere to a brook and from there to a *scearden beorg* (scarred hill).

The Anglo-Saxons also inherited a countryside in which lay roads, tracks, earthworks and barrows constructed by their predecessors; these were distinct and permanent enough often to serve as convenient boundary-marks between the communities whose fields were slowly approaching them on all sides.

30. BISHOPSTONE   Wiltshire

A good deal has been written about parish shapes and the general significance of large and small parishes. The elongated parishes climbing the slopes of Lincoln Edge must represent a virtually simultaneous movement of colonisation, each village set at the spring-line on the scarp slope, and from each the clearance of the ground above and below the village proceeding at about the same pace. The final symmetry is striking: villages are fairly evenly spaced and the pre-enclosure maps show that each elongated parish had its meadow land down in the plain, its arable fields on the lower slopes and its pastures in the heath on the upland.

Similar conditions with appropriate local modifications will be found in many other parts of the country. The sweep of country shown in fig. 30 includes the villages that lie along the lower slopes of the chalk downs in the Vale of the White Horse. In the foreground is the village of Bishopstone, six miles east of Swindon. The northern boundaries of the parishes, on the left, are as much as two miles from their villages, while the southern boundary of Bishopstone lies three miles away on the downs, well back from the crest of the ridge.

[6] Dr G. B. Grundy has published several county studies in which Anglo-Saxon charters were compared with the large-scale Ordnance Survey, e.g. *Saxon Charters and Field Names of Gloucestershire*, I and II (1935–6). The county volumes of the English Place Name Society now devote attention to the relevant charter material and include a summary of the bounds with identifications.

[7] A long, straight parish boundary suggests where further investigation of the presence of a pre-Saxon roadway might be made.

Fig. 30. Panorama looking NE from Bishopstone along the chalk escarpment, April 1949.

The question of medieval population density is relevant to the shape and size of parishes. Small parishes are not usually matched by small medieval populations. Indeed, the small parishes usually indicate that there has been much competition for the ground; closely set communities have managed to survive with an area of fields which in less fertile soils would have been insufficient to support a village. With the attractive, fertile soil went a high population density.

The very large parishes were usually found in areas where both terrain and documents indicate settlement initially sparse and soils relatively inhospitable. Men were living at considerable distances from each other, and in many instances making a livelihood from pastoral or forest resources so that nucleated villages were not necessary to existence. The scattered communities were not able to maintain a church, so that one centrally placed church had to serve a large area. The large parishes of medieval Lancashire and Cheshire derive from such conditions, and later colonisation in these counties is reflected in the growth of chapelries to serve the growing communities within the great mother

parishes. Miss D. Sylvester has reckoned that in 1669 Cheshire had only seventy-five parish churches (excluding the city of Chester), while there were about four hundred townships, each of which would contain a village, a hamlet or a dispersed scatter of cottages. The parish of Malpas had twenty-four such constituent townships and Prestbury had thirty-two.[8]

The late arrival of a settlement in an area with older communities and well-established parish boundaries would disturb their symmetry (see Hedon, fig. 93, and New Buckenham, fig. 97). But the growth of new medieval communities usually derived not from new urban creations but from villagers cultivating lands neglected by their ancestors; occasionally it derived from new industry. Mines and quarries are often located where the land is unsuited for agriculture, as if Nature had contrived a consolation prize. Thus, the development of lead-mines in Nidderdale called for reconsideration of the bounds of the great parish of Ripon, and in 1361 the new mining townships were formally assigned to the

[8] D. Sylvester, 'Rural settlement in Cheshire', *Trans. Hist. Soc. Lancs. and Chesh.* CI (1949) 1–39.

church at Sawley which was more conveniently placed than Ripon: 'there are places called Daker and Bewerly formerly a waste moor in our parish utterly devoid of men and extra-parochial, but it is now found that not a few Christian faithful of both sexes have newly begun to live there'.[9]

The parish bounds of Marlborough show a similar readjustment, but provoked here by the expansion of an old-established urban community. The Anglo-Saxon borough had been cut out of a rural parish, Preshute, whose bounds completely surrounded it, just as New Buckenham and Hedon were surrounded by the parishes in which they were planted. But in the thirteenth century, as Marlborough expanded, the population overspilled into Newland at the east end of the borough, across the bounds of Preshute parish. Thus townsmen of Marlborough who dwelt in Newland found themselves owing tithes as they were residents also of the rural parish into which the town had spread. Preshute's claim was supported in 1252 by the bishop, but two years later eight 'principal burgesses and the householders of Newland' built themselves a chapel there (now the church of St Martin) and pledged themselves to maintain its priest.[10]

In small detail, the adjustment of boundaries is nowhere better seen than in the half-mile length of the narrow strip, a few yards wide, which Castle Rising (Norfolk) pushes into its eastern neighbour. The strip is made up of the river, the millrace and the site of the mill and its pool. To allow access from Castle Rising the bounds took on this curious and significant alignment. Sudden disturbances of symmetry in parish bounds are always suggestive.

The parish boundaries which are oblivious of a town's walls (as at Bristol or Wallingford) make it likely that the walls are a later arrival on a scene where territorial bounds were already too well entrenched in tradition and privilege for anyone to think of altering them.[11] The multiplication of parishes within a town is similarly an indication of urban growth, and the direction of growth can be sometimes inferred from their shape and relation to the mother church. Conversely, as towns became less wealthy and popu-lation ceased to expand, some churches became superfluous. The amalgamation of parishes and the decay of churches within the city of York between 1420 and 1550 mirrors a diminished prosperity, the reverse of the hopeful half-century after the Norman Conquest when the city had added so many new churches to its streets.

Although, in general, parish bounds delimit a single compact area there are interesting exceptions where islands of one parish are found within another. In these cases the principle of overlordship has been too strong. These 'detached parts' of parishes were assigned to the endowment, not of the surrounding parish, but to the distant church of the lord in whose possession they were. The force of overlordship was strong enough, even after a lapse of several centuries, to preserve under the title of Northamptonshire eight small separate parcels of land within the Huntingdonshire parish of Catworth. These 'parcels' comprised a holding of one and a half hides held by the Abbey of Peterborough which, in Domesday Book, was surveyed under Northamptonshire.

Equally informative about early conditions are what might be called the 'blurred' parish boundaries, the existence of areas common to more than one parish. Examples of this 'blurring' can be found in the North Yorkshire Moors and on the Pennines near the borders of Yorkshire, Lancashire and Westmorland. They are very late survivals of the principle of intercommoning, the sharing of boundary ground by all the parishes which abut upon it. The adjacent villages of Thorpe Waterville and Achurch, on the Nene, carried the joint occupation even further: the arable lands of the two villages were intermingled in one set of open fields and there was intercommoning on the pastures.

An earlier stage in such a practice is probably responsible for the occasions in the Midlands and Southern England where a number of parishes meet at a point. Each parish extends a long, thin finger to meet its neighbours. These 'wheel-spoke' meetings usually occur on heath or rough pasture and they would seem to derive from the partition of ground previously shared by all, the centre of the wheel sometimes being a common pool. Nine parishes meet in this way at D. House (TL 867758) on the Bury St Edmunds to Thetford road. The nine parishes once turned their animals into the heath without being very much concerned about individual boundaries.

Three quarters of a century ago, J. H. Round[12] pointed out that Canvey Island, with its mosaic of detached portions of parishes some eight or

[9] *Memorials of Ripon* I. Surtees Soc. LXXIV (1881) 203.

[10] Marlborough: H. C. Brentnall, 'The origins of Preshute', *Wilts. Arch. and Nat. Hist. Mag.* LIII (1950) 294–310.

[11] J. Tait, *The Medieval English Borough* (1936) 56, for the parish of Frome Belet cutting the walls of Dorchester.

[12] *V.C.H. Essex* I (1903) 369; maps also in H. C. Darby, *Domesday Geography of Eastern England* (1952) 242–3; for another fenland complication see H. C. Darby, *Medieval Fenland* (1940) 68.

Fig. 31. The Devil's Dyke looking SE from the edge of the Fens at Reach (foreground) with the villages of Burwell and Swaffham Prior to left and right, respectively; April 1969.

ten miles away on the mainland, was a relic of a system under which all these parishes had rights in the common marshland pasture. The modern parish boundaries are also fantastically inter-mixed in Tilney Smeeth (Norfolk) where seven villages intercommoned on the marsh.

The partition of former common lands some-times led to compromise: either the solution of leaving an area common to more than one par-ish, or some such Box and Cox arrangement as that which affected two farms in Swinton near Rotherham. Each year they changed their parish: from one Easter Day to the next they were in Mexborough parish, and then for the next year were reckoned in Wath-upon-Dearne parish. This, in its way, would have been less incon-venient than to own property which always straddled the boundary of two parishes. There are stories of Rogation Day processions making their way through the Halls of Oxford colleges in their meticulous pursuit of the parish boun-dary; and Mr H. C. Brentnall recorded the con-venience which a Marlborough innkeeper derived when his house lay in two parishes. To

avoid giving settlement to his servant by a year's continuous residence in one parish he moved him once a year from one wing of the inn to another.

31. REACH AND THE DEVIL'S DYKE
Cambridgeshire

The Devil's Dyke, constructed after the end of the Roman period and, in all probability before the seventh century, is one of the great linear earthworks of Britain. In this view (fig. 31) the entire length of the dyke can be seen, from the fenland margin which appears as mottled ground at the foot of the photograph, across Newmarket Heath in the middle distance, to its southern end near Ditton Green among the trees, top centre. Until recently the dyke formed the boundary between parishes for the whole of its seven and a half miles. In the foreground, the land east of the dyke belonged to Burwell, the village on the left; the land west of the dyke lying in the parish of Swaffham Prior (right). Reach (centre) situated at the very edge of the Fens, has

85

a landing-place, or hythe, at the head of a canal, Reach Lode, by which it is linked with the River Cam. The goods carried on the canal will have included, incidentally, many loads of stone from the large quarry which is visible in the photograph as a light-toned area immediately south of Reach. The Burwell Rock worked here was locally much prized as a building-stone by reason of its hardness. The village straddles the dyke which was shortened to make space for the medieval *Fair Green* and, until modern reorganisation, Reach was bisected by the parish boundary which continued to follow the line of the dyke. There can have been no village here when the boundary between Swaffham and Burwell was determined. In the fourteenth-century tax-lists Reach always appeared twice, with some of its inhabitants in 'Reach, the hamlet of Burwell' and others in 'Reach, the hamlet of Swaffham': but both groups faced each other across the one village street. When, after centuries of division, Reach itself was made a parish (ecclesiastical in 1901, civil in 1958/9) the boundary was rearranged to take land from each of the parent neighbours. The *Bran Ditch* and *Fleam Dyke*, other Cambridgeshire earthworks, are also used as parish boundaries, as is frequently the case with Roman roads.

Sources

For the Cambridgeshire dykes see C. Fox, *Archaeology of the Cambridge Region* (1948) A20–1 of Appendix IV; C. Taylor, *The Cambridgeshire Landscape* (1973) 235–7 and fig. 19; R.C.H.M. *Cambridgeshire* II (1971) 85–90.

The question of the relation of parish boundaries to minor earthworks has not been thoroughly studied, but it may be suggested as a profitable subject. Why, it may be asked, is the Wansdyke spurned as a parish boundary for twelve miles of its course west of Marlborough, yet serves as a boundary east and west of Lacock for twelve miles continuously when it runs beside a Roman road? What of the relation of parish bounds to the great hill-forts? – that of Walbury Hill, for example, divided between Combe and Inkpen parishes with the bounds of Woodhay coming up to the north-east perimeter. Barbury Castle on the Marlborough Downs is bisected by a parish boundary which here follows a ridgeway on the scarp edge for a nine-mile semicircle from Ogbourne to East Kennett.

The course of English parish boundaries is often so suggestive of settlement history, and of the character of the landscape at the time when bounds were cast, that it is frustrating to be ignorant of the period when this delimitation took place. All that can be said is that it was later than the conversion to Christianity but could not have reached anything like its modern complexity until a large number of villages had acquired a church or churches, each with an endowment of glebe and a title to fees and tithes from the surrounding area. It must also have been earlier than the Anglo-Saxon boundary-charters.[13]

[13] For the growth of the parochial system, see F. M. Stenton, *Anglo-Saxon England* (1943) 147–52; there are also interesting suggestions in C. C. Taylor, *Dorset* (1970) ch. 2.

IV. A LOCAL STUDY

> Water and fire succeed
> The town, the pasture and the weed.
> T. S. ELIOT, *Little Gidding*

32. THE GIDDINGS   Huntingdonshire

This detailed discussion of the settlement history of one small area for which air photographs of all the villages are available may serve as an example of such studies. The adjacent parishes of the three Huntingdonshire Giddings were chosen because the photographs reveal much of interest, while open-field maps drawn in 1541 and in 1858 exist for the mother village.

There were already two Giddings in Domesday Book. By the time of the earliest surviving ecclesiastical records each village had its own parish church. Despite this independence, both the overall shape of the three parishes and their common name suggest an original unit of settlement of some 4000 acres, perhaps based on Great Gidding, which has been split into three as daughter villages were founded. It seems likely that the first subdivision of the original parish took place well before the Conquest, and a further division soon afterwards.

In 'Gidding' each village bears the name of 'Gydela's people'. The suffix 'Great' had already been added to the northernmost village by 1252. Little Gidding was assessed with Great Gidding as one unit in Domesday Book but Steeple Gidding was independently assessed. It is likely that Little Gidding was separated by Viel, son of Richard Engayne, soon after the Conquest. The separation of Steeple Gidding from the original great parish took place at an earlier and unknown date. Since in pre-Conquest documents Steeple

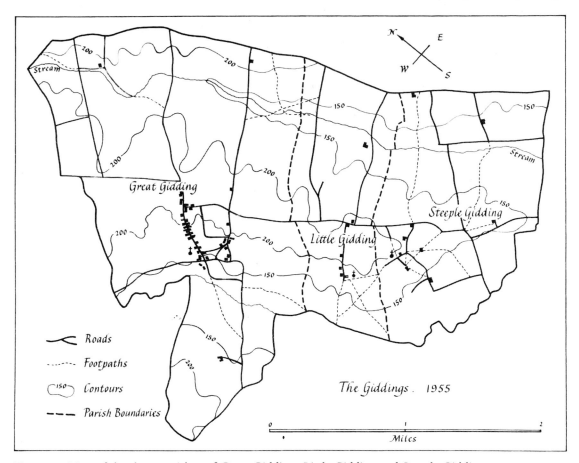

Fig. 32A. Map of the three parishes of Great Gidding, Little Gidding and Steeple Gidding.

Gidding belonged wholly to the Abbot of Ramsey, it may have been cut from the southern part of the original territory as a gift to the abbey.

The parish boundary of the 'original' parish corresponds to the outline of the modern map (fig. 32A). It will be seen that the parish bounds, which now subdivide this area into three, run parallel, as if a deliberate division had been in mind. The villages lie between the 150-foot and the 200-foot contours on the western slope of a ridge of land running north and south. The parishes each comprise an area of low-lying ground near a stream on the west, the slopes on which the villages stand, and higher ground to the east of the villages including the crest of the ridge. Beyond this the ground falls to a second stream. Two of the villages are served only by a cul-de-sac leading off the ridge-road, and this must originally have been the arrangement at Great Gidding too. The modern road (B660) takes a sharp, right-angled turn at the south-western end of Great Gidding, there being no direct line available for it.

A study of the 1-inch map shows that the 'ridge-road' to the east of the Giddings is represented by a continuous line of lanes, green roads or footpaths for a considerable distance. In 1541 it was 'the way to Huntingdon'. It leaves the present Great North Road near Alconbury and would rejoin it at Wansford, at the crossing of the Nene. An older crossing lay at Castor, the point at which Ermine Street reached the river. The diversion of the Great North Road to Wansford may have captured the traffic from the 'Gidding ridge'.

Each of the Giddings had its open fields. The fate of the three sets of fields was strikingly different. Alongside the Great Gidding map of 1541 (fig. 32B), showing fields but not the detail of strips, can be set the open-field map surveyed in 1858 (fig. 32C). Even at this late date there had been hardly any enclosure, and almost all the 2050 acres of the parish are seen to be occupied by the villagers' strips which were enclosed that year; open commons survived until 1869. Little Gidding and Steeple Gidding, on the other hand,

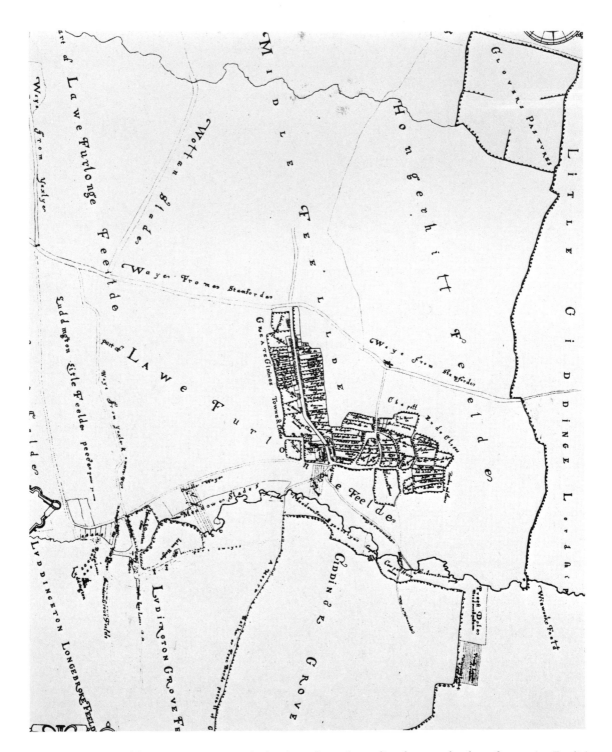

Fig. 32B. Great Gidding in 1541; a part of what is perhaps the earliest large-scale plan of an entire English parish. Note the windmill at the T-junction of roads, centre. A windmill tower stands in the same position today.

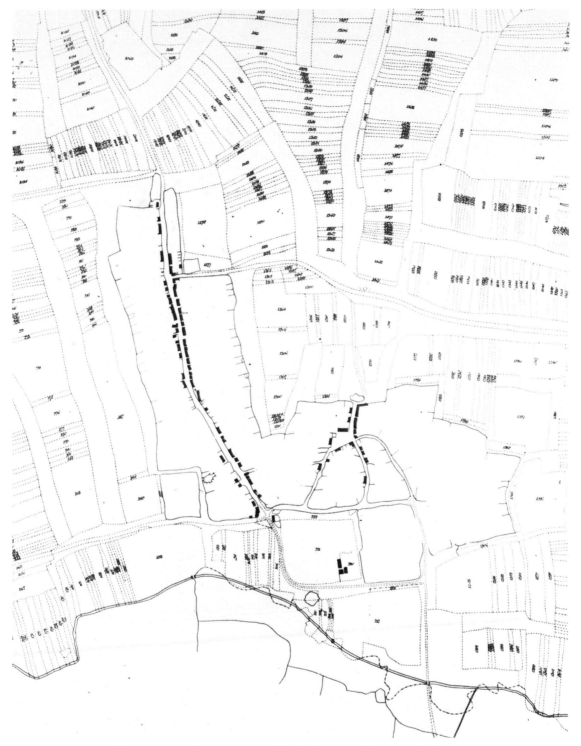

Fig. 32C. Great Gidding in 1858, still unenclosed. The field-areas without subdivisions were cow-commons, the hay from which was divided amongst the village by lot until the final enclosure in 1869.

lost their open fields at an early stage. The shrinkage of these two villages to a mere scatter of houses is apparent from the photograph (fig. 32D), and it seems likely that their fields must have been enclosed in the sixteenth century for pasture, with the almost total depopulation of the two settlements.

In 1594 there was a dispute involving the tith-able land in Little Gidding. Evidence was taken from local witnesses and brought back to the Court of Exchequer in London. Henry Stretton of Hempston testified that in 1566 the fields had been arable and unenclosed: 'and the said fields are now enclosed with hedges and converted into severall closes, neyther is there remayning any howses of husbandry nor eny land in Till-adge savinge yt wch is in the occupacion of John Bedell gent. as farmer unto Humffrey Drewell esq.' The witnesses proceeded to enumerate the scattered strips of glebe land as they remembered them lying in the three fields: thirty-one strips making twelve acres in Middle Field: eleven strips making three and a half acres in Kinverslade Field; and ten strips making four and a half acres in Parsongrove Field. In 1566, Stretton stated, there had been six houses, now there were none. In 1549 Drewell had 600 sheep on the commons here. These six houses must have represented a decline from the days when the village had all its seven hundred acres under cultivation. There were at least eighteen households in 1327 and thirty-one in 1279.

Great Gidding, which may be taken as the mother settlement, had about twice the area of Steeple Gidding and almost three times that of Little Gidding (table 1 below). For this reason it is not very rewarding to compare the number of taxpayers or the number of shillings paid in tax, for it is only to be expected that the larger village would pay more. It is more useful to examine the tax paid and the number of taxpayers *per acre*. For the purposes of the calculations it has been assumed that the whole of the three parishes was under cultivation in the early fourteenth century. The open-field map does indeed show that virtually all Great Gidding was eventually divided into strips and furlongs, and since both Steeple and Little Gidding are known to have abandoned arable for grass by the end of the sixteenth century it seems reasonable to suppose that the peak of arable cultivation in all three parishes was reached before and not after the Black Death. Indeed, if the acreages given in the Gidding portion of the Hundred Rolls of 1279 are realistic acres of modern size, it will be seen that almost all of the 2050 acres of Great Gidding were then in cultivation together with 600 out of Little

Gidding's 713, and 1080 out of Steeple Gidding's 1091.

On that assumption, the relative position of the three villages is set out in table 2 below.

Table 1

	Great Gidding	Little Gidding	Steeple Gidding
Domesday hidage (1086)	10 hides		7½ hides
Modern area: acres	2050	713	1091
'Acres' under cultivation in 1279 including fallow field	1940	600	1080
Households (all classes) in 1279	73	31	34
Tax paid in 1327	77s. 7½d.	30s. 5½d.	32s. 6¼d.
Tax paid in reassessment of 1334	133s. 5½d.	46s.	53s. 1½d.
Number of taxpayers in 1327 (probably number of households of substance)	52	18	20
Census of 1801: persons	420	47	77
Census of 1921: persons	271	42	62

Table 2

	Great Gidding	Little Gidding	Steeple Gidding
Households per thousand cultivated acres, 1279	37	50	30
Taxpayers per thousand cultivated acres, 1327	26	30	19
Tax paid per thousand cultivated acres, 1334	68s. 9d.	76s. 8d.	49s. 2d.
Population per thousand acres, 1801	205	67	70
Population per thousand acres, 1921	132	60	56

There is much interesting matter in table 2 which lies outside the scope of this book, but it will be noticed that Little Gidding was more intensively exploited than Great Gidding and, if the medieval assessments can be trusted, with probably a denser population and a slightly higher tax-assessment per acre. But while Great Gidding shows the common experience – a population in 1801 at least equal to that of the fourteenth century but a subsequent fall in the nineteenth century – the other two parishes (including outlying farms) have since the late sixteenth century had less than half the density of population of the mother village.

If the assessments and numbers of households for Little and Steeple Gidding are added together and the total compared with Great Gidding the results shown in table 3 are obtained.

Table 3

Date	Mother settlement	Daughter settlements	Daughters' total as per cent of mother
1086 (hides)	10	7½	75
1279 (area, acres)	1940	1680	87
1279 (households)	73	65	89
1327 (tax)	77s. 7½d.	62s. 11¾d.	81
1327 (households)	52	38	73
1334 (tax)	133s. 5½d.	99s. 1½d.	74
1801 (census)	420	124	30
1921 (census)	271	104	38

It will be seen that until the early fourteenth century mother and daughter settlements kept very much in step. The greatly inferior position in the last two hundred years is due, as has been seen, to the sixteenth-century change in land-use which removed both ploughs and ploughmen. Lest it should be objected that the steadiness of the ratio between mother and daughter settlements arises from the fact that the tax-collectors deliberately made it so, always dividing the sums due from the Giddings in approximately the same 100:80 ratio, it must be emphasised that the figures from 1279 and 1327 are from lists of named villages, and that the sums by which villages were assessed in 1334 were designed to correspond to the actual capacity of each. Two later reassessments are extant, for 1433 and 1448: in these, the relief for 'impoverishment' at Great and Steeple Gidding was only 18 per cent, not very far from the county average; but at Little Gidding it was 28 per cent in 1433 and 39 per cent in 1448. Unfortunately the reassessments for other years have not survived, but if these two years are typical, Little Gidding was already on the way to being the group of six houses which alone stood to face Humphrey Drewell in 1566. In the early fourteenth century there had been at least three times that number. The Plague alone cannot explain the shrinkage: for had it struck more fiercely at

Little Gidding than at its neighbours, their fortunes might well have been evened out by the mid-fifteenth century after a flow of men into the vacant holdings from the other two Giddings or from farther afield. Neither the density of settlement nor the tax-assessments suggest that Little Gidding was any less fertile than its neighbours. It looks as if the policy of the landowners before Humphrey Drewell had something to do with the retreat of settlement.

Studies of the distribution of lost and shrunken villages in other parts of the Midlands show a similar pattern of lost and surviving settlements set side by side. There is nothing to suggest, therefore, that Little Gidding and Steeple Gidding represent small or marginal villages from which settlers retreated when land-hunger lessened. They represent the more common Midland experience of adjacent settlements whose owners decide to make different use of very similar soils. In Little Gidding and Steeple Gidding the houses of husbandmen have largely disappeared. In Great Gidding the open fields remained until 1858 when the surveyor found himself in a medieval landscape.

Thus, in the mother village, the landowners and their tenants had found it profitable to continue with arable and had been unable to persuade each other that hedged arable was superior to open fields. In the other two villages a grass crop had seemed to be the more profitable, and the open fields had disappeared before any one could map them.

The photograph, fig. 32D, shows what remains of Steeple Gidding and Little Gidding after the husbandmen left the village streets. In the foreground are the church, rectory, farm and farm-cottages that make up the hamlet of Steeple Gidding, here seen from the south-east. The grass field to right of the church is scarred by earthworks of former streets and houses. South of the church, a chain of three rectangular fishponds still contains water, and, nearby, the earthworks of the manor house are covered by open scrub. These fishponds are the 'fisheries in Gyddinges Abbott' granted by the queen in 1589 to the Boton family, once the tenants of Ramsey Abbey and later the chief landowners in the parish.

T. S. Eliot has reported what you find when you reach Little Gidding:

when you leave the rough road
And turn behind the pig-sty to the dull façade
And the tombstone....
    There are other places
Which are also the world's end, some at the sea jaws,

91

Fig. 32D. Steeple Gidding and Little Gidding; looking NW, August 1965.

Or over a dark lake, in a desert or a city –
But this is the nearest, in place and time,
Now and in England.

In the view, looking north-west, much of 'the dull façade And the tombstone' shelters in the trees; the parish church of St John, which was used as a barn at the end of the sixteenth century, was rebuilt in 1625 and again in 1714. The Ferrars family, through whom the church is principally known, lived at Little Gidding Hall. The building no longer exists; its site is possibly marked by the moats, now covered by scrub and hedges, where the trees thin out to the right of the church to leave a rough grass field between them and a straight, unfenced lane. Few remains of the village are to be seen; yet in 1279 there were thirty-one households here, beside the Engaynes' manor house, and eighteen households were substantial enough to be taxed in

1327. There were only five households in 1428. Much of the ground is scarred and uneven as if it had formerly been built upon. The wood and scrub cover a considerable area, and may conceal further house-sites.

The village of Great Gidding (fig. 32E) is an exception to this story of decay: its fortune, moreover, may be traced from the two surviving open-field maps. The 1541 map (fig. 32B) must be one of the earliest large-scale plans of an English parish. It is minutely informative about the position of cottages and crofts but it only indicates the position of the open-field land in a general way. By contrast, the map of 1858 (fig. 32C) plots every strip in the open fields but is less detailed for the village streets: the surveyor was satisfied to mark the position of houses and to sketch the outer boundary of the enclosed crofts; the boundaries between gardens have

Fig. 32E. Great Gidding; looking N, June 1952.

not been completed.

The lack of change between 1541 and 1858 is remarkable; apart from the building of one house and two outbuildings in *Lawe Furlonge Feelde* the village had hardly altered. No reduction of open-field land by piecemeal enclosure had taken place, and the enclosed pastures at the parish fringe were still the only area not minutely divided into strips.

One particular feature of the village plan deserves comment. The street pattern consists of two contrasted sections: there is the regular succession of forty-seven cottages and gardens along the main street where the church also stands. These have crofts behind them, and the far hedges of the crofts make a neat frontage to the fields. At the south end of the village, however, quite a different picture appears. A loop of lanes serves an irregular scatter of cottages known now (as in 1541) by the name of *Chapell Ende*. There is no regular frontage for these cottages nor for their crofts, and the road serving them winds around two island properties.

In the air photograph (Fig. 32E), where the village is viewed from the south, this loop of streets at Chapel End occupies the foreground, with the long main street at the left centre. The church is near the left margin. In Chapel End the third street of the loop has disappeared since 1858; other cottage-sites are now unoccupied: the population of the village shrank by one-third during the nineteenth century. The small closes of the earlier map have been partly replaced by wood and plantations (right foreground) although the outer boundary of the hedges in 1541 is still marked by trees. The windmill at the crossroads towards the top right-hand margin has lost its sails, but it stands where the mill of 1541 stood and probably on the site of the mill mentioned in a survey of 1296. The *Waye* which passes it no longer bears much traffic *from Stamforde*, and the strips of *Hongerhill Feelde* among which it stood have been replaced by hedged fields. The open-field strips in the map of 1858 correspond in detail to the ridge-and-furrow seen between the windmill and Chapel End.

93

Signs of ridging within the former closes among the trees suggest that *Chapell Ende* was an extension of settlement over land which had been earlier in use as arable, and this would not be out of character with the irregular street pattern noted in this quarter. Great Gidding may thus have had a period of expansion at a time subsequent to the settlement along its regular main street frontage.

Sources

V.C.H. Hunts. III (1936) 48–53, with map of 1541. The original of this map was then in the possession of Sir Michael Culme-Seymour, at Rockingham Castle; 1279: *Rot. Hund.* II. 619, 626 and 631; 1296, windmill: C. 133/80/2; map of 1858: U.L.C., Maps bb. 66.93.33–4; table I: 1327, E. 179/122/4, 1334, E. 179/122/77; 1594 tithe suit, E. 134/27 Eliz., Hunts. no. 23; 1549 sheep census, E. 179/122/146.

V. THE JOURNEY TO THE MARGIN

In the general absence of documents the progress of settlement before the Norman Conquest can only be inferred from evidence of the kind discussed in this chapter, and from the related disciplines of field-archaeology and place-name-study. With Domesday Book the progress of settlement becomes much more certain. It is true that the mention of a name in Domesday Book is no guarantee that any village in the modern sense existed but, where the number of ploughs and ploughmen is given, some assessment of the relative size of the vills can be made as an assurance that the 'vill' was more than two or three houses in an isolated clearing.

In the plains of lowland England, including the coastal plains of the north-east, the map of Domesday settlements bears a close resemblance to the modern map. For example, in one small compact area for which the medieval evidence has been assembled,[14] the Ainstey of York, there were thirty-seven vills in 1086, excluding the suburbs of the city. Only two more villages were added by the end of the fourteenth century, and as seven villages had disappeared, six of them by 1332, the area then had fewer villages than at the Conquest. Since the end of the fourteenth century, four more villages have been lost or have shrunk to one house, so that the present number of villages in the Ainstey is smaller than at any time since 1086.

Except on inhospitable soils, the main progress of rural settlement between Domesday Book and the early fourteenth century produced not more villages but more fields. The principal expansion of population in this period (which estimates put at about threefold) depended on the extension of the field-land of existing villages. It was between 1086 and the early fourteenth century, and probably in the last hundred years of that period, that village fields at last reached out towards their parish boundaries. Where acreages are given in the survey of 1279,

[14] *Yorks. Arch. Jnl* XXXVIII (1953) 230.

as at Gidding (p. 90) it can often be seen that the field-land already extended almost to the edge of the parish.

This advance of settlement between Domesday Book and the tax-lists of 1334 took two forms, not necessarily mutually exclusive. On the one hand, improved techniques, additional ploughs, more people and a rising land-hunger were pushing fields and settlers into places where colonisation had previously seemed too difficult or too unrewarding. This process would be accompanied by new villages, like the Newtons, and the Newboroughs. It was a moving frontier, which might have been seen within this period along the edge of the Wash, among the northern hills, in the moors of the south-west and along the Welsh Marches.

The second way in which additions were made to the available land was the less spectacular advance of assarting, land being won from adjacent wood, heath and marsh and added to the fields of old-established villages. Here, there was no single moving frontier but many, and the creation of new villages was unnecessary so long as the newly acquired land could be reached and farmed from existing settlements. The extension of field-land by assarting has already been illustrated in the account of the open fields in chapter 3. By it, furlong was added to furlong until the complete pattern of the sixteenth-century parish maps was achieved.

The gap in time between the early fourteenth-century tax-lists and the Elizabethan maps may seem too large to be bridged in a single sentence. May not much of the extension of field-land be attributable to the fifteenth and early sixteenth centuries? In fact, the general agrarian history of England suggests a stabilisation and, in some regions, a retreat of settlement in the early fourteenth century, a contraction pushed further by the losses of manpower in the mid-fourteenth century plagues. The result of this was that some mid-sixteenth

Fig. 33. Cholwich 'township'; a view looking N over Dartmoor, June 1952.

century villages might have arable fields occupying no more ground than in the years before the Black Death (1349). In such circumstances it would have been quite possible for an Elizabethan to see land under scrub carrying marks of old ploughing-furrows, as described in the passage from Norden quoted near the beginning of chapter 3 (II). Although no single photograph can be representative of the assarting movement of the thirteenth century in the Midlands almost every one of the views of medieval fields must somewhere bear witness to it.

33. CHOLWICH TOWN   Devonshire

An interesting combination of the two forms of advance can be demonstrated in western Devonshire. In districts where early settlement had not been as thorough as in the Midlands, the new creations of the later Middle Ages could be placed in the wide spaces left by the Anglo-Saxon villages, not as additions to the field-land of the older villages, but as the fields of scattered farms and hamlets newly founded. This produced the combination of nucleated villages and outlying farms characteristic of the western half of Devonshire. The poll-tax receipts for Devon in 1377 show the result of this double wave of settlement even after it had been checked by the plagues: there were villages with as many tax-payers as would have been found in the Midlands, but also small townships with fewer than twenty taxpayers each. Some of them possessed parish churches and were to appear in the returns of 1428 as 'having fewer than ten persons holding house'.

This western colonisation is illustrated by a compact farm on the moorland edge, still in use, and by abandoned fields elsewhere, where advances of the thirteenth century have not always been maintained.

The 'township' of Cholwich lies in the parish of Cornwood, at the 650-foot contour on the very margin of Dartmoor. Before the advent of the china-clay industry the expanse of moorland shown in the photograph (fig. 33) had very limited economic value. The less favourable soils made it unlikely that such areas would be occupied as early or as densely as the valleys and plains. Scattered settlements are the creation of small groups or single families arriving fitfully at the frontier. The low agricultural output in grain and grazing which they could hope to achieve with their resources made any great density of population impossible; with such soils and so wet a climate non-arable pursuits would loom large in the farming lives of settlers. In order to make the most of pasture, rough grazing, forests, and fenland fishing it was not necessary for people to live as close together as in the ploughing villages of the English plains.

The farm of Cholwich and its occupiers has been taken as a model study by Professor Hoskins. In the early thirteenth century when all over England men were pushing forward in the last great burst of medieval colonisation, the lord of Cornwood granted some 200 acres of *Cholleswyt* to Benedict, son of Edric Siward, a small peasant freeholder. The eastern bounds of the grant were formed by the River Piall which flows in a wooded valley on the right-hand side of the photograph. On the left are the fields which the farmers cleared of boulders, 'hauling ... with their bare hands clearing their little fields'. The granite boulders taken from the fields went to make houses, while the high banks of the lane which runs down the photograph, and the hedge banks, have solid foundations of such stones.

The lane leads down to Cornwood, a small nucleated village more than two miles away. In the thirteenth century a number of other farms akin to Cholwich were carved out of the poorer land on the parish margin. Professor Hoskins showed that this pattern of the nucleated village and the scattered farmsteads of late colonisation is characteristic of other parts of Devon. He has also produced evidence to suggest that these settlers took into their territory some tracts of land which had already been used casually as temporary 'outfields' by the Cornwoods of the county; with the establishment of the Cholwiches, permanent occupation by a single adjacent farm replaced intermittent, short-term cultivation by the distant villagers.

Similar close correlation between late, non-nucleated settlement and the free status of settlers has been observed in many parts of England. The family who came to Cholwich to make a home of it for the first time were freemen. Hoskins observed:

> In the large parish of Cornwood ... practically every farm for some miles appears to be the holding of a free tenant from the thirteenth century onwards.... The western manors running up to the moors relied upon a host of free tenants to reclaim their extensive waste in severalty, acre by acre and field by field. The open field was rarer, the customary tenants relatively fewer, from the nature of the problem of colonisation.

The rarity of open fields and the paucity of bondmen are phenomena which recur in the marginal colonisation of the eastern fens and the northern hills.

Sources

W. G. Hoskins and H. P. R. Finberg, *Devonshire Studies* (1952), 78–93; C. D. Linehan, 'Deserted sites and rabbit warrens on Dartmoor', *Med. Arch.* x (1966) 113–44, esp. fig. 58; Cholwich lies at SX 587618.

34. CATHERTON COMMON   Shropshire

Fig. 34 shows an area near Farlow three miles north-west of Cleobury Mortimer, photographed from the north-east, late of a summer evening. On the north-eastern slope of Clee Hill, on land at the margin of cultivation where soils offered poor prospects for farming, settlement was encouraged by opportunities to make a livelihood from quarrying or mining, as the local geology might determine. Here the reclaimed land was not incorporated in any system of communal fields but formed the holding of squatter colonists and their families. This detachment, in every sense, was also marked by the island-like character of the occupied areas and by the typically irregular boundaries between surviving commons and enclosed fields, as if they were determined more by the ambit of tethered stock than by a line for the convenience of a ploughman. Elsewhere, these 'islands' are now merged into continuous fields but their shape shows clearly that they too were once isolated: a similar pattern – a landscape with field-boundaries surviving from a period of piecemeal settlement – can be seen in the very different circumstances of marshland reclamation in fig. 111A.

Exploitation for mining of the rough and now furze-grown commons is attested by the numerous circular mounds, each with a central depression, like the homes of giant sand-bees. Each depression marks the site of a pit dug down to a shallow seam of coal; the waste rock from the excavations now forms the surrounding

Fig. 34. Catherton Common; looking SW, July 1963.

mound. The close spacing of the pits and their random scatter indicates the piecemeal nature of the mining. The mounds in the foreground are seen to be much smaller than those in the centre of the photograph, although the size of the depressions is not dissimilar. Since the earth has been thrown out as spoil, the size of the waste tips must relate to different depths of working. At least three disused pits lie within fields on the left of the present common and seven more in fields on the right, suggesting that the squatters' encroachment on the common continued after mining had ceased. These coal pits have not yet been dated: they may be post-medieval.

35. GARROW   Cornwall

In general our photographs have been restricted to those which can be matched to surviving historical evidence such as maps and documents. The intrinsic interest both of Catherton Common and of the area shown in fig. 35 has

suggested a departure from this discipline so that we find ourselves in the position of many of our readers who, we suspect, will use the photographs and commentaries in this book as examples with which they may compare sites and earthworks of interest to themselves.

The area of fig. 35 comprises the sloping ground on either side of a shallow curving valley south-east of Bodmin in St Breward parish. The situation is analogous to that of Cholwich and Catherton Common except that the remains of former cultivation take a different form. However, the equivalent of the single-farm settlement can be seen in the rectangular fields of cleared ground by the farm in the far distance. These regularly planned fields are probably a late rationalisation of less regular boundaries, as can be seen from the field banks in the moorland to the left. The whole of the rocky ground on the right carries cultivation ridges not unlike those found in the Outer Hebrides and elsewhere. These ridges are overridden, here and there, by

97

Fig. 35. Garrow, looking NW; remains of agriculture on Bodmin Moor, April 1966.

earthen banks, seemingly devised to contain the cultivated area within rectangular plots. The limit of cultivation fades away up the slope into a rock-strewn hillside.

The land in the middle distance carries similar ridges, though these can only just be distinguished on the photograph. These narrow ridges have been gathered within eleven roughly parallel earthen banks, and close examination suggests that the ridges do not quite extend to the upper end of these enclosures. The sinuous dark mark crossing the hillside from right to left is a modern track.

Is the whole system medieval, representing an early attempt at cultivation of this waste moorland?

Excavations at Garrow Tor were undertaken by Dorothy Dudley and E. Marie Minter in 1962.

Fig. 36. Chelmorton; looking NE, August 1953. A Peak District village with walled fields of early and late enclosure.

They excavated a group of nine house-sites on the south-east side of the Tor (SX 146780) and also at this group of fields, which are illustrated in their report by a photograph looking E across the valley towards the hill-slope. These moorland strips might well have been thought pre-medieval, were it not that thirteenth-century pottery was found within them, comparable with that from excavations at the village itself.

Hut circles of Iron Age character are common on the moor; in particular a group of four such circles which lay in the way of medieval farmers was incorporated into a small paddock which interrupts the seventh and eighth rectangular plots near the point where the modern track makes a pronounced bend.

Source

Dorothy Dudley and E. Minter, 'The medieval village at Garrow Tor', *Med. Arch.* VI–VII (1962–3) 272–94 and plates. The report gives a useful list of many other medieval sites in Cornwall, both villages and fields. National Grid ref. SX 142777.

36. CHELMORTON — Derbyshire

Altitude alone does not make a village agriculturally marginal. The village of Chelmorton (fig. 36), seen here from the south-west, is a street-village of the simplest type with all its farmhouses and cottages strung out along a straight road. Such villages are found all over the English lowlands; but the fields in the foreground are 1100 feet above the sea; the church, in a tree-ringed enclosure at the far end of the valley, is at 1250 feet; and the plateau to the right of it, at over 1300 feet.

The use of the phrase, Peak District, sometimes conjures up the impression of Pennine wildness. The villages which stand between the Manifold, the Dove and the Wye have very little of the atmosphere of *Wuthering Heights* . As far north as Buxton they continue to be as nucleated as any village south of the Trent. The neighbours of Chelmorton – Blackwell, Flagg, Taddington, Earl Sterndale and Monyash – are all within a three-mile circuit.

It is unlikely that anyone would now write, as in the *Victoria County History of Derbyshire* (1907): 'the manorial economy of Derbyshire naturally resembled that of the rest of England', but since the settlement history of the Peak is still largely unwritten this photograph can only indicate some of the interesting questions which remain unanswered.

Settlers in this part of Derbyshire chose the open plateau rather than the deeply incised dales, but the shape both of the fields and the villages suggests that the settlers were not primarily pastoral farmers but men seeking land for ploughing. The long, narrow fields of Chelmorton resemble exactly those of other villages (e.g. Brassington, fig. 53), where 'open fields' have been enclosed by the simplest method possible, the encircling of a block of strips with a fence or wall. A novel feature, not to be found farther south, is the nature of the boundary: the stone cleared from the surface of the ground has been utilised for dry-built walling, and hedges are lacking. As Celia Fiennes commented, as she rode through the Peak, 'you see neither hedge nor tree but only low drye stone walls round some ground'. A few trees have now been planted as windbreaks or for ornament.

The limestone walls mark out two distinct field-patterns. In the foreground and on the higher ground in the distance are rectangular fields which have probably arisen from the enclosure of common fields and pasture in 1809. The remaining fields, nearer the village, are long and narrow. Some adjacent fields appear to have been amalgamated, but in general the width of these fields is the width of the street frontage which a single farmstead occupies in the village. These elongated crofts are intersected on the right-hand side of the photograph by a road which takes the steep slope at an easy gradient; the older road up to the plateau probably followed the natural cleft behind the churchyard to which the main street leads.

The village is protected by hills from the north and east winds, but the altitude, the rainfall and the soils of the Carboniferous Limestone plateau can never have been conducive to good grain yields, so that the village might well have been among the first to change the traditional local balance between arable and grass. The form of arable farming here in the early Middle Ages has not been discovered, but with so much grassland available it would not be surprising to find some form of infield–outfield cultivation. If that were so, the long, narrow fields might represent an early piecemeal enclosure of the infield, and the remainder of the parish, with its rectangular fields, the former reservoir of grassland of which each year a small part was drawn upon for temporary cultivation. In 1630 the J.P.s of the county reported that the villages hereabouts were 'mostly long inclosed'.

In 1334 the tax-assessment of the village was sixty-two shillings, as high as that of any village down in the valley of the Trent. Its neighbours appear elsewhere in the list, so there is no doubt that this sum was assessed solely on Chelmorton. The prosperity of Peak Forest villages farther east might be explained partly by lead-mining but there are no visible lead-workings in this parish.

Sources

Map *c*. 1640: M.P.C. 78; deeds: *Derbys. Arch. Jnl* n.s. II; enclosure award (1809): County Record Office; W. E. Wightman, 'Open field agriculture in the Peak District', *Derbys Arch. Jnl* LXXXI (1961) 117–18.

37. THE DEEPINGS Lincolnshire

The communities of Deeping were in the Middle Ages at once limited and supported by the surrounding fens. The photograph (fig. 37), looking west-north-west, shows clearly what a barrier to settlement was afforded by fens such as those on the left of the river when the task of drainage was beyond the capacity of early medieval techniques. The ground on the right of the river in Lincolnshire, which stood slightly higher, could be reclaimed and occupied. The arable fields and common pastures of Deeping lay behind the houses on the right. The community was settled along its river frontier, facing the Welland which served as a route for traffic and trade. The medieval crofts were able to develop on one side only of the village street and they can be seen extending back from the road. Many of these crofts are still hedged or have straggling trees along the line of former hedges; others have been thrown together, their old boundaries still visible in the grass.

Country such as heaths and dense woodland, which offered obstacles to easy settlement, led to the growth of scattered communities. Fenland and marsh, on the other hand, limited the degree to which individuals could maintain a separate economic existence. The effort of reclamation and the continuing need to maintain defences against flood-waters have always called for a communal effort, and the characteristic village of the medieval fenland is a nucleated settlement set wherever natural conditions provided a firm foothold from which to begin the work of draining and cultivation. Such footholds were

Fig. 37. Deeping St James, Deeping Gate and Market Deeping; looking WNW, June 1951.

afforded by silt islands surrounded by salt and freshwater marsh, like the line of villages from Spalding to Lynn; or, as at Deeping, by the bank of a river. The expansion of settlement, as more land became available by reclamation, took place along the line of the bank so that the largest villages are not dense clusters but a long chain of houses.[15] Deeping St James in the foreground is continuous with Deeping Gate, and Deeping Gate with Market Deeping in the distance. These neighbouring communities seem to feel themselves distinct; at coronations and jubilees they

[15] Post-medieval drainage has added a more scattered settlement along the newer dykes.

have tug-of-war matches over boundary-ditches into which the losers are forcefully pulled.

The recorded population in 1086, which may be regarded as the heads of households only, numbered fifty in East Deeping (as Deeping St James was then called). Part of this area was owned by Peterborough Abbey, six miles to the south, and the creation of a third village at Market Deeping was described in the chronicle which embodied the monastery's traditions: 'Building upon the embankment numerous tenements and cottages, in a short while the abbot formed at Deeping a large vill, marking out gardens and cultivated fields. At the same time he changed the chapel of St Guthlac into the parish church of the new vill.'[16]

The multiplicity of economic interests in a large village like this at the edge of fens is shown in the reeves' accounts of the manor of Market Deeping. These are in six divisions, and six men rendered account. There were keepers of the meadow and of the river-bank: one profits from the river, the other guards against it. A third kept the market-tolls, for the village was an important centre for boats coming from the 'mainland' of Kesteven for the marshland produce: fish, eels, osiers and wildfowl. A fourth accounted for the carriage of timber, probably for the river defences. A fifth had charge of the banks and ditches of the smaller watercourses which formed the field-boundaries and the drains of the reclaimed land. A sixth rendered account to his lords for the products of the marsh; the fishery in Deeping had been one of the assets of Peterborough Abbey noted in Domesday Book. Like other fenland villages, the taxes paid here in the early fourteenth century were considerably in excess of the 'mainland' villages a few miles westward. Once reclaimed, the fertile soil could maintain a density of rural population surpassed nowhere in England.[17]

Sources

1086: *The Lincs. Domesday. Lincs. Rec. Soc.* xix (1924) 128, 173–4; reeves' accounts: S.C. 6/909/16.

[16] The pseudo-Ingulph, quoted in H. C. Darby, *Medieval Fenland* (1940) 44.

[17] The densities are from an unpublished analysis of the 1334 and 1377 tax-returns by M. W. Beresford. A study by Professor H. E. Hallam elucidates the topography of early medieval settlement and reclamation in the Lincolnshire fens: *Settlement and Society* (1965).

VI. THE MIGRANTS

Almost nothing is known of the failures among the earliest settlements. These sites have long ago been swallowed up in the fields of their more successful neighbours; only such a chance as disclosed a Sutton Courtenay of the Anglo-Saxon period in a gravel pit to the west of medieval Sutton (in Berkshire) will reveal places where an early Anglo-Saxon village had no medieval successor on the same site.

Here, a few illustrations are given of the migration of villages after centuries of apparent prosperity. In the more spectacular movements, such as that of Old Sarum to Salisbury (fig. 84), both documents and earthworks are available for study. For smaller villages it is unlikely that the movement will be documented. Usually there is only the evidence of earthworks, which may be difficult to read, but when remains of a parish church are included amongst them the evidence for an ancient village site becomes emphatic.

The historical fact of migration may be embodied in a folk-myth. The real cause of the isolated church is forgotten, but the fact is preserved by distortion and imagination until a fiction is realised which the villagers can find more credible than the cold fact. Churches carried away by the devil, and stones that insisted on walking to lonely sites, are the subject of popular myths.

The migration can sometimes be dated by a subsequent amalgamation of parishes. The villagers of Kiplingcotes in the Yorkshire Wolds, who abandoned their village at some unknown time in the later Middle Ages, removed their chapel bells to rehang them in the church tower of Middleton on the Wolds.

In short-distance migrations, the process may have been much more gradual than the evictions often associated with total depopulations. Where the houses now cluster along some main road that was previously shunned, the attractions of buying, selling and innkeeping may have lured first one household and then another, so that a considerable time would pass before the church and the manor house were left isolated.[18]

At Cublington (fig. 38) the village seems to have been abandoned and then resettled. The possibility of such a retreat and qualified return cannot be excluded elsewhere: for example, during the mid-fourteenth-century plagues. The inquisitions *post mortem* printed in the *County History* of Northumberland often describe total devastation in one year and a fair-sized list of tenants a generation later. Even Cistercian depopulations were sometimes reversed: both Fountains and Jervaulx were forced to refound villages when in the later fourteenth century the abbeys had insufficient capital to replenish the damage the Scots wars had done to their granges. Some of these granges (such as Baldersby) had once been created by destroying a village, and a village had to be created again.

[18] For example, Potterspury (Northants.) on the main road A5 three miles north of Stony Stratford; Shenley (Bucks.) four miles south of Stony Stratford; Stevenage (Herts.).

Fig. 38. Cublington; looking E to the village over earthworks of the deserted village, December 1968.

38. CUBLINGTON Buckinghamshire

The small village of Cublington, five and a half miles north of Aylesbury, achieved national fame since our first edition through its spirited resistance to the siting of an international airport within the parish. As we shall show, there is good evidence that an old tradition of the village being emptied by the Black Death and later re-settled is more than an imaginative folk-story, and for this reason alone the earthworks of the first village that appear in fig. 38 are of great archaeological interest. However, as far as we know, the defenders of Cublington in 1970 did not argue that one devastation in the life of a village was quite enough.

Fig. 39A. East Witton; looking E, July 1953.

Within the church of the small village, which appears in the background of the photograph, there is a monumental brass commemorating a rector, John Dervyle, who died in 1410, as 'the first rector of the present church'. Taken by itself, this might mean no more than that the church fabric had recently been rebuilt, but there is good evidence, apart from surviving earthworks, that the first church lay some distance from the present village in a field at the centre of fig. 38. In his visitation of 1519 Bishop Atwater of Lincoln was scandalised to find a desecrated graveyard, and ordered that 'the graveyard where the parish church of this place formerly stood' should be fenced off from the pastures to exclude animals, and then perambulated with the glebe lands each Rogation Day.

The oldest surviving terrier of the glebe, dated 1601, does describe this small close as an addition to the glebe land which was scattered in selions in the four open fields, *Weyld, Meade, Broncott* and *Holcombe*. These fields remained open until the parliamentary enclosure of 1769, so that the depopulation of Cublington cannot be assigned to the conversion of arable to grass which so exercised the minds of Bishop Atwater's contemporaries.

Nor can the Black Death be the sole cause of the abandoned village. In 1341, Edward III was granted the ninth fleece, lamb and sheaf from country parishes. The return of the jury which assessed Cublington has been printed in the *Nonarum Inquisitiones*. It is clear that eight years before the Black Death the village was already

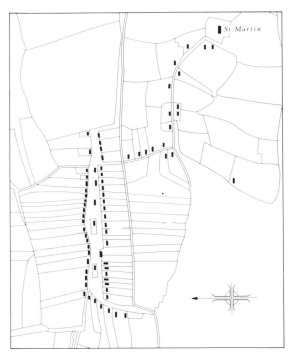

Fig. 39B. East Witton in 1627. Redrawn after the plan by William Senior.

of the first village. Clearest to see is the conical mound known locally as *The Beacon* which is probably a small fortified motte, an early stronghold of the lord of the manor; there are traces of rectangular buildings in the bailey below it. The church site now lies again as Bishop Atwater found it in 1519, unfenced within a grass field and open to animals. There is no sign of foundations, but the boundary-ditch of the churchyard is clearly visible a little above the Beacon, separated from the motte by a hollow-way which narrows to left and then branches: the right-hand fork joining the present village street and a smaller left-hand fork extending as far as a hedge beyond which it is lost in a ploughed field. The significance of the church-yard earthwork was first recognised by Hadrian Allcroft in 1908, and he reported that thirty skeletons had been disinterred there. In 1925 Mr Pelham Maitland confirmed the site of the church by excavation. The patches of rank vegetation near the lower margin of the photograph conceal further earthworks but no clear traces of village houses appear. Uninterrupted ridge-and-furrow of former ploughlands in the background helps to delimit the village site.

Sources

V. C. H. Bucks. II (1908) 27, III (1925) 338; R.C.H.M. *Buckinghamshire* II (1913) 98; H. Allcroft, *Earthwork of England* (1908) 548; visitation of 1519: *Lincs. Record. Soc.* XXXIII (1940) 44; *Nonarum Inquisitiones* (1807) 327; 1283: C. 131/38/8; 1304: C. 133/118/17; 1346: C. 135/81/10; 1334 and 1446 taxes: E. 179/77/65; glebe terriers: Bodleian Library, MSS. Arch. Oxon., and Lincs. Archives Committee, Lincoln; sketch plan of Maitland's excavations on the site of the church, made available by the Rev. J. W. H. Faulkner, vicar of Aston Abbots.

39. EAST WITTON
Yorkshire, North Riding

East Witton lies in Wensleydale, one and a half miles south-east of Middleham, at the junction with Coverdale. The photograph (fig. 39A) is a view looking east over the village down the side valley. The commanding position of the church of St John at the head of the village green makes it easy to assume that the two are integral, and that the antiquity of the green is authenticated by the company it keeps with the church. The fact that the fabric of the church is wholly nineteenth century may raise some first doubts, but there are many ancient foundations with wholly nineteenth-century architecture, bearing witness to the thoroughness of restoration or the piety of a rebuilder. This church was in fact newly built

on the verge of decay: 'there are two carucates of land in the said parish of Cublington which lie fallow and uncultivated, and thirteen houses stand empty. Their tenants have gone away because of their poverty. Sheep and lambs are few, and there is no one in the parish substantial enough to be taxed to the fifteenth '

Nine years earlier there had been sixteen households wealthy enough to pay the taxes, and only seven years earlier, when the village's capacity to contribute to the tax of the fifteenth had been assessed, the villagers were rated at forty-two shillings, a sum not much below the local average. (After the resettlement the new village was rated at 23s. 6d.) In 1283 there had been at least thirty-nine households.

It does not seem possible that a sudden deterioration in the fertility of the soil could have taken place in seven years. The surveys of the manor in 1283 and 1304 show respectively 394 and 300 acres of demesne arable. In 1346 they show only 160 acres, but even this reduced amount indicates that the village was not completely empty.

Whatever the reason, the old site was abandoned soon after 1341. Perhaps the Black Death was the last blow. Sixty years later it was re-settled and a new church built.

In the foreground of fig. 38 are the earthworks

by the Earl of Ailesbury in 1809 in honour of George III's jubilee. East Witton had an older church of St Martin at Lowthorpe some distance from the village, where the enclosed area of God's Acre may still be seen. A large-scale plan of the village and fields survives among surveys of the Jervaulx estates made in 1627 by William Senior, 'Professor of Arithmetique, Geometrie, Astronomie, Navigation and Dialling, well-wisher to the Mathematiques' as the cartouche modestly declares. St Martin's was then standing, with seventeen houses set at intervals along a lane leading south-eastwards from the present village. The old church is shown at the top right-hand corner of fig. 39B based on the plan of 1627, and its site is marked on the photograph (fig. 39A) by a clump of trees in a corresponding position. There are now even fewer houses along this lane, settlement having become concentrated at the green. The modern church stands upon land that was part of the *East Field* in 1627: the plough-strips are still visible in the adjoining meadows.

The map of 1627 sets aside suspicions that the neat lay-out of East Witton is the work of a paternal squire of the eighteenth or nineteenth century. Although the Earl of Ailesbury rebuilt the village in 1809, the houses and gardens now occupy exactly the same position as they did in 1627, while five small cottages squatting on the green itself have been removed and a row of six cottages across the west end of the green is now reduced to two houses. Apart from the seventeen houses on the lane to the old church, the plan of 1627 shows twenty-two houses on the north side of the green and twenty-five on the south. In the Dissolution Survey of 1536 there had been fifty-three households. To say when migration took place is not possible without the manorial records. In the fourteenth-century tax-lists East Witton ranks third in the wapentake. It had 220 taxpayers in 1377. Lying at the junction of Coverdale and Wensleydale, East Witton would have been well placed for a market-centre. It stood, moreover, on the edge of Jervaulx Abbey park, the nearest village to the abbey gate. The abbey park had once been part of the demesnes of East Witton manor but by 1287 the abbey owned five-sixths of the parish and may well have been responsible for the development of the new village site around a new market-place suited for the Monday market and the Martinmas cattle-fair first held in 1307.

The road from Ripon to Coverdale runs along the village green but the present main road up Wensleydale, having passed the new church of East Witton, then diverges northwards through a right-angle turn avoiding the former market-place. Such a siting for a plantation-settlement with commercial ambitions would have been rather odd but close examination of the Ordnance Map shows that the Wensleydale road originally crossed the River Cover half a mile west of the present bridge, at a point where a green lane comes down from Middleham to the river to continue on the East Witton side as a footpath leading straight to the west end of the green. The footpath and green lane on opposite banks point to a former crossing, superseded by the existing bridge which is no older than the turnpike. By the original route both the Coverdale and Wensleydale traffic traversed East Witton market-place. If the original road eastwards from East Witton passed the old church of St Martin this suggests that the earlier route along the south side of Wensleydale continued down the dale by Ellingstring.

The re-orientation of East Witton aligns the axis of the village green almost upon Jervaulx Abbey, emphasising the likely role of the abbey in changing the plan of the village. The present main road from East Witton to Jervaulx on the line of the turnpike, follows a direct route from the village to the abbey.

A Cistercian abbot by the conventions of his Order would not be allowed to bring a lay community to the gates of his abbey, although, as Bury or Abingdon show, other Orders were able to encourage commercial settlements alongside their Houses. A development at East Witton, two miles west of Jervaulx, broke no rules. Other developments of this kind and period aspired to borough status (chapter 9 below) but no documentary evidence has yet been found for burgages at this village, although the plan resembles that of many petty burghal plantations elsewhere in England. But if never more than a village, there is a likelihood that East Witton, one of the most often-quoted examples of a 'green-village', may turn out to be secondary in its present form.

Sources

Map of 1627: Jervaulx Abbey Estate Office; *V.C.H. Yorks, N.R.* 1 (1914) 280–6; survey of 1536: S.C. 11/19/20; S.C. 11/4/24.

40. MILTON ABBAS Dorset

The fate of Milton Abbas, a market-village ten miles north-east of Dorchester, was briefly if slightly inaccurately summed up by Eden in his 'State of the Poor' (1797) – 'the town is now

Fig. 40A. Milton Abbas; looking SW, June 1950.

converted into a fishpond'. The fishpond is a rather diminutive term for the lake fashioned by Capability Brown and his landscape engineers in the late eighteenth century with its north end covering part of the site. An impression of its size can be gathered from the portion which forms the end of the vista down the modern village street. The Earl of Dorchester's aim was not simply to drown the village in the fashion of modern reservoir engineers. A new but smaller village was built out of sight of the Abbey House (fig. 40A).

The landscape gardeners were able to turn *High Street* and *Market Street* into smooth lawns and gardens. The market-place, where men had bargained since King Athelstan's charter, disappeared under a shrubbery. The churchyard became another lawn, the headstones being broken up or buried. Its neighbour, the Grammar School, migrated to Blandford. From the

west gate of the abbey, with only a lake and park in view, it is impossible today not to admire the audacity of Joseph Damer in conceiving the wholesale removal of a village of more than a hundred houses, a considerable engineering feat at any time. Only here and there on the steeper valley slopes do surviving earthworks show the site of the crofts in *Back Street*.

Fig. 40A, a view from the north-east, shows the new village which was created as a complement to the destruction of the old. Lying snugly in the bottom of a side valley, it was planned with a sense of space and form. The cottages were spaced evenly along the single street with a regular punctuation of chestnut trees, some of which survive. The gardens climb the hillside in orderly step and behind them is a masking plantation. That on the right has been recently felled and not replanted. Half-way down the left-hand side of the street is the new

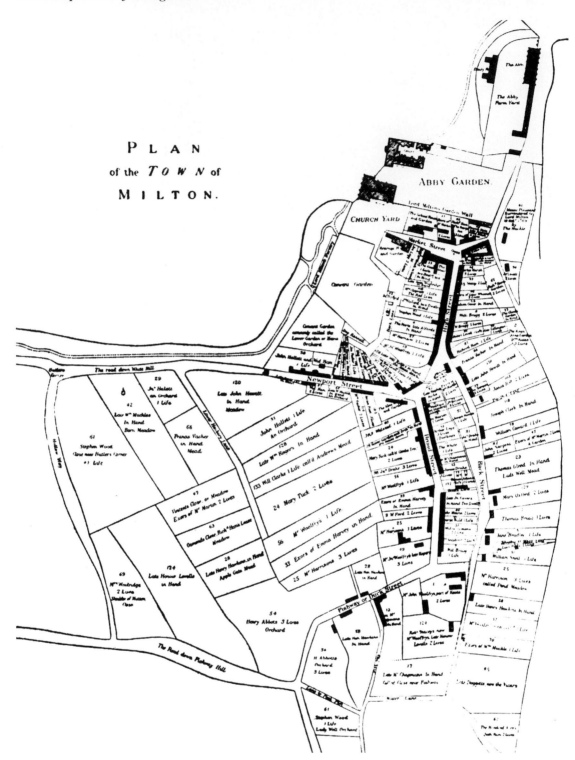

Fig. 40B. Milton Abbas in 1771; after William Woodward.

church opened in 1786 to replace the *Abbey Church* which the villagers had used as their parish church since 1298. Opposite it stands a small group of almshouses brought from the old site. Wide grass verges give an air of spaciousness and at the lower end of the valley the road widens into a triangular green with the lake beyond. The plan of the destroyed village (fig. 40B) is reproduced from a copy[19] in the possession of the Rev. C. J. Collis of Whitechurch. It dates from the time when Lord Milton was calculating the removal of the village, a survey being necessary to see what obstacles lay in his way. Each plot has marked on it the number of lives to run before leases expired. Others are 'in hand'. Near the *Abby Garden* there is 'Mount Pleasant, Surrendered to Lord Milton 10th Oct. 1769 by Tho. Muckle'. Several plots were occupied by Mr Harrison, a local solicitor, with three lives yet to go in the unexpired lease. It was this Harrison, victor in a lawsuit against the proprietor, who was the principal opponent of the destruction of the town. It is usually said that twenty years' patience was required before all the tenements

[19] The original plan, some 5 ft by 8 ft in size, made by William Woodward in 1771 after a survey of 1769, has been presented to the Brotherton Library, Leeds by the Rev. Dr C. K. Francis Brown.

were available for destruction. Then as Eden reported, 'he pulled down the houses as the tenants died off, and removed the church to a distant spot, where he erected very substantial cottages for such of the inhabitants as could not procure a more substantial habitation.'

The plan shows that the old town had more than a hundred houses standing in 1771. The focus of the streets was the small triangular market-place with its cross. Before the Dissolution this would have stood immediately outside the abbey precinct, as at Battle or Ramsey. With more than 700 years of markets and fairs the town had not failed to prosper: this is, indeed, not a case of a feeble light extinguished.

Sources

Hutchins, *Dorset* IV, 382; H. Pentin, 'The old town of Milton', *Proc. Dorset Nat. Hist. and Arch. Soc.* XXV (1904) 1–7 and plan, frontispiece; F. M. Eden, *State of the Poor* (ed. A. G. L. Rogers, 1928) II. 177; Dorothy Stroud, *Capability Brown* (1950) 81–2 and 90; partial survey of 1472: S.C. 12/7/71; plan by kindness of Rev. C. J. Collis; R.C.H.M. *Dorset* III, *Central*, part 2 (1970) 182–200, with plan of remains of the town; Joseph Damer (1717–98) was created Baron Milton in 1753 and Earl of Dorchester in 1792; an air photograph of the abbey was published in D. Knowles and J. K. St Joseph, *Monastic Sites from the Air* (1952) 34–5.

VII. SHRUNKEN VILLAGES

The shrunken English village is a phenomenon which has been very little studied, and until the general availability of air photographs after the war of 1939–45 it was difficult to realise the number of villages with traces of former homesteads and streets outside their present built-up area. Nor is there any single historical explanation of what the air photographs reveal. Some shrunken villages fall within the period of 'deserted' villages described in chapter 6, section III, change in land-use or the exhaustion of some local economic asset having made it impossible for the village to maintain more than a fraction of the former population. Decay of a castle, exhaustion of a quarry, diversion of a road, competition of foreign imports, a change in fashion or the silting of a harbour: these are particular and local causes which may be invoked.

Unless documentary or archaeological evidence is available, unanswered questions may remain. Were all the former houses of which there is evidence in the photographs in occupation at one and the same time? Are the modern cottages of the village also underlain by medieval

houses, or has the village migrated a short distance to its modern position from a site now distinguishable only in terms of earthworks or other marks?

Even where auxiliary evidence proves that there has been simultaneous occupation of both existing and abandoned sites, general agrarian history suggests a wide choice of explanations, quite apart from the specific and local catastrophes mentioned above. Agrarian change has produced a shrinkage of village populations on more than one occasion. The depressions of the late nineteenth century and of the thirties of the present century did much to reduce the rural population in certain districts; the coming of machinery has enabled economies to be made in man-power without any retreat of cultivation; migration to towns has drawn steadily on the villages, as successive census reports show. Similarly, the enclosures made in the late sixteenth and early seventeenth centuries had the object of more effective farming of consolidated holdings; even where there was no move from corn to grass the consolidation might cause a fall in the

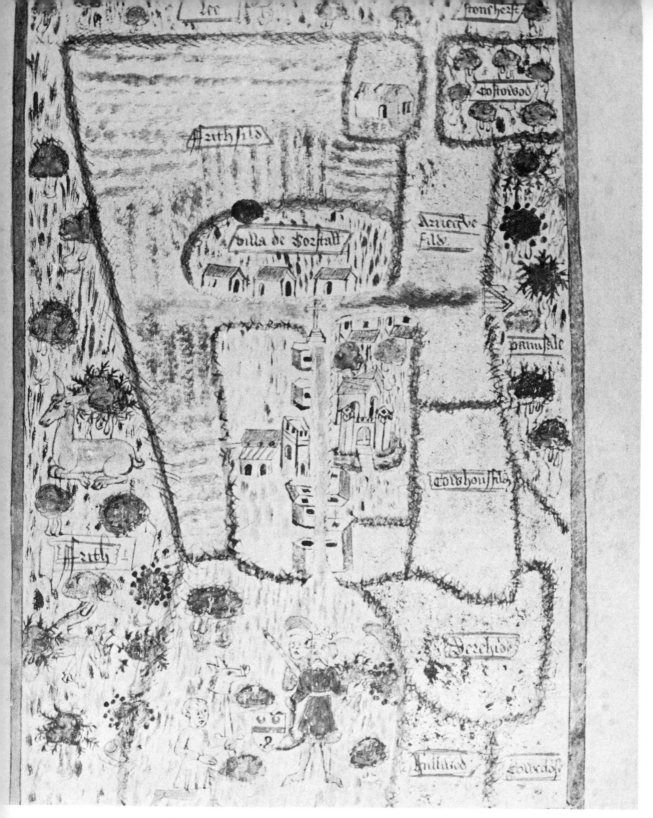

Fig. 41A. Boarstall in 1444. This plan, bound in the Boarstall Cartulary, is probably the earliest plan of an English village.

Fig. 41B. Boarstall; vertical photograph, February 1970. Scale 1:2300.

demand for labour, that 'decay of hospitality' which Tudor pamphleteers bemoaned.[20] Even earlier, in the late fourteenth and early fifteenth centuries, there were settlements, usually near the margin of cultivation where the difficulty of making a living from the soil led to the abandonment of hopes and the incorporation of arable fields with those of a neighbouring village. How many villages are smaller now than they were in the Middle Ages may be judged from the descriptions in the more recent county *Inventories* of the Royal Commission on Historical Monuments.[21]

Deductions about shrunken villages from the evidence of earthworks alone may be very misleading if no account is taken of new building elsewhere. Parliamentary enclosure, in particular (see chapter 6, section v), encouraged the building of farmsteads amongst newly enclosed fields allocated to the farms, and therefore away from the old village centre. While some of the village farmsteads were then put to use as labourers' cottages, others decayed and would leave just such a pattern of earthworks as air photographs show. Similarly, the imparking movement could create model villages in one place and leave the marks of deserted house-sites in another, without diminution of the total population; while, at any time, rehousing in 'new model' dwellings might be the cause of 'deserted' villages. Shrunken and migrant villages present many problems of interpretation. There are medieval village sites where no medieval buildings survive above ground at all (as Downtown, fig. 51); others, like Wharram Percy, of which the church alone survives; and again others like Brauncewell (fig. 50) where the manor house, vicarage or a modern farm yet stand among the earthworks. What, though, if there is also a second farm or a third? . . . and so on? Is the original size of the village important? Is a 'village' where three houses now survive more 'deserted' if it originally comprised thirty households than if it had been reduced from only six?

In most instances a verdict of 'shrunken' would have to be returned on the evidence of earthworks alone since there may be no plan

[20] For a reduction in the number of village houses from thirty-six to eighteen at the time of rebuilding and reorganisation in 1567 see *Northumberland County History* v. 208 (High Buston) and examples in B. K. Roberts, 'The regulated village' (typescript circulated 1972).
[21] Shrunken villages and their earthworks are described in R.C.H.M. *Northants.* I, *Cambs.* I and II, and *Dorset* II part I, IV and v. The sectional prefaces to these *Inventories* discuss the remains of reduced and of deserted settlements in their region.

available of the village at its greatest extent. However one of our examples, Boarstall, is recorded on a plan of 1444 which is often claimed to be the oldest large-scale plan of any English village; for another, Ogle, a map of 1632 shows former houses and crofts where now earthworks alone survive; and for a third, Chippenham, there is a map of 1712 and excellent earlier documentation. Our choice of illustrations for shrunken sites has not been random but in the tradition of matching the evidence of field-archaeology with written historical sources.

41. BOARSTALL   Buckinghamshire

The plan of 1444 (fig. 41A) appears in the parchment volume drawn up for Edmund Rede the younger, to document his family inheritance. In 1412 Edmund's father, also Edmund, acquired Boarstall by marriage with the fitz Nigels who had been royal foresters of Bernewood, the surrounding district, since the late twelfth century. The landscape in the photograph (fig. 41B) has nothing of the forest about it, but the 1444 plan has three open fields surrounded by seven named woods amongst which appear beasts of the chase. At the bottom is drawn a kneeling man who offers a boar's head to a king and receives a shield with the fitz Nigel arms in exchange. Yet Boarstall was clearly a nucleated village with its houses arranged along lanes that form a 'T'. The houses appear crudely drawn but quite recognisable, and at the centre of the village on opposite sides of the longer street are the church and a moated manor house with a castellated gate-tower. The village was surrounded by open fields, the ridges of several furlongs are clearly indicated; they do not all lie in the same direction.

Both church (consecrated in 1418 and rebuilt in 1818) and gate-tower can be seen near the centre of fig. 41B, with water filling three sides of the rectangular moat. The church stands to the east of the moat in the sweeping curve of the lane which crosses the figure from the middle of the bottom margin. In 1444 this lane ran straight, passing between the now vanished manor house and the church. The standing cross shown on the plan at the T-junction has also gone. A house with a date-stone of 1874 stands across the lane from the church, while a range of modern barns is seen just to the north of the gate-tower. In the grass field above, south of the moat, ridge-and-furrow shows, with a headland running towards the manor house; between this headland and the lane there are at least three croft divisions. The demographic history of Boarstall is not known

Fig. 42A. Ogle; looking SW, December 1967.

but there is some evidence to corroborate the plan of 1444. In 1452 an agreement between the villages of Oakley and Boarstall carried the seals of twelve inhabitants of the *villula* of Boarstall. In 1525 there were 35 taxpayers and in 1662 the hearth tax accounted for fifteen houses as well as the manor with its 25 hearths.

Sources

H. E. Salter and A. H. Cooke, eds. The Boarstall Cartulary, *Oxford Hist. Soc.* LXXVIII (1930) does not reproduce the map which is bound with the cartulary in the Bucks. County Record Office. The map will be treated in R. A. Skelton and P. D. A. Harvey, eds., *Local Maps and Plans from Medieval England* (forthcoming); 1525: *Bucks. Rec. Soc.* VIII (1944) 32; 1662: E.179/80/354; R.C.H.M. *Buckinghamshire* I (1912) 57.

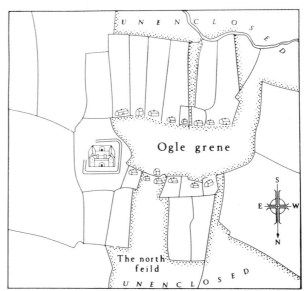

Fig. 42B. Ogle in 1632, after the plan by Huntingdon Smithson.

42. OGLE   Northumberland

Those who have not visited Northumberland can hardly realise how far north the characteristic settlement features of the Midland plain continue, with extensive ridge-and-furrow, and mainly nucleated villages. Villages made up of two parallel lines of houses or *rows* facing each other across a broad green are better known

from County Durham but the vestiges of a village of this type can be seen in fig. 42A.

Ogle lies five and a half miles south-west of Morpeth. The village was surveyed in 1632 for the Earl of Newcastle, and the plan, which is

Fig. 43A. Chippenham; looking NNW across the park, November 1965.

now among the Portland muniments, shows clearly the castle within a rectangular moat at the east end of *Ogle Grene*, and the two rows: eight houses on the south side of the green and seven on the north. The photograph, looking south-west, has nearly the same orientation as the redrawn plan, fig. 42B. The plan shows very large enclosures east of the township (the plan gives the names '*West* Fence' and '*West* Cowpast' for some reason) and four new crofts of 4, 3¾, 4 and 3½ acres taken from that part of the otherwise unenclosed *north feild*, that is represented by the parcels of ridges in the foreground of fig. 42A: the more prominent banks at intervals may mark these newer divisions. The houses standing within small crofts on the plan can be matched to the earthworks beside the green, along the centre of which is a hollow-way. On the plan, an isolated house encroaching on the green appears south of the two houses built on unenclosed land between crofts, and there is a corresponding earthwork in the photograph. On the south side

of the green the line of former crofts can be seen diverging from the present road frontage but some of the crofts are occupied, or re-occupied, by houses. The boundary-bank of the medieval crofts is clear to see on both sides of the village.

A plan of 1830, not published here, shows that the north row had then totally disappeared and the south row was reduced to two farmsteads, nine cottages and one other house, all on the line of a new estate road across the former green, explaining the divergence noted above; another farm occupied the castle site and four others had been built out in the fields. The village continued to shrink during the nineteenth and twentieth centuries as the demand for farm-labour fell, and depopulation has been arrested only in recent years with several new houses on the north side of the estate road occupying part of the green but leaving untouched the earthworks of the former north row, as the photograph shows.

The present lay-out of houses at Ogle pro-vides a warning against views of village mor-

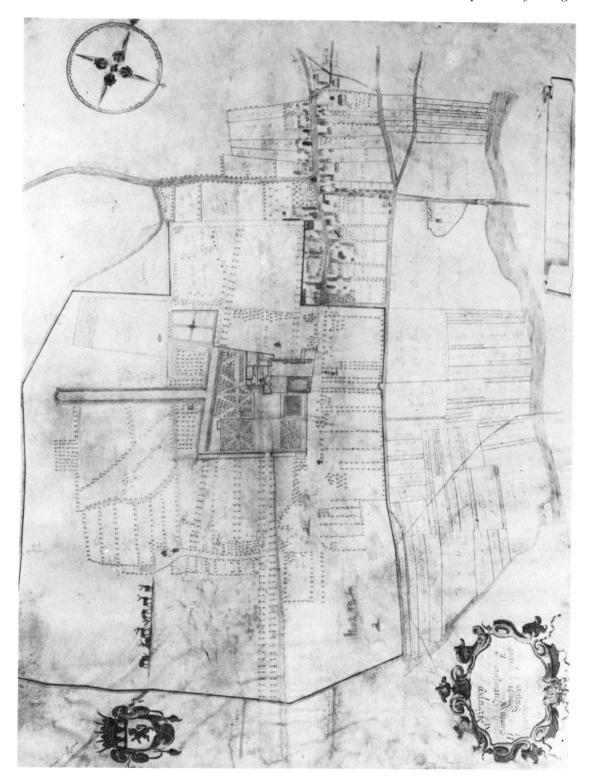

Fig. 43B. Chippenham in 1712; plan by Heber Lands.

phology based on the Ordnance Map, from which Ogle appears to be a small street-village; the road on which these houses lie is modern and the abandoned farmsteads show a quite different form, a village of green and rows.

Sources

Plan of 1632 by Huntingdon Smithson: Notts. Record Office, K4/18; plan of 1830: Northumberland Record Office, ZMI B12/xxvII/1: this information was kindly communicated by Mr Stuart Wrathmell; for rows: B. K. Roberts, 'Village plans in Co. Durham: a preliminary statement', *Med. Arch.* xvi (1972) 33–56, and pls. vii–viii.

43. CHIPPENHAM   Cambridgeshire

Here the shrinkage of a village raises for the historian different problems of interpretation. What could be more typical at first sight than the two rows of cottages outside the park gate (fig. 43A, centre)? However there is a plan of 1712 by Heber Lands which shows that the creation of a landscape park around Lord Orford's house had been achieved by the removal of forty houses; the pattern of surviving hedges within the park then recorded the crofts which formerly continued High Street southwards from its present limit, and, as South Street, led westwards to the two cottages then remaining. The plan also shows that the present space outside the park gates did not exist in 1712, for the houses of High Street then abutted the road. Documents of the same period show that another feature of the existing village, the road to the right beyond the churchyard, was not medieval but a New Street with fourteen houses provided for some of those evicted villagers whose crofts were thrown into the park. In 1702 licence was obtained from Quarter Sessions to close the imparked portion of High Street and the whole of South Street; the diversion created the dog-leg turns in the present road. None of the trees now standing in the park are on the lines of the hedgerows of 1712, and the double avenue leading south from the house has also gone; its line ran across the present cricket pitch in the centre foreground.

Yet, as Dr Margaret Spufford has shown in her detailed study, even the plan of 1712 fails to reveal the original condition of medieval Chippenham. At the peak of population in the late thirteenth century, there had been about 150 households all occupying crofts in the two main streets which formed the L-shaped village. By 1377 there were fewer than half this number, and even in 1544 after two centuries in which the population might have recovered from the Black Death, a very thorough survey recorded only sixty households. The sites of sixty-four crofts, empty and 'clere decaied' were noted among the occupied houses. The late-medieval shrinkage assisted the would-be imparker, and the villagers who continued to farm the remaining open fields so consolidated their holdings that, at the new apportioning of the land effected by the parliamentary enclosure of 1791, only eight farms had to be created.

Sources

Survey of 1544: Cambs. Record Office, R.55/7/5/1; plan of 1712 by Heber Lands: R.58/16/1. Other details from Margaret Spufford, *A Cambridgeshire Community: Chippenham from Settlement to Enclosure*, Univ. of Leicester Dept. of English Local History Occasional Papers no. 20 (1965) esp. endpaper map reconstruction of 1544; and the same author's *Contrasting Communities* (1974) 58–93.

6

THE DISSOLUTION OF THE MEDIEVAL LANDSCAPE

We wish the hedges and they who made them in the ditches.
THE OXFORDSHIRE RIOTERS OF 1596,
quoted in *Three Oxfordshire Parishes. Oxford Historical Society* XXIV (1893) 61

An arrangement which can maintain itself with unhappy ease ... the common field husbandry can maintain itself centuries after every one has called it a nuisance.
F. W. MAITLAND. *Township and Borough* (1898) 25–6

I. INTRODUCTORY

I mean not all Inclosures ...
THE DOCTOR in *The Discourse of the Commonweal*, 1549

The medieval landscape was in perpetual dissolution. One of the most characteristic creative activities of the time, the colonisation of fresh land, made continual encroachments upon the old-established forests. On a smaller scale, the advance of technology in the later Middle Ages spread the scars of pit, quarry and forge among the fields. The exploitation of rivers by new weirs and millraces altered the drainage of fields. On a larger scale, ironworks, town hearths and shipyards were to rob the remaining sixteenth-century forests of their oaks. The perennial exploitation of the soil was to bring seriously decreasing yields especially to those communities settled on poor land near the margin of cultivation. There were other natural changes, for a period of five hundred years is long enough to embrace major tempests, the silting up of estuaries and the diversion of rivers to new courses. The histories of Dunwich, Stonar, Winchelsea, Rye, the Romneys, Chester and the Dee ports are enough to emphasise this aspect of change.

Nevertheless the greatest assault on the traditions of the medieval farming landscape came not from Nature but from men. By Norden's day a fresh attack on the fens and marshes of East Anglia was imminent, carrying the work of medieval colonists one stage further. The same years saw a renewed assault on upland wastes. But there was an important difference between this later colonisation and the assarting described in chapter 3. The newly won land was now passing directly into individually owned plots with hedges as the sign of ownership.

To possess such enclosed plots was also the declared ambition of many landowners and tenants who were farming in the old-established fields. Stubborn resistance to such an ambition was also widespread, and from time to time the government backed this resistance, although hesitatingly since it was aware of the technical advances which enclosed fields made possible and since it drew political support from among the enclosing landlords. The very existence of Norden's profession and the increase in its numbers between 1550 and 1640 are, as Professor Darby and Professor E. G. R. Taylor have shown, clear indications that landowners were willing to pay to possess an accurate description of their property, and to see how best the landscape might be transformed to a new pattern and the fields put to new uses.[1] Even where a landlord was satisfied with the old ways, the zeal of his neighbours for change often drove him also to acquire a map or survey as a defence if lawsuits should threaten.

An accurate survey provided information about such matters as the extent of the commons, and therefore where a lord might lawfully or unlawfully increase and enclose his pastures. The naming and numbering of the demesne strips was a prelude to the extinction of open-field farming by an agreed exchange of properties and the extinction of the right to graze the fallow. In woodland, the trees were counted so that timber could be cut and sold. The whole

[1] H. C. Darby, 'The agrarian contribution to surveying', *Geog. Jnl* LXXXII (1933) 529–35; E. G. R. Taylor, 'The surveyor', *Econ. Hist. Rev.* XVII (1947) 121–33.

tenor of Norden's *Dialogue* is that it is false economy not to employ a surveyor. In that part of the book where the surveyor defends himself against the suspicions of the tenantry it is obvious that this association between the arrival of a surveyor and an increase in rent or the resurrection of forgotten duties was the prime cause of such suspicions.

In some respects the Elizabethan village-maps show a landscape already in transition. Some open fields have already been swallowed into parkland, like those at Castle Donington (fig. 60). Some have been lost to grazing for more than a century, as at Burston (fig. 46), where the change in land-use had brought about the disappearance of the village itself. Contemporaries also recognised that certain counties were 'old enclosed' and no one could recall when the enclosure had taken place. Kent and Devonshire were often cited as examples, approvingly by those who favoured enclosure. Recent research has proved that part even of Devonshire once had open fields, though when they disappeared remains to be settled.[2] The late thirteenth and early fourteenth centuries are the probable time, and a similar date may one day be assigned to those other villages in the south-west, the Welsh Marches and the north-western counties where medieval deeds indicate the presence of open fields while seventeenth-century topographers describe a completely hedged or walled landscape.

Apart from the Elizabethan villages already long-enclosed, the surveyor's usual task was to survey and measure fields which in their aspect revealed a confused mixture of medieval and modern practice. The furlongs across which Shakespeare walked from Stratford to Shottery were still 'open',

> Between the acres of the rye
> These pretty country folks would lie,

but the road to Mary Arden's cottage lay through enclosed fields, and in the Lucys' park of Charlecote the deer and merino sheep were already grazing the grass of former ploughlands. Ten miles to the south of Stratford bridge was the village of Whitchurch, enclosed and depopulated in the lifetime of Shakespeare's father: yet its neighbour, Crimscote (fig. 6) was still unenclosed when Victoria ascended the throne.

It is this intermingling of different experiences in adjacent villages which makes the chronology of enclosure far from easy to expound, and makes many exceptions to even the simplest rules. The intermingling itself is easy to explain; it arose principally from the chance distribution of two crucial factors which determined whether enclosure was to be hindered or hurried in a particular village. One factor was the personality of the landlord and other proprietors, the zeal for change, the divergent attitudes to profit by radical innovations. The other was the great variety of tenurial security possessed by the different villagers, varying from those whom the lord could evict in the 1460s without causing the slightest stir, to those whom the surveyors compiling the first large-scale Ordnance Maps found still working their open-field strips. In explaining the wholesale early enclosure of the west and north-west it is proper to invoke regional differences of soil, climate, crops and husbandry, but in the examination of local differences within the broad belt of open-field counties the factor of terrain seems subordinate to personalities and legal status.[3]

The illustrations in this chapter are arranged approximately in chronological order, from the early enclosures through to the late parliamentary apportionments of land. It must, however, be observed that a selection which proceeds by chronological order of final enclosure cannot show how far all open fields had already made limited concessions to the improving farmer long before their final dissolution, indeed often preserving themselves thereby. But since these concessions had been mainly in the direction of modified cropping and limited exchanges and consolidation of holdings they made very little difference to the aspects of open-field geography with which an air photograph is concerned. The tenants' names might vary until John Jones had ten adjacent strips in one furlong, and the crops might change and the fallow rotate differently: but so long as strips and furlongs remained there was little in these important changes which would leave any mark for an air photograph to record. Only if these partial rearrangements produced economies in the employment of labour will the undetected changes in the fields be reflected in the earthworks of decayed labourers' cottages in a shrunken village.

[2] For a discussion of early enclosure see C. C. Taylor, *Fields in the English Landscape* (1975) ch. 5.

[3] For modern accounts of local enclosure chronology see *V.C.H. Leics.* II (1954) 254–64; Mary E. Finch, *The wealth of five Northamptonshire families, 1540–1649. Northants. Rec. Soc.* XIX (1956).

II. DISSOLUTION BY RETREAT

Ill fares the land, to hast'ning ills a prey,
Where wealth accumulates, and men
decay; . . .

But a bold peasantry, their country's pride,
When once destroyed can never be
supplied.
A time there was ere England's griefs
began,
When every rood of ground maintain'd its
man; . . .

OLIVER GOLDSMITH, *The Deserted Village*

In the two centuries following Domesday Book settlements on the whole increased in size and in number. There were losses to the sea by erosion and to rivers by flooding, but there are more villages named in the *Nomina Villarum*, a list of hamlets and villages compiled in 1316, than in Domesday Book of 1086; although some villages known to have been in existence in 1086 must have had both their population and their acres silently numbered in the later account of a neighbouring manor. To take an example from one county, in Norfolk the *Nomina Villarum* adds seventy new names to the 726 separate placenames in Domesday Book, but sixty-nine names recorded in 1086 were not thought worthy of inclusion in 1316. Thirty-five of these have no subsequent record as villages so that it is reasonable to conclude that they had already decayed by 1316, being reduced to insignificance at the same time that, elsewhere, new settlements were being born.[4]

44. GRENSTEIN   Norfolk

The disappearance of a village community soon after the Norman Conquest makes the identification of its site difficult and in all English counties there are some Domesday names which have been linked to no modern feature nor to any surviving earthworks. The site of one small early medieval village which has left faint traces is illustrated in fig. 44. This village was first observed as slight earthworks in 1933–4 but since then the site has been ploughed and is now to be seen, as here photographed in 1960, as crop-marks. The site lies near Grenstein Farm in Tittleshall parish, west-north-west of Mileham, central Norfolk.

[4] K. J. Allison, 'The lost villages of Norfolk', *Norfolk Archaeology* XXXI, pt. 1 (1955) 122.
[5] Excavations were carried out by Dr Wade-Martins in 1965 and were briefly reported in *Med. Arch.* X (1966) 212–14 but a full account has yet to be published.

The marks reveal a village of simple plan: a main street bordered by a row of crofts on the west side, giving on to a green. There is a pond at the far end of the crofts, with a nearby well. The plan is similar to that of the small deserted village sites of the Yorkshire Wolds, particularly Raventhorpe by Leconfield. The importance to archaeology of a village which was abandoned so early is evident; the more regrettable, then, that the site should have been ploughed.[5]

Dr K. J. Allison has examined the maps of the locality which were drawn by Haiwarde in 1596 and are now among the Holkham muniments. The maps record that the village site had been completely absorbed into the fields of Tittleshall, while the green in front of the houses had been preserved as *Dowes Grene*. Nearby, Haiwarde marked the 'site of the manor of Callis', which seems to have been an alternative name for Grenstein. There are references to the manor in 1250 and 1266 which are printed by Blomefield and the only later record to be found is the survival of a lane named *Greynston Street*, in 1474. This is probably the *Gramston Lane* (and *meadow*) which appears on Haiwarde's map. The large field-pond on the right of fig. 44 was surveyed in 1596 and marked on the map as *Harber's Pitt*.

This small community would seem to have decayed in the late thirteenth or early fourteenth century and its field-land was absorbed into the furlongs of Tittleshall, though perhaps not immediately. In the fifteenth century some decaying villages of the Lincolnshire Wolds, probably on 'marginal' land, joined forces with a neighbour and amalgamated their two sets of fields which were thereafter worked from only one centre, the other village and its church being abandoned. These marginal villages were occupied in times of land-hunger or when the choice of territory was limited; given the opportunity to think again and revise the decision, men chose to farm elsewhere.

Sources

Map of Tittleshall (1596): Holkham MSS., maps 4/73a; 1198: *Publications of the Pipe Roll Soc.* n.s. XXVII (1950) nos. 85 and 118; Blomefield, *Norfolk* V. 1070–4; *Feudal Aids* III (1909) 540; K. J. Allison, 'The lost villages of Norfolk', *Norfolk Archaeology* XXXI (1955) 148 (Gramston). National Grid ref. TF907198.

45. TUSMORE   Oxfordshire

The village of Tusmore lay in the north-east of

Fig. 44. Grenstein. The site of the deserted village; looking SE, April 1960.

the county five miles north of Bicester. In 1279 it comprised sixteen villein families, four freemen and three cottars. These twenty-three house-holds were not very wealthy; when villages were taxed in 1334 Tusmore paid about half the local average. But in the collection of 1355 it paid nothing, for the village had been completely depopulated by the Black Death. Fig. 45, a view to the west, looks over the grounds of Tusmore House to the earthworks of the former

village, which appear in grass fields near the centre of the photograph. A small stream has been dammed to make a pool visible amongst the trees at the bottom left-hand corner; the name of the village means 'Thur's pool'. The banks in the grass of the parkland were the boundaries of crofts and there are faint hollow-ways marking streets. Traces of plough-ridges appear in a cricket ground to the right of the pool.

The total destruction of the village is affirmed

Fig. 45. Tusmore; looking W, April 1963. A village depopulated by the Black Death.

by the wholesale tax reduction of 1355 and by the licence granted in 1357 for Roger de Cotesford, lord of the manor, to 'enclose his hamlet of *Toresmere* and the highway from *Cotesford* to *Sulthorne* passing through it, the hamlet having been inhabited entirely by Roger's bondmen but now void of inhabitants since their death in the pestilence. Roger is to make a new road on the north of the hamlet.' This 'new road' is the road that now skirts the north pale of the park, beyond the top margin of the photograph, on its way from Souldern to Cottisford.

Sources

1279: *Rot. Hund.* II. 825; 1334: E. 179/161/12; 1355: 161/30; 1357: *Cal. Misc. Inq.* III, no. 258; D. Miles and T. Rowley, 'Tusmore deserted village', *Oxoniensia* XLI (1971) 309–15; since 1971 parts of the site have suffered damage from farming operations. National Grid ref. SP 562308.

It is now certain that many of the depopulations locally ascribed to the Black Death are as ill-explained as those blamed on Oliver Cromwell.

The sheep-depopulations of the period 1450–1550 were responsible for much that has been blamed on the Black Death.[6] But the general easing of the pressure on land following the plagues was a powerful stimulant to minor readjustments within villages where arable cultivation continued. Conditions of tenure had to be eased, and the abdication of the lords of manors from direct working of their demesne estates made way for the division of the property among the peasantry who then held it at rent. The gathering together of adjacent strips into single ownership or occupation, characteristic of the earliest open-field maps, dates largely from the 150 years after the plagues and was vigorously aided by an active market in small parcels of land. A limited amount of such reorganisation was to the villagers' advantage, but over-consolidation in a few large blocks was to prove dangerous when ambitious men cast their eyes at the arable fields.

[6] Park-making sometimes followed upon the contraction of population, as at Castle Bolton (fig. 59) and Harewood (fig. 21).

Fig. 46. Burston; looking S, March 1966. A village depopulated in the late fifteenth century.

III. DISSOLUTION BY ATTACK

When the oxe and sheepe shall feede where good houses stood ... who will not say it is the bane of a common wealth, an apparent badge of *Atheisme*, and an argument of apish ambition, or woolvish emulation?

NORDEN, *Surveior's Dialogue*, 179

The next broad stage to be distinguished in the advance of the hedge is the period between about 1450 and 1550 when the attractions of animal husbandry moved many landlords to pass over wholly from arable to pasture, solving the problem of enclosure at a single blow. Once the arable strips had passed out of use there was no obstacle to laying out large, hedged pastures. The abandonment of ploughing did away with the need for ploughmen, and with the evacuation of the village houses there were no rival claimants for common rights. The shepherd and his dog had all.

In these depopulations it was not the poor dividends from arable farming which pushed the landlords over to grass but simply the better dividends from stock and wool. Land was not tumbling to grass because it was near the economic margin but because even good arable paid better as pasture. The sheep-depopulations are therefore more scattered geographically than the older, abandoned (marginal) villages and display the characteristic intermingling with late-enclosed villages to which attention has already been drawn.

The hedged fields which derive from sheep-enclosures of the Yorkist–Tudor period may be recognised most readily by their association with easily identified earthworks of deserted villages such as are illustrated here. Unless subdivided in recent years, the fields of this period are usually much larger than those set out by other forms of enclosure and tend to be bounded by curved rather than by straight hedges.

The freshness and clarity of the earthworks of deserted villages do not depend solely on the length of time since depopulation. Subsequent land-use and the type of soil are more important determinants. Earthworks of the lost villages on the light soils of Norfolk are poorly preserved. Some Yorkshire villages have had their sites completely ploughed over with the return of arable cultivation under the improved techniques of the last hundred and fifty years. The type of building material is also relevant; houses with stone foundations will leave substantial remains beneath the grass in those districts where other sources of stone are readily available for later builders. Timber houses in clay country had little durable material by which their outline could be preserved, and there was, moreover, a great temptation for neighbours to take whatever stone they could find. Thus, some of the early depopulations on the Wolds are better preserved than early sixteenth-century depopulations on Warwickshire clays.[7]

46. BURSTON   Buckinghamshire

The enclosure and depopulation of Burston, a hamlet in the parish of Aston Abbots, is dated by the evidence given before Wolsey's Commission of Inquiry in 1517. According to the jurors, John Swafield had evicted sixty people from the village in March 1488; after the eviction, the value of the land rose from £13 1s. 8d. a year to £40. This improved value is explained by the new use to which the land was being put, 'predicte villa hamelettum et Manerium de Byrdeston totaliter et integre in pasturam ovium modo utitur et habetur'. Not far away were the depopulated Cottesloe, Creslow, Fleet Marston and Littlecote: it was country where the arable fields were vulnerable when wool became an attractive alternative. Only a few years after Wolsey's commissioners, Leland passed this way and noted the excellence of the pastures at Burston.

Burston lies three and a half miles north-north-east of Aylesbury on the west bank of a tributary of the Thistle Brook. The photograph (fig. 46), taken from the north, shows that a large field between Lower Burston Farm and the stream contains evident traces of the former village. A wide main street crosses the field diagonally, making a sharp turn near the farther hedge to avoid the stream. In the nearer part of the field the ground is neatly divided by the boundaries between crofts; a narrower lane serves this area, branching from the main street near the right-hand corner of the field. The crofts have a clearly defined straight limit along the waterside at the left of the field.

Sources

I. S. Leadam, *Domesday of Inclosures* (1897) 161–2; *V.C.H. Bucks.* III (1925) 328; M. W. Beresford 'Glebe terriers and open-field Buckinghamshire', *Records of Bucks.* XVI (1953–4) 1–28. National Grid ref. SP842188.

47. QUARRENDON   Buckinghamshire

The church and manor house at the abandoned site of Quarrendon have already been shown in fig. 19. The earthworks of fig. 47 lie to the south-east of the church in one of the large fields characteristic of the period of sheep-enclosures. At the corner of the photograph is an angle of the moats seen in fig. 19. The earthworks in the background lie on a low ridge from which the ground falls gently to the stream at the farther side of the field. The long bank in two lengths at right angles is said to be the remains of fortifications of the Civil War, the incisions being embrasures for cannon. The remains of the village lie on the nearer slope.

Like Burston, there seem to be croft boundaries that are irregular in one part of the village and regular in another. The regularity appears on the left-hand side, below and to the left of the Cromwellian earthworks, where the ridge-and-furrow ends at the line of a boundary-ditch. On the right-hand slope of the hill and over the whole foreground the ditches make no regular pattern. The street which, judged in terms of the width and depth of the well-worn hollow-way, would seem to have been most in use comes diagonally down the hill to a circular mound, after which it bends to the right towards the church, beyond the bottom right-hand corner of this photograph, but shown in fig. 19. The earlier figure also shows a puzzling second village site separated from these earthworks by a broad meadow and a meandering stream, but not separately documented. If both sets of earthworks were part of a single Quarrendon, the position of the church, otherwise very much on the edge of this village, becomes more rational, and the settlement may prove to be one of those with more than one original nucleus.

No report of depopulation here was made to Wolsey's Inquiry of 1517–18. The church at Quarrendon was altered and decorated in the late sixteenth century although it seems likely to have been used only by the Manor. In 1636 Quarrendon was described as 'an ancient enclosure depopulated' and such language is unlikely if the depopulation had been as late as the reign of Elizabeth. Three thousand sheep grazed hereabouts in 1570 and the Lees' mansion, of which the church became virtually the

[7] The subject of depopulation is more fully discussed in M. W. Beresford, *The Lost Villages of England* (1954).

Fig. 47. Quarrendon; looking SE, December 1965.

private chapel, was built about 1560. Nothing was said of any enclosure here when another Royal Commission visited the county in 1565 at a time when a host of small enclosures for more efficient mixed farming was producing a 'decay of hospitality' which caused the Earl of Leicester to write to Burghley in January 1566: 'I never saw in so riche a soyle so many miserable and power [sc. poor] people.' This Commission had cognisance of enclosures since 1550; there had been another Inquiry in 1548 covering the years 1518–48, so that it would seem that Quarrendon was depopulated before 1485, the limit beyond which Wolsey's Commission of 1517–18 could not enquire.

Sources

V.C.H. Bucks. IV (1927) 100; R.C.H.M. *Buckinghamshire* I (1912) 273; 1565: E. 178/424 and E. 159/357/Mich. m. 523; 1566: S.P. 12/39/31; plan: Hadrian Allcroft, *Earthwork of England* (1908) 479. The site lies at SP806156.

48. COWLAM Yorkshire, East Riding

On the crown of the Yorkshire Wolds near Sledmere lie more than a score of abandoned village sites to testify to the retreat of settlement from those parts, a process which continues in the area even today. In our first edition we offered a photograph of the great grass field adjoining Cowlam Manor Farm, six miles north-west of Great Driffield, a large cluster of farm buildings of various periods surrounding a red-brick church of 1852. The original church mentioned in Domesday Book, of which only the Norman font survives, was no more than a ruined chancel in 1713 when a Faculty was granted to contract it to a length of seven feet and to pull down the steeple, the parish 'being depopulated with not any inhaibitants save two shepherds'. The exact date of the major depopulation of Cowlam is not known. There were fifty-four persons taxed in 1377, and the village may have been larger than this before the plague since it obtained a remission of more than half its tax in the years 1352–4.

There may have been depopulation here at the time of the sheep-enclosures elsewhere on the Wolds; in the early eighteenth century Cowlam was made up of extensive rabbit warrens on the high chalk, scattered holdings in still-unenclosed fields, and great expanses of open pasture. Arch-

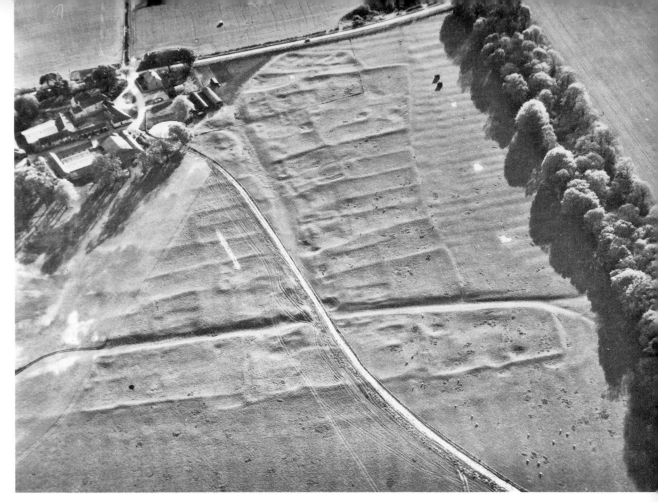

Fig. 48. Cowlam; looking SW, May 1968. A depopulated village on the Yorkshire Wolds.

bishop Sharpe noted in about 1700: 'the Town they tell me has now no inhabitants but the parson and 2 shepherds . . . the tithe barn is fallen down . . .' It was an empty landscape to which the Sykes family brought Improvement with such striking success. A Miss Sykes commissioned the red-brick church of 1852 now crowded among the barns in the farmyard. In 1783 Cowlam Manor had nearly 2000 acres of land, three quarters of which were rabbit warren and only 200 acres arable; the area of arable doubled by 1801 in the Napoleonic Wars, and by 1844 the Improvement was complete, the warrens destroyed, hedged fields everywhere, and 1564 acres under plough.

The Census of 1841 shows that there were forty-four inhabitants in the great farm from which the fields were worked: the farmer's family and a small army of resident labourers, mostly unmarried and many under eighteen. The deserted villages of the high Wolds that are neighbours to Cowlam – Cottam, Croom, Swaythorpe, Pockthorpe and Towthorpe – were each worked in the same way from a farm of the Improvement period with its characteristic wind-break plantations standing on or adjacent

to a large grass field where the foundations of the former village have successfully deterred the ploughshares, even in times of war.

We wrote in our first edition that the light covering of grass on the wall-footings of locally quarried chalk blocks had preserved the village plan as well as anywhere in England. The new photograph, taken in 1968, shows, centre left near the farm, that deep ploughing of a part of the field had then smoothed out the earthworks and strewn the chalk of walls and boundary banks into blurred soil-marks; the whole of the field has now been bulldozed and ploughed.[8] Currently, the outline of the village still appears indistinctly as soil-marks in winter and as crop-marks in summer.

The crofts of Cowlam were laid out regularly along both sides of a broad street, represented by the hollow-way extending down the centre of the photograph. A modern farm-track cuts across the crofts, which at their farther limit are obscured, on the left, by farm-buildings at the top of the photograph. The boundary between

[8] Permission was given to Mr T. C. M. Brewster to excavate one croft in 1971–2 in advance of this stage of destruction: no excavation report is yet available.

125

crofts and open fields is marked by the limit of the ridge-and-furrow. The row of crofts to the right of the village street stops where three or four selions intervene between the last of the house-sites and the public road.

The nearer end of the village is delimited by a prominent boundary-bank enclosing a long, narrow area almost the full width of the photograph. The ridge-and-furrow stops short of the line of this bank as the terminal heaps of plough soil show. The older limit so marked has a curved end near the plantation-belt. Manor houses are sometimes set apart from villages in this way, but the earthworks here are not clear enough for detailed interpretation.

The earthworks marking the site of the village houses suggest two forms of building. There are long, narrow peasant houses similar to those excavated at Wharram Percy (eight miles to the north-west) and, near the modern road, groups of buildings gathered around a courtyard, perhaps a more developed farm with accommodation for animals, separate from the dwelling. Earthworks of these two types are found together in the villages of Towthorpe and Duggleby, and there are excellently preserved earthworks of a similar courtyard-farm at an isolated position (SE 843695) near Settrington.

Sources

C. 1700: Borthwick Institute, York, papers Bp. Dio. 3, f 124; M. W. Beresford, 'The lost villages of Yorks.' *Yorks. Arch. Jnl* XXXVIII (1952) 60; The 1st edn O.S. six-inch map has an accurate survey of the earthworks; Alan Harris, 'The lost villages and the landscape of the Yorks. Wolds', *Ag. Hist. Rev.* VI (1958) 97–100; June Sheppard, 'The East Yorks. agricultural labour force in the 19th Century', *ibid.* IX (1961) 43–54; Alan Harris, *The Rural Landscape of the East Riding of Yorks., 1700–1850* (1961) esp. 29, 99 and 102. Cowlam and other Wolds villages were noted and planned in Robert Knox, *Descriptions etc. of East Yorks.* (1855) esp. 142–6.

49. WOLFHAMPCOTE AND BRAUNSTONBERRY
Warwickshire and Northamptonshire

The village of Wolfhampcote, six miles south of Rugby, was enclosed and depopulated in 1501, the enclosure being reported to Wolsey's Commission in 1517: *villam in ruinam positam*. Depositions in lawsuits of the early seventeenth century show that the vicarage was rebuilt in 1625 and by 1641 the arable land was again largely under cultivation. But the restoration of the plough did not bring the ploughmen back to village houses in Wolfhampcote. Two hamlets,

Nethercote and Flecknoe, have survived; the latter is a normal-sized Warwickshire village.

The photograph (fig. 49), taken from the north-east, emphasises the isolation of the church which is seen to the right of the railway embankment. The white lane now leads only to three cottages and the former rectory. The lines of streets and crofts are visible in the distance, covering an extensive area to the right of the lane on the far side of the small River Leam which crosses the centre of the photograph. The canal, top right, is the Grand Union, carried across the valley on an embankment, replacing an earlier contour course.

A puzzling and interesting feature is the similar set of earthworks on the nearer side of the river. These earthworks, so like those of a deserted medieval village, do not join those of Wolfhampcote; there is an interval of level ground where the water-meadows lay. This second 'village' might be assumed to be no more than an extension of Wolfhampcote north-eastwards over the Leam, were there not an insuperable objection. The river is both parish boundary and county boundary. That a village should have extended into another parish and county without some consequential adjustments of boundaries would be almost unprecedented. By a fortunate chance the bounds of Braunston were described in a charter of 956, and there is no doubt that they followed the Leam.

No documents suggest that there is a lost hamlet of Braunston in this quarter of the parish. The lost hamlet of Fawcliff has been located at Braunston Cleeves in the north fields of the parish. Although Braunston is only two fields away from the edge of the photograph there are no signs of earthworks in the intervening space to suggest an original continuity of the built-up area. There remains only the possibility of an early migration from this site up to the ridge-back where the manor house, church and village now stand (fig. 22).

The thirteenth-century manorial surveys speak of the manor of *Braunston and Braunstonberry*. The whole area shown in the photograph is still known as Berryfields and the field with the earthworks as Chapel Field. The present Castle Inn, where the London road crosses a stream, only just outside the lower margin of the photograph, used to be called Berry Bridge Inn. The moat in the centre of the photograph, with two isolated trees at its corner, must be the site of the manor. The ditch is linked with the outfall of a large fishpond now represented by the flat, unridged, narrow field to the right, which is still called Fish Weir Field. In a

Fig. 49. Wolfhampcote and Braunstonberry; looking SW, January 1966.

survey of thirteenth-century date the demesnes of Braunstonberry included an area of meadow known as *Fiswere*. The remains of the dam which retained the water can be seen at the farther end of the field, and the north edge of the pool is marked by the ends of plough ridges near the right-hand margin of the photograph.

The 'chapel' of Chapel Field is probably a chantry-chapel of the de Ros family in or near this manor house. The Rev. H. E. Ruddy, who has assisted the elucidation of this interesting site, has pointed out that the Northamptonshire maps of both Norden and Morden place a village of Ovencote here, but in 1656 Dugdale had stated that 'Ovencote' was a vulgar corruption of Wolfhampcote. The earliest known form of this name is no older than 1518, so that no lost village of Ovencote is indicated.

The extensive earthworks to the left of the moat and fishpond are certainly more than the outbuildings of a manor. Excavations may someday decide whether this settlement is the precursor of Braunston, a group of houses around the *burh* from which *berry* derives, or an early hamlet in Braunston which had decayed before Domesday Book was made.

Sources

Baker, *Northants*. 1. 266; the 'Bury Fields' were already 'old enclosures' at the time of the parliamentary enclosure in 1775; M. W. Beresford, 'The deserted villages of Warwickshire', *Trans. Birm. Arch. Soc.* LXVI (1950) 98–9. National Grid ref. SP530655.

50. BRAUNCEWELL   Lincolnshire

The first air photograph of a deserted village ever to be published is that of Gainsthorpe, a Lincolnshire village. Lincolnshire was also the first county to have a gazetteer of its deserted villages, namely Canon C. W. Foster's 'Extinct Villages and other Forgotten Places', which was compiled by reference to Domesday Book (1086), to the *Nomina Villarum* of 1316 and to early fourteenth-century tax-assessments. This gazetteer extended to twenty-six printed pages, but did not include Gainsthorpe or Calcethorpe, two sites where prominent earthworks may still be seen, nor Goltho, where no fewer than

Fig. 50. Brauncewell; looking WSW, February 1969.

twenty-seven crofts could be distinguished around the church before the site was bulldozed and ploughed. Another omission by Canon Foster was Brauncewell in Dunsby parish, four miles north of Sleaford. In 1086 there were twenty-five heads of households as well as a church; there can be no confusion with Dunsby, for that was recorded separately with twenty-eight households. Both places appear in the tax-assessment of villages in 1334, Brauncewell at 53s. 5¾d. and Dunsby at 24s. 7d. There were fewer than ten households in Dunsby by 1428.

The last institution took place in 1506, and twenty years later the living was amalgamated with Brauncewell: there are a number of similar parish amalgamations in the Lincolnshire Wolds as the late medieval population shrank. For example, no priest was instituted at Wykeham after 1396 when the living was joined to South Cadeby, itself later depopulated, and the church at Calcethorpe was in ruins by c. 1450.

Like many sites in stone country, the village earthworks at Brauncewell lie in a grass field surrounded by land that has long been under plough. Modern farm-buildings obscure part of the site but the traces of the medieval village are remarkably clear: not only croft boundaries but even individual houses. In the right-hand half of the field some thirteen crofts can be counted: in the left-hand half, some eight crofts can be distinguished up to the long barn, and beyond the farm lie other earthworks. The line of the former village street enters the near end of the field as a hollow-way which can be traced between the crofts to the right-hand end of the long barn. Earthworks marking houses can be distinguished along its course, and elsewhere, for example to the right of the barn. The church stands amid the distant trees to the left of the modern farm-road.

Sources

C. W. Foster and T. Longley, eds., *The Lincs. Domesday. Lincs. Rec. Soc.* XIX (1924) xlvii–lxxii, 59, 128 and 195; Gainsthorpe, vertical photograph, taken April 1923: *Ant. Jnl* (1925) 30.

51. DOWNTOWN   Northamptonshire

This site lies near the head of the Avon close to the county boundary with Leicestershire, three miles south-west of Husband's Bosworth. Its earthworks represent two rows of broad crofts facing each other across a long and narrow green which continues the line of the hollow-way seen at the foot of the first photograph. The site was cut through by the Market Harborough branch of the Leicestershire and Northamptonshire Union canal constructed in 1809. Villages having regular greens of this sort are infrequent in the Upper Avon valley. The existence of a distinct boundary-bank confirms the simplicity of the plan, while the ridge-and-furrow which, as soil-marks or earthworks, surrounds the village on all sides, shows that this is indeed the entire village. The clearest earthworks are those that indicate the bounds between crofts, and between crofts and green; house-positions are difficult to define, possibly because building was largely in wood. The village must always have been small and its documentation is slight, since it was never assessed for taxation separately from its neighbour Stanford on Avon.

Only two years separate the two photographs. In this short interval trees have been uprooted, hedges removed, and the earthworks levelled so that the site, now scarcely detectable, lies in one great sweep of arable land. The photographs thus demonstrate more dramatically than any description how vulnerable in the face of modern agricultural techniques are these comparatively slight, even if extensive, remains of the medieval landscape. Not only have the earthworks been completely levelled, but with continued ploughing, causing disturbance of foundations and destruction of further stratified levels, the scientific value of the site will largely be lost.

There had been earlier attempts to plough the site, and Bridges, the county historian, noted in about 1720 that there were 'large foundation stones and causeys' turned up on ploughing, but the first photograph shows so little disturbance of the earthworks that the eighteenth-century ploughmen, and the later ploughing-up campaigners of the two world wars must have been deterred by the stones they encountered. There is no record of any discoveries made when the canal was being dug.

Sources

K. J. Allison *et al.*, *The Deserted Villages of Northants.* (Univ. of Leicester, Dept of English Local History, Occasional Papers no. 18 (1966)) 38; R.C.H.M. *Northamptonshire* III (forthcoming). National Grid ref. SP 615802.

52. WEST WHELPINGTON
Northumberland

In 1827 John Hodgson, vicar of Kirkwhelpington, wrote an account in his *History of Northumberland* of the deserted township that lay in the western part of his parish, and concluded it appropriately with two lines from Goldsmith's *Deserted Village*. He began:

The village of West Whelpington stood proudly on the northern margin of the Wansbeck, on an elevated plain, which slopes gently towards the east, and is defended on all sides and especially on the south by a whinstone precipice. It was of oblong form, about 440 yards long, and consisted of two rows of houses inclosing a large town green ... Its name occurs in the parish register up to 1715. One of the [Stote] family when he took the whole of it to rent 'put out 15 farmers here', according to the phrases and account of a person who was his servant, and is still living at the age of 86. The place is now remarkable for the distinctness of its ruins.

Probably as a result of this account, the site was marked on Greenwood's county map, surveyed in 1827–8, and the bounds of the township are known from the tithe map and apportionment of 1884, showing 3758 acres of which only eighty-two acres were then arable; the area of Cornhills farm, the nearest surviving building to the site, then comprised 546 acres, most of it made up of the former open fields of the village, the ridge-and-furrow of which is so marked in fig. 52, a view of the site from the north.

Fig. 51A. Downtown; looking SW. Earthworks of a deserted village, April 1963. Compare fig. 51B.

The 'distinctness of the ruins' observed in 1827 can be seen in the areas untouched by quarrying or by recent excavations. The croft boundaries are exceptionally clear. Quarrying of the whinstone began in 1937 at the south-east corner (left) of the little plateau. In recent years the threat of total destruction has prompted first a trial excavation in 1958–60, and, since 1965, annual excavations directed by Dr Michael Jarrett, in advance of the workings which are expected to remove the whole plateau by 1985.

The cover of earth is very shallow all over the

Fig. 51B. Downtown; the same view as fig. 51A in March 1965.

hill, and this has presented its own problems for the excavators. The settlement pattern has proved to be just as complex as at Midland sites; as the work proceeded the distinct turf-covered banks were found to represent only the latest phase of the occupation of West Whelpington.

Extensive stone-robbing had taken place and many of the banks were composed of stone tumbled from former walls but not removed, rather than of wall stones in place. Nor were the croft boundaries which give such a regular appearance to the site always in the positions

Fig. 52. West Whelpington; looking SSE, January 1967. The deserted village is being destroyed progressively as the hill on which it stands is quarried away.

they now occupy. They were found to overlie buildings of many periods, both on the more regular north row, which had been assumed to be an original feature, and on the more sporadic south row, assumed to be an addition like the spaced-out groups of crofts which close each end of the green. 'Most of the banks which can be traced at the present day', concludes the excavation report, 'seem to indicate the village of the seventeenth century rather than a medieval predecessor.' Excavation has suggested that the basic change was from a number of detached medieval houses, apparently scattered more or less at random, to what was almost a planned lay-out around a green. As at Wharram Percy, successive seasons of work have not brought repetition of uniform features, but complexity and evidence of considerable changes in the village plan in the centuries before its final depopulation in about 1720.

Sources

M. G. Jarrett, 'The deserted village of West Whelpington', *Arch. Aeliana* 4th ser. XL (1962) 189–225 and XLVIII (1970) 183–202, with earlier air photographs; *Med. Arch.* XV (1971) 173 and XVI (1972) 203. National Grid ref. NY975838.

IV. DISSOLUTION BY AGREEMENT

Unnecessary statutes unfit for this time ... these snares that might have lien heavily upon the subject ... either are repealed or not continued.
SIR EDWARD COKE, FORMER CHIEF JUSTICE, in *The Third Part of the Institutes* (1644)

The heyday of sheep-depopulations was over by 1550, checked by popular hostility, government action and the recovery in the relative profit of corn as against wool. By the early seventeenth century it was becoming possible to view enclosure and conversion to pasture as two dis-

Fig. 53. Brassington. Enclosure observing the bounds of open-field furlongs; looking WNW, December 1967.

tinct processes. Even as staunch an opponent of enclosure as the author of the *Discourse* had scrupulously exempted from censure the enclosure which did not 'dispeople villages'. The opponents of enclosure continued to invoke the fears aroused by the word 'depopulation', but there is good evidence that it had ceased to be relevant to the enclosures of Norden's day. Here and there (particularly in Northumberland) depopulation of a whole village accompanied enclosure, but in general the Stuart enclosures aimed rather at improved arable farming or at mixed farming within the hedged fields. The elucidation of enclosure history in the period between the last Anti-enclosure Act of 1597 and

the flood of local Enclosure Acts which begin about 1720 is confused by an apparent attack on enclosure by James I and Charles I. They saw that fines for enclosure prohibited by the Act of 1597 made a useful addition to a slender purse, but the significance of their action is lost if seen as a continuation of the old attack on enclosure. The fine gave *permission* to enclose. As the quotation from Coke indicates, these enclosure fines, being a non-parliamentary source of royal income, brought the Stuart Enclosure Commissions into disrepute.

Yet, if by 1644 the hostility to enclosure had abated in official circles, there was still reluctance to grant any overt approval or any machinery by

133

which an enclosure might receive public sanction. This did not come until the Hanoverian parliaments began to accept local bills, each providing for the enclosure of fields under certain conditions. In the intervening years enclosure took place either by purely private agreement for which no public sanction other than enrolment was sought, relying on the good faith of the contracting parties and their descendants, or by fictitious lawsuits in Exchequer or Chancery.[9]

If an enclosure took place by private Act a local historian may easily track it down either in the index to the parliamentary *Journals* or in that of *Acts, Local and Personal*. Mr W. E. Tate's county *Lists* are also available. But not all the seventeenth-century records of Chancery and Exchequer have such accessible place-indexes, and their name-indexes do not differentiate an enclosure case as such. Nor are the proceedings of the Stuart Enclosure Commissions easy to trace. As a consequence the illegal enclosures of the early sixteenth century are better known than the agreed enclosures a century later. A chronology of enclosure, parish by parish, has been reconstructed for Leicestershire by Dr Joan Thirsk.[10]

53. BRASSINGTON Derbyshire

The combination of a low sun and snow cover has accentuated the ridge-and-furrow in grass fields at Brassington, four miles west of Wirksworth. The view is to the west towards rather higher ground near Dovedale where the land is divided into rectangular fields of the type produced by eighteenth-century parliamentary enclosure. In the foreground, however, the whole agricultural landscape is of a different pattern, one where agreement largely prevailed between landowners, so that the limits of each existing open-field furlong have been taken as ready-made boundaries for the majority of the new fields, thus minimising the expense of lawyers and surveyors. It is a paradox that open-field strips within a modern landscape are now best seen at Braunton (fig. 13), where an unusual conservatism has preserved them, and here at Brassington, where agreement by progressive landowners led to early enclosure of the western quarter of the parish and so effectively 'fossilised' the medieval strip pattern; the remainder of the parish lay open until 1808.

The hedges reproduce the pattern of pre-existing features so closely that the sides of the fields generally have the same reversed $\int$-shape as the former selions; in fact, today's boundaries preserve the swing of the ploughteams in the colonising centuries. To find so extensive an area where the furlongs of the former open fields have the same 'grain' is unusual; only in fields in the foreground and near the left margin have the blocks of ridges a markedly different alignment. Indeed, for the most part, at the ends of the furlongs, the access-ways, indicated now by lanes with continuous lines of hedges crossing the photograph from left to right, are themselves generally parallel, save where they converge at the edge of Brassington village by the right-hand margin of the photograph. Here, the change of direction and slope combine to produce a triangular furlong, or 'gore', now represented by a modern field of the same shape.

Sources

W. E. Wightman, 'Open field agriculture in the Peak District', *Derbys. Arch. Jnl* LXXXI (1961) 111–25, esp. 113; enclosure map of 1808: Derbys. County Record Office (the help of Miss J. C. Sinar, County Archivist, is acknowledged).

[9] Sources for pre-parliamentary enclosure are described by M. W. Beresford in F. J. Fisher, ed., *Essays in the Economic and Social History of Tudor and Stuart England* (1961) 40–69.

[10] Joan Thirsk, 'Agrarian history, 1540–1950', *V.C.H. Leics.* II (1954) 199–264, esp. Appendices.

V. DISSOLUTION BY ACT OF PARLIAMENT

This is now a Science, which in its Infancy was confessedly understood very imperfectly....
REV. HENRY HOMER,
An Essay on the Nature and Method [of]
the Inclosure of Common Fields (1766) 61

However complicated or long drawn out the procedure, the principle of enclosure by Act of Parliament was simple. Those promoters who could convince a parliamentary committee that a majority of the proprietors in a village favoured enclosure were allowed to override the objections of the dissenting minority, the actual reallocation being carried out by a body of commissioners like those who drew up the plan for the new fields of Ilmington shown in fig. 5B. The chief task of the commissioners was to ascertain existing rights and to compensate the owners by allocating compact fields with straight boundaries and right-angled corners. The proprietors then took their fields for hedging and ditching. Some built new outlying farms away from the village centre, and rearrangement of the old lanes

Fig. 54. Padbury. Fields S of the village, looking W, April 1953. Straight field-boundaries drawn at the enclosure of 1795 radiate from the village across the 'furlongs' of the medieval fields.

leading to the fields was usually necessary.

This type of enclosure is well documented and has been much described in print in recent years. It can be seen in detail at Ilmington (fig. 5A), and its occurrence has been silently passed over in the commentaries on many other photographs. Locally, its progress may be studied in the Acts themselves, in the Awards made by the commissioners and sometimes in the minutes and papers of the commission. Where no maps and Awards have survived, careful examination of hedges and fields may enable a comparison to be made of the old and the new landscapes, the one of ridges and furrows and the other of overriding hedges. With practice, a distinction between the small fields of 'old enclosures' and the larger, more regular fields delineated by the enclosure commissioners may be recognised even in a modern landscape wholly made up of hedged fields and bare of ridge-and-furrow. What the air photograph cannot recall is the raw newness of the quickset hedges, the ditches and the gates in the first few years after the completion of an enclosure, as raw as the contemporary canal

works and early railway cuttings. The parallel is not inept: many of the surveyors who worked on these transport improvements had been apprenticed in the school of enclosures, just as a barrister piloting an Enclosure Bill past the committee might well have as his next brief a Turnpike Bill or a Canal Bill.

54. PADBURY   Buckinghamshire

With fig. 54 the commentary comes full circle. In fig. 7A the topography of the open fields of Padbury was illustrated. In this view looking west, the ruler of the enclosure commissioners has been laid across the medieval landscape. The straight lines of the new hedges radiate from the village, and other hedges have been laid between them in order to define plots of the right size, to compensate the owners of open-field holdings for the loss of their scattered strips. The hedged fields in the photograph straddle two of the great medieval Fields of Padbury. Those on the left were made up of furlongs from the old West Field; the boundary between it and the old East

135

Field was the balk or access-way which can still be seen between the ridge-and-furrow, leaving the top right-hand corner of the small square field (centre) and swinging away leftwards towards the end of the village. Inside this small square field lies a ring-earthwork consisting of mound and ditch: this may be the site of a medieval windmill.

The Bill to enclose some 2400 acres in Padbury passed through parliament in 1795. In their *Report* to the Board of Agriculture, published in 1794, James and Malcolm urged that Padbury stood in great need of enclosure, and within a year of the Act the commissioners' Award was enrolled with the Clerk of the Peace at Aylesbury. A landscape which had taken centuries to create was only a year in dying.

Sources

W. E. Tate, *Hand-list of Bucks. Enclosure Acts and Awards* (1946) 25, 35; Act and Award: County Record Office, Aylesbury; other documents: All Souls College, Oxford.

7
VILLAGE PLANS

I. INTRODUCTORY

Hamlet. Do you see yonder cloud that's almost
  in shape of a camel?
Polonius. By th' mass, and 'tis like a camel
  indeed.
Hamlet. Methinks it is like a weasel.
Polonius. It is back'd like a weasel.
Hamlet. Or like a whale?
Polonius. Very like a whale.

Hamlet, III, ii, 378–84

As the quotation from *Hamlet* suggests, we consider that the classification of English villages by their shape should be accepted with caution. Since the work of Meitzen and Demangeon, the principal contribution to the study of village morphology has been that of geographers. Perhaps because of its initial association with Meitzen the study has never lost the character of a search for a body of general principles which would elucidate settlement history in the pre-cartographic age. It is not therefore surprising that the general principles most canvassed are geographical and that physical influences are those which are best known.

Explanations cast in physical terms are least unsatisfactory in the broader classifications. The extent to which geography can promote understanding of settlement history is seen in recent trends in the study of English local history. No historian today would think of neglecting the influence of local physical conditions on the shape of a village and the choice of site.

Yet in all systems of classification the very categories which are chosen are pre-suggestive. If villages are grouped by shape, then it is suggested that shapes are more than the chance combination of many variables. Thus, to quote a recent summing-up by a French geographer, himself not indifferent to the shape of settlements but forced into caution by the very complexity revealed by his studies:

The village is a complex organism and to classify it is equally difficult. It cannot be done by the use of one single yardstick, even one combining several features like that of 'form' used by Demangeon. Even less by preconceived racial theories like those of Meitzen. The village is the child of a combination of forces, not without their own internal contradictions, whose influence can only be seen in the whole history and archaeology of agriculture. It quickly acquires a momentum of its own which gives it power to modify even the very structure of the elements which created it.[1]

In the early stages of gathering material for this volume it was hoped that a representative collection of village plans could be assembled and, indeed, that the main grouping of these chapters would be by shape. As the work progressed there was a gradual shift of emphasis towards the point of view expressed in the quotation from Tricart. The broader classifications by plan, the street-village, the crossroads-village, the bridgehead-village, have easily discernible patterns, and the simplicity of the pattern usually brings a ready explanation. Yet it is not in the understanding of primitive village forms, so simple as to be all but self-explanatory, that air photographs are likely to provide most assistance in elucidation. When a student goes into the English countryside armed with a system of classification he will either find villages so simple in shape that interpretation comes easily, or so complex that he will feel impelled to create yet another category. On every hand, to take physical influences alone, not one but several forces have clearly been at work. It would seem more realistic to begin with a statement that villages exhibit a great variety of shapes and everywhere reflect organic growth and particular local influences, and then to add the rider that certain repeated influences may occasionally and profitably be seen in isolation.

It is with such an intention that the photographs of villages and towns have here been assembled. Others may consider this approach too pragmatic, and no doubt schemes of classification will continue to be devised. Local variations are so many that it may be questioned whether any system of classification can ever be

[1] J. Tricart, *Cours de Géographie Humaine* I (Paris, n.d., 1950?) 187.

realistic enough to aid historical research and indicate stages in the development of a village earlier than those known from documents. The elaborate formulae by which Professor Griffith Taylor[2] has classified modern towns confirm such pessimism; we are still, however, open to conversion.

Since historians have learned much in the last thirty years from geographers' essays in classification[3] it may be well to point out that some systems have too easily assumed that the pattern of fields and houses on the modern map is *ipso facto* medieval. The air photograph is an

[2] Griffith Taylor, *Urban Geography* (1949) 87.
[3] A. Demangeon, 'Villages et communautés rurales', *Annales de Géographie* XLII (1933); *Problèmes de Géographie Humaine* (1943) 261–331; D. Sylvester, 'Rural settlement in Shropshire', *Trans. Shrop. Arch. Soc.* 4th ser. XI (1928) 213; R. E. Dickinson, 'Town plans of East Anglia', *Geography* XIX (1934) 37–50; B. M. Swainson, 'Rural settlement in Somerset', *ibid.* XX (1935) 112–24; H. M. Keating, 'Village types of Nottinghamshire', *ibid.* 283–94; D. Sylvester, 'Rural settlement in Cheshire', *Trans. Hist. Soc. Lancs. and Chesh.* CI (1949) 1–38; W. Page, 'Notes on the types of English villages and their distribution', *Antiquity* I (1927) 447–68 and contributions to *V.C.H. Herts*; C. W. Atkin, 'Aspects of Herefordshire Settlement', M.A. Thesis, Univ. of Liverpool; H. Thorpe, 'Some aspects of rural settlement in Co. Durham', *Geography* XXXV (1950) 244–55.

essential instrument for testing such an assumption. The views of shrunken villages, migrations, consolidated fields and abandoned road systems should induce caution. Even the Tithe Award maps, a favourite quarry, can be dangerously modern in this context.

The under-representation of the scattered and often shapeless dispersed settlements has been confessed and explained in the first chapter. It must be emphasised again that what is representative does not always lend itself to photography, lest this book suggest that medieval England was a country of nucleated villages, its land cultivated in open fields and its towns laid out in a few standard patterns.

The following pages can only bring together some of the more definite patterns imparted to villages and towns by their early development. In particular, the influence on a plan of certain dominating buildings has seemed apt for photographic illustration, while the examples of encroachment may draw attention to topographical features in towns and villages which have been overlaid by modern development and their formative influence in earlier times consequently overlooked.

II. REGULAR AND IRREGULAR SHAPES

Antony. It is shap'd, sir, like itself; and it
  is as broad as it hath breadth; it is just
  so high as it is. . . .
Lepidus. What colour is it of?
Antony. Of its own colour, too.
  Antony and Cleopatra, II, vii, 41–6

Many of the commonest settlement patterns are illustrated elsewhere in this book in connection with aspects of villages other than their shape. Here, only one regular shape, the simplest of all, has been taken for separate illustration in order that the logic of regular shape might be briefly examined: the village with houses centred upon one street. This category may be considered to extend from villages with a single built-up frontage, through villages with houses facing each other along both sides of a street, to villages set at a crossroads where two frontages are multiplied into four. There is thus a double regularity to take into account, the regularity of houses in relation to a street frontage; and the regularity of streets themselves: the perfectly straight street or the right-angled crossroads. In contrast with this regularity may be considered a village such as Badby (fig. 56) where the streets form loops and figures-of-eight, and the houses are set around more than one green.

The simplest shape, the single row of houses on one side of a street, is not here illustrated. It can be seen in fig. 37 (the Deepings) and in fig. 90 (Airmyn) where the houses are set facing the river from which many of the villagers derived a livelihood. The double frontage can be seen at Appleton and Braunston (figs. 55, 22) where it is not difficult to imagine an earlier stage with fewer houses set along a shorter street, with church and manor house at the head. In its initial stage such a street-village hardly calls for explanation. It would be a natural form in the early days of settlement wherever a community wished to be compact and required a central thoroughfare to and from the fields. The axis of the street-villages must reflect the direction of some local track which may have been initially no more than a way to a stream, to the fields or to pasture. It would presuppose a considerable degree of regional organisation if the axis of an early street-village were part of a long-distance track or even set so as to give a straight course to a neighbouring village.

Among the physical influences likely to determine the direction of this axis may be counted the straight lines found in Nature: a river-bank, a marsh-edge and a long, narrow hog's back of elevated or better-drained ground. Airmyn has already been mentioned as determined by the line of the river; and the Deepings by river and fen.

Meitzen first drew attention to the significance of the simple street-village as a stage in forest clearance, the cleared land being worked from the back of each house and extending outwards, as colonisation continued, in long strips into the forest. If this happened in England it has left little trace on surviving open-field maps where the furlongs show little of this regularity, but there are signs in such villages as Middleton (Yorks. N.R.) that the simple English street-village might have developed in such a way.

Since so many English villages grew by continuous and slow clearance of woodland it would be surprising if more examples of this process could not be found by local observation. But growth only along a single street can scarcely be considered a natural development. A long street-village is diffuse and difficult to defend, with its villagers living progressively farther from each other than if the same length of frontage formed a web or grid. The extremes of street development did not occur until the coaching-villages of the eighteenth century expanded in a long ribbon along the turnpike, but such medieval villages as Long Buckby (Northamptonshire), Long Houghton (Northumberland) and Long Sutton (Lincolnshire) were so set out and named before coaches and turnpikes. Long Melford (Suffolk) shows how a village which originally clustered round a triangular green developed later into a long street-village by ribbon development.

If, indeed, there is any rational explanation for a village plan persisting as a single street it must lie either in the great attraction of a particular thoroughfare, so that no new building was begun elsewhere, or in the prohibition of building on field-land behind the original street. The formative years in village plans are well beyond the reach of documents and there can only be supposition in this matter. Fondness for a main-road frontage presupposes trade and traffic. Reluctance to allow new houses on adjacent land suggests that assarting was in progress just beyond the crofts, and that new buildings were tolerated only at the end of the street where no one was assarting.

It must be remembered that initial decisions about the siting of houses in relation to a street would not be easy to reverse. Crofts and field-

land once assigned, there would be little enthusiasm for a 'general post' which disturbed boundaries. The initial decision which set a church and a manor house at one end of a street might also have an impeding effect on the later development of houses in that direction, confining them to the other end of the original street frontage.

Where villages are themselves focused on an important building (such as a monastery, or a castle gate) a line of development along the approach road is self-evident. The same is true of villages related to a bridgehead. But monasteries, castles and bridges are much later arrivals on the medieval landscape than most villages. If a village is known, perhaps through Domesday Book, to have antedated a castle or monastery and yet is seen to have a street plan focused on such a building, the relation of fields and streets ought to be minutely examined to see whether there has not been a change of position to accommodate the houses to the new centre. At both Abingdon and Peterborough,[4] for example (although neither is a single-street village), it is known that monastic influence brought about a complete change in the alignment of the houses.

While a Roman road, itself, was seldom used by the Anglo-Saxons, its existence seems sometimes indirectly to have encouraged street-villages: as when the axis along which houses spread was a track joining the original centre of settlement to the road. The course of Ermine Street north of Lincoln provides examples of street-villages set at right angles to the line of a Roman road, along the lanes which run down from the road to the meadows and marsh. In the same way, although not near a Roman road, the three Giddings (fig. 32A) can be seen to lie on parallel tracks, each extending from a ridge-way to a stream.

The boundaries of divisions in any system of classification will be difficult to draw, and the street-village may easily appear in the guise of a 'green-village' wherever the houses are set far enough back from the street. Similarly, some of the small towns which have long, narrow, triangular market-places may have acquired them by widening one end of a street, while elsewhere the broadening of a long street provided ground for a market-place. Thus Burford (fig. 75) might have appeared in this section had it prospered less.

55. APPLETON-LE-MOORS
Yorkshire, North Riding

Appleton-le-Moors, four miles north-west of

---

[4] Peterborough: *V.C.H. Northants.* II (1906) 425; Abingdon: *V.C.H. Berks.* IV (1924) 430.

Fig. 55. Appleton-le-Moors; looking N, January 1967.

Pickering, is in form a classical street-village of the strictest regularity. Seen from the south in fig. 55, the houses face each other along the two sides of a main street which has narrow grass verges. There are no side-roads. The regularity of the pattern is continued in the crofts which are of the same length on either side of the main street. Consequently, the two back-lanes at the ends of the crofts are also straight and parallel. Until enclosure, in the last century, all the houses

of the village were contained within these bounds. As at Nun Monkton, there is now no uniform width for a croft, since the decay of some cottages and the enlargement of others has occasionally thrown adjacent crofts together into a larger unit.

At Appleton the two back-lanes form a well-defined boundary between the crofts and the field-land. There is evidence from some depopulated villages of a track following the perimeter

Fig. 56. Badby; looking N, April 1964.

of the crofts as do the back-lanes at Appleton. The passage of animals, carts and men along the lanes lowered the surface until this perimeter 'ditch' was two or three feet below the level of the crofts. The fact that the land on only one side of the boundary was being ploughed would tend to accentuate the contrast between the croft and the field-land. The 'mound' and 'ditch' that gradually developed by this process may have been used to defend the crofts from wild animals, and the sown field-land from domestic cattle.

To judge from the poll-tax assessment of 100 persons in 1377 there may have been as many as fifty households in the years just before the Black Death; there would certainly be room for twenty-five crofts on either side of the main street. Miss Pamela Allerston has argued that these regularly formed villages which are so characteristic of the Vale of Pickering, were the result of a regrouping of settlements, presumably by a seigneur, in the course of which some settlements were deserted. The now-lost Domesday vill of *Baschebi* is suggested as the

former partner of Appleton, since thirteenth-century charters for Appleton refer to lands in the lost vill which lay about a mile to the north. There is no direct evidence to link the imposition of a regular form on Appleton with the time when *Baschebi* was abandoned. The mere proximity of a deserted site to a regular village proves nothing; desertion occurred in the neighbourhood of villages of all shapes.

Sources

V.C.H. Yorks. N.R. I (1914) 524–5; P. Allerston, 'English village development from the Pickering district', *Trans. Inst. Brit. Geog.* LI (1970) 95–109, citing the Cartulary of St Mary's Abbey in the Dean and Chapter Library, York: MS. XVI A1.

56. BADBY   Northamptonshire

Post-war building in Badby has accentuated rather than obscured the street pattern of this old village, two miles south-south-west of Daventry. This type of pattern, a double loop of roads, has an air of casualness very different from the disciplined street-village and carries with it an implication of growth at once slow and continuous, unrestricted by any sacrosanct area of fields, or major-road frontage along which it was imperative that new buildings should be set. The hedged road that crosses the top of the photograph (fig. 56) in a confident curve is a by-pass created in turnpike days so that a traveller from Daventry to Banbury could avoid the mesh of village streets.

Villages having looped streets are commonly found among the wooded country on the Northamptonshire–Warwickshire border, the north-eastern extension of the Cotswold scarp. It may reflect a husbandry in which field and forest, champaign and bocage, lived side by side; in which the medieval village had carried through into its period of expansion something of its earliest form of a group of houses in a clearing. This air of unrestrained freedom of movement is emphasised in Badby by the tendency of the streets to widen into greens at the slightest opportunity.

The woods to the south which appear in the foreground of the photograph come to within two fields' distance of the churchyard and help to give the village a thirteenth-century air with uncleared woodland on its fringe. At Badby the woodland was never completely turned into fields. In this stretch of woodland the men of Badby intercommoned with their neighbours of Fawsley. In 1245–6 the Abbot of Evesham, who was the lord of Badby, enclosed the woods as parkland. At the Dissolution it passed into the hands of the Knightleys, the squires of Fawsley who had already turned most of Fawsley over to grazing, destroying the village, building their great house and laying out ornamental lakes, with the parish church on a peninsula between them.

Sources

Baker, *Northants.* 1. 253; *P.N. Northants.* (1933) 11–13; E. 179/155/28, 31 and 35; an account of archaeological remains in Badby village and parish will be found in R.C.H.M. *Northamptonshire* III (forthcoming).

III. CASTLES IN VILLAGES AND IN ISOLATION

The Elizabethan surveyors' opinion of castles was strikingly modern; while a few might be preserved as royal palaces (after suitable alterations for comfort's sake) and some others, particularly on the coast and the borders, might be useful as barracks, in general they were a survival from obsolete military practice and an out-moded fashion of aristocratic aggressiveness. When surveyors came upon a castle their calculations were unchivalrous; they thought only of the sum the lead would fetch and the scrap value of the timber: this is how John Norden, for example, approached Sheriff Hutton Castle when the estate was being surveyed[5] for Sir Arthur Ingram in 1624. The former seat of kings and, more recently, of the Council of the North was viewed as if Sir Arthur had become the reluctant heir to derelict property.

Long after the medieval castle had passed from the practical politics of civil war and national defence it retained some glamour as the proper architectural form in which even a domestic residence of a pacific nobleman ought to be built. Kirby Muxloe (fig. 18) shows the earlier stages of this transition, at the end of which battlements have become but an ornament and towers have shrunk to majestic pepper-pots. By the time of Norden, the castellar form, even as a mask, was

[5] B.L. Harl. MSS. 6288.

passing out of fashion as rapidly as civil war. When a civil war did arise in 1642 on issues quite different from baronial factionalism many castles had to be hastily refurbished from their dilapidation and decay. At the end of the Civil War the wholesale 'slighting' made it unlikely that any of them would ever be used again.

No one was more realistic about castles than Elizabeth I. Within three years of her accession she sent out a commission to survey the castles, houses, parks and buildings belonging to the Crown.[6] Such as were superfluous to military needs were to be converted to farms if any one would take them; and, if not, they were to be pulled down and the materials sold, reserving the lead for the queen's use.

Yet not all superfluous castles were pulled down; for many, the surveyors reported that building-stone was so cheap locally that it would not pay to demolish the castle; in others the value of the timber would not exceed the costs of demolition. In November 1609 James I ordered another survey of royal castles in order to see what could be raised by their sale and to reduce the cost of maintaining them.[7] Thirty-seven castles were viewed, including some of the most famous. The use to which the buildings were

[6] C. 66/972/m. 31 d.
[7] S.P. 14/49/82.

being put was carefully noted. For many, it was a variation on the words *decaied* and *utterlie decaied*. In a few (as at Pembroke) the herbage of the court and moats was let for a shilling or two. In seven castles the Assizes were still held, and at Brecon the Assize Hall was the only habitable portion. Others had a few rooms used as prisons: another popular use was for archives. The court rolls and records of the Honour were lodged in Clitheroe Castle; Pickering Castle housed the records of the Liberty; Bolingbroke Castle (fig. 61) was 'a very convenient house but very chargeable for repairing, and onlie used for keeping of courtes and rolls there'. In Tutbury's favour it was urged that the castle was near many of the royal chases, an argument which might have been thought to appeal to James I. Clitheroe had been used by the auditors of the Duchy of Lancaster but because of 'the chardge of reparacions' they had moved elsewhere. At Caernarvon only the gatehouse was usable. Altogether the castles had proved less profitable than the monasteries which had at least furnished quarries for gentlemen's residences (Fountains) and even house-room for a battery of looms (Malmesbury) and a wire-works (Tintern).

It is a far cry both in mood and in valuation from these Elizabethan and Jacobean surveys to the instructions for the valuation of castles in the *Extenta Manerii* of 1275–6 when a castle might be among the most highly esteemed assets of its owner, royal or noble.

The aerial camera, by reason of its distant viewpoint, is able to record in a single comprehensive photograph both castles themselves and their surroundings including the natural and artificial defences. Since the photographs in this book were not chosen to illustrate military architecture or political history the sample of castles is not representative. They range from a simple motte (e.g. Toddington, fig. 2A) through the developed fortresses of kings and barons at the height of their rivalry and power, to the urbane, castle-like country residences of the late fifteenth and early sixteenth centuries (e.g. Kirby Muxloe, fig. 18) in which the drawbridge serves only to admit hunting parties and the moats only for fishing.

The warlike castles of the king and the feudal aristocracy had not been built for pleasure or sheer display. The element of display entered into the calculations, for an impressive castle might terrify a possible rebel or rival, yet the most impressive castle was one where the defences had successfully resisted the test of siege, and domestic and international politics provided opportunities for such tests before

long. A castle is very largely a reflection of developments in the art of war.

As improved techniques of attack and defence reacted on each other the elaboration of castles placed them outside the reach of all but the wealthiest. For a lord with a lesser income the seigniorial badge could be no more than a moated manor house. The castle, which began as a motte to which almost any territorial magnate might aspire, ended as the mark of the man with money to burn. The headquarters of the Honour, the petty kingdom of retainers revolving around the little king, the baron, it could only be built and manned by the twin forces of allegiance and money. Just as, in the last analysis, the lord of a manor was supported on the broad backs of the villeins on his demesnes so the castle rested on the income from the baronial estates. Money was needed to buy and transport materials, and labour for the building and maintenance. In some of the border territories local customs were coloured by the assumption that the defence of a castle was the principal service by which land was held and for which society existed.

The lords who built most, and most often, were those whose incomes from land were large or whose credit with Jew or Italian stood high. Some fortunate lords with towns and market-places at their gates could supplement their revenues from the profits of markets or of charter granting. The less fortunate might hope to do well from the prize money of international wars conducted according to the rules of chivalry.

Just as the castle towered over the manor house, and the barons over the lords of single manors, so the king, greatest baron of them all, was best placed to maintain and multiply his castles. If he could amplify his sovereignty he might determine which of his barons built castles and might declare other castles adulterine. He had sources of income in addition to those of a great landlord: profits of justice, customs dues, taxes on the property of clergy and laymen, forfeitures. He had the power of impressing masons and of conscripting general labour, the means by which the Welsh castles (figs. 100, 101, 102) were built. The number of royal castles should have been enough (had other things been equal) to raise him safely above barons who built and held castles only by his pleasure. But other things were not equal. When a castle was held by a Percy (Warkworth, fig. 62) or a Bolingbroke (fig. 61) maintenance of public order depended upon the good faith of the holder, but when this wavered, no moats, keeps and drawbridges could save the last century of the Middle Ages from civil warfare.

With the distasteful memories of this disorder men gave grateful allegiance to the Tudors who promised security and, in the main, fulfilled their promises. Memories of baronial disorder contributed to the neglect of castles in the sixteenth century and the indifference with which they were regarded when reckoning royal or aristocratic property. The audience who saw Richard II descend into the base court of Flint Castle (fig. 100) to kneel before Bolingbroke in Shakespeare's chronicle play hoped that an English castle would never again be garrisoned against a king. Pomfret Castle, the scene of Richard II's murder, was described in the survey of 1609 as 'very much decaied and . . . needful to be repaired forthwith'.

The first examples in this section show how the dominating influence of castles might be expressed by a whole village plan being related to the castle gate. The final photograph is an example of a castle without a village nearby. Elsewhere, as at Pleshey, the village followed the castle; the Mandevilles extended the works of the castle to embrace the village area, anticipating in miniature Caernarvon or Denbigh.

An open area in front of the castle gate was the natural place for a market or fair under the supervision and protection of the lord, and in the commonest plan for a village dependent on a castle the houses stand around a market-place, or down the sides of a broad street leading to the gates. Warkworth (fig. 62) has but a single street; at Corfe (fig. 58), there are two; Donington (fig. 60) has signs of an original open space covering the whole distance from castle to church. At Corfe the church faces the castle gate across the market-place; at Bolton and Bolingbroke (figs. 59 and 61) the church adjoins the castle; at Warkworth, where the church is older than the castle, the whole length of the village street separates the two; at Brough the two are contiguous; at New Buckenham (fig. 97) the castle chapel proved inadequate for the little town at the castle gate and the townspeople eventually founded their own church. At Devizes and Denbigh (fig. 102) there is a similar duplication of churches.

Other examples of castles in relation to streets and houses will be found among the urban photographs of chapter 8. Some of these towns were from their beginning many times larger than any contemporary village, but others are merely castle-villages that have prospered from the activity which the castle and the markets brought to them; in essence, their plan is no different from those shown here. Had the owners of Old Bolingbroke stayed there longer the village might have become another Alnwick.

57. CHURCH BROUGH AND MARKET BROUGH   Westmorland

Brough occupies a commanding position eight miles south-east of Appleby on the Pennine road from York over Stainmore to Carlisle and Scotland. A rounded knoll beside the Swindale Beck had been chosen by the Romans as the site for a fort, and the same site was taken, probably by William Rufus, for the Norman castle which guarded this key route to the north. In such a position the castle and the village at its gates were the objects of frequent attacks originating across the Border. Both Edward I and Edward II came here in the course of their campaigns, and the village was burned after Bannockburn (where its owner, Robert, Lord Clifford, had fallen) and again five years later.

The air photograph (Fig. 57), taken from the south-west, shows how the castle is set within the rectangular earthwork of the Roman fort (bottom left), occupying no more than a third of it. On the far side of the castle the Roman ditch was possibly incorporated in the defences; on the near side, in the middle of which stands the gatehouse, a new ditch was dug. The remainder of the Roman fort lies without the area of the castle. Its grassy platform can be easily distinguished; trees and scrub mark the line of its defences.

The knoll on which fort and castle stand falls away to the stream on the north, and to a marshy hollow on the south. The village of Brough grew up to the east of the castle. Its plan is the familiar open market-green with houses set back along two frontages and the whole dominated by the castle. A fragment of a market-cross still stands at the end of the green, but farm buildings have encroached on the green at the castle end. The church is seen to lie away from the street on lower ground nearer the camera.

The relation of castle and green is exactly that of Warkworth and Castle Donington, and it is reasonable to suggest that Brough was planned as a market-village by the lords of the castle. In the Pipe Roll of 1197 the 'burgesses' of Brough appear. The parish church began as a chapelry of Kirkby Stephen designed to serve the castle-dwellers and perhaps also those who were already beginning to live by trade at its gates; and there is nothing to suggest a village here before the Normans built the castle.

At some later date medieval traffic took a route a little distance up the valley from Brough.

Fig. 57. Church Brough with Market Brough beyond; looking NE, July 1952.

A second village, known as 'Lower' (or Market) Brough, to distinguish it from Church Brough, developed along this road by a stream-crossing. The market community can be seen as a compact line of houses on both sides of the Stainmore road in the middle distance. This second settlement was already in existence in 1196 when burgesses were tallaged. This second settlement had a market by 1281, and a charter was given to it in 1330. The profits of a fair are mentioned in 1314. Since Market Brough grew up along a large main road it has only a small market-place just off the wide street.

When a survey was made of the possessions of the Lord Clifford who died at Bannockburn in 1314, there were two dozen cottages in Market Brough; at least thirty houses stood in Church Brough by the castle, that is more than the present number. It may be that the repeated attacks and burnings of Brough gave the lord or the villagers an opportunity of second thoughts about the more useful site, and that the charter of 1330 marks the real beginning of the dominance of Market Brough. This continued to be an important local market and the centre of an annual fair to which animals were driven in the eighteenth century from as far away as the Scottish Highlands. It also did well in coaching days, and the petrol engine has restored to it travellers whom the railways had escorted away on routes well down in the plains.

Sources

W. D. Simpson, *Trans. Cumb. and West. Arch. Soc.* n.s. XLVI (1946) 223–83; tallage: *Pipe Roll Society*, N. S. VII (1930) 98; 1314: C. 134/39; 1379: E. 179/195/17, 189 taxpayers in the two Broughs.

Fig. 58. Corfe; looking N, April 1957.

58. CORFE   Dorset

Corfe Castle stands in the only broad gap through the Purbeck Hills on a site pre-determined by nature for defence. It is seen in the photograph (fig. 58) from the south. Even as ruins the design is impressive. The inner ward occupies the crest of an isolated hill, with supplementary defences formed by the two outer baileys, one on the left of the summit and the other extending between the main gate and the inner ditch. The lords of Corfe naturally wished to hold their markets and fairs in the protection of the castle. Charters for markets were granted in the first half of the thirteenth century. However, the village that grew up below the castle gate was not granted borough status till 1572, although it had long laid claim to possess a pre-scriptive right.

The castle gate overlooks the church and a small market-place where the base of the market-cross still stands. There were only two streets in medieval Corfe, East Street and West Street, and the village plan was captured in this simplicity by the surveyor Ralph Treswell in 1585. His castle plans, which date from the next year, show the inner buildings of the castle as they were sixty years before their destruction in the Civil War. In Treswell's plan of the village there are twenty-nine houses in West Street and thirty-four in East Street. The two streets were then less built-up than now. West Street ended where it now turns sharply away towards the left of the photograph and the built-up frontage of East Street was of similar length. The only buildings outside these two streets were the two mills that stood by the streams which run on either side of the castle hill. The main road took, as it does now, the right-hand (east) gap on its way to Wareham.

Medieval Corfe was a town of craftsmen. In the two streets lived the master marblers who

146

Fig. 59. Castle Bolton; looking ENE, July 1955.

fashioned the Purbeck 'marble' before it was shipped to decorate cathedrals and churches in England and France. The port of Ower lay through the gap, three miles over the heath, and no doubt Edward I had this valuable export in mind when he planned the port of Newton to serve the Island. Footpaths and bridle-roads from the quarries converge on East and West Streets. Villagers who dig in their gardens find layers of 'marble' chippings from the medieval workshops, and the surface of local bridle-roads is scattered with broken pieces fallen from carts or put down to give a surface and foothold in bad weather.

Sources

Hutchins, *Dorset* (ed. of 1761) I. 469ff; maps of 1585 and 1586 from Kingston Lacey reproduced there, 482; marblers: G. D. Drury, *Proc. Dorset. Nat. Hist. and Arch. Soc.* LXX (1948) 74–99; R.C.H.M. *Dorset* II, *South East,* part 1 (1970) 52–78, 81–97.

59. CASTLE BOLTON
Yorkshire, North Riding

Since 1378 the village of High Bolton has been dominated by the castle of Sir Richard Scrope, who had obtained permission to 'crenelate his manor with a wall of stone and lime'. The building contract between the lord of the manor and 'Johan Lewyn mason' has been published elsewhere; it was made at Bolton, presumably in the Scropes' older manor house.

Castle Bolton stands deep in the Pennines on the north side of Wensleydale. The photograph (fig. 59) shows the village lying between the moorland edge on the left and the valley-side fields on the right. The long, narrow fields to the right of the houses look like early enclosures. The grass field around the castle once formed part of the castle park (foreground); earlier still, before the Scropes made their park, it was part of the open fields of East Bolton.

High Bolton was a hamlet of Wensley, the riverside village after which the dale is known. In the first years of the fourteenth century the Scropes expanded their estate, based on Bolton, by purchasing the manor and advowson of Wensley; in 1315 they acquired all the lands in Bolton which their predecessors had given to Rievaulx Abbey, by offering equivalent territory elsewhere. In 1314 they had been allowed to make a park along the riverside by diverting the old road from Swaledale which came down through Redmire and Low Bolton to cross the Ure at *Slapwathe* (Slapestone Wath). This track, probably the 'Road going from Richmond to Bolton' mentioned in a grant to Rievaulx, *c.* 1173, was diverted to the present course of the main road after a local enquiry *ad quod damnum*. These acts of territorial consolidation gave the lords of the hamlet of Bolton the seignory of the mother- and market-village of Wensley and a considerable estate to the west of it. They were the work of Sir Henry Scrope (d. 1336), Chief Justice and Chief Baron of the Exchequer.

A generation passed before the first Lord Scrope of Bolton completed the process by building the castle on the valley side 300 feet above Wensley. The erection of the church of St Oswald (seen to the left of the castle) probably followed; the first documentary reference is in 1399, and the plan to make Wensley church collegiate provided for priests to serve Bolton and Redmire.

The main street of Castle Bolton was originally part of the 'high' road, which runs just below the moorland edge along the north side of the dale. Before the construction of the castle and its park the 'high' road would have continued westwards on a contour course swinging south with the curve in the dale towards the former village of West Bolton. Much the same line is now followed by a footpath. A 'low' road by the river has also been diverted; an abandoned stretch passes alongside earthworks of the deserted village of Thoresby, a mile south of Castle Bolton.

The castle was defended in the Civil War, but in the later seventeenth century the centre of gravity moved away again. Bolton Hall was built in a riverside park to the west of Wensley, while Leyburn became the local market-centre. It is not impossible that the present formal plan of the village was designed at the building of the castle when an earlier plan was obliterated. On the other hand, the village may have been a 'street-green' settlement before the castle came into existence at its head. Its neighbours along the scar have this form also, although not quite so markedly.

Sources

V.C.H. Yorks. N.R. 1 (1914) 271; E. 179/211/34 and 211/87; building contract: L. F. Salzman, *Building in England* (1952) 454–5.

60. CASTLE DONINGTON
Leicestershire

In villages dependent on a castle it is usual to find the streets, market-place and church lying at the foot of the stronghold, in the fashion of a Corfe, but at Castle Donington, eight miles south-east of Derby, the contrast is not between the castle and village, but between the low ground of the surrounding country and the town and castle both together on a hillside. In the photograph (fig. 60) the village is seen from the north-east; beneath the aircraft the ground is already falling away to the meadows of the Trent valley over which the castle commands wide views near the confluence with the Derwent.

The main road from Nottingham to Ashby-de-la-Zouch can be seen by-passing the village on the right; before turnpike days the road took the left fork into the village arriving at the bottom-right corner of the wedge-shaped grid of streets. From each of the other three corners of this grid travellers could also enter and leave.

Nothing is left of the castle but its great mound, now tree-covered. This occupies the foreground of the photograph with houses and gardens on the level top where the castle buildings stood. In 1564, when royal surveyors inspected the ruins, they found the remains of five towers but nothing worth reclaiming in the way of iron, glass, tiles or slate. They reported that it would cost more to dig and remove the fallen rubble than to quarry fresh stone in the local hills. They found fruit-trees growing in the moat, the 'crab trees' of another survey of 1580, and the ancestors of the trees in the photograph. The fruit-trees of 1564 were in their turn probably descended from the 'Castle Orchard' recorded in 1352.

More than half the central block of the village is occupied by the church and churchyard. The neat layout of the street pattern at the castle gate, with the church at the centre of the grid and roads leaving at the four corners, is one which appears in other market-towns and is only slightly obscured in this photograph by the turnpike road. This turnpike follows the line of a lane called *Bondgate*. The customary tenants alone appear in rentals of this street, for the burgess-houses lay within the main grid near the castle and church.

The most prosperous days of the village were

Fig. 60. Castle Donington; looking SW, July 1948.

when its lords lived in the castle, but the burgesses were particularly fortunate when Edward IV, who held the castle, abandoned it for a hall in the park by the river, nearly two miles away. He was anxious to enclose his park and, in order to extinguish the villagers' right of common within it, he granted all his demesne lands, totalling 406 acres, to the tenants, who were already extensive field-occupiers. In no rental do the burgesses appear solely as house- or shop-owners. A series of surveys shows how densely inhabited was the little grid of streets before the enclosure of 1777 thrust some of the farmhouses out into the fields. Today, even with the ribbon-development along the main road, Castle Donington is still a remarkably compact town.

In the census of 1871 there were 616 families and almost that number of houses. In the poll tax of 1379 there were 142 households containing in all 225 persons who did not succeed in evading the tax; in the collection of 1377, when there was less evasion, 280 persons had paid tax. No rentals are known earlier than the Black Death, when the number of households might well have been nearly 200. The church was enlarged to hold additional parishioners on more than one occasion before the end of the fourteenth century, and the fine spire is of this period.

In the rentals of 1462 there were 164 occupied dwellings. The terrier of 1656, quoted by Farnham, had a total of 102 houses. In the hearth tax of 1666 forty hearths in the hall were taxed and ninety-two other households appear in the schedule. Unfortunately no early map of the village has been found.

Sources

Nichols, *Leics.* III. 770; Farnham MSS.: City Museum, Leicester; rentals and survey: D.L. 43/6/3–6 and

Fig. 61A. Old Bolingbroke; looking E, March 1957.

44/105; poll tax of 1377 (the poll tax of 1379 is wrongly ascribed by Farnham to this year): E. 179/133/25; R. H. Hilton, *Economic Development of some Leicestershire Estates* (1947) 157–61.

61. OLD BOLINGBROKE Lincolnshire

Old Bolingbroke lies six miles south-east of Horncastle on the southern edge of the Lincolnshire Wolds where the castle, built here *c.* 1220–30, commands the land route along the edge of the dry ground above the fens near the end of Stickney Causeway, the link between Boston and north Lincolnshire. The prefix 'Old' is comparatively recent; in the nineteenth century a New Bolingbroke was built in the fens.

Bolingbroke was the administrative head of the great feudal Honour which took its name from the village and which in turn named the son of John of Gaunt, the future Henry IV, who was born here.

The foundations of the castle stand in the centre foreground of fig. 61A. Since the photograph was taken, the remains have been excavated and consolidated by the Department of the Environment, in whose guardianship the Duchy of Lancaster has placed the site. To the right of the keep is the outer ward, or *Rout Yard*, and, within it, an embanked rectangular enclosure. A *rout* was an animal pound, perhaps for the strays of the great fenland commons of the Honour, and Dr Thompson suggests that the prominent

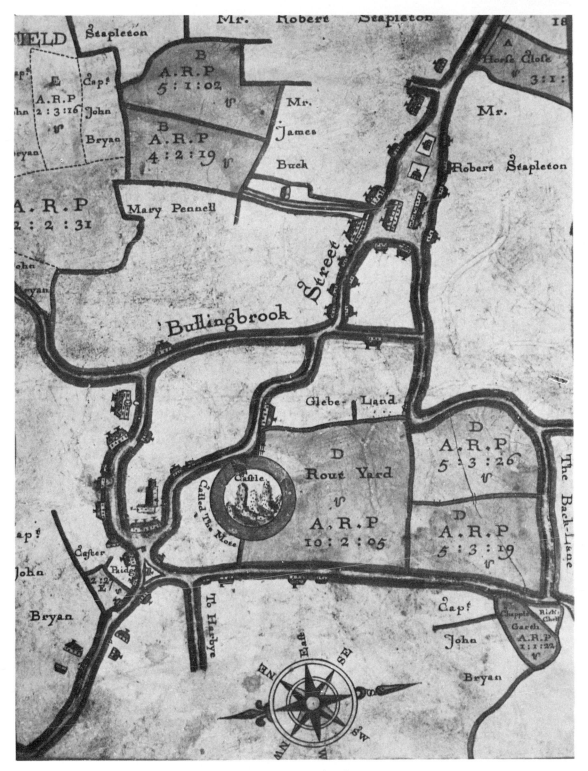

Fig. 61B. Old Bolingbroke in 1718; part of a map by Jared Hill.

rectangular mounds enclosed a watering-pond for impounded animals. In Domesday Book there is already mention of a market, the New Market; the village was the head of a wapentake; and the value had risen by one-third since 1066. The Crown survey of 1608 shows Bolingbroke still the centre of a great estate extending in a twenty-mile circuit, with sheep and corn villages on the Wolds, fishing villages in the fens and a strip of salterns on the coast.

The map reproduced as fig. 61B (wrongly attributed and dated in our first edition) was made by Jared Hill in 1718. It shows that the relation of village to castle was more complex than at Brough or Warkworth. Beyond the castle (to the east) is the usual convergence of roads with an open space, in which, by 1608, there were three fairs a year and a weekly market. The wedge shape of the former market-place is accentuated in the photograph by the foreshortening of perspective. Although Bolingbroke in 1718 was no more than a large village, the cartographer marks four groups of houses that had encroached upon the market-place and the photograph shows that, with the decay of the market, the process has gone further.

It will be noticed that the name *Bullingbrook Street* was given in 1718 to the twisting lane which leads from the market to the group of streets and houses north (that is, left) of the castle. The fact that the church stands in this group, and not in association with the market, suggests that this may be the original nucleus of settlement before the needs of a 'new market' (the Domesday Book term) brought into being a more formal layout, and this suggestion, which we made in 1958, is borne out by Dr M. W. Thompson's identification in 1965 of the earthwork on Dewy Hill overlooking the church from the north, as an eleventh- or twelfth-century fortification.

In 1921 the village had a population of 304; in 1377, even after the plagues, there were 117 taxpayers, or perhaps 170 souls all told. The castle was slighted after the Civil War; the market and fair fell into decay and Bolingbroke remained no more than an agricultural village. The plan of 1718 shows some forty-five houses. The nineteenth-century census volumes repeatedly comment on the falling population here, giving as the cause migration to large manufacturing towns and emigration.

Sources

1086: *The Lincs. Domesday. Lincs. Rec. Soc.* XIX (1924) 86; written survey of 1608: D.L. 42/119; Jared Hill's map of 1718: M.P.C. 118; M. W. Thompson, 'The origins of Bolingbroke Castle', *Med. Arch.* X (1966) 152–8 and sources there cited; pls. XI–XII include an air photograph of Dewy Hill.

62. WARKWORTH — Northumberland

The first positive evidence for a castle at Warkworth dates from a royal grant of 1158. A narrow meander in the river Coquet a mile above its mouth provided a fine defensive site. The river-crossing must have been in use many years earlier and the village and church have a long civil history: in 737 the King of Northumbria presented the estate and the church to the abbot and monks of Lindisfarne.

The tempestuous political fortunes of the owners of the castle have resulted in frequent forfeitures to the crown, so that there is an unusual number of surveys of the town. Moreover, the late sixteenth- and early seventeenth-century earls were conscious of the advantages to be gained from carefully kept rentals and frequently commissioned surveys; these are preserved amongst the muniments at Alnwick and Petworth.

The photograph (fig. 62) gives a view of the village from the south. The borough houses stand along the single main street which extends from the castle down to the bridge. This street widens at its lower end in front of the churchyard into an open space for markets. The general relation of river, castle, main street and bridge is very similar to that at Appleby, but it will be noticed that both the main gate at Warkworth Castle and the alignment of the defences point southwards towards open moorland. The village did not lie at the front of the castle gate as at Castle Donington and Brough. The gardens and crofts of the borough houses ran straight down to the river on either side, short and steep in their fall on the west and long and gentle on the east. A narrow back-lane behind the houses on the east of the main street shows that the crofts here were originally no longer than those on the west. The road which swings east at the castle and follows the river bank is a modern diversion.

In a survey of 1249 there were sixty houses in the borough and 'New Town'; ninety-five appear in a rental of 1498, sixty-four in 1569, seventy-four in 1585, eighty-five in 1616, seventy-seven in 1623 and seventy-one in 1667. The rental of 1616 shows that the right-hand side of the road leading from castle to bridge had a frontage of thirty-eight burgess houses. Thirty-nine houses can be counted on the photograph.

Fig. 62. Warkworth; looking N, July 1961.

The Tudor surveys all agree that the prosperity of Warkworth had then declined. At some unknown time in the past an extension of the borough to the far bank of the river had taken place to accommodate the seamen whose boats sheltered here. As the crow flies, Warkworth is little over half a mile from the coast, but the course of the Coquet had changed by the time of Clarkson's survey in 1567, which records the maritime tradition:

it was thought good for divers causes that those persons which should trade for traffic by sea (as mariners or fishermen, owners of ships and merchants only excepted) should inhabit and dwell together. So there was set forth one parcel of ground for them to inhabit upon as this day called the *Newe Towne*.

The motive for this segregation of seamen is not clear, nor indeed whether they had permanent houses at New Town. In any event the segregation was quite deliberate, rather like that of clothier and husbandman at Castle Combe (p. 268), for the 1567 survey continues its report of the tradition: 'the part of that borough which is betwixt the castle and the bridge was appointed for the inhabiting of such as was merchants and

other handycraftsmen'. No more details of the craftsmen were given. The only other assets mentioned in 1567 are the quarries for grindstones, the salt-pans in the estuary (the *salt-goats* (= cotes) of the 1623 map), and a coal seam which was proving 'too great a charge'.

The survey of the forfeited estates made in 1569 by Humberstone paints a rather gloomy picture:

the borough standyth on the northe parte of the Castle at the foote of the hyll meanely buylded and inhabyted wyth many pore men, which have no trade of lyvyng but onely fysshyng to the Sea, and some land not suffycyent to maynteyne ther famyly, for the most parte of the land in Warkworth ys in demesne and graunted by the lord to fermors.

The great park of the castle occupied most of the parish by this time and of the 311 acres of demesne which had been under plough in 1249 almost all had been incorporated in the park.

The town must also have suffered from the decay of the castle after 1572, when Thomas Percy was executed for his part in the Rising of the Northern Earls and the later Percies made Alnwick their home. In 1617 James I saw 'goats

153

and sheep in every chamber, almost in the dungeons, where they lie every night...'. The photograph shows the great fifteenth-century keep and the gatehouse at the opposite side of the courtyard. Around the courtyard walls are the remains of the domestic offices of the castle, namely the hall, chapel, kitchens, pantries and stables. These date from a period before the construction of the elaborate keep which, Dr W. Douglas Simpson has argued, was less a fortress than an elaborate house for the domestic life of its baronial owner. The excavated foundations of the chapel, planned by the first earl to house his college of priests but never completed, extend the whole width of the courtyard.

The photograph takes in a wider sweep of ground than that used for the first edition and therefore includes one of the oddest modern consequences of the Middle Ages: the long strip of caravan sites, each in a little plot, along an unfenced road leading to the sea (top right). Dr B. K. Roberts has pointed out that each of these plots appears on the Tithe Map *c.* 1840 making up a block of land, named 'The Tens' and 'New Town Butts' intruding into Birling parish. They can be related to the selions of Warkworth *Nova Villa* (or New Town) where it had been intended (before 1249) to create a second borough for mariners and fishermen. In a rental of 1498 twenty tenants shared these selions which were still regarded as part of Warkworth even though lying across the river in Birling parish; in a survey of 1569 the abortive New Town site was described as 'not inhabited, the grounde or rigges thereof is nowe used and occupied by the burgesses of Warkworth'. The *rigges* were presumably the selions once destined for burgage plots, had the borough taken root. In recent times the owners of the plots redeemed the failure of the thirteenth century by seizing the economic chance of the 1950s and letting their plots for caravans which were thus drawn up in ranks all the way to the sea, beyond the right-hand border of fig. 62. More recently the county planning authority has cleared the site, and built a caravan park on the sea edge, leaving the plots again 'not inhabited'. As far as we know, no one locally was aware of the ghosts that were being stirred.

Sources

Castle: W. D. Simpson in *Arch. Aeliana* 4th ser. XV (1938) 115–36; Department of the Environment, *Guide* (1949); survey of 1538: E. 36/173, fol. 64; town: documents of 1249, 1498, 1567, 1585, 1616, and 1667 printed in *Northumberland County History* v (1899); Humberstone's survey of 1569: E. 164/37, fol. 151;

Map of 1623 by Robert Norton in *Mayson's Survey*: Alnwick Castle MSS., reproduced in *N.C.H.* v. 137; the selions of New Town: M. W. Beresford, *New Towns of the Middle Ages* (1967) 474 and documents cited there; Dr B. K. Roberts drew our attention to the Tithe Map and the caravans. Robert Newton, *The Northumberland Landscape* (1972) 150–4 and fig. 15 makes Warkworth itself a planned medieval borough from the reign of Henry II although he admits a 'substantial village in the eleventh century' (*ibid.* 152); thus 'planned' perhaps but not planted. Recent maps of the Ordnance Survey show that Birling parish has been absorbed by Warkworth.

63. SHERIFF HUTTON
Yorkshire, North Riding

At Bolingbroke the position of the church in relation to the castle indicated a primary centre of civil settlement associated with an early motte and bailey castle. The siting of the church and the two successive castles in the village of Sheriff Hutton, nine miles north of York, has a similar significance emphasised by the existence of two greens or market-places.

The Howardian hills sweep in an arc to the north and north-east of the low-lying Foss marshes, part of the medieval Forest of Galtres, which once extended virtually to the city walls of York. The gap cut through these hills by the Derwent was protected by a castle at Malton, and the route skirting the northern edge of the marsh by a simple motte and bailey defence built *c.* 1140 by Bertram de Bulmer, sheriff of York, at the village then known as Hutton. This castle was built next to the church at the end of the village street which followed the crest of a hill. In fig. 63 the churchyard is seen to adjoin land in ridge-and-furrow (top centre); to the right in a square grass field lie the motte and bailey earthworks of the sheriff's castle now carrying a small group of trees. Ridge-and-furrow shows clearly in the light-toned field farther to the right, and less distinctly on the darker-toned field below the castle earthworks. These cultivations continue to the very edge of the earthworks, so that the castle may have been intruded into arable cultivation (see Yelden, below).

The main street widens to a triangular green in front of the church, and the shadows show that the street surface throughout the village has been deeply worn by the passage of traffic in former times; had Hutton been deserted, it would have had hollow-ways of the type already noted above (p. 17) as characteristic of village streets. Far from being deserted, Hutton prospered by the presence of the Nevills, who descended from a daughter of Bertram the sheriff. In 1335 a park

Fig. 63. Sheriff Hutton; looking E, April 1956.

was created from the woods on the carr to the south of the village, and later enlarged by incorporating much of the field-land of the deserted village of East Lilling. In 1378 a market-charter was granted; the rectangular market-green can be seen on the right of the main street in the middle distance. Four years later John, Lord Nevill, was granted license to build a new stone castle 'on a plot of his own ground'.

The plot chosen for the Nevill Castle lay at the western end of the village in a position to take advantage of a slope to the south. The ruins of this castle with four corner towers similar to those of Bolton (fig. 59) stand in the foreground. The trees to the right mark the line of a ditch cut along the hill-slope, and of the lower moat and fishponds.

The manor reverted to the Crown at the death of the Earl of Warwick in 1471, and was favoured both for the quality of the hunting in Galtres and for its proximity to York. Henry VIII established the court of the boy Earl of Richmond at the castle from 1525 to 1536, and it was later used for meetings of the Council of the North. In 1622 James I sold the park to the monopolist, Sir Arthur Ingram, and Charles I leased the castle site in 1624. A survey made at that time by Norden described the castle as already in decay although the Crown did not formally dispose of it until 1685:

the case of a stately castle, the inward materials transported, the walls ruined ... the forms of certayne decayede fishpondes ... the bowells of this worthy pile and defensive howse are rent and torne and the naked carkas lately by his Majestie alienated. To this Castle garthe adioyneth Sherife Hutton parke well stored with fallow deere and sett with neere 4000 decayed and decaying okes.

In recent times the inner courtyard has had barns built in it, as the photograph shows, while surviving cellars and rooms in the towers are used for farm animals and as rubbish tips.

Sources

V.C.H. Yorks. N.R. II (1923) 172–97; Norden's 1624 survey: B. L. Harl. MS. 6288 and Leeds City Archives, TN/B/4/1; 1765 survey: B/4/2; the Temple Newsam MSS. at Leeds City Archives contain another copy of

Fig. 64. Yelden; vertical photograph, November 1972. Scale 1:2800.

this survey as well as others of 1765 and 1774 (TN/B/4/1–3) and many papers dealing with the eighteenth-century enclosures.

64. YELDEN   Bedfordshire

The motte and bailey castle at Yelden, built by 1173–4 perhaps a generation later than the first Sheriff Hutton castle, was already in ruins in 1361, twenty years before the Nevill Castle at Sheriff Hutton was projected. These remarkable earthworks comprise a motte, still standing forty feet above the bottom of the defensive ditch, and two irregularly shaped baileys. The ditches are now largely dry, but were formerly fed by the Til Stream which is at present contained in an artificial course to the right of the earthworks; after heavy rain, water flows again

Fig. 65. Cainhoe Castle (Clophill), and other earthworks; looking WSW, May 1971.

in the ditches. No stonework of the castle survives above ground. Stone-robbers' trenches suggest a square building in the upper bailey, while minor irregularities in the surface of the baileys and hollows on the top of the motte suggest the former presence of other structures. Excavations of the small circular mound near a pond to the left of the street undertaken nearly a century ago indicated the existence of a round tower there.

The parallel ditches seen to the left of the castle have been interpreted as part of the defences, but they are too shallow to have served any such purpose.[8] In this photograph they are seen to

[8] This identification was made in 1904 when the study of village earthworks had hardly begun.

form part of a series, all lying at right angles to the village street and ending to the left at a long straight boundary-ditch. A matching series of ditches can be seen behind cottages to the right of the street, towards the top of the photograph. Thus, the castle, like Sheriff Hutton, was perhaps built upon land forming part of the area of an already existing village. If this identification is correct, the builders of the castle took in more than half of five crofts, supplanting the houses to which they belonged.

Sources

V.C.H. Beds. I (1904) 289–91 with plan, III (1912) 175–9; excavation: *Trans. Beds. Arch. Soc.* XVI (1882) 261–3.

65. CAINHOE CASTLE (Clophill)
Bedfordshire

The best strategic site for a castle was not necessarily in or near an existing village, and especially in hilly country. Hilltop villages of refuge with a castle, so common in the more disordered parts of medieval Europe, are rare in England, and even the founders of boroughs displayed a preference for sites straddling commercial routes rather than for the defensible heights favoured by castle-builders. Isolated castle sites are particularly frequent in the period of simple earth mottes. The later and larger castles, in which a lord and his retainers were present for at least part of the year, and to which was added the amenity of a park, however isolated when first built, were bound to attract further settlement.

The motte and bailey at Cainhoe may be such a castle. Both Clophill and Cainhoe manors were held by the family of d'Aubigny, but the castle which was to become the head of the barony was not built at the existing village of Clophill. The extensive minor earthworks beside this motte and bailey at Cainhoe suggest a dependent settlement attracted to the castle. When the lord of Cainhoe manor died in October 1375 the inquisition *post mortem* found that there were ten cottages which were empty and in the lord's hands, unlet 'since the pestilence'. What was the relation of this settlement to the village of Clophill? The medieval church of Clophill itself is more than half a mile from that village. Was there once a village by the church? Clearly the whole pattern of local settlement hereabouts invites further study.

Sources

V.C.H. Beds. I (1904) 291–2, II (1908) 320–5; inquisition of 1375: C.135/243/8. National Grid ref. TL098374.

IV. VILLAGES AND MONASTERIES

A number of sites that might have been included here are illustrated in other sections, while in Knowles and St Joseph, *Monastic Sites from the Air*, several photographs of monastic houses showed also the nearby villages. Battle (*Monastic Sites*, 26–7) was a market-town where the relation to a monastery gate is as plain as at Nun Monkton. Only when a religious order tolerated a village in its immediate vicinity is a clear relationship between village plan and monastic house to be expected. Most of the great Cistercian houses stand aloof from villages in their solitude and, as is well known, this solitude was sometimes achieved by the destruction of older villages which stood near to the site chosen for the abbey or for one of its granges. It should also be remembered that in England only a small number of medieval monasteries are contemporary with the first four hundred years of English villages. Unless a lord gave up his manor site, any new monastic house would have had to adapt itself to an existing village plan. Similarly, some very prosperous monasteries in towns came too late to influence the basic plan, although by their presence they might set limits to subsequent building.

Villages which prospered from association with a monastic house were likely to develop into market-towns and some few of them into monastic boroughs. This explains why some of the better-known monastery-gate settlements do not appear until Part Three of this book (e.g. Bury St Edmunds).

A characteristic monastic building set far away from village and town was the grange, the agricultural outpost of the house. Usually situated in open country, it acted as a collecting centre for the produce of the scattered monastic properties in the locality. If it stood in a compact block of monastic land it could also serve as a working farm, sometimes almost a ranch. A wealthy Cistercian house such as Fountains would have many of these outposts, some in the Pennine pastures, some in the Dales, some near the abbey and some thirty miles away in the arable fields of the Vale of York. They were manned by the lay-brothers, the *conversi* for whom the same solitude was sought as at the abbey: the removal of villagers from the site at Greenbery near Scorton (Yorkshire, North Riding) is well documented.[9]

The area covered by the permanent buildings of a grange need not have been very large, probably little more than the house, outbuildings and yards of the farms which have succeeded them. There are granges which have not continued as modern farms, and here the plan of the medieval buildings might well be recovered, but no effective air photographs are yet available. The sale of the monastic estates at the Dissolution seems to have made very little difference to the topography of most granges. Where the Dissolution surveys detail fields and areas they tally closely

[9] W. T. Lancaster, ed., *Fountains Cartulary* (1915) 330.

with those of the modern farm on the grange site which may well bear the name of *Grange*; although the popularity and prestige of the name in the last century has been such that by no means every *Grange* is medieval any more than every *Manor House* is a true manor.

The names and location of the monastic granges could easily be recovered from the surveys in the records of the Court of Augmentations, for which there is now a typescript *index locorum* at the Public Record Office, London. Many of these surveys have been published by local record societies, and Dugdale's *Monasticon* contains summaries of a great number. For any student of local history to trace the granges of his neighbourhood should not be difficult; until recently this has been a neglected study.

The monastic granges in their role of 'collecting centres' assisted the development of that local specialisation which was characteristic of thirteenth-century monastic estates. One grange would specialise in corn, another in stock-rearing, others respectively in stock-fattening, in sheep, in marshland products, in salt-pans and in timber. The monastery which could embrace all these specialisations among its network of granges was a fortunate and wealthy one, but most of the large houses possessed four or five granges with a diversity of occupations. Fig. 107 shows Bentley Grange, an outpost of Byland Abbey, where iron-mining and smelting were carried on.

In the troubled economic circumstances of the later fourteenth century, abbeys might find their granges an encumbrance. The more compact grange estates were often leased as going concerns, so that the monasteries enjoyed a regular cash income from the leases instead of the annual waggon-loads of produce. In 1342 Jervaulx let to tenants its most distant grange, Horton in Ribblesdale, and the land was never directly farmed by the abbey again.[10] The lease-books of Fountains,[11] extending over the last forty years of the abbey's life, show all the granges leased out.

In the Vale of York there was an interesting reversal of earlier policy after the Scottish invasions of the early fourteenth century brought dislocation and damage to the granges. In 1318 the Abbot of Fountains complained of 'grangiae et loca exteriora destructa et combusta ac depredata'. The cost of rebuilding and new equipment was beyond the resources of the abbeys. They cut their losses and offered to divide up the land

among any who would come to be their tenants. In this way villages which had been expelled at the making of the granges nearly two centuries earlier returned to their original site. In 1342 the Abbot of Jervaulx had 'made towns of his four great granges of Rookwith, Aikber, Newstead and Didderston'.[12] At the time of grange-making Walter Map had written[13] of the Cistercians' methods 'And because their rule does not allow them to govern parishioners, they proceed to raze villages and churches ... not scrupling to sow crops or cast down and level everything before the plough-share, so that if you looked in a place that you knew previously you could say "and grass now grows where Troy town stood".' The Troys were now being rebuilt.

66. OLD BYLAND
Yorkshire, North Riding

The present position of Byland Abbey, four miles from Rievaulx, is the result of a migration from a site in Ryedale, north-west of Helmsley, so close to Rievaulx that the bells of the two abbeys caused confusion. When the abbey had first settled in Ryedale it removed and rebuilt a village which occupied its chosen site. In similar situations other Cistercian houses destroyed whole villages; but this village was rebuilt over a mile away on a bare plateau four hundred feet above the Rye. The photograph (fig. 66A) shows the new site, Old Byland as it is called, from the south-east. There is a little valley on the left, a tributary of the Rye which flows in a deep cleft not far to the east. Above the valley the ground is almost level, and was all taken in as the village fields; the East Field lay in the distance covering almost the whole of the visible area. Old Byland and its neighbourhood are depicted on a plan of 1598, of which a part is reproduced as fig. 66B.

The name of 'Old Byland' given to this new village is confusing: it is only 'old' in relation to the present hamlet of Byland near the existing abbey ruins. It is 'New Byland', 'eidem nomen primum imponentes', compared with an older monastic site on the riverside near the farm now known as Tile House (SE 566867). In Saxton's plan there were 'Town Ings' to the south of Tile House. In Domesday Book, a century before the

[10] *Cal. Misc. Inq.* II, no. 1797.
[11] Yorks. Arch. Soc. MSS.

[12] *Cal. Misc. Inq.* II, nos. 385, 453, 455, 489; E. 359/14 m. 12d; *Yorks. Arch. Jnl* XXV (1920) 161; *Memorials of Fountains* I. *Surtees Soc.* XLII (1862) 203–5; C. Platt, *The Monastic Grange in Medieval England* (1969) esp. 222–3 and 226.
[13] *de Nugis Curialium*, Distinction 1, ch. XXV, 49 (M. R. James' translation), *Cymmrodorion Record Series* no. 9 (1923).

Fig. 66A. Old Byland; looking NW, March 1956.

coming of the monks, there had been a church in that first Byland. The church in the present village includes much twelfth-century work and must be that which (the chronicle says) the monks gave to the village they transplanted.

The new settlement has a simple plan. Its houses lie back from a broad green which is not itself on a through route. The road enters at one end by a right-angled turn and leaves by another. Saxton's plan shows a single back-lane, still visible in the distance of fig. 66A. In the small valley beside which the monks set the houses of the new village there are springs, which are, perhaps, the source of the stream described in the chronicle as 'Stutekelde' (*Keld*=spring, and cf. *kell troughe* on fig. 66B).

There is no reason to think that the village was ever very large; thirty-three persons were taxed in the poll tax of 1377, and at the Dissolution of the abbey there were nineteen tenants in the 'villata'. Half a century later a boundary dispute in the Court of Exchequer caused the surveyor Christopher Saxton to be sent to make his plan.

Some of the witnesses, in giving evidence, looked back to the days when the Abbot of Byland had kept his flocks up on this plateau: 500 ewes at Great Murton, 1000 in Old Murton (possibly the lost Dale Town), 700 in Wethercote, and in Old Byland 'what nomber he cannot tell', said Christopher Kilvington. In the census of 1861 there were only thirty houses in the whole parish.

Sources

Dugdale, *Monasticon* v. 343, 351; poll tax: E. 179/211/29; Dissolution survey: E. 315/397, fol. 81; Saxton map and depositions of 1598; E. 178/2779 and M.P.B. 32; fragment of depositions in *Hist. MSS. Comm. Var. Coll.* II. 109.

67. NEWLASS GRANGE
Yorkshire, North Riding

Like Old Byland, only two miles to the west, the small village of Newlass stood on a comparatively level plateau into which the Rye and

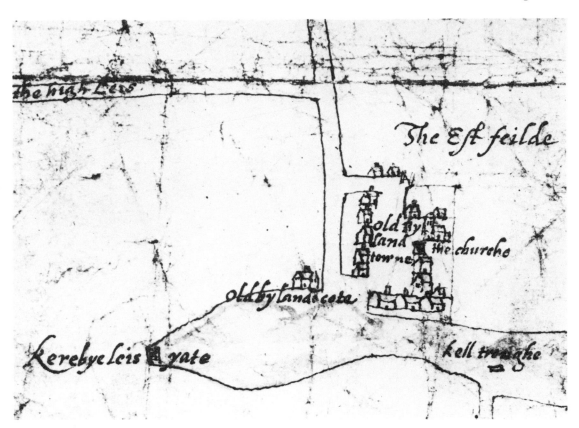

Fig. 66B. Old Byland in 1598; plan by Christopher Saxton.

its tributaries have cut deep valleys. Newlass was 'new laithes', distant barns belonging to Helmsley two and a half miles to the south-east, but on territory which was eventually given to the Cistercian abbey of Rievaulx. It was country where both arable and pastoral agriculture have always been possible. Medieval plough-ridges can be seen (fig. 67) in the grass field to the right of the farm-buildings, and all the other fields are still under agricultural rotation.

In the two grass fields adjoining the farm, New Leys, which preserves the name of Newlass, there are extensive earthworks, some of them clearly marking the foundations of rectangular buildings. The earliest documentary references to Newlass, as Dr Platt has shown, are not to a grange but a small village community. It was a grange by 1301 and in the later years of the abbey it became a specialist sheep-rearing grange, which, in 1539, was made up of 'the grange, the great shephouse, the rabbit warren and a third building'. If the grange is represented by the present farm there are two earthworks in the photograph which may fit the description of the others. In the left-hand of the two fields is a large rectangle, apparently later than the ridges

which can be faintly seen in the grass, and in the right-hand field, near the dividing hedge, there is a rectilinear enclosure perhaps to be interpreted as a building with yard attached. The site of other small buildings may be detected here and there. The zig-zag course of a boundary-bank crossing these two fields may have been partly determined by further buildings. The steep valley sides would have provided plenty of cover for the rabbits.

Sources

1301: E.179/211 12, mm. 13 and 17d; Rievaulx Cartulary. *Surtees Soc.* LXXXIII (1887) 313 and 345; C. Platt, *The Monastic Grange in Medieval England* (1969) 222–3. National Grid ref. SE581865.

68. TEMPLE BRUER   Lincolnshire

The Knights Templars' village of Bruer was planted, like Baldock their new Baghdad (fig. 99), in open country and in heathland, as the name indicates (*bruer*=heath). The foundation charter of the preceptory (*c.* 1150) delineated an area 'de terra vastata et brueria' on the plateau south of Lincoln 'between the road

Fig. 67. Newlass Grange; looking W, November 1968.

to Sleaford and the road to Stamford'.

Although there is no entry in Domesday Book, the survey of the Templars' estates in 1185 gave a separate section to Bruer and a separate *summa* of its income, treating it as a full manor. By 1185 the village was already a generation old. Around the preceptory there had settled thirty-seven tenants inhabiting thirty-four crofts. Ten of the villagers each held field-land amounting to a single croft and a single bovate, probably of twenty-four acres. The villagers paid the Templars a rent in money, in hens and in services, *boon-works* being rendered. The surnames of the tenants in 1185 indicate peasant migrants from local villages. A weaver and a shepherd apart, occupational names are markedly absent, in contrast to the list of tenants that same year in the equally new foundation of Baldock.

The site lies six miles north-west of Sleaford. There is now but a single large farm beside a fragment of the Templars' buildings. There is little doubt that an entirely new village of Temple Bruer was planted here, settlers being encouraged by the Templars who needed a labour force for cultivation of their lands, while the uniformity of the holdings in the 1185 survey suggests a simple, rough-and-ready allocation of land for the maintenance of the incoming peasantry. But the Templars had no intention of Bruer remaining solely an agricultural village, and a weekly market began to be held in the third quarter of the twelfth century. A brief rental of 1316 seems to indicate arable holdings and rent-paying villeins at that date, while accounts from 1328 to 1332 show an annual surplus of more than 200 bushels of grain sent annually to market, and from 2700 to 4500 sheep shorn here each year. About 1000 of these fleeces were from the Bruer flock, the remainder from other local estates of the Order for which Bruer formed a collecting and administrative centre, rather like the granges of other Orders.

The subsequent fate of the village is not known. It was never well placed in relation to long-distance traffic, being midway between the Lincoln–Stamford and Lincoln–Sleaford roads which formed the boundary of the heath in the foundation charter. The Templars were equally

162

Fig. 68. Temple Bruer; looking SE over the preceptory (left foreground) to the site of the deserted medieval village, revealed by soil-marks, February 1969.

unfortunate in an attempt to establish a roadside market at Walshford Bridge in their Yorkshire manor of Ribston, and the Knights Hospitallers failed at the Fosse Way site of Eagle, Lincolnshire, in 1348.

When Leland visited Bruer in 1538–9 he saw 'great and vaste Buildinges, but rude at this Place, and the Este end of the Temple is made *opere circulari de more ...*'. An engraving of the ruins published by Samuel Buck in 1726 shows part of the circular church with an adjacent tower. The tower alone remains standing, but excavations carried out in 1908 by W. H. St John Hope revealed that there was a walled precinct occupying most of the field to the west of the farm. No signs of this appeared in the photograph in our first edition: the new plate (fig. 68), looking from the north-west, shows the tower, now in a farmyard, while in the arable field at the bottom of the photograph, faint soil-marks suggest vanished buildings. Moreover, the site of the lost village now appears as soil-marks.

A shallow dry valley, one of many in this part of the plateau, curves away to the south-east from the farm; it is joined by a second valley, their combined course leading to the upper left-hand margin. They can be distinguished as lines in dark tone due to the increased depth of soil on the valley floor. The vanished village of Bruer occupied the first few hundred yards of the valley below the farm. The main street seems to have followed the valley floor past a triangular spinney to a field where soil-marks show clearly. There, small white patches on the floor of the valley may be scatters of limestone rubble from ploughed-up foundations of houses on a green. Dark patches, sometimes outlined in white, suggest at least seven house-sites on each side of the village street. The trees of the spinney then intervene on the left, while on the right, in the near field, large rectangles can be discerned, probably the remains of croft boundaries. In all, twelve or more may have existed, each corresponding with a house-site.

Sources
W. H. St John Hope, 'The round church of the Knights Templars at Temple Bruer', *Archaeologia* LXI (1908) 177–98, pls.xix-xxi; survey of 1338: *The Knights Hospitallers in England, being the Report of Prior Philip de Thame to the Grand Master Elyan de Villanova* for AD *1338*. *Camden Soc.* LXV (1855); of 1316: D.L. 29/3882/242; of 1328–32: E.358/18 mm. vi,xix,xxxviii and 19 m.xxx; B. A. Lees, ed., *The Templars' Inquest of 1185* (1935) clxxxi; bounds of 1201: *Curia Regis Rolls* I (1923) 452. National Grid ref. TF010535.

V. VILLAGES WITH GREENS

A small green could probably have been found in a large number of medieval English villages. Before the time of metalled roads most villages had their house-frontages set back far enough from each other to permit a grass space, the village 'street' over which traffic moved as it thought fit. In times of little traffic there was uninterrupted rough grazing for tethered animals, while a pond somewhere in this space served for ducks and geese. Even where village houses had been placed so close that only a double cart's width separated one frontage from another there were crossroads, forks and T-junctions where the course of traffic left a central 'island' of grass. In the more dispersed Midland villages having several 'ends' (or outlying hamlets), the area of green might be extensive and it would be more true to say that houses were scattered along the green than that the green lay amongst the houses. Encroachments, allotments, metalled roads and cottage-gardens have greatly diminished the area of these 'casual' greens.

There is a small number of villages in all counties where the green is of greater area and of more significance in the village plan. The increased area is usually accompanied by a greater regularity of shape. The great triangular green around which stood the village of Nun Monkton, with the priory gate at the apex of the triangle, is illustrated in fig. 1.

Professor Thorpe has examined and analysed the villages of County Durham with large and regular greens, and his studies have been extended into Northumberland and southwards into Yorkshire and the Midlands.[14] He has shown that, in Durham, 101 out of 232 villages have greens, and that these are divided almost equally between three categories, 'street-green', 'broad-green' and 'indefinite-green', the latter only partly enclosed by houses. Houses which face the greens (often completely enclosing them) are old farmsteads, and where the common rights are still guarded these perimeter farms are usually the sole possessors of grazing rights.

[14] H. Thorpe, 'The green villages of County Durham', *Trans. Instit. Brit. Geog.* XV (1951) 153–80.

Encroachment on greens, like encroachment on market-places, must always have been possible with the assent of the lord and the common-right holders, and may well have taken place on other occasions without too nice an enquiry into the legal position. Schools and chapels are frequently found, the lord and commoners having agreed to the endowment; smithies were sometimes tolerated.

The regular green with farmsteads set around it will usually have a corresponding back-lane between crofts and the field-land, making an outer ring-lane. Streams flowing down the centre of the green and ponds set at intervals within it also occur widely. Professor Thorpe's analysis of the alignment of the street-greens in Durham has shown that 84 per cent lie with their longer axis on, or within 30 degrees of, the east-west line. Only a small proportion of these east-west alignments are determined by local physical features. The question arises, what caused one alignment to be more popular than another when extensive level ground near a settlement made it equally possible to face in any direction? The most likely answer lies, as in the question of the alignment of street-villages, with some existing trackway, possibly only of very minor character, which the first settlers found or created. In default of this explanation, chance factors or cultural traditions, which only a detailed examination of English and continental greens will reveal, may provide the key.

The deliberate placing of houses to leave a central green suggests that either the demarcation of this area or some advantage in the position of the houses was in mind when the form was first adopted. The central green can only have been required for animals; to drive them into a central stockade in troubled times has great advantages and is an idea that would easily come to mind. A ring of houses with their fenced or stockaded enclosures would be readily adaptable for defence, and would afford a well-marked perimeter conveniently served by the outer ring-lane when it had to be manned. Some form of perimeter earthwork might soon develop, even if it only consisted of the balk

Fig. 69. Milburn; looking E, July 1952.

marking the start of the open fields. The very small number of villages that have well-defined defensive earthworks may be held to show that large-scale defences were exceptional.

The illustrations chosen for this section show two village greens, one from the north and one from the east of England. Other photographs of greens (some much encroached upon) appear in figs. 1A, 2A, 28A, 39A, 42A, 52. In the smaller market-towns the market-places occupy sites which might well have been greens at an earlier date, just as abandoned market-places sometimes reverted to greens: the village green of Sheriff Hutton (fig. 63), for example, was the market-square when the Council of the North had its quarters in the castle.

69. MILBURN   Westmorland

No chance development in a growing settlement could have produced the deliberate pattern of this village (fig. 69), which lies just below the Cross Fell escarpment, six miles north of Appleby. Nor is there any question of the green being an extra-wide street. The roads of the district by-pass Milburn, and the lanes approaching from the main road come up to it in curving sweeps. The lanes into the fields leave surreptitiously by narrow gaps at the two upper corners of the green; short lengths of an original back-lane may be traced behind the houses on the right. The green at Milburn is a parade-ground to which the lanes give access, and not itself a much expanded lane. The only encroachment is that of the school. The parish church of St Cuthbert (not within the figure) is curiously placed some distance away beyond the main road. This may indicate that the village has moved, but no earthworks of an abandoned site have been traced in the fields near the church.

Fig. 70. South Elmham All Saints; looking NNW, April 1953.

A ring of narrow, hedged fields all but surrounds the village. Most of these contain plough-ridges, and they probably derive from early enclosure of strips of arable nearest to the village, the first land to be cleared from its natural state, and later, the first to be allowed to pass into individual ownership when other arable had become available by the spread of the fields. With the slopes of Cross Fell immediately behind the village there can never have been a shortage of pasture. Of the eight square miles of Milburn parish, less than half lies below the thousand-foot contour: the parish boundaries, like those of its neighbours, run back to the crest of the Pennines. Yet the early fourteenth-century tax-quota would not have disgraced a village in the Vale of York.[15]

[15] Milburn paid 31 shillings in 1334; this compares with an average of 27 shillings for the fertile parts of the Yorkshire plain.

The villages with regular greens which have been mentioned so far have been set in country characterised by open-field farming. Even as far north as Durham they are the villages of husbandmen and open fields, as is shown by the language of the *Bolden Book* and of the later bishops' surveys, and until the open fields were enclosed the majority of houses were found around the green. Of all the 'nucleated' village forms the green-village most deserves this description.

In these regular greens the grass has something of the character of a lawn. The more irregular greens, on the other hand, bear both in their wider extent and irregular shape the marks of being merely relics of heathland which has been retained as an open space after houses have grown up round about. This type of green has not the deliberateness and formality of a lawn; it is more like a garden which is still under grass because a new householder has not bothered to attend to it. Besides the farmhouses that lie round the edge of the green, there will be other old-established farms scattered elsewhere in the parish. The village church may be in an isolated position and not even near the green. Conditions such as these are commonly found in districts where there is much surviving heathland, such as the Weald, west Dorset or the Wyre Forest. They occur in a modified form in Suffolk and Essex where the reclamation of field-land has been carried much further.

70. SOUTH ELMHAM ALL SAINTS
Suffolk

In north Suffolk, between Bungay and Halesworth, there is a concentration of ruined, vanished or isolated churches equalled only in Norfolk or on the Lincolnshire Wolds. South Elmham is a curiosity in itself. The name is borne by seven adjacent parishes, making up an area of more than 6000 acres. The parishes are distinguished by the addition of saints' names, giving the local signposts for miles around a touch of ecclesiastical purple. Thus, there are South Elmham St Michael, South Elmham St Peter, South Elmham St Nicholas, South Elmham St James, South Elmham St Margaret and South Elmham St Cross. The seventh village is more comprehensive in nomenclature, being South Elmham All Saints.

None of the seven villages is particularly large. Including outlying farms, there was a total of some 200 farms and cottages in the first census of 1801. In 1327 there were 143 households wealthy enough to be taxed. The isolated and semi-isolated churches of Suffolk and Essex pose difficult problems of interpretation, like those of Herefordshire and Worcestershire west of the Severn. Often there is no village nucleus and all the farms in such parishes are widely scattered. The farms in the Elmhams and in the neighbouring four Ilketshalls are considerably dispersed, yet this is not an indication of late settlement; the villages and their separate churches are recorded in Domesday Book. The subdivision of the original territory represented by the combined Elmhams, as also that of the Ilketshalls, is a mysterious one, for which no certain explanation can yet be offered.[16]

Fig. 70 shows the largest of the Elmham greens, that at South Elmham All Saints. Its size and the incompleteness of the present built-up frontage are not the only distinctions of this green-village. Only a few yards over the parish boundary, approximately the lower margin of the photograph, is the parish church of Rumburgh. The parish church of South Elmham All Saints is still standing and in good repair but it will not be seen on the photograph. It lies a mile to the north-west, down a farm-track, within a large moated enclosure, near the earthworks of the manor house. Only a single farmstead occurs beside it.

No traces of earthworks of a former village can be seen near the isolated church, so that a migration is unlikely.[17] The occurrence of isolated and sometimes ruined churches bearing the names of villages which now exist only as a scatter of buildings round a small green some distance away, is an interesting feature of settlement in central and western Suffolk.[18] In this area, the relationship between village and church is to be thought of in different terms from those customary in the nucleated villages of the Midlands.[19]

[16] N. Scarfe, *The Suffolk Landscape* (1972) 112–27 and fig. 8, identifies the Elmhams as the *ferding* (farthing or quarter) of a Hundred, but despite several references to the importance of the Suffolk greens is not able to offer anything new to explain their isolation from their churches.

[17] South Elmham All Saints had been amalgamated with St Nicholas in 1737, St Nicholas having previously been amalgamated with St Mary's (Homersfield) in 1362.

[18] E.g. Linstead Magna with ruined church (TM 318763); Sotherton (TM 442796); Frostenden (TM 479818); Badley (TM 063560).

[19] Since the above comments were published in 1958 Dr Wade-Martins' work on cognate green-and-isolated-church settlements in Norfolk has begun to reveal something of the complex settlement history behind the modern forms. The Anglo-Saxon village site around North Elmham church was not utilised in the Middle Ages except as a green and a clay-pit, the villagers presumably being elsewhere. The question cannot be separated from the general one of multiple settlements and migration (above, p. 102).

PART THREE

THE TOWNS

8

FEATURES IN THE TOWN PLAN

I. INTRODUCTORY

Between village and borough there is no insuperable gulf. . . .

F. W. MAITLAND, *Township and Borough* (1898) 35

The exploration of villages and fields in Parts one and two began by setting air photographs alongside maps and surveys of the Tudor period. When the wealth and corporate life of the towns are considered it may seem surprising that the number of urban maps available for comparison is so small. A much larger proportion of those that do exist has, indeed, been engraved and printed, since publisher and bookseller could hope for many customers in populous towns like London, Norwich and Cambridge, which were among the first to have printed maps. These maps, and a few others known in manuscript, prove that it was not lack of skill which prevented the employment of surveyors to measure town streets, but the absence of those ambitions and uncertainties which drove rural landowners to commission maps. Only one danger seemed capable of arousing the authorities to employ surveyors, the fear of invasion. As the enclosing landlord needed to know his rights, so the coastal towns and ports needed an accurate plan of their defences when faced with a type of warfare different from that which the medieval walls had been built to oppose. Among the Cottonian manuscripts and the State Papers there is an interesting collection of Tudor town plans which have defences as a common feature[1] (see Berwick, fig. 79B).

The towns delineated in these plans, together with the much larger number without plans, occupied a different place in Elizabethan life and sentiment from the fields and villages so far considered; in size, wealth, function, and sometimes

in shape, the urban community of Norden's day was becoming so different from the village that Maitland's 'gulf' seemed very wide. The old-established towns looked jealously at the extension of privileges to newcomers, forgetting how many of the old-established had once themselves been newcomers.

Tax-lists and muster-rolls show that most Tudor towns were not only more densely populated but also wealthier than their village neighbours. The concentration of economic power had come through workshops and counters rather than by ploughs and animals. Fertility of soil may explain why one Elizabethan village was four times the size of another, but not why a town could be forty times the size of a village.

The protection afforded by walls and the freedom from feudal obligations had provided a climate in which trade and crafts could flourish more luxuriantly than in a village, and even when privilege hardened into jealous restriction of competition there were still enough advantages in town life to prevent every townsman and every occupation from fleeing countrywards. Administration, in particular, had become town-centred, and towns which were ports had a second chance of calling a new world into existence to redress the balance of declining crafts. Coastal towns might complain that Elizabethan London was taking the bread out of their mouths but they at least did not have to worry about the flight of the clothing crafts to the industrial villages.

Urban society, whose early growth had offered a way of life which was non-feudal and non-rural, an environment suited to crafts and trade, was nevertheless closely linked to the countryside, its reservoir of population and raw materials, the hinterland for its exports and imports. In York the metal trades used Yorkshire iron, the textile industries the Pennine and Wolds wools, the leather-workers the skins from local flocks and herds, the same animals which supplied the butchers of the Shambles. The oaks of the Forest of Galtres were used by

[1] The B.L. maps are in MSS. Cot. Aug. I, i; a typescript *List* of manuscript maps earlier than 1600 which have been found in the public records has now been compiled: Round Search Room, Public Record Office; Professor P. D. A. Harvey is editing a collection of annotated facsimiles of all known plans earlier than 1500.

tanners, carpenters and boat-builders, while the masons repaired churches and town walls with stone from the same limestone quarries that had been exploited for the original buildings. Lead for roofs was brought down the Ouse from Nidderdale and Swaledale; and, if the retailers of food and drink are added, the list covers all the principal occupations of the tax-list of 1381 and of the Elizabethan *subsidies*.

Unwin once attributed the growth of medieval towns to a geographical potentiality, a legal title and a social force. The air photograph may catch a glimpse of the first, but it is more adept at picturing some of the concomitants of growth, particularly the broad delineation of urban topographies.[2] The skill of townsmen, the enterprise of merchants, the degree of self-government, the character of the governing factions and the stringency of law and ordinance; these are subjects crucial to urban history which find no direct reflection in an air photograph. It has also been necessary to select only those towns where the medieval plan has not been too greatly altered or shrouded in the last two centuries, while flying restrictions have also precluded certain urban views. Other towns proved too large for their principal features to be embraced in a single oblique photograph.

Fortunately, between 1400 and 1700, town topography changed much more slowly than social structure. There was no revolution comparable to that which redivided the open fields by quickset hedges. The town plans of Norden and Speed, although not always completely representational, scarcely ever show streets, wharves, bridges, markets or walls in positions different from those indicated in rentals three centuries earlier. The fabric of houses had improved with the widespread use of stone and brick, but there was no general replanning, a task which would have roused even more of a hornet's nest than general enclosure.[3] The Dissolution of the religious houses made certain urban plots available for building, but it is unlikely that more than a handful of Tudor towns had populations growing fast enough to need more living room than could be satisfied by the taking in of orchards and gardens.

The crafts and commerce of towns can be illustrated here only by the growth of streets and houses, the product of these urban skills. In places the countryside still bears the scars of medieval industry (chapter 10), because the working of iron, salt and wool are no longer carried out in the same districts. But towns have usually continued as the seat of manufacture on a scale which effectively obliterates archaeological traces of medieval industry. Yet even before the Industrial Revolution it is unlikely that the industries of medieval towns would have formed a good subject for air photography. For cloth-making perhaps a row of tenter-frames on the grass; from dye-houses and breweries a little smoke; from the millraces and windmill sails it might be deduced that power was being harnessed, but much manufacture was being carried on without water-power in small workshops whose smoke was indistinguishable from that of the homes.

The characteristic of all the Tudor towns, in distinction to villages, was the very number of roofs which sheltered such activity. In their present density of population the air photograph may catch something of the crowded topography of medieval towns, of which York and Nottingham are first taken as general examples before passing to particular features in later sections. York is chosen because it preserves much of the medieval form; the walls still stand for most of their circuit, the street plan is little confused by subsequent development. Consequently the analysis of the medieval topography is straightforward. Nottingham, in contrast, lost its medieval walls long ago and much of the old street plan is obscured by overriding 'urban-motorways' or other development. Yet the shape of the Anglian and Norman boroughs may still be traced amidst the modern city, despite several centuries of piecemeal rebuilding to meet the changing needs of the citizens.

[2] There is as yet no comprehensive study of urban topography in England. The *Historic Towns* atlas of the British Isles, ed. M. D. Lobel, when completed, will be an essential source; two collections have so far been published, in 1969 and in 1975. The subject has been approached in T. H. Hughes and E. A. G. Lamborn, *Towns and Town Planning* (1923), a study with wider scope than the title might suggest, and recently in M. W. Barley, ed., *The Plans and Topography of Medieval Towns in England and Wales* (1975), in M. Aston and J. Bond, *The Landscape of Towns* (1976) and in C. Platt, *Medieval Towns* (1976). Some excellent local studies, with plans, have appeared in the *Archaeological Journal*, *passim*. Recent regional surveys included in the *Handbooks* of the British Association's Summer Meetings have sometimes dealt with urban matters.

[3] The important influence of the open fields on a town's economy and plan was first discussed with reference to Cambridge, in F. W. Maitland, *Township and Borough* (1898). More recent local studies on this theme include C. J. Bilson, 'The open fields of Leicester', *Trans. Leics. Arch. Soc.* XIV (1925–6) 10–19; D. Charman, 'Leicester in 1525', *ibid.* XXVII (1951) 19–29; R. M. Butler, 'The common lands of the borough of Nottingham', *Trans. Thoroton Soc.* LIV (1950) 45–62; J. D. Chambers, *Modern Nottingham in the Making* (1945).

71. YORK

The dominant feature in the townscape of York is the Minster. In the vertical photograph (fig. 71), its south facade is illuminated by bright sunshine and the towers cast long shadows across the grass of the precinct to the north. The Minster was consecrated in the seventh century, but the earliest influence still evident in the topography of medieval York is the Roman fortress within which the great church stands (see the key). The fortress, some fifty acres in area, was founded in about AD 71–2, at a little distance from the north-east bank of the Ouse. A civilian settlement, which later attained the status of a *colonia*, grew up on the opposite bank. The medieval wall around the south-west part of the present city probably follows the boundary of the *colonia*. The wall can be traced on the photograph (fig. 71), as the thin line of the thirteenth-century stone wall runs along the crest of the broad, grassy rampart of the eleventh century, appearing from the air as a cordon of open ground between the densely built-up city and its suburbs. On the north-east bank, the influence of Roman works on later development is more certain. The rectangular fortress was re-occupied in the Anglo-Saxon period and subsequently, from 867, by the Danes. The population of the city increased to overflow the limits of the fortress and to spread across the habitable land between the rivers. By 950 a new earthern rampart had been built far out beyond the Roman south-east wall (see the key-map). The city continued to grow and the medieval circuit came to encompass the fortress on the north-east bank and the land beside it down to the Ouse and to the Foss, the *colonia* on the south-west bank, and, lastly, a kite-shaped area south-east of the Foss. The circuit of the defences, as remarkably preserved as any in England, encloses an area of 263 acres, about half that of the city of London.

The key-map shows the main medieval features visible on the vertical photograph, the position of earlier lines of defence, the sites of medieval churches, and, in addition, the extent of the now vanished pools of the Foss which are missing links in the defences of the city. The Ouse at York is crossed by a railway bridge (top left of the photograph), and by three road bridges of which only the middle one, *Ouse Bridge*, was medieval. The other two, which are modern, stand conveniently to mark the points at which the walls of both parts of the city come down to the water's edge. At these points, where the river offered a passage through the land defences, a boom or chain was hung to complete the circuit. The north-west and north-east walls, framing the Minster in their angle, preserve the corresponding walls of the Roman fortress. The line of one of these walls was extended south-eastwards towards the Foss, the line of the other was followed to the western angle-tower and then along part of the south-west side, before the medieval wall turned away to the river-bank, ending at the *Lendal Tower*. The position of the abandoned fortress walls is marked on the key.

The southern side of the city was defended by two castles which William I built in 1068 or 1069. Both were destroyed by the Danes in September 1069 but were rebuilt by the end of that year. Of one, the *Old Baile*, the motte is now a low mound, crowned by trees; the ditches and ramparts are partly incorporated in the town wall. The other castle was built on the neck of land between the rivers: a low-lying site at some distance from the heart of the city. Documents record that houses had to be demolished to clear the ground; evidence that settlement had spread thus far from the fortress by 1069. After its early destruction the castle was strengthened with water defences achieved by damming the Foss to form a broad pool on the east side. This work caused a further flooding a little way up-river where a second, much larger, pool was formed. Domesday Book records that 'the King's pool destroyed two new mills worth twenty shillings and of arable land and meadows and gardens fully one carucate' (about 150 acres). The dam also blocked the Foss to navigation and confined the city's wharves to the Ouse waterfront. The castle, built first of timber, was twice destroyed and rebuilt in 1069 and in 1190, was reconstructed in stone by Henry III in 1245–70 and has undergone much alteration since then. All that now remains is the motte and Clifford's Tower and part of the bailey wall; the moats are filled in and now provide space for roads and car-parks.

The early growth of a suburb south-eastward along *Walmgate* over the Foss necessitated the construction of defences for its protection; *Walmgate Bar* and, presumably, the rampart through which it gave passage, were in existence by the mid-twelfth century. This sector was not given a wall of stone until 1345. Outside the north-west wall, St Mary's Abbey was established, the foundation stone being laid in 1089. In 1266 the abbey precinct was enclosed with a wall to form, between *Bootham* and the Ouse, an annexe to the city. Much of the plan of the abbey church, of which the foundations have been laid bare by excavation, can be distinguished between trees (fig. 71).

Fig. 71. York; vertical photograph, November 1972. Scale 1:12 000.

Just as the walls partly adopt and partly ignore the Roman plan, so do the medieval streets. The axial NW–SE road of the fortress is still followed approximately by *Petergate*, from *Bootham Bar*, which is the only medieval gate on the site of a Roman one, to a point near the junction with *Goodramgate*. *Stonegate* records in the name its Roman origin but its course to the north-east gate was interrupted by the building of the enlarged minster and the growth of an ecclesiastical precinct. The north-east gate was moved to *Monk Bar* at the mid-point of the extended wall. The site of the Roman bridge across the Ouse is lost, but it may be presumed to have lain where the line of *Stonegate* would meet the river.

Micklegate, on the south-west bank, runs at first from the entrance of the *colonia* towards the same point, but shortly diverts towards the medieval crossing at *Ouse Bridge*. The expansion of the settlement eastward beyond the fortress before the Norman Conquest is attested by several features: the number of Anglo-Saxon churches beyond the limits of the fortress, the extended defences built by the Danes, and a record of houses destroyed to clear a site for William I's castle. Additional evidence is found in the placing of the principal market-places. The oldest, which came to be known as the *Thursday Market*, lay near St Sampson's church, of which the parish boundary (see key-map) pays scant heed

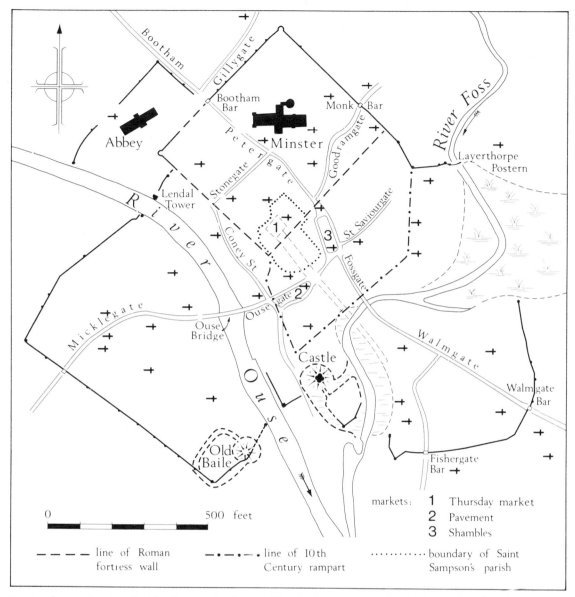

Key to the medieval and older features in fig. 71. The Latin crosses mark positions of medieval churches.

to the line of the Roman wall. A second medieval market-place occupied an oval space, now built over, where *Pavement* joins *Ousegate*, below the modern market-place. The similar arrangement of the streets near the *Shambles* implies encroachment on a third market-place outside the Roman south-east gate, and two 'flesh-benches' here (*duos bancos in macello*) were mentioned in Domesday Book. In the later Middle Ages, York had markets for specialised commodities in almost every available open space, from the riverside fishmongers' staithes to the butter-market in Micklegate on the south bank. Neither the cathedral church of St Peter nor the castle had a market-place outside it. Together, the *Shambles*, *Pavement* and *Thursday Markets* made up one of the ancient, pre-Norman wards, each bearing the name of *shire*. This area was *Marketshire*, and the first Guildhall may have stood in it and not, as later, by the river. The city's three great annual fairs were held outside the walls in the more spacious atmosphere of *Gillygate* (= St Giles' Gate) top left, part of the suburb of *Bootham* (= of the booths).

Fig. 72. Nottingham; vertical photograph, July 1971. Scale 1:8000.

The air photograph gives a good impression of the web of narrow and winding streets. The density of the medieval population is suggested by the number of churches marked on the key, but can also be given quantitative expression. The five acres of the parish of St Sampson, in which *Thursday Market* lay, maintained in 1377 a population of eighty taxpayers per acre, more than 2000 times the density in the parishes of the adjacent countryside and more than twice the average density in the city of London. In 1377 neither city could have recovered from the Black Death, so the early fourteenth-century populations were probably higher. The survival of another tax-list from 1381 indicates that St Sampson's was a parish in which the metal-using crafts were concentrated, just as the next parish had nineteen butchers listed one after the other as if the collectors were moving down the Shambles. And as significant as the density are the surnames; of the hundred or so male taxpayers thirty-eight had surnames taken from Yorkshire villages whence their paternal ancestors had been attracted by city life.

Sources

R. H. Skaife, *Historical Map of York* (1864); G. Benson, *Later Medieval York* (1919), plans; 1377: E. 179/217/13; 1381: J. N. Bartlett, 'The lay poll tax returns for the city of York', *Trans. E.R. Ant. Soc.* XXX (1953) 1–91; G. T. Clarke, 'The defences of York', *Yorks. Arch. Jnl* IV (1877) 1–42; A. Raine, *Medieval York* (1955); *V.C.H. City of York*, (1961); R.C.H.M., *City of York* I (1962), II (1972), III (1972), and IV (1975); the York Archaeological Trust maintains a programme of excavation in the city wherever opportunity offers. The results have greatly increased knowledge of the history of York and will no doubt continue to do so.

72. NOTTINGHAM

The area of our vertical photograph corresponds to that of the plans of Nottingham in the *Historic Towns* atlas, and the commentary is based on the historical account there given by Professor Barley and Mr Straw. The principal plan in the atlas reconstructed the topography of the county town *c.* 1800. At that date there were many more medieval buildings, domestic and public, sur-

176

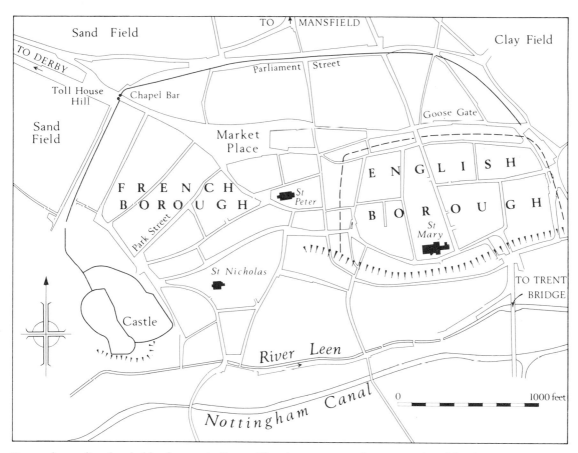

Key to the medieval and older features in fig. 72. The plan represents the topography of the city as it was *c.* 1800. The difficulty of matching an ancient to a modern townscape will be evident; the River Leen, for example, is no longer visible.

viving in the streets of the town than today, and some ground within the medieval walls was still not built over, especially in the south-west and north-east. A vertical air photograph on the scale of fig. 72 would hardly distinguish a medieval roof, had any now survived, but it does show the influence of the medieval street pattern on the town centre, despite nineteenth-century railway lines and marshalling yards and twentieth-century urban motorways. In 1800, and indeed in 1939, virtually every street in the town followed the line of a street either of the Anglian or the Norman borough. The town wall and ditch did not survive long enough to be themselves an impediment to building development, but their influence was stronger than in most English towns. Nottingham has often been cited as a nineteenth-century town whose courtyard housing and congestion were a result of the restricted area of land available. Outside the borough development was only possible along the Derby and Mansfield roads leading from the west and north gates of the medieval borough.

The boundary of the nineteenth-century town followed the line of the medieval defences even though almost all visible traces of these had long since gone. The impediment to building on land outside the borough arose rather from the presence of two large unenclosed common fields, *Sand Field* on the north-west and north, and *Clay Field* on the north. For political as well as economic reasons these were not enclosed until 1845 when streets such as those towards the top left-hand corner of fig. 72 could be built.

Consider, for example, the broad road across the top of the photograph, starting at a large roundabout (top left). This roundabout is on Toll House Hill, an open space outside the north-west gate of the town, *Chapel Bar*, which stood till 1743; the present road is the widened Parliament Street, formerly *Backside*, but in the early seventeenth century sufficient space between then existing building-lines for so wide a street was only possible because it followed the line of the filled-in town ditch and the demolished wall, occupying their combined widths. The curve of this road at its eastern end follows that of the medieval defences, coming round to the east gate.

A second and narrower road leading south-eastward from the roundabout on Toll House Hill soon widens into an open triangle, but readers who have studied the encroachments on medieval market-places in other photographs will at once recognise that the three blocks of properties to the east have invaded what was once a much longer market-triangle; the most western of the three is the present open market-place, and the city hall has been built on the middle block where the stocks and pillory once stood. The apex of the triangle, at the right-hand end of the third block, is a key point in the interpretation of the historic plan of the medieval town, and we shall return there in a moment.

After these conservative street-lines, one radical departure: the third of the roads coming into the town from the roundabout where we began is broader than either of the two so far considered, and its direct course was driven in the 1950s right across old street-lines. The clearest of these is Park Street, running from the south-west corner of the market-place to the castle and crossed by the new road at a small roundabout (centre left). The present buildings of Nottingham castle, set on a crag 133 feet high, are not medieval. The line of the medieval walls can, however, be followed round the open grass of the inner bailey, while trees and formal gardens mark the site of the outer bailey.

Nottingham's defences and street-lines have been treated as medieval. In fact, the streets and market-place so far described, having defences set out in the first half of the twelfth century, lie outside the original core of the town. This 'French' borough, as it continues to be called, was an appendage, enlarging an existing Anglian *burh*, the 'English' borough, with its own defences, streets and church. Within the new ambit of defences – some 120 acres – the northern and western walls of the *burh* were abandoned, and by 1086 houses had been built over the ditch. But the distinction survived; in the Middle Ages each borough had its own sheriff and bailiff. To trace the perimeter of this thirty-two acre *burh* in modern street-lines we must return to the apex of the triangle at the east of the market-place. Like the castle and the churches of St Peter and St Nicholas, the market-place was a new creation, lying wholly outside the *burh* which William I found as the shire town. The

apex of the triangle leads into Goose Gate, a street which was laid out along the northern side of the earthen wall and ditch that protected the *burh*. The Norman borough followed the Anglian line of defence only on the east and south. On the east, this took the form of a rampart and ditch: the existence of an east gate has already been indicated. On the south a fifty-foot sandstone cliff provided a natural line of defence overlooking the Trent crossing.

The modern road to the Trent bridge is the broad avenue crossed by the railway, bottom right, and in building the approach roads to this avenue the original plan has been obliterated. The vanished defences of the *burh*, within the Norman borough, lie for the most part between two rings of streets (see the key): an inner ring along which the house-plots extended back to the shelter of the town rampart, and an outer ring, developed in the Norman borough. As building progressed along the outer ring the significance of the early circuit of defences was lost until eventually its course was only preserved in terms of property boundaries. The inner perimeter road is best seen on the south side where it passes by St Mary's, the town's first church, and on the west where it curves northwards in correspondence with the defences of the *burh*.

The ground to the south of the boroughs has been completely transformed by the construction of a canal and railways, occupying meadows on the flood-plain of the Trent. The wider road to the Trent bridge now starts at a roundabout lying near the south-east corner of the *burh*. The road is in turn crossed by, then crosses, railways, to pass through half a mile of Victorian suburbs before reaching the Trent.

Sources

M. D. Lobel, ed., *Historic Towns* I (1969), Nottingham section; K. C. Edwards, *Nottingham and Its Region* (1956) 363ff; J. D. Chambers, *Modern Nottingham in the Making* (1945); R. M. Butler, 'The common lands of the borough of Nottingham', *Trans. Thoroton Soc.*, LIV (1950); recent excavations within the *burh*: *Med. Arch.* XVII (1973), 147–8, 170. A. Rogers, 'Parish boundaries and urban history', *Jnl Brit. Arch. Assoc.* 3rd. ser. XXXV (1972) 51–6, draws attention to the market-place lying outside the two new Norman parishes of St Peter and St Nicholas. The present site would seem therefore to be secondary: the primary site has not been determined. Perhaps it lay at the castle gate.

II. THE MARKET-PLACE

The urban features considered separately in succeeding pages were all to be found in medieval and Tudor York: walls, defences and gates, castles, cathedrals and monasteries, market-places and wharves. They may be considered both as products of medieval economic life, not essentially different from a windmill or a field, and as formative influences on the topography of a town. Walls which were integral to the survival of a town at one stage in its history might become physical barriers to expansion in another. Market-places remained in active use longer than walls but were early determinants of the alignment of streets and the position of houses, shops and manufactories. Walls and market-places were to the town what the fields were to a village: the sign of past achievement and of assets to be carefully guarded; the means by which the daily life of the community continued to be sustained; and, rightly used, the means to future prosperity and expansion.

A market-place was a feature of almost all towns, and some, like King's Lynn, Thirsk and Hertford, had two, for no town existed without trade although many managed to survive without either walls or a castle. The figures which follow illustrate a few towns where the market-place has had a significant role, but many other photographs inevitably have included this feature. Its importance is seen in the newly planned towns (chapter 9), not all of which had walls and gates, but every one a market-place.

The market-place showed that petty, day-by-day barter and sale, natural to any community, had begun to loom large enough to need space for concourse of townsmen and country visitors, their goods and animals. In the larger towns, even before the expulsion of money-changers from the churchyards, more elbow-room had been needed than could be found in front of a church porch. In some towns the main street was wide enough to make a market out of a former green; elsewhere, the street was widened uniformly; in others the market-place assumed the characteristic square or triangle which the air photographs so commonly reveal. Usually the market-place was laid out too early in a town's history for documents to show whether or not houses had to be cleared to make it.

The existence of a market-place was also a sign that the privilege of conducting a market, and often also a fair, had been obtained. The grant of such permission was an important way by which territorial landowners, from the king downwards, could augment their incomes. It also provided a centre from which the lord's household could be provisioned, and a convenient place to market the surplus from his demesne when his own needs had been met. Like the grant of a borough charter, it enabled a landowner to share in the proceeds of trade, and by offering opportunity for trade it gave townsmen the chance of earning income which the king or the lord would share. If the townsmen contracted to pay a fixed annual sum for their charter the risks of profit and loss had been passed on to them with every incentive so to organise trading that losses never came into the question. Such organisation was best served by a fixed and public venue at fixed times and by keen scrutiny of all other dealing. Only in the largest fairs, when the congregation of traders was too great to be confined to the market-place, does trading seem to have been allowed to spread outside the usual bounds. The great fairs at St Ives (fig. 73) show this pressure on space pushing the booths out along the side-streets into the fields, over the meadows and even on to the arable strips in the open fields north of the town. What did it matter if crops were trampled for a few weeks in spring time when the rent paid for a stall or the profit made by trading was more than compensation? When the merchants had gone, St Ives reverted to its role of a small market-town with the calmer weekly concourse of local dealers confining themselves to the long street-market-place, sufficient for ordinary needs.

In the earlier medieval market-places the shelter for goods, tradesmen and clients was as temporary as it had been in the churchyards. Early town rentals record payments for permanent buildings along the street-frontages, ordinary houses which were also *shoppae*: but with these often went the right to set up booths in the street facing the particular house. Thus the market-place began to fill. In addition there were payments to the market-authority from those townsmen whose houses did not abut the market-place and who needed to bring out their stalls to display their goods. Finally there were the out-tradesmen, craftsmen-merchants and villagers who came in only on market-days or at fair times.

The diminished area of many medieval market-places can obscure appreciation of their medieval scale. A town in which Market Street broadens for only a few yards and is surrounded by narrow streets may suggest a false deduction: that little stock was set by having room to trade.

Fig. 73A. St Ives; vertical photograph, May 1967. Scale 1:4450.

But from the air, as indeed by the intelligent study of a large-scale map, the unity of the original great triangles and squares can be restored despite their fragmentation by the encroachment of post-medieval building when townsmen were hungry for house-room and tradesmen anxious for permanent shelter.

As Chelmsford (fig. 96) shows, permanent encroachment was not necessarily a sign that the trading function of a town had ceased and that townsmen had become careless of access to their market-place. On the contrary, the erection of substantial wooden or stone buildings might indicate that there was enough trade to make it worth while having a permanent stall there, even at a correspondingly greater rent. The lords of the market, whether king, seigneur or burgesses, saw that it was to their interest both as traders and as rent-receivers if the canvas-roofed stall were to become a tiled *shoppa*.

The greatest resistance to encroachments on market-places would come in towns where the business of the market was centred principally upon animals. Leather, cloth, pottery, shoes,

yarn, food: all these commodities need only shelf and counter room, while animals need pens or tethering-posts. Many towns solved the dilemma in the nineteenth century by building sheep- and cattle-markets on their perimeter near the roads along which the herds came, and ultimately near railway sidings.[4] No such solution was possible in the Middle Ages when it was the essence of a market that it should be held in the fullest light of day and that its entrances and exits should be in as public positions as possible.

The interests of the consumers and of the market-authority ran in the same direction. The medieval market was haunted by the shadow of scarcity, particularly by scarcity artificially contrived. The enemies of society and good order were the men who bought large quantities to secure a corner in a commodity; and the men who sought to side-track the market by intercepting the seller on his way to the town. The

[4] Royston has a post-medieval market-place (fig. 77) to the south-east of the old market, probably to avoid congestion of the main thoroughfare where the medieval market lay.

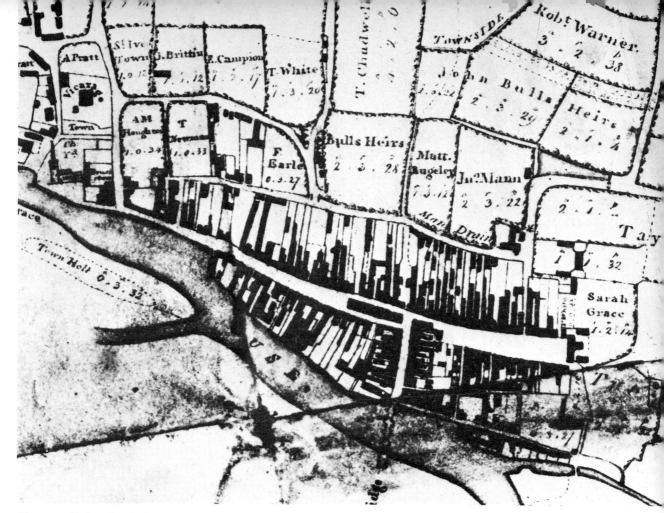

Fig. 73B. St Ives in 1808.

topography of the market-place cannot be appreciated if it is regarded only as a place of congregation. It is a place of supervision and regulation.

In a walled and gated town the entrance and egress of market-goers could be rigorously watched. In the smaller and unwalled towns and especially in towns planned *de novo* there is often a significant concentration of roads leading to the corners of the market-place, so that the stream of rural traffic had to pass along controlled channels. The photograph of Castle Donington (fig. 60) shows this feature well.

The close relation of the market-place to the church is found even in towns where there is no dominating seigniorial castle. Thus the church may occupy an island in the market-place or, most commonly, stand at one end or at the side of it. There is no doubt that the earliest places of congregation were at the church door and in the churchyards, just as the earliest occasions for congregation were the days when people were drawn to the festivals of the church year. The close connection between the day of the patronal

saint of the parish church and the day of local fairs has often been noticed, and it is clear that the ordinary weekly market was commonly held on Sunday when the parishioners were brought together at church. It took a great deal of papal exhortation and royal orders before the markets forsook Sundays and the booths left the churchyard. In the larger towns it is probable that the space required would already have necessitated a street-market as well as a churchyard-market, but in smaller towns the heyday of the street-market may date from the time when churchyards fell in disfavour, that is in the late thirteenth century; the Statute of Winchester (1285) ordered 'henceforth neither Fairs nor Markets be kept in Church Yards for the Honour of the Church'. In the monastic boroughs it was only natural for the market-place to be set outside the abbey gate within the view and protection of its lord.

The photographs which follow show market-places which vary in size and position. Many of them still form the focus of their town. An old-established market-place set in accordance with the economic advantage of one period was always likely to find itself marooned if economic conditions changed; for example, an old main road giving way to a new route which by-passed the market-place. As well as deserted villages, England has its deserted market-places. Local examples come to mind in many areas, but two striking Yorkshire examples are the great cobbled market-place of east-bank Thirsk rather like a Hogarth drawing without its characters; and the grass-covered square of Sheriff Hutton lying between the church and the castle (fig. 63).

73. ST IVES   Huntingdonshire

The topography of this important medieval commercial centre shows clearly the two stages in its development: the addition of trading activities to an already well-established agricultural village. In the manor of Slepe, on the banks of the Ouse, Domesday Book recorded twenty-nine ploughs. The parish still contains 2325 acres of fields and meadows, 1400 acres remaining unenclosed open fields until 1801. The township was acquired by Ramsey Abbey late in the tenth century. A church was recorded in Domesday Book and its successor can be seen beyond the island in the Ouse, at the west (left-hand) end of the modern town which stands on the north bank (fig. 73 A).

Ramsey Abbey's estates extended from the Nene southwards to the Ouse. The road from Ramsey enters St Ives to the right of the church, and the original centre of the agricultural village lay thereabouts, probably by a ford. It was the riverside potentialities of Slepe which induced the abbey to make something more of this property.

A bridge was constructed farther downstream so that traffic from Ramsey then entered the town by the church, turned along the river bank and then turned again to the bridgehead. Once across the river, a direct road led to Ermine Street and London. A wooden bridge is known to have been standing in 1107.

By that time, the travellers crossing the bridge would be more interested in St Ives than Ramsey. In 1110 the abbey obtained licence to hold a fair during Easter week on the open ground between the church of Slepe and the bridge, and the Ramsey Cartulary shows successive grants of permission to abbey tenants to build permanent houses along two main frontages between church and bridge.

These buildings marked out a long, narrow triangle with the church of Slepe at its apex (left) and the early eleventh-century priory at its base

beyond a green. Three streams of traffic led into this great marketplace, or *Strata* as it appears in medieval rentals: one at either end, from Ramsey and Ely, and the third across the river from the south.

The contrast between the cluster of houses at Slepe and the ordered frontages of houses in the market-town is clearly distinguishable in fig. 73 B, a map of the town in 1808, and in the modern appearance of the town. A back-street (now called East and West Streets) runs behind the main street for the whole of its length. Narrower lanes in similar positions behind the houses in Bridge Street appear in the map of 1808.

In and among these streets the fair grew to be one of the four great annual occasions in England when medieval buyers and sellers met to do business. Its peak of prosperity was the thirteenth century. In the late fourteenth century the abbot's income from tolls and fines had fallen, and there were empty tenements.

The name of Slepe had given way by 1200 to that of the saint whose bones were laid here early in the eleventh century, but the distinction between the old village and the new *vicus*, the *Strata* (Street) of St Ives, was still remembered in Ramsey rentals and in the divisions of the Exchequer tax-assessments.

The integration of field and town life at St Ives was not broken. It was only a step from the cluster of houses at the bridgehead, where the abbey stored carts and packs, to the open fields and the riverside grazing. There was never a great concentration of manufactures here; the occupation was trading, and the great international fair lasted only one week. When the strangers had gone the abbey's tenants could turn their minds again to the agricultural tasks which fall in the period after Eastertide.

St Ives never achieved municipal standing. Its courts were the courts of the Abbot of Ramsey as lord of the manor, and he obtained the profits of tolls and jurisdiction. The houses and stalls were rented from him at customary tenures, and in most buildings he reserved the right to occupy or let rooms at fair-time. With traders from so many towns and countries, jurisdiction was always a profitable asset. Along the main streets were the Rows, named after their merchandise or their merchants. Thus, in the records of the Court of Pie Powder and the Ramsey Cartulary there occur Barkers' Row, Spicers' Row, Skinners' Row and Canvas Row; Ypres Row, French Row, Lincoln Row, Beverley Row and Leicester Row. These names indicate the nature of the trades. The French merchants were selling their wine, and the English cloth merchants were

Fig. 74. St Neots; looking NW, with Eynesbury in the foreground, April 1959.

offering the fine quality cloths of the weaving cities. Henry III set the fashion of purchasing here all the cloth for the annual issue of royal liveries. Wool and hides were also dealt in, while petty disputes involved men from Fish Lane and Barbers' Lane.

The old wooden bridge was replaced by the present bridge about 1414. The stone, it may be noted, came from Barnack (fig. 106). It is no longer possible to see the original width of the *Strata*, fully forty yards, as it was in the Middle Ages. With the contraction of the market, the centre of this space had already been partly built over by 1808 (fig. 73 B) and there has since been further encroachment at its eastern end (fig. 73 A).

Sources

V.C.H. Hunts. II (1932) 210–23; R.C.H.M. Huntingdonshire (1926) 213–20; 1279; *Rot. Hund.* II. 603; temp. Edw. I: S.C. 11/10; 1396: S.C. 11/320; map of 1808: U.L.C., Maps bb. 66. 93. 7.

74. ST NEOTS   Huntingdonshire

St Neots (fig. 74) is set on the right (east) bank of the Ouse, half a mile from the trunk-road (A1)

which leads northwards on the opposite side of the valley. The traffic which passes through its market-place is mainly east–west traffic from Cambridgeshire to Northampton or Leicester. Superficially, St Neots and St Ives have much in common: each stands on a navigable reach of the Ouse; each has a shrine of a remote saint; at each a bridge has replaced a ford, and a T-shaped street plan has developed. But St Neots was essentially a local market-town and never the centre of a great fair. Lying fifteen miles upstream from St Ives, with Huntingdon intervening, St Neots was less well placed to compete for seaward traffic.

Eynesbury was the Slepe of St Neots, an older agricultural settlement on higher ground a few hundred yards from the river. The expansion of the settlement seems to date from the transfer of the relics of the saint from Cornwall in the late tenth century. It was not until 1113 that the priory at the saint's shrine came to possess the whole manor of Eynesbury, which was less integrated with the market-town than Slepe. However, St Neots had a field-area of 3700 acres and was no more shop-bound all the year round than St Ives.

The bridge at St Neots which replaced the ford at Eynesbury (Eaton Ford) has been the dominant factor in the development of the town plan. The rectangular market-place was formed in Bridge Street itself, possibly because the priory lay in this quarter. The broad, open space can just be distinguished to the right of the bridge. On the left of the bridge, as at St Ives and Godmanchester, a raised causeway carries the road across the flood-meadows. The site of the priory to which the town owed its medieval prosperity, and indeed its very existence, is now covered by a brewery comprising the large buildings on the east bank of the Ouse above the bridge. As at St Ives the continued local market function of the town maintained prosperity, and very little medieval work is now to be seen. The right background is dominated by the parish church of St Mary, the sign of the separation of St Neots from Eynesbury in 1214, but it, too, was largely rebuilt between 1400 and 1530, and the proud west tower is early Tudor. A plan of 1757 shows the market-place covered with houses, encroachments that have now been cleared. The church of Eynesbury, the parent village, stands in the foreground.

Sources

R.C.H.M. *Huntingdonshire* (1926) 220–8; maps of 1757: U.L.C. Atlas 1/93/4/18–20, 24, 33; rental, temp. Henry VIII: S.C. 12/31/22; G. C. Garham, *History of Eynesbury and St Neots* (1824); *V.C.H. Hunts.* II (1932) 337.

Not every monastic house attracted settlers to its gates and created a market-place within sight and jurisdiction of the abbey. The northern Cistercian houses in particular, with remote situations and an initial tradition of isolation, present a marked contrast to foundations like Battle and Ramsey. The absence of a market-place did not preclude commercial activity; there were few more active traders than the monks of Fountains, Kirkstall, Rievaulx or Jervaulx. Yet none of these had market-places and villages.[5] When the abbeys of the dales sought market-charters it was for a dependent village some distance from their gates. Bolton Priory obtained one at Appletreewick, and Jervaulx at East Witton (fig. 39). The Templars were more active creators of markets and market-towns (figs. 68 and 99) and showed a willingness to call one into existence if no settlement was already there, but they were

not always successful. In 1227 they obtained a charter for a weekly market and fair at Walshford Bridge on the Great North Road, but within thirteen years found it more advantageous to transfer the place of trading to the town of Wetherby, three and a half miles farther south at the Wharfe crossing.

The next two towns (Burford and Chipping Campden) have much in common with St Neots and St Ives. But their closest kinship is with the smaller market-villages having a wide main street and a total number of houses that was never large. Burford and Campden are the nearest approach to the town which is but a 'grown-up' village, Maitland's 'gulf' being here, in the topographical sense, at its narrowest.

75. BURFORD   Oxfordshire

At Burford, seen in the photograph (fig. 75) from the south, the whole of the broad main street served as the market-place. Thanks to the patient work of Mr R. H. Gretton the history of this Cotswold borough, seventeen miles west-north-west of Oxford, has been well explored.

Medieval Burford was centred upon the long High Street which led from the 'ford by the *burh*' at the Windrush crossing, early replaced by a bridge. The river may be seen near the top of the photograph, with the diverted millrace following a more circuitous course to the 'Town Mills' just to the left of the bridge.

Although Burford was not walled, the built-up area has remained remarkably compact. The upper part of the High Street, in the foreground with the double row of trees, lay outside the medieval town. Sixteenth-century documents show new houses creeping out in this direction. Nor did the medieval town extend beyond the line of Pytts Lane, the open street on the right and parallel to High Street. A survey made in 1552 records sheep driven to water down this lane from the pastures on the higher ground.

The main London to Northleach road has by-passed Burford since 1812. The medieval road, however, took a riverside course, crossing the High Street in the centre of Burford, where stood three of the medieval inns, the George, the Crown and the Bull. High Street itself forms part of the main road from Lechlade to Stow-on-the-Wold and Chipping Norton.

The parish church, much rebuilt and redecorated in the century after 1390, stands in the background at the north-east corner of the town. Its guild-chapel of the Blessed Virgin, built in the thirteenth century, was extended eastwards in the fifteenth to reach the south

---

[5] Whitby is an exception, though the vertical distance between the riverside port and the cliff-top abbey effectively isolated the latter. The position was prejudiced by the pre-Conquest abbey site.

Fig. 75. Burford; looking N down the High Street to the River Windrush, April 1961.

porch. This chapel can be seen projecting beyond the west (left) end of the church. When the estates of the chapel were surveyed in 1547 the town was described as 'a very great market town replenished with much people'. A survey of 1552 records 140 houses, and a rental of 1596

185

Fig. 76. Chipping Campden; looking NE, April 1953.

adds another forty. At the end of the seventeenth century there were 130 houses claiming full burgage rights, and a plan drawn in 1797 shows about a hundred houses on each side of High Street, approximately the same number as in the photograph.

After the opening of a local quarry many of the inns, houses and shops were wholly or partially rebuilt in stone, although a number of survivals show that the upper storeys might be left with plastered wattle and daub even when the base was stone.

The open fields and the common pasture lay upon the higher ground, south of the town, where two completely agricultural hamlets, Upton and Signet, were included in the parish; there were fifty taxpayers in these in 1377.

The burghal history of Burford is curious. Sir Lawrence Tanfield bought the manorial rights from the Crown in 1617 and within three years a succession of lawsuits showed that the claims of

the townsmen to possess a fully fledged borough were illusory. In 1086 Burford was a village of some forty households. Between 1088 and 1107 the village had been granted the right to have a Gild Merchant as well as other privileges associated with the setting up of a borough: the inhabitants were to pay a money rent; they could dispose freely of their property; and a market was granted. But the privileges went no further. The townsmen never paid a fee-farm and they never had the return of writs. In 1617 they knew that there were sums paid to the lord of the manor from the market-dues and thought that these represented the fee-farm. The fatal weakness of their case was that no charter could be produced. Even when King John was temporarily lord of the town there was no widening of the burgesses' privilege by a new charter: Burford was a seigneur's borough.

It is surprising that the lords of Burford had been content with such legal confusion at the time of prosperity in the later Middle Ages. Set at the junction of important Cotswold roads the town was well placed as a market in wool and cloth. A record of tolls granted for the repair of the bridge in 1322 gives a long list of the goods coming in to the markets and fairs, *de rebus venalibus ultra pontem transeuntibus*: livestock, hides, meat, fish, metal, wood, charcoal, wine, cheese and dairy products as well as fleeces and woollens.

Sources

R. H. Gretton, *The Burford Records* (1920); M. S. Gretton, *Burford Past and Present* (2nd edn 1929).

76. CHIPPING CAMPDEN
Gloucestershire

There is no reason why the broad market-street of a town should be as straight as at Burford. Local geography often imposed a sinuous course upon village streets and a market-place might then have to develop in a cramped position.

Chipping Campden, in the Cotswolds, some ten miles south-south-west of Stratford-on-Avon, lies in the valley of a small stream which may be traced from the bottom left-hand corner of the photograph (fig. 76) along the foot of the gardens as far as the mill at the centre of the right margin. The view is to the north-east down the valley. The stream was harnessed for the town mills, but the houses have preferred the higher ground above the valley floor. The enclosed land lying between the stream and the townsmen's crofts constituted the *Sheppeys* or sheep pastures, perhaps for the flocks brought down at shearing-time. The main feeding-grounds for the town flocks were the hills in the west and south of the parish, where, in 1273, the lord of the manor had the right to turn out a thousand sheep to grass.

The line of the broad main street follows a contour course along the valley, and the marked curve at the farther end is the turn of the road up a side valley which eventually brings it to the edge of the Cotswold scarp and so down to the Severn plain. The church and manor house (top right) stand on a spur.

At the market-place, famed for its wool sales, the main street has a characteristic broadening, the original width of the open space being masked by encroachments. Three groups of buildings now occupy an island site. Beyond a group of private houses comes a car-park, and then the town hall; after another space there is the market-hall erected by the lord of the manor,

Baptist Hickes, First Viscount Campden, in 1627.

Amongst the buildings facing the market are the Woolstaplers' Hall and the old Grammar School. The dwelling-houses on High Street, many of them much as the woolmen left them, have long, narrow crofts with a back-lane behind them. The two back-lanes enclose the medieval borough, in which a survey of 1273 shows seventy-five burgages, fifteen other houses and seven shops. Although not walled, the limitation of the advantages of burgess status to those who occupied this area has acted just as effectively in restricting the development of building along other frontages until the last two centuries when the privileges of the borough have been of less importance.

Campden was never divorced entirely from its field-land. The burgesses themselves owned field-land, but those parishioners who actually worked the land tended to be gathered in the adjacent hamlet of Westington across the stream. The borough was never a large one and the town is still compact and half-rural, a bowshot from the fields. The thirteenth-century lords of the manor derived part of their income from the burgage rents, but they also had 320 acres of arable in their demesnes with a further 672 acres occupied by the villeins. The borough was connected with the surrounding countryside in another way, for its burgesses' principal occupation in the later Middle Ages was the buying and selling of wool from the Cotswold flocks.

The first creation of the borough was the grant made by a Hugh de Gonneville who owned the manor shortly after 1173. Sir Baptist Hickes, a wealthy London mercer who acquired the manor by purchase in 1604, conferred new benefits on the town. In 1605 he obtained a new charter of incorporation with four fairs a year, two for the lord and two for the corporation. He gave the town its market-hall, almshouses and a conduit, and for himself built a new manor house in 1613 on a site to the south of the church. This house was burned in the Civil War and only an isolated fragment remains as a ruin in the park behind the present Manor House.

The church is one of the most justly famed in the Cotswolds. Its size and ornamentation testify, like Lavenham and Long Melford, to the prosperity of the burgesses whose memorial brasses still lie within it. But the benefactors were not manufacturers of cloth as in Suffolk. The Grevels, Welleys, Lethnards, Gybbys and Bradweys were wool merchants dealing in Cotswold fleeces, thriving on the custom, first of the Italian and Flemish clothiers and then of

Fig. 77. Royston; looking S along Ermine Street at the crossing with the Icknield Way, May 1962.

the English manufacturers. Campden itself was never the centre of any substantial weaving industry.

In the tax-lists of 1334 the total sum due from Campden was 340 shillings, about one-third the amount due from Gloucester itself. Since the town stood and fell by wool it did not suffer that seventeenth-century stagnation which afflicted the rural industry in East Anglia; wool was still in demand even if methods and location of manufacture changed. Later burgesses of Campden did not replace medieval houses by Georgian, and the beauty of the High Street and the church continues to attract visitors. No black and white photograph can do justice to the colour and texture of the buildings or the stone 'slatts' on the roofs, both taken from the now disused quarry on Conduit Hill, two miles south-west of the town.

Sources

P. C. Rushen, *History of Chipping Campden*, London, n.d. [1911]; 1273 survey: C. 131/2/6; 1294: C. 131/70/26.

77. ROYSTON   Hertfordshire

Ermine Street on its way from London to York climbs the long dip slope of the chalk hills and descends to the upper tributaries of the Cam, turning a little to take the steeper scarp slope. Before it reaches the plain it is crossed by the Icknield Way which follows the foot of the escarpment and here forms the boundary between Hertfordshire on the hills and Cambridgeshire on the plain.

Such an intersection of roads sounds like a geographer's prescription for a market-town of venerable antiquity. In fact, Royston is a comparative newcomer, with its legal and administrative status in the later Middle Ages pointing unmistakably to its position as a youngest child. Although the town was compact, gathered around the four arms of the cross-roads, it straddled the territory of five parishes and two counties. It required the Act of Parliament of 1540 to give it independent status:

Forasmuche as the Towne of Royston is a markett Towne situate and bilded to gither and extendeth itself into Fyve severall parishes whereof never a Parrisshe churche of them is within twoo myles of the said towne and somme of them be three myles ... forasmuche as the towne of Royston is a greate and a common thorowefare for the Kinges subjectes and liege people travayling from many and sundry partes of this Realme and in the said Towne is also wekely a great markett whereunto greate and frequent resorte is of all thinhabitauntis of the Countery therunto adioyning ...

It is clear that in 1540 Royston was far from being a no-man's-land. Yet at the time when men first gathered there it was no more than a place where four roads met in open country. Any men working in the fields near the crossroads went home in the evening to one of the five villages adjacent to the crossing. In the late twelfth century there is the first recorded mention of *Crux Roys*, a wayside cross near which a house of Austin Canons had been founded (1163–84). The priory lay within Newsells manor in Barkway parish and acquired the manorial rights in its foundation charter.

In 1189 the priory obtained the right to hold a market and fair: a second fair followed in 1213

and a third in 1243, so that the roadside settlement was well set on its path as a market-town with an enviable position. In the early thirteenth century it ceased to be known as 'Rhohesia's Cross' and acquired the *-ton* ending. By the time of the Act of 1540 there were at least twelve inns, although the priory, which had played so large a part in its foundation, was then dissolved. In the early seventeenth century the town became a fashionable social resort when James I made it his hunting headquarters.

The priory and market-place have each imposed their mark on the town plan though both have been transformed. The photograph looks south; the Icknield Way is the broad street that extends from side to side of the plate. Ermine Street crosses it at right angles. The parish church which stands by the side of the Icknield Way near the left margin is made up of the chancel and choir of the priory church, bought by the townspeople 'to their great charge' in order to have a church of their own, and the ruins were refurbished about 1600. The encroachment of houses and shops upon the great open market-place of Ermine Street has left only two narrow streets, one on either side of an island of buildings. The newer, wedge-shaped market-place in the south-east quarter of the town, has replaced the medieval market-place, but is far smaller in size.

Sources

V.C.H. Herts. III (1912) 253; R.C.H.M. *Hertfordshire* (1911) 172–5; E. 179/81/40 and 109; Act: 32 Henry VIII, c. 44.

III. THE TOWN WALLS

Thus have I, Wall, my part discharged so,
And, being done, thus Wall away doth go.
A Midsummer Night's Dream, v, i, 203–4

The walls of towns such as Berwick and Chester impress themselves on the mind of any traveller who climbs them or who walks in the streets which lie in their shadow. The psychological effect on medieval travellers is difficult to estimate. Such a town was seen to have citizens wealthy enough to build and to maintain great earthworks, stone walls and gates. The burden of repair and maintenance in most towns was laid squarely on the burgess community who might meet the charges either in proportion to the number of tenements owned, or from the common chest. In other towns the burden was

shared among country manors which might be considered to benefit from the various roles a town played in the province.[6] To the unwanted visitor in time of civil and national wars the walls presented a stern façade; to those sheltering within them they signified the protection dear to the hearts of traders and craftsmen.

The walls show on a larger scale the same search for physical security which produced the walled precincts of abbeys, the walled cathedral close of Lincoln or St David's and the walled farmhouses of the type of Markenfield. The walls of Norwich had a circuit of two and a quarter miles; those of York measure two and three-quarter miles, and those of Chester two

[6] E.g. the walls of Malmesbury were allocated for repair in 26 sections, *Eng. Hist. Rev.* XXI (1906) 123.

miles; at the other extreme is the tiny area encompassed at Totnes, too small for the modern market-town. The very fact that new walls were being built and old ones strengthened quite late in the Middle Ages indicates that they still had a very live importance. Townsmen did not spend money on walls for ornament: in the pacific centuries when walls became unnecessary there was no enthusiasm for their maintenance and many have completely disappeared from view.[7]

The combined advantages of personal safety and trading privilege go far to explain why the more important medieval manufactures sheltered in towns and why the more important and profitable bargains tended to be struck at urban counters. The same protection brought administrators to the towns. As in the eleventh century the moneyers had struck their coins in the shelter of *burh* defences, so in the thirteenth century the itinerant judges came to the great towns for their assize-courts.

A town offered the best guarantee of personal safety which a troubled world could afford, and, to those who purchased the privilege, it provided the best opportunity of access to market-places crowded with people having money in their purses and goods in their packs. To the less ambitious countryman in flight from his manor, the walls of a town symbolised the protection which town customs and privileges might offer him should his lord seek to reclaim him.

In such towns as Denbigh, Berwick or Chichester, where the wall is largely free of modern buildings, it is possible from the air to form an appreciation of the defensive strength of the position and to see the distinct separation of streets and fields which the walls emphasised. The wall, even in disuse, was a considerable barrier to the spread of streets. It usually marked the outer bounds of an area with valuable privileges reserved for its residents, and to live five yards outside was to lose those privileges just as effectively as to live five miles away. The wall also discouraged extra-mural building by sheer difficulty of access. Even if the upper stone-work was pillaged for building, the substantial earthworks, many of them older than the stone walls, were difficult to breach, and there was no advantage in pillaging earth. Until the

barrier was passed, the growth of town-housing could only take place at the expense of empty crofts and yards within the walled area.

Differences in street level are commonly found inside and outside the walls, and the two areas develop different street patterns. Since so many of the interior streets were laid out at a time when the wall was in existence, they have no ambition to go beyond its circuit. Thus there are marked culs-de-sac, each with its closed end along a significant line or curve; and quite commonly there is an inner ring-lane marking the line of the inside of the wall and etching its shape in the modern urban landscape.[8] Small streets feed into this ring-lane but, except where there were gates or posterns, there is no corresponding egress from it. The line of the medieval wall at Leicester reveals itself very clearly in this way.[9] At Berwick (fig. 79) the amputation of an old street-line, effected when Tudor walls were built embracing a smaller compass than the walls of Edward I, illustrates the restriction upon development that a wall might impose, and Alderman Lee has recently shown the line of the 'old borough' walls at Northampton by following similar clues.[10]

It is surprising how late in the Middle Ages certain towns acquired the walls now visible. Political circumspection and the need for money usually necessitated an appeal to the Crown and the grants of *murage* are well recorded. They were at once a licence to build and a licence to collect tolls. The grant of murage may mean no more than the improvement of an older earthen rampart by additions in stone or the replacement of timber by stone. Some earth defences, such as Wallingford (fig. 80), seem never to have been crowned with a wall. Other grants of murage indicate an extension of the walled area of a town. Just as medieval Chester and York had extended their walls beyond the Roman compass, so Bristol twice enlarged its original walled area, the second occasion in 1247–8 involving the purchase of part of a marsh, the cutting of a new channel for the Frome and the filling in of the old river-bed.

The relation of an urban castle to the mural defences was often close. In the new towns of

---

[7] A. Harvey, *The Castles and Walled Towns of England* (1911), has the fullest published list of towns with mural defences, and see also H. L. Turner, *Town Defences in England and Wales* (1970), and M. W. Barley, ed., *The Plans and Topography of Medieval Towns in England and Wales* (1975). There are at some towns remains of ramparts or walls beyond the present limit of buildings, as at Lydford, Devon; Wareham, Dorset; and Winchelsea, Sussex.

[8] In 1310, when the walls and ditches of Southampton were obstructed by the encroachment of gardens, it was ordered that a clear circuit, 12 feet wide, should be restored along the inner face of the walls: *Cal. Misc. Inq.* III, no. 154.

[9] D. Charman, 'Leicester in 1525', *Trans. Leics. Arch. Soc.* XXVII (1951) 19–29; *The Walls of Norwich* (Norwich City Council, 1910).

[10] F. Lee, 'The origins of Northampton', *Arch. Jnl* CX (1953) 164–74.

Edward I the castle and walls were conceived as part of the same plan. In other towns the walls are patently an afterthought. At Totnes there is a hint in the alignment of walls and castle mound that the building of the Norman castle caused a small change to the line of pre-Conquest defences, and Domesday Book has several entries showing town houses being destroyed to make way for castles.

The walled towns, arising from the insecurity of invasion or baronial warfare, are not evenly distributed on the map of England. There is a concentration on the southern and eastern seaboards and on the Borders. In the Midlands only the county town was usually walled; in Warwickshire the walls of Coventry are no earlier than the fourteenth century. But the list of England's largest towns in the poll tax of 1377 shows that only Boston, among the first ten, lacked substantial defences and even there there was a ditch. All but three of the forty largest towns and cities were defended.

By the time that Tudor topographers recorded the appearance of towns, and cartographers sketched their bird's-eye plans, the degree of insecurity was much smaller. But on the Border and along the coastline there were walled towns which still formed part of the anti-invasion plans of Henry VIII and Elizabeth. The military associations of many of the earliest surviving town plans have already been stressed, and all the Tudor monarchs called for reports on coastal town defences and executed, or planned, repairs and extensions. The ports received particular attention, and Berwick (pp. 193–5) shows how the pre-existing Edwardian walls were replaced by elaborate defences in the best Italianate manner complete with gun-emplacements.

The defences were not seriously tested in the sixteenth century by any foreign invader, and when towns had to defend themselves in the seventeenth century it was in civil war. In the more peaceful centuries which succeeded, the maintenance of walls was a luxury which did not commend itself to towns of shopkeepers and tradesmen, so that fewer town walls than were seen by Celia Fiennes or Defoe now survive to be recorded by the aerial camera. Yet even where substantial remains no longer exist above ground, a maze of built-up streets may reveal much to those who have learned to use air photographs as sources of urban history.

78. CHESTER Cheshire

The bird's-eye plan (fig. 78A) of Elizabethan Chester shows that there were already suburbs outside the three landward gates. The air photograph (fig. 78B) gives a view from the opposite direction, looking south towards the north gate where a line of trees marks the course of the wall high above the deep rock-cutting occupied by the Shropshire Union canal. In the top right-hand corner is the Roodee, the reclaimed marsh, once tidal but now a level meadow used as a racecourse and showground. The river has moved three hundred yards from the western walls of the town where Braun showed ships moored at the west gate.

The city still has its entire circuit of medieval wall incorporating for much of its length the older wall of the Roman fortress. There was a Mercian stronghold here in 910 on the high ground above the Dee, and medieval Chester grew from the expansion of this site into the ruins of the fortress of the Twentieth Legion which were eventually enclosed in the medieval wall. In the reign of Edward the Elder (899–925) Chester's mint was one of the most important in the country. Four, possibly five, of the parish churches were already in being by the Norman Conquest and from 1075 to 1107 the church of St John outside the east gate was the seat of the first Norman bishop of Mercia. In the early Middle Ages Chester prospered as a port for Wales and Ireland and as a frontier town. Until the silting-up of the river began in the early fifteenth century it was the natural headquarters for both war and trade with these countries, a strategic position recognised in the creation of the earldom of Chester, taken into the king's hands in 1237 and given to his eldest son.

By the sixteenth century Chester shared with many old-established towns certain general complaints of distress and empty houses. The silting-up of the estuary was progressively forcing shipping towards the quays of the Wirral and there was effective, growing competition from Liverpool on the Mersey, once no more than a minor harbour within the jurisdiction of Chester. In the nineteenth century Chester's position made it an important railway junction, a garrison-town and an administrative centre, so that houses now stretch far beyond the walls on either side of the river.

The whole of the north wall of the Roman fortress is incorporated in the medieval defences. On the left-hand side of the photograph the town wall can be seen making straight for the river from the tower at the north-east angle, but before the river is reached there is an indentation to the right, after which a parallel course is resumed. This indentation marks the point where the Roman circuit was extended, prob-

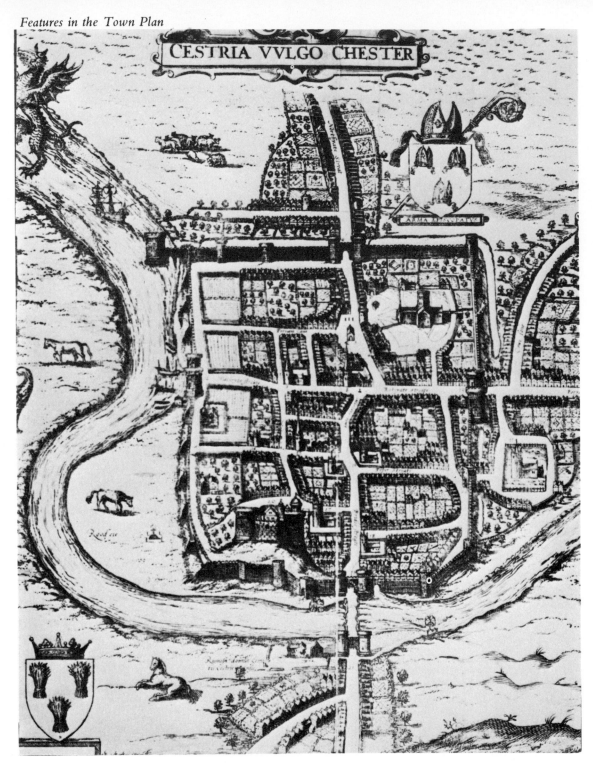

Fig. 78A. Chester in about 1580; plan by Braun, looking N.

ably in the early Middle Ages, to take in a greater area of ground. The medieval wall of this enlarged circuit follows the riverside. turning back along the edge of the Roodee just beyond the castle. On the west (right-hand) side of the town the narrow white band of the wall is visible, being set well outside the Roman defences, the line of which is approximately that of the

Fig. 78B. Chester; looking S, July 1948.

long street parallel to the present west wall and ending at the castle gates. The general shape and alignment of medieval Chester were thus formed under Roman influences but the main streets do not exactly follow the Roman lines. The open space into which the road through the north gate widens is the market-place with St Werburgh's church on its left. Much of the north-east (bottom left-hand) quarter of the city was occupied by the monastery of St Werburgh whose church Henry VIII took for a cathedral. The south-west corner (top right) is dominated by the castle; the present buildings were erected between 1789 and 1813.

Sources

Graham Webster 'Chester in the Dark Ages', *Jnl Chester and N. Wales Arch. Soc.* XXXVIII (1951) 39–48; historical account and plans in *Arch. Jnl* XCIV (1937); *Official Guide* (18th ed.); H. J. Hewitt, *Medieval Cheshire* (1929); R. C. Jarvis, 'The head port of Chester', *Trans. Hist. Soc. Lancs. and Chesh.* CII (1951) 69–84; D. Knowles and J. K. St Joseph, *Monastic Sites from the Air* (1952) 8–9.

79. BERWICK-UPON-TWEED
Northumberland

The plan of Berwick from the Burghley papers (fig. 79B), printed in this book for the first time, was drawn by Rowland Johnson in about 1575, at a period when the coastal defences were being mapped. It shows, as does the photograph, that the new defences, constructed between 1559 and 1640, took in a much smaller circuit than the walls of the medieval town. The old fortifications included nineteen towers and an eighty-foot wide ditch dug to a depth of forty feet. They were linked to a castle in the south-west corner which was replaced between 1545 and 1558 by a new extra-mural fort now supplanted by the railway station.

The defences of Berwick had been in the minds of Elizabeth's predecessors for more than four centuries. Along the Cheviots ran what contemporaries called the 'Debateable Land' and Berwick might well have been called the 'Debateable Town'. Between 1174 and 1482 it changed hands thirteen times and was in dispute

Fig. 79A. Berwick-upon-Tweed; looking SE, July 1948.

on innumerable other occasions whenever England and Scotland were at war. Thus, Edward I's walls were strengthened by Bruce after he had won the town in 1318 and again by Edward III after its recapture. The new Elizabethan defences embraced an area only two-thirds that of the medieval town and followed the old town walls for only part of their course. The superfluous length was abandoned, the stone taken for new works and some of the earth banks carted away to form the immense new ramparts with their five spear-head bastions in the Italianate style.

In fig. 79A the town is seen from the Scottish side with the peninsula which was chosen for fortification extending between the sandy shore and the Tweed. Remains of the medieval fortifications can be seen near the railway viaduct on the right, and to the left where the Bell Tower stands isolated on a short stretch of Edward I's wall. The much wider Elizabethan ramparts now form a grassy promenade linking the five huge spear-head bastions.

Just as the medieval wall limited the spread of houses over the fields in the foreground, so the Elizabethan enclosure left some houses stranded in the undefended suburbs. Two thoroughfares were cut across by the new defences. The plan, fig. 79B, shows them clearly; the lower is Mary Gate, with Wallace Green above. Both can be seen in the photograph where Wallace Green is a wide cul-de-sac ending between the nearest bastion and the clump of trees (left). To the right of the bastion Mary Gate now runs beneath an arch in the Elizabethan defences and then continues down the curve of Castlegate to pass through the medieval rampart at Mary's Gate which stood in the foreground above the railway. The gun-emplacements on the new bastions on the left are well preserved. The trees in the angle of the wall all but mask the church of Holy Trinity built in 1650–3 as a tardy replacement for the parish church of St Mary near the castle which had been pulled down to make space for the new defences. Above the tree-grown churchyard stand the eighteenth-century barracks. In Johnson's plan this area appears thinly settled, two windmills

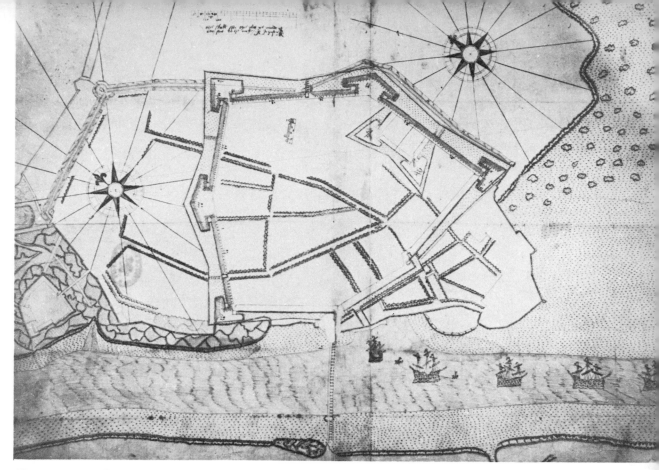

Fig. 79B. Berwick-upon-Tweed in about 1575; plan by Rowland Johnson.

being shown, each sited on a bastion of a fort which was superseded by the Elizabethan defences. The farthest bridge over the Tweed in fig. 79A is of seventeenth-century date, replacing the fourteenth-century bridge washed away in 1607, but shown on Johnson's plan. An earlier bridge existed at the end of the twelfth century.

The Elizabethan project also involved shortening the seaward walls by a direct line from the bridge to the 'King's Bastion', but in 1639 the defences were taken back to the sea-edge and the Edwardian line restored in this sector. Edward I's town had just under a hundred burgesses. In 1377, an unsettled time to collect taxes, there were 135 to pay the poll tax. At the time of Johnson's plan there were about 450 houses in town and suburbs.

Sources

Plan: Hatfield House MSS.; Fuller, *History of Berwick* (1799); Scott, *Berwick upon Tweed* (1888); poll tax; E. 179/158/32; 'circuyte of the wawlles of the town and castell' (1537): E. 36/173; plan, *c.* 1545: M.P.F. 137; survey of 1587: B.L. Cot. Tit., F. XIII, fol. 269; I. MacIvor, *The Fortifications of Berwick upon Tweed* (Department of the Environment Official Guide, 1972, emended 1974).

80. WALLINGFORD · Berkshire

The earliest defences of Wallingford were constructed about the time of Alfred. The existing defences are rectangular in shape with the east flank guarded by the Thames. On the other three sides there were a ditch and earthen rampart, probably never crowned with a stone wall. From the 'Burghal Hidage', a list drawn up in the reign of Edward the Elder (899–925) Mr P. Hunter Blair has calculated that the defences thrown up by Edward's predecessor, Alfred, would have been about 3300 yards in circuit. The length of the existing rampart, together with the river frontage, is in fact 3030 yards. In fig. 80A, a view looking north, the south side of the earthwork is marked by bushes behind a row of houses in the foreground. The west side may be picked out near the left-hand margin of the photograph by the line of trees and shrubs growing upon it. The north-west angle is visible, and also part of the north side until the line is lost among the trees which hide the grass-covered mound of the castle. Here the town ditch joins the castle defences. The erection of the castle in this north-east quarter is recorded in Domesday Book, and to clear the ground for it the king

Fig. 80A. Wallingford; looking N, June 1951.

sacrificed eight of the 276 closes which he owned in the town. The castle was well placed to guard the important river-crossing where a ford, from which the town was named, was early replaced by a bridge. The north-west quarter, now largely open ground, was principally occupied by Wallingford Priory, its precinct and its gardens.

There is no surviving plan of the Elizabethan town, but a very detailed rental enables the main features to be reconstructed in the accompanying sketch-plan. Anyone journeying west from London would cross the bridge and enter by the east gate with its chapel, the Mary of Grace, dedicated to the use of travellers. From the bridge the High Street leads straight to the west gate which stood where the west wall is breached by a modern road. For those who wished to rest in Wallingford or to do business in its market-place there was a choice of inns.

The market-place has been partly covered by buildings which leave only narrow lanes on the north and south approaches; occupying almost its full width stands the parish church of St

Mary the More. In 1584, when the rental was first drawn up, there were empty plots on the east side of Wood Street and much open ground in the southern part of the town. The grid of streets did not go farther west than Goldsmiths' Lane and the west wall was flanked by orchards and gardens.

The grid of streets enclosed by the walls of Wallingford seems to be the result of deliberate planning, for walls, gates, streets and market-place make a unity. It might also be expected that the boundaries of the four modern parishes of All Hallows, St Mary's, St Leonard's and St Peter's, formed by the amalgamation of the eleven medieval churches, would conform to these regularly spaced houses and gardens. In fact there is no such apparent conformity and, indeed, some of the boundaries cross the town walls and take in stretches of the surrounding countryside, as fig. 80B shows. They may, therefore, represent the last trace of a pre-urban agricultural community which Alfred decided to fortify to protect the Thames crossing. Only excavation of walls and house-sites would show

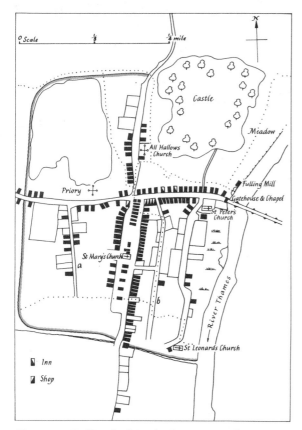

Fig. 80B. Wallingford in the late sixteenth century. The plan is based chiefly upon the rental of 1584; the lines of dots mark parish boundaries; (a) marks Goldsmiths Lane, (b) Wood Street.

whether the regular street plan accompanied the building of the walls or whether the 'utter destruction' of the town by the Danes in 1006 gave its rebuilders the opportunity to match the parallel walls with parallel streets.

The surviving tallage and 'company' rolls from 1227–96 indicate the wide range of crafts and trades occupying the burgesses who sheltered within and maintained these walls and who profited by the fine natural situation of the town. The number of burgesses listed in this period never exceeds 170 while the 'companies' numbered 430 members in 1227. Of these 156 are specifically listed as 'foreign', and it is probable that others lived in the surrounding district, like one Richard of Gatehampton, a fuller who worked in a (now lost) village of that name; away in the Thames-side and Chiltern villages the peculiar advantages of doing business within a walled town were making themselves felt. As time passed these advantages became less important and when more crossings of the Thames

were bridged (e.g. at Culham in 1415) Wallingford ceded both industry and trade to others better placed. In 1439 it was reported: 'many burgesses have departed from the town so that there are only four parishes inhabited nor more churches sustained and beneficed.'

Sources

Survey of 1584, revised 1606: E. 315/369; company and tallage rolls: Berks. Record Office, W/FC 1–11 and W/FT 1–9; copy of 1584 survey: W/F/Ab 1; P. Hunter Blair, *Anglo-Saxon England* (1956) 78 and 293; *Anglo-Saxon Chronicle* (Rolls Series) I, 256–7; *V.C.H. Berks.* I (1906) 119, 121 and 325, III (1923) 517–46; *Med. Arch.* II (1958) 223 and XI (1967) 284.

81. TOTNES   Devonshire

The medieval walls of Totnes (fig. 81) enclose a densely built-up town, oval in shape, which guards the upper reaches of the Dart. It lies on a ridge above the river, nine miles from the sea, twenty miles south-west of Exeter. The main street starts at the Dart bridge, top centre, but does not enter the walled town until the east gate which may be distinguished just above the church. From there the two streets marking the line of the walls curve to left and right towards the foreground; the oval walled area ends where the right-hand curve again crosses High Street at the former west gate, below the castle. The shorter diameter of the town is at most 200 yards, and High Street has only 300 yards between the gates.

The Anglo-Saxon *burh* had a mint in 975, and the town was one of the four Domesday boroughs in Devon. The Norman baron to whom William I granted the town founded a priory here and built a castle at the end of the town farthest from the bridge. The medieval walls include the area of the great castle motte, an artificial mound encased in a layer of puddled clay and crowned by a circular shell-keep seventy feet in diameter. The lower bailey, to left of the mound, its defences now hidden by trees, probably did not lie wholly within the defences of the *burh*, so it would seem that the erection of the Norman castle necessitated both the destruction of houses and a small extension of the town area. In the Middle Ages houses had already spread along the 400 yards of road which led from the east gate to the riverside wharves where a 'sea-mill' was turned by the tidal waters. A second borough was planted by the Pomeroy family in about 1250 on the other side of the Dart bridge in Berry Pomeroy parish, with fifty burgesses in 1293.

197

Fig. 81. Totnes; looking ESE, June 1962.

Fig. 82. Lydford; looking SW, April 1966.

When Totnes Castle fell out of use in the mid-thirteenth century the borough took over many of the seigneurial functions, just as, after the Dissolution of the monasteries, the burgesses acquired the priory and its precinct to enlarge their churchyard and to build a guildhall, a prison and a school. The parish church was completely rebuilt by communal effort of the townspeople between 1432 and about 1460, with a tower of red sandstone from quarries at Stoke Gabriel, four miles down river.

After the decay of the castle the principal source of prosperity for the townspeople was in trade and in clothmaking. The craftsmen in the earliest guild roll of 1206 included smiths, fullers, merchants, carpenters, fishers, tanners and shoemakers; but in a small town so near the open country there were always agricultural interests to diversify the basis of prosperity. The town had three swine-wardens and three ale-tasters in 1444–65, and wardens of the three markets, which lay one 'within the gates', and one outside each of the two main gates. With High Street packed with stalls and tethered horses, to say

nothing of the pillory, men and their bargains were pushed into the suburbs. The need for building-space caused the crofts to be built over, leaving only narrow passages as tunnels to the inner courtyards. This room exhausted, houses were built outside the walls.

The size of medieval Totnes may be gauged from the tightly packed buildings and from such tax-lists as survive. In 1416, tax-lists indicate the extent of the extramural development:

	Within the walls	Outside the walls
Burgesses	48	47
All taxpayers	73	114
Tax paid	77s. 1d.	77s. 10d.

Thus, about as much of the town's wealth lay outside the walls as within. The poll tax of 1377 had found 303 taxpayers of either sex and in 1255 a jury had reckoned that the burgess rents numbered 277, a much larger number than in 1416. Such a contraction may well have taken place, but the 277 should probably be compared with all 187 taxpaying households of 1416. An

199

estimate for fifteenth-century Totnes of some 200 households which tax-collectors felt to be worth visiting, will not be far wrong.

Sources

H. R. Watkin, *The History of Totnes Priory and Medieval Town*, 3 vols. (1917). All the information here is taken from this calendar of documents, with the exception of the poll-tax receipt: E.179/95/42m. 13; see also W. G. Hoskins, *Devon* (1954) 504–8 and plan; C. F. Rea, *Trans.Dev.Assoc.* LVI (1924) 202–13; Berry Pomeroy: M. W. Beresford, *New Towns of the Middle Ages* (1965) 420.

82. LYDFORD   Devonshire

The narrow neck of land seen in fig. 82 has the gorge of the River Lyd on the left, joined by the wooded gorge of a minor stream in the upper part of the photograph. Guarded by these slopes, the site was chosen by Alfred for fortification as one of the four Devon *burhs*. It was a commercial and administrative centre for north-west Dartmoor in Anglo-Saxon times, for coins were minted here from the reign of Ethelred II (979–1016) onwards. Until 1198 the lord of Lydford Manor was supervisor of the Dartmoor stannaries; in 1195 a tower was added to the castle as a prison for those convicted by the stannary courts.

It had always been presumed that the earth rampart in the foreground across the width of the plateau was the north-west part of the town defences, with a gate where the present road enters. In 1962 opportunity arose for excavation in the area of the early Norman fort, the bank of which can be seen in the top right-hand corner of the town, beyond the church. The Anglo-Saxon town wall was found under this early fort, the construction of which probably accounts for the forty houses said in Domesday Book to have been destroyed since 1066. The line of the town wall can be followed from this corner in either direction round to the rampart in the foreground. Outside the gap in the rampart representing the north gate the roads fork; within the confines of the town the main street continues straight past the castle keep and the church of St Petrock to leave by a presumed south gate, and then to turn left outside the line of the defences (marked by a hedge) and descend to the ford in the gorge after which the *burh* and town are named. Only a fraction of the former town area is now built over but the excavations of 1962–6 showed that burgage plots were laid out, bounded by ditches at right angles to the chequer road system. One of the roads in the grid is represented by the lane running along behind the rampart in the foreground, and another by the second, parallel lane, half way to the castle keep. The early Norman fort, together with the church, has obliterated any Anglo-Saxon streets on the right-hand side of the main street beyond the keep, but two hedgerows on the left-hand side may follow former street lines.

Sources

W. G. Hoskins, *Devon* (1954) 427–9 and fig. 15; *Med.Arch.* IX (1965) 170–1; X (1966) 168–9; XI (1967) 263; XIV (1970) 83–103, esp. fig. 35.

IV. CASTLES AND CATHEDRALS

A town where the plan is dominated by a cathedral is only a special case of a town dominated by a church and not very different from a town situated at a monastery gate. That a cathedral and a castle should occur together is likely enough. In the choice of a centre for his see a bishop would not be averse to the advantages of protection offered by a defended town. The migration of episcopal seats between 1050 and 1086 from such pre-Conquest cathedral towns as Sherborne, Crediton, Dorchester, Elmham and Selsey can be seen partly as a migration to larger and better-defended urban centres at Old Sarum, Exeter, Lincoln, Norwich and Chichester. The transfer of Lichfield to Chester (St John's) in 1075 was to a church standing outside the walls of a town, but it was short-lived. The move from Crediton to Exeter was 'to give the bishop security against raiders', while the defensible position of the monastic church of Durham had already in 994 brought about the transfer of the see from Chester-le-Street.[11] As will be seen, the circumstances under which a bishop of Salisbury built New Sarum were not such as to endear him to castles and their garrisons, but it is significant that even the new Salisbury could not manage without a rampart. Thus in the early twelfth century all the English dioceses were centred upon defended towns.

[11] For these moves see F. M. Stenton, *Anglo-Saxon England* (1943) 658–9.

Fig. 83. Durham; looking NNE, July 1964.

83. DURHAM   County Durham

While both Durham (fig. 83) and Old Sarum (fig. 84) were independent settlements before the transfer thither of a see, only Durham owes its very existence as a town to the foundation of a church. Although the cathedral, castle and walls at Durham were eventually as closely integrated as they ever were at Sarum, the defences are not all so old as the church.

One of the chance compensations for the industrialisation which has marred the landscape of so much of County Durham is the superb view of the city offered to travellers by train as they cross the viaduct into Durham station. The air photograph (fig. 83), taken from the south, provides an even better view of the city as a whole, embracing cathedral, castle, town and river. It displays the strategic importance of the site and makes it possible to see the city with something of the respect which the Monk of Durham paid to Bishop Flambard: 'though nature had made a fortress of the city, he made it stronger and more imposing with a wall.' He linked the parted banks of the River Wear by building an arched bridge of massive stonework. The encircling wall, once from thirty to fifty feet high, has largely disappeared, but the other

201

Fig. 84. Old Sarum; looking W, December 1965.

architectural works of the Norman bishops – the monastery, cathedral and castle – remain.

The cathedral was served by a monastic community whose cloisters can be seen on the near (south) side of the great nave. The bishop was temporal lord of the Border palatinate with powers far beyond most temporal lords. The conjunction of cathedral and castle provides a visible sign of the union of powers in the prince-bishops.

The growth of Durham was rapid. When the body of St Cuthbert was brought here for safety in 995 there was a settlement at Elvet on the east bank near where St Oswald's Church now stands (right-hand margin of fig. 83). The wooded rocky site on the other side of the river was not particularly attractive for agriculture. On this rock a church was built for the saint by 998, and ramparts were in existence by 1006. After the Conquest, the church became a Benedictine monastery and a fitting cathedral for the Norman bishop began to be constructed. Palace Green, on the far side of the cathedral, has the castle buildings ranged around it, with the great mound and (reconstructed) keep at the town end. In military terms this is the inner bailey of the fortress, with the cathedral and monastery in the outer bailey, the whole encircled by the river and strengthened by the wall. The castle is now garrisoned by the University, founded in 1833.

Beyond the keep, sloping down on to the neck of the river meander, is the medieval city which occupied some fifty-eight acres. The market-place, to which main roads lead from the bridges, lies in front of the tall spire of St Nicholas' church, a mid-nineteenth-century building. Part of the open space can be seen. In the fourteenth century, after experiencing several raids, Bishop Bek extended the walls to embrace the market-place. Expansion of the urban area was limited by the nature of the site, but Speed's plan shows suburbs beside the three main approach roads, two near the bridgeheads and the third spreading out along the narrow neck of the peninsula eastwards to Hartlepool, a port and walled town.

The city owes both its medieval bridges to bishops, the older being Framwellgate Bridge (left) near the original ford. Bishop Pudsey built Elvet Bridge and founded the extramural borough of Elvet. The weir near the left margin provided power for the monks' corn- and fulling-mill. The weir beyond Framwellgate Bridge was for the bishops' mill to which the whole town owed suit.

Sources

V.C.H. *Durham* III (1928); Monk of Durham, *Anglia Sacra* (Rolls Series) I. 708; D. Knowles and J. K. St Joseph, *Monastic Sites from the Air* (1952) 2–3.

84. OLD SARUM   Wiltshire

The second illustration in this section is of a site with a long history before either castle or cathedral was established there. No town in England has defences more ancient in origin. The earthworks, comprising a massive rampart and ditch which enclose an oval area of some 30 acres, are the defences of a hill fort of the Iron Age. The site was later re-occupied in the Dark Ages: King Alfred, it is recorded, ordered the defences to be strengthened. There is no doubt that the castle and the cathedral of Old Sarum followed William I's transfer to this site of the seat of the bishop who occupied the amalgamated sees of Ramsbury and Sherborne between 1075 and 1078. William I also elaborated the existing defences of the hilltop with an inner ring earthwork or bailey, almost 300 feet in diameter, about the same length as the cathedral; at the same time the seat of county government was moved from the town of Wilton, embodied in the shire name.

There had undoubtedly been a Roman *Sorbiodunum* and an Anglo-Saxon *Searisbyrig*, where Edgar's *witan* met in 960, where Aethelred II had a mint, where a church of St Ethelreda was founded early in the eleventh century, and where the Danes went in 1003. Yet the Roman town site has eluded the spade, although Roman roads converge near this hilltop, and extensive excavations on the hilltop alongside cathedral and castle have not succeeded in recovering any trace of the Anglo-Saxon or Norman borough. The bounds of Old Sarum, a small enclave, make it clear that the royal borough was cut out of the bishop's manor of Stratford, the village where the Roman road crossed the river. King and bishop shared its revenues and the strips of their tenants lay intermingled in its fields.

There is no evidence for the size of the Norman borough; it need not have been large. In the twelfth century its tax was less than that paid by Wilton, then no longer the county town, and William of Malmesbury was willing to accept the place as a cathedral but hardly as a 'city'. Surviving burgage plots outside the earthworks of Old Sarum have been identified in a plan of about 1700, on the narrow hedged lane to the small village of Stratford sub Castle, which can be seen alongside the river in the distance in fig. 84. The long survival of Old Sarum as a rotten parliamentary borough meant that there was always a premium on remembering where the eligible burgage plots lay when it came to elections. From 1734 to 1747, for example, the deserted site and its ten electors were represented by the elder Pitt.

The Norman cathedral and borough were abandoned together between 1220 and 1227 when Bishop Richard planted the city of New Sarum (now Salisbury) in the meadows of the Avon, leaving the great earthwork and its buildings as 'Old Sarum'. In 1377, 150 years after the final migration to Salisbury, the poll-tax collectors found only ten persons over sixteen years of age in the shell of the old city, compared with 3226 in the new. Stone for Salisbury was taken from Old Sarum both for the initial building and for repairs of cathedral and walls. Leland visited Old Sarum at a time when the newly dissolved monasteries all over England were about to become quarries, but in the ruined Lady-chapel of the cathedral he saw fragments of walls that had been put to the same use for the previous three hundred years. The castle had been falling into ruin since at least the early fourteenth century, and in 1400 even the county gaol was in ruins, and it was to Thomas Compton, groom of his Chamber, that Henry VIII granted the liberty of knocking down and carrying away 'the stone walls called the castle of Old Sarum'.

We are left, therefore, only with the certainty of a small borough and the cathedral and castle, the excavated remains of which can be seen in fig. 84. A modern path enters the inner ring by a high footbridge leading through some fragments of the gatehouse. The two most substantial ruins visible within the bailey are the great tower exposed on the right and the postern at the farthest (west) end. From there a wooden bridge led out towards the west gate of the town. By 1092 a cathedral had been built in the outer bailey. As the chronicler wrote: 'Bishop Roger made these buildings, wide in their extent, lavish in expense, most beautiful in appearance.' Between about 1125 and 1138 the cathedral was enlarged and a cloister added on its north side. The full length from east to west is over 300 feet and the transepts are seventy-five feet wide. In the nearer (north-east) angle of the building a square, grassy platform marks the site of the twelfth-century cloisters; the much lower floor of the crypt beneath the chapter-house can be seen beyond, with some of the walls still standing above ground. The boundary between the cathedral precinct and the houses of the soldiers and citizens is visible on the nearer side of the cathedral as a line of earthwork supporting a clump of trees.

This crowding together of church, soldiers and townspeople led to much conflict between the bishop and the castle after 1130, when the bishop's authority over the castle had been replaced by that of a castellan. In 1217 the dean and chapter petitioned the Pope, complaining of their insecurity and dependence on the whim of the garrison commander. There are picturesque stories of the clergy making their way one Rogation Day to the site of a new town, and the foundation stone of a new cathedral was laid in 1220 in the meadows by the Avon, two miles away. The townspeople followed and the streets of Salisbury were laid out, chequer-board fashion. In 1227 the new cathedral replaced the old.

Sources

V.C.H. Wilts. VI (1962) 51–68; *Proceedings of the Society of Antiquaries of London* XXIII–XXVIII (1911–16); *Old Sarum, Official Guide* (1965), with plan by D. H. Montgomerie; R. A. Brown *et al.*, *History of the King's Works* II (1963) 824; P. A. Rahtz and J. W. G. Musty, 'Excavations at Old Sarum', *Wilts. Arch. and Nat. Hist. Mag.* LVII (1962) 353–70 and 'The suburbs of Old Sarum', *ibid.* LIX (1964) 130–54.

V. TOWNS AS PORTS

For as long as trade and a strategic position were determining factors in the prosperity of a town it was only natural that the largest medieval towns were those with good communications. While land transport for bulky and heavy goods was restricted by the power of draught animals and by the capacity of carts, the towns with the best long-distance communications were those which stood beside estuaries or navigable rivers. The ports of the east and south coasts, lying on good navigable rivers and facing those foreign ports most important to English trade, possessed these geographical advantages to the full. They also had behind them productive hinterlands. With the exception of Bristol and Chester (which stood in a particular relation to Ireland and Wales) the western ports were less fortunately placed.[12]

A medieval port has no characteristic topographical feature now to be discerned from the air other than its proximity to water. The most prosperous medieval ports have been submerged under the modern paraphernalia of docks, breakwaters and jetties. The results of excavations at a site like Stonar, by Sandwich, must be awaited to learn what features of a medieval port the spade may reveal.[13]

With boats of shallow draught the physical equipment of a medieval port could have been

[12] For accounts of medieval foreign trade see *Cambridge Economic History of Europe* II (1952); E. Power and M. M. Postan, eds., *Studies in English Trade in the Fifteenth Century* (1933); E. M. Carus-Wilson and O. Coleman, *England's Export Trade, 1275–1547* (1963).

[13] F. W. Hardman and W. P. D. Stebbing, *Arch. Cant.* LIII (1940) 62–81, LIV (1942) 41–61, LV (1943) 37–49.

Fig. 85A. Old Romney; looking NW, June 1953.

small. Groynes and breakwaters were necessary to amplify the natural protection provided by a haven against high seas and winds; in an age before gunpowder, protection against marauding strangers could best be offered by some seaside fortifications of the conventional land type. The larger ports needed ample lengths of quays with deep water and cranes and warehouses for storage. As Professor Carus-Wilson has written, 'while every tide left a muddy deposit on the irregular and unpaved quay of Bordeaux, Bristol had not only paved its streets and piled its strand, but had bound its Key and its Back with freestone'.[14] Where there was no port to serve developing needs an inland community might feel it necessary to create one. Thus Newton (Dorset) was planned as a port for Purbeck; the new Edwardian towns of North Wales were at once markets, garrisons and ports; and, on the Northumberland coast, the Percies and the monks of Alnwick were led to build themselves

a new port at Alnmouth to ensure their supplies, and to capture some of the benefits of coastwise trade.

Although piracy, invasion and wrecks were always to be feared, two long-term enemies dealt severely with the fortunes of coastal towns. Ancient ports like Shotwick and Dunwich have been put out of business by the silting of channels and the erosion of cliffs. Again, changes in consumers' tastes; political changes which made foe into friend and enemies out of good customers; and the reorientation of commerce: all have affected the rise and fall of ports.

Ports derived their activity in the last analysis from production or consumption in towns and villages. Occasionally the most valued commodities in a customs account will be the fine-quality manufactures of the craftsmen of the port itself, but more often they are the products of inland towns or the raw materials of the countryside. Through the ports there flowed in the goods which the economy lacked or had in short supply: some, like cloth, wines, fruit and wax, were for whoever could afford them;

[14] E. M. Carus-Wilson in Power and Postan, eds., *Studies in English Trade*, 190.

205

Fig. 85B. New Romney; looking ENE, June 1958.

others formed the raw materials of industry: dyes, mordants and fuller's earth. Stone and roof-tiles came from abroad and shipbuilders looked to the Baltic for timber, tar, hemp, canvas and sailcloth. In addition, every port was some sort of fishery, and for fish and other preserved flesh there was a constant movement of salt cargoes. In all respects the coastal ports and the inland markets and fairs were mutually dependent.

Nor was the role of the medieval and Tudor port confined to imports and exports. The coastal waters, even to a small extent those of the west, formed a main artery of domestic communications. London drew on the fields of East Anglia for its grain, which was carried by river and sea. The stone of Purbeck and Barnack was moved by water just as Pennine millstones found their way over the North Sea as ballast. At the end of our period it was the Tyne barge and the coastal collier which brought the London wharves their 'sea-coal' from Newcastle.

85. OLD AND NEW ROMNEY Kent

The Cinque Ports of the Channel coast offered the shortest crossing to the Continent and held a significant place in English society long before William I landed near one of them. Domesday Book records that the borough of Romney discharged its burgesses from any further obligation to the king 'by reason of service at sea'. In the twelfth century its share of the Cinque Ports' fleet was five ships, each with a crew of twenty-two. A century before the battle of Hastings New Romney had a mint and the record of one of its churches goes back to 740.

The medieval coastline between the cliffs at Hastings and Folkestone was made up of shingle beaches broken through by the estuaries of the Brede, Tillingham and Rother. Among these were low-lying islands on which such settlements as Old Winchelsea, New Romney and Lydd were gathered, all of them now joined to the Kent mainland. Tudor maps of Rye and New Winchelsea show the River Rother flowing

Fig. 86. Fowey; looking NNE, July 1953.

to the sea past the walls of Rye, a course only followed since the great storm of 1287. This river previously flowed south-eastwards to the south of the Rhee Wall, and by it lay the ports of Old and New Romney. Old Romney was probably silted up before 1086 and the air photograph (fig. 85A), a view from the south-east, shows the parish church, large enough to take most of the modern population of the whole Marsh, but it stands with only a few houses nearby. The main road follows the line of the Rhee Wall and dike. To distinguish former roads from dried-up watercourses is difficult and so no certain indication can be given of the former extent of Old Romney. The oval enclosures near the top right-hand corner mark the probable site of two moated manor houses. Air photographs of the fields surrounding the ruined churches of the Marsh (e.g. Midley, one and a half miles south of Old Romney) show the same absence of definition in former buildings and streets.

New Romney stands two miles nearer the sea set amongst reclaimed marshland, now parcelled into fields. In the photograph (fig. 85 B) it is seen from the south-west. The old coastline of the Rother estuary is marked by a curving stream and belt of trees, beginning top centre and forming the limit of a modern housing estate, top right. The new houses are built where ships were once moored. The great Norman parish church with its square tower and triple roof-ridges can be seen at a road junction on the near side of the belt of trees. To the east of it lay the main quay.

In plan, the town formed a grid, consisting of four long streets with short cross-streets making the steps of a ladder. The view is in the direction of the long streets, and the grid is best preserved to the left of the church where all four streets remain.

Sources

V.C.H. Sussex IX (1937) 34; Gordon Ward, 'The Saxon history of the town and port of Romney', *Arch. Cant.* LXV (1952) 12; poll tax: E. 179/240/256; J. A. Williamson, 'The geographical history of the Cinque Ports', *History*, n.s. XI (1926–7) 97–115; J. A. Steers, *The Coastline of England and Wales* (1946) 316–41; MS. maps of Romney Marsh: Hovenden maps, All Souls College, and B. L. Cot. Aug. I, i; of the Rother (1571): M.P.F. 212 (see *Geog. Jnl* CXIX (1953) 200–7 for date).

Fig. 87. Alnmouth; looking N, May 1957.

86. FOWEY   Cornwall

The ports of Devon and Cornwall developed later than those of Kent and Sussex; apart from tin, their hinterlands yielded a poorer harvest to load into ships and their population provided no large market for imports. Only with the development of trade with Brittany and Gascony were these western ports able to exploit an advantage of position both for trading and for preying on those who traded. Leland wrote of Fowey (c. 1535) 'waxinge riche, partely by feates of warre, partely by pyracie it fell all to merchaundize ... so that the town was haunted with shippes of diverse nations, and their shippes went to all nations'. A. L. Rowse has said of Fowey's piratical days: 'the town seems to have prospered by them; for it was in those years that they were building the splendid tower of their church, erecting the blockhouses with a chain across to guard the entrance to the haven, while Thomas Treffrey built his fair house of Place and embattled it'.

The photograph (fig. 86) looks north over Polruan to the west shore of the long, narrow haven which continues as an estuary far into the countryside. Drowned river valleys served as arteries for trade and made the coastal towns of Cornwall both ports and markets. Fowey was granted fairs by Richard I, and a market-charter in 1316. It has little coherent plan. Its streets are the alleys between the various buildings which have grown up on the limited area of level ground alongside the quay. These buildings are set as irregularly as boats on a strand at low tide, and modern traffic moves through it at a crab's pace. The spread of building on the cliffs is modern: a view of the Tudor town, half map half picture, is included among the collection of defence plans in the Cottonian manuscripts. There had been many attacks by French fleets in the fifteenth century, and in 1457 the manor house was 'embattled'. As late as 1667 a Dutch fleet attempted an attack.

From the port books and customs accounts Dr Rowse has shown that Fowey in the sixteenth

208

Fig. 88. Yarmouth; vertical photograph, July 1968. Scale 1:6300.

century was still ahead of Falmouth in trade; its ships, laden with the produce of the up-country tin-mines, waited for the wind like the ships portrayed in the old maps while French, Irish and Welsh ships came along the coast to land unsweetened wine, linen mantles, charcoal and timber.

Sources

Lysons, *Magna Britannia* III. 107; maps in B. L. Cot. Aug. I, i and Sloane MS. 3233; partial survey of 1649: E. 317 Cornwall 15; A. L. Rowse, *Tudor Cornwall* (1941) 70–5, 108–10.

The history of as flourishing a port as Boston shows that no pre-Conquest ancestry was necessary for a port so to prosper that it ranked high among English medieval towns in wealth. At Boston (p. 217) this prosperity has left its mark most clearly in the great parish church and the market-place at its door, but modern buildings obscure traces of the ancient port. In this section new, post-Conquest coastal towns are represented by Alnmouth and Yarmouth (Isle of Wight).

87. ALNMOUTH   Northumberland

As the survey of 1567 put it, Alnmouth was 'sett at an angle or corner of the lordship of Lesburie, given forth by the lord of Alnewyk to one certain nombre of persons'. The simplicity of its plan and its coastal situation derive from the plantation of a new borough on the edge of the parish of Lesbury at some date before 1147. For the lord of Alnwick it was useful to have a sea-haven only five miles from his castle at the mouth of the river along whose valley supplies came. Two hundred and ninety-six acres were carved out of the fields of Lesbury at a point where the River Aln curved around a neck of land. The river has since broken through the narrow neck, and the ruined parish church of St Waleric lies in the foreground, now separated from the town by the river. With its harbour gone, Alnmouth is today a retiring seaside vil-

209

Fig. 89. Torksey; looking N, April 1953.

lage whose street plan is unchanged since the twelfth century. It is seen in the photograph (fig. 87) from the south.

Although they had field-land allocated to them, the burgesses of medieval Alnmouth were occupied at the wharf-side as well as at the plough. In 1207 port- and market-charters were granted and the tax-list of 1296 shows a substantial list of townsmen. The surveyor of the Percy estates found only the memory of former prosperity in 1567: 'The scite of the towne doth nowe marvelousleye weyre with the vyolence of the wynde and sea whereby the haven is much indamaged and ys not nowe so good as [when] yt was taken forthe of this lordship of intente it should be planted with suche persons as wold traffique by the sea.' The surveyor laments the decay of fishing; only one-third of the sixty households were fishermen's. Francis Mayson's survey of 1622 reported 'Alnmouth is not nowe used at all for any trafficke but by fishermen that

fish upon the coastes with small boats and cobbles'.

Sources

Surveys of 1567 and 1622, map of 1624; Percy MSS. Alnwick Castle (seen by kind permission); extracts in *Northumberland County History* II. 413, 424, 475, 482; projected fort: B.L. Cot. Aug. I, i, 60.

88. YARMOUTH   Isle of Wight

Yarmouth was probably also a post-Conquest creation, not far from the Bishop of Winchester's new port (Newtown) set at the edge of his rural manor of Swainston and across the Solent from Richard I's new port of Portsmouth. In the photograph (fig. 88) the town appears almost as an island, isolated by mudflats on the west and south, with few modern buildings outside the perimeter of the old walls. In the late twelfth century the third earl of Devon granted burgess privileges to the inhabitants although self-government did not come until 1440. Like Hedon (p. 219) the newness of the foundation is attested by the absence of field-land; Yarmouth comprised only fifty-eight acres.

Badly ravaged by the French in the late fourteenth century, the port shared the Tudor decay of Southampton; a note among the State Papers records only a dozen houses in 1559 and a ruined church. A 'castle' built at the entrance to the harbour in the invasion scare of 1543–7 became a coastguard station in 1883, and subsequently a hotel. The modern town, which does not occupy the whole of the walled area, is a small port and a popular watering place. In 1861 the Census showed 142 houses: a rental of the town in 1299 lists 181 burgage plots owned by 130 proprietors, an average density of three plots to an acre.

Sources

V.C.H. Hants. I (1900) 525 and v (1912) 286; 1299; S.C. 11/579; 1379 (thirty-five taxpayers): E. 179/173/41; 1559: S.P. 12/7/58.

89. TORKSEY   Lincolnshire

Not all medieval ports were on the coast. So long as navigable rivers served as thoroughfares, settlements along their bank might develop as local ports where goods for and from the hinterland could be shipped. Torksey, an important Anglo-Saxon port, stood on the east bank of the Trent sixty miles from the sea and was a point of trans-shipment for Lincoln, ten miles to the south-east, to which it was joined by a canal, the Foss Dyke. Transfer of goods from the Trent ships to smaller barges was necessitated by the restricted waters and shallow depth of the Dyke. This canal was made by the Romans and in the Middle Ages formed part of a continuous waterway from Boston to Yorkshire and the Midlands. There were periods of silting up and periods of energetic clearing: for example the lock seen in fig. 89 dates from the latest reconstruction in 1740, but five years earlier the antiquary Stukeley had seen loaded waggons driven over the silted channel.

The periods of neglect cannot themselves be the cause of the decline of Torksey as a port; rather, the neglect arose from the shrunken volume of trade which sought to come this way. In the course of a long inquiry into the bounds of the borough in 1237 the jurors expressed themselves in metaphor, 'of old, Torksey was the key of Lindsey just as Dover is the key of England'.

The Anglo-Saxon *burh* with its mint and the Domesday borough of 213 burgesses held their own by virtue of close legal and economic ties with Lincoln. As yet there was no port of Boston at the mouth of the Witham, but the post-Conquest development of that new town alongside the church of St Botolph drew traffic from Lindsey. In the late thirteenth century Boston replaced Lincoln as the staple market for wool and the later decline in the export of raw wool and its diversion to home looms may also have reduced the westward movement of ships from Lincoln along the Foss Dyke. The *Valor* of 1534 reported that one of the three parish churches of Torksey was in ruins, and a few years later Leland noted: 'the olde buildinges of Torkesey wer on the south of the toune but there now is litle seene of olde buildinges more than a chappelle wher men say was the paroch chirch of olde Torkesey'.

The decline seems to have been most pronounced in the late fourteenth century. In 1377 Torksey was about twice the size of neighbouring villages but no longer the prosperous town of two centuries earlier when townsmen could cheerfully give fifty houses to endow an Augustinian priory and another seven to a Cistercian nunnery. The priory was dedicated, as was proper in a mercantile community, to St Leonard, the patron saint of those imprisoned for debt. In 1385 it was complaining that 'the tenements are unoccupied by reason of the scarcity of labourers and our rents extinguished' and at the Dissolution the surveyors noted the nunnery as 'a beggarly power [poor] ruynose howse' – a far cry from the days of two religious houses and three parish churches. The survey of 1237 occupies fifteen feet of the Patent Roll; and it shows that Torksey was a good town in which to own a stake. Seventy-three dwellings belonged to various religious houses in the Midlands and the king's tailor had acquired eight others. The borough also owned the Trent ferry and had possessed a fair from 1218 and a weekly market from time immemorial. The long list of dutiable articles helps to explain why the town flourished: '... herrings, ling, greenfish, cropling, corn, lead, iron, wool, wine, woad, teasels, alum, fuel, straw, hay, manure, coal, casks, turves, grindstones, mill-posts, mill-machinery, planks...'

Convoys of potato-lorries now constitute the principal transport passing through Torksey. The air photograph shows the shrunken town which once stretched from the Foss Dyke in the foreground towards the railway half a mile distant. Near the canal bank lay the nunnery and

Fig. 90. Airmyn; looking N, June 1951.

one of the parish churches, of which foundations have been turned up by the plough in the angle between Trent and Foss, but no traces are now visible from the air. The surviving church of St Peter can be seen near the right-hand end of the railway-bridge. The 'Castle', a ruined façade facing the Trent in a meadow to the left of the modern village, is an Elizabethan mansion incorporating stone from the old priory. The third parish church, St Mary's, has also had its stone pillaged for other uses. It is a far step from Aethelred's mint and the privileged town which Domesday Book recorded as sharing all the privileges of the city of Lincoln, being free of all tolls and customs and serving the king by virtue of the duty of escorting his messengers to York

with its ships. Only in the Trent barges, one of which lies stranded on the bank, is there an echo of the ships which went north to the Humber, or of the riverside nunnery dedicated to St Nicholas, the patron saint of sailors.

Sources

1086: *The Lincs. Domesday. Lincs. Rec. Soc.* XIX (1924) 11–13; 1334 and 1377: E. 179/136/293 and 196/40; *Inquisition Post Mortem* of 1377: C. 135/262; many documents concerned with Torksey are printed or summarised in R.E.G. Cole, 'The royal burgh of Torksey', *Reports and Papers of the Assoc. Arch. Socs.* XXVIII, pt. 2 (1906) 451–530; J. W. F. Hill, *Medieval Lincoln* (1948) 307–13 and plan, and *Tudor and Stuart Lincoln* (1956) 128–34.

90. AIRMYN   Yorkshire, West Riding

In 1253 the Abbot of St Mary's, York, claimed that his predecessors had founded the little town of Airmyn within the parish of Snaith on the east bank of the River Aire half a mile above its confluence with the Ouse and two miles west of the modern port of Goole. Just as indented harbours imposed their pattern on the houses and streets of Cornish ports such as Fowey, so a river-bank invited settlement to spread out along it. The photograph (fig. 90) gives a view of Airmyn from the south. The shape of the town, with its houses facing the Aire, points to a preoccupation with the river and the opportunities it provided for earning a living by fishing, fowling and carriage. But there were also six square miles of field-land beginning behind the village crofts, and extending southwards deep into the profitable peat turbaries of Inclesmoor.

For modern road traffic the bridge nearest the mouth of the Ouse is still in Airmyn parish, at Booth Ferry; boats for crossing the rivers here have always been as important as those carrying goods up and down them. In the poll tax of 1379 two of the fifteen villagers wealthy enough to be assessed were ferrymen. There were also a chapman, a wright, a butcher, a draper and two smiths in what must have been, compared with the smaller modern village, quite a commercial community.

The ferry at Airmyn would take travellers from London and the south across the Ouse to the market-town of Howden set among the marshes, and thence to Beverley, Hull, Market Weighton or Malton. The importance of a ferry in the economic life of a district was recognised in medieval public law by the right of the lord of a manor to take tolls and by the duty which devolved upon him to maintain it. With few bridges and many streams too deep to be forded, a ferry was a public utility which custom and law were not willing to see lapse. In the last century many of the smaller river-ferries have disappeared from the landscape. Their former existence may be indicated on Ordnance Maps and can often be deduced from the course of roads and footpaths which end in open country on opposing banks of a river.

Sources

1253: P.R.O. Curia Regis Roll 151 m. 27; 1318: C. 143/244/1; 1379: E. 179/206/48 m. 23; Inclesmoor, plans of *c.* 1407: M.P.C. 56 and D.L. 42/12f. XXVIII.

9

THE PLANNED TOWNS, 1066–1307

I. INTRODUCTORY

Let them come who know best how to devise and array a new town to the best profit of the king and of merchants. (Edward I's writ of summons to the Parliament at Bury St Edmunds, 1296.)

PALGRAVE, *Parliamentary Writs* I (1827) 49

The towns illustrated in the previous chapter achieved recognition as urban communities at very different times. In English towns like Leicester and Chichester urban life had been resurrected within the broken Roman walls well before the Domesday survey affords an opportunity to assess, however roughly, the degree of urban status possessed by those places to which the clerks gave the ambiguous title of 'borough' or in which burgesses were recorded. To have been favoured as the site of a fortified *burh* in Anglo-Saxon times was no guarantee of continued urban prosperity, as the subsequent history of places such as Burpham (Sussex) shows, while a number of Domesday boroughs can no longer claim to be towns today. Yet the majority of the towns with the largest recorded populations in the poll tax of 1377 are those which Domesday Book shows as already in being in 1065. Occasionally a reference in the *Anglo-Saxon Chronicle* shows one of these towns coming into existence, but, in general, their pre-Domesday development is shadowy. The recurrence of rectilinear street plans in some of them (e.g. Wallingford) suggests a deliberate laying out of a town, but there are others where the development seems to have been protracted and organic.

Similar differences are to be found among the towns which rose to prominence after Domesday Book. There are some, like Bristol, dismissed with hardly a notice but certainly in existence in 1086. Others, including those illustrated in this section, only came into being as a deliberate act of 'plantation' in the twelfth, thirteenth and fourteenth centuries. The planting of new towns comes to an abrupt end just before the mid-fourteenth century and was not to be

renewed in England until the development of industrial towns of the last two hundred years.

Town 'plantation' in the early Middle Ages was considerable, and to say with Sir Arthur Bryant[1] that 'every English town, with the possible exception of London, has grown out of a village' is quite untrue. The pioneer survey by Tout[2] had already shown that this was hardly so and no fewer than 172 planned towns in England can now be listed.

These 'plantation'-towns were the work of territorial lords: kings, barons, bishops and abbots who saw that their income could be supplemented by establishing a new town on what had previously been either agricultural land or waste. Here was another community to render an annual fee-farm to its seigneur; another body of craftsmen and tradesmen on the royal demesne under the king's protection, paying tallage and contributing when taxes were assessed upon movable property. The plantation of new towns is only one specialised aspect of the well-known multiplication of boroughs by seigniorial grants to old-established villages.

The number of new towns was limited partly by fears that there was only a fixed amount of trade to be shared and partly by the king's reluctance to see too many additional fortified centres. Many of the planned towns of the twelfth and thirteenth centuries were fortified, some, like Devizes, by association with a newly built castle. The compact block of streets and houses was usually surrounded by defences, whether ditches or walls, having entrances protected by gates.

The new towns are marked by regularity of plan. In the older towns that simply grew up from villages, new streets had to accommodate themselves to existing buildings and natural features. The new towns were able to begin with no such restrictions and no venerated buildings. Their founders laid out a grid of parallel streets

[1] Arthur Bryant, *The Story of England* (1953).
[2] T. F. Tout, 'Medieval town planning', *Collected Papers* III (1934) 59–92.

forming symmetrical building-plots of standard size, with central market-places, and spaces for churches and religious houses. The apotheosis of urban geometry is seen in New Winchelsea, never completed (fig. 103B). The late arrival of a town can also be deduced if its parish-boundaries cut into the smoother lines of older rural parishes among which the town has been planted. Chipping Sodbury and Hedon, with their tiny parish areas and virtually no field-land, are obviously towns carved out of rural parishes, and at some new towns, like Hull and Market Harborough, the mother parish long insisted upon a dependent status for the town's church.

The second part of this chapter illustrates some of Edward I's activities as a builder of towns in England and Wales. It is sometimes said that Edward's early years in France taught him the importance and art of town-planning, but the number of new English towns of the twelfth and thirteenth centuries shows that there was also an English tradition on which the king could draw. As a boy he had looked down from Clarendon towards the streets of New Sarum, while as Warden of the Cinque Ports he must have noticed the symmetry of the streets of New Romney and Sandwich. John, perhaps better known for the sale of borough charters to older communities, had founded New Woodstock and Liverpool, and Richard I had founded Plymouth. Where kings led, bishops were not slow to follow. Chelmsford and Devizes are the work of bishops, and Royston, Baldock and Battle were monastic enterprises. The most impressive English migration, that of a city from Old to New Sarum, was also the work of a bishop.

Although only complete re-planning and planting of towns are discussed here, the plans of some of the smaller medieval boroughs, such as Leeds, suggest that there the grant of borough status to an old-established village was accompanied by the deliberate laying out of burgess plots away from the old centre of gravity (in Leeds, the parish church). It is difficult to pursue this investigation without much better documentation but sometimes plans are most suggestive of a migration.

The full chronology of medieval town 'plantation' shows marked periods of enthusiasm and coolness.[3] The Middle Ages ended with a century and a half of virtual stagnation in this respect, and even when the economy developed new industries in the sixteenth century these did not encourage new towns. The heirs of Edward I and the town-planners whom he summoned to his parley at Bury in 1296 and to Berwick in 1297 were such pioneers as the Ashworths of Turton, the Greggs of Styal and Sir Titus Salt of Saltaire.[4]

[3] Since our first edition a gazetteer of sites and a survey of the whole subject has been published in M. W. Beresford, *The New Towns of the Middle Ages: Town Plantation in England, Wales and Gascony* (1967). Except for the correction of errors, the substance of our text is unchanged.

[4] For some planned towns of the nineteenth century see W. Ashworth, 'British industrial villages in the nineteenth century', *Econ. Hist. Rev.* 2nd ser. III (1951) 378–87. In the seventeenth century Charles I had planned a fenland settlement of Charlemont near Manea, Cambridgeshire (*V.C.H. Cambs.* IV (1953) 136) and Stuart plantations in Ireland had produced the new town of Londonderry on the ruins of Derry: the plan is among the Lambeth Palace Archives. In the eighteenth century deliberate planning had extended Bath (1729–75), and created Edinburgh New Town (1767), very much as five centuries earlier a bishop of Salisbury had added the new borough of Newland at the edge of the older town of Sherborne, Dorset (*Somerset and Dorset Notes and Queries* XIV (1915) 22.

II. FROM DOMESDAY BOOK TO EDWARD I

91. BURY ST EDMUNDS   Suffolk

In many towns Domesday Book records a fall in the number of houses between 1065 and 1086 to make room either for a new castle or for enlargement of one already existing. At Bury, however, the record is much more cheerful. In the twenty years since the death of Edward the Confessor the town houses had spread over the field-land:

... all this account refers to the town as if it were still as in the reign of king Edward. But the town is now contained in a greater circuit including land which was then being ploughed and sown ...

There follows an indication of the occupations of those living in the new houses:

here are 30 priests, deacons and clerks together, 28 nuns and poor people who daily pray for the king and for all Christian people; 75 bakers, ale-brewers, tailors, washerwomen, shoe-makers, robe-makers, cooks, porters and agents ... Besides whom are 13 reeves over the lands of the abbey who have a house in the town, and under them 5 bordars. Now 34 knights, French and English, with 22 bordars under them. Now altogether there are 342 houses on the demesne of the land of the abbey which was all under the plough in the time of King Edward.

Here was a lay community 'daily waiting on Saint Edmund, the abbot and the brothers'. In

Fig. 91. Bury St Edmunds; vertical photograph, August 1967. Scale 1:4750.

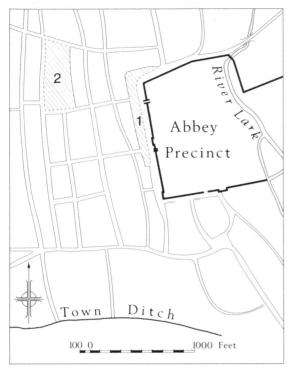

Key to fig. 91 showing (1) the market-place on Angel Hill, and (2) the later 'Butter Market'.

laid out to the west of the old, took the form of five north–south streets, all parallel to the west front of the precinct. The town was protected on the east by the River Lark, on the south by a town ditch and on the north and west by a defensive wall, built in the twelfth century.

The arable land over which the new borough was spreading at the time of Domesday Book had been part of the West Field. The South Field came up to the town ditch, and the East Field lay over the river behind the abbey precinct on the right. These fields played only a minor part in the lives of the townspeople, and the abbey, too, had other estates to maintain it and was by no means dependent on its 400 acres of demesne at Bury. While the cellarers' chequer shows that the fields of Bury were not unprofitable to the abbey in yields of grain and stock, the sacrists' accounts make clear that the real importance of the urban property lay in house-rents, market-dues and tolls. One significant sign of the commercial basis of the town is the market-place (2) which was built in the new town to supplement or replace the old market-place at the abbey gate. This new market-place, now called the 'Butter Market', lay among the grid of streets. It can be seen, much encroached upon, in the top left-hand corner, breaking the symmetry of the parallel roads of the town which Abbot Baldwin created.

Sources

V. B. Redstone, 'St Edmund's Bury and town rental for 1295', *Proc. Suff. Inst. Arch.* XIII (1909) 191–233; M. D. Lobel, *Bury St Edmunds* (1935); J. T. Smith, 'A note on the origin of the town-plan of Bury St Edmunds', *Arch. Jnl.* CVIII (1951) 162–4; rental of 1593; S.C. 12/15/2.

some ways it also resembled the communities of servants and shopkeepers who gathered around the walls of a castle, for the Abbot of St Edmund's was a great feudal magnate, charged with the upkeep of lands, the collection of revenues and participation in local and national administration. A constant coming and going of visitors, whether to the shrine of St Edmund or to the baron-abbot, provided opportunities for those who made their living out of ministering to travellers and pilgrims.

Three hundred and ten persons were recorded in the older *burh* of 1065. This *burh* in its turn had arisen from a great expansion of the village of Boedericesworth after the bones of St Edmund, king and martyr, had been brought here in 908 and a monastery founded. Both stages in the expansion have left their traces on the plan of the town. The vertical photograph (fig. 91), shows how the abbey and its precinct intercept the straight route of Northgate Street and Southgate Street, forcing the main road to make a detour along the front, or west wall, of the precinct. At the north-west corner of the precinct lies the open market-place on Angel Hill (1), just outside the great abbey gate.

The post-Conquest expansion has left its mark on the plan of Bury. The new borough,

92. BOSTON   Lincolnshire

Boston was originally 'Botolph's Town'; a church dedicated to St Botolph is probably the second of two churches in the marshland parish of Skirbeck that are mentioned in Domesday Book. In 1090 the Earl of Richmond gave the rectory of this church to support the abbey of St Mary at York. No urban element is indicated by the Domesday Book references to the earl's property in Skirbeck, and the earliest documentary reference is from 1113 when a town craftsmen, a brazier, made a gift to Croyland Abbey. The town is most likely to be a Norman development, like the earl's borough of Richmond (Yorks) itself.

The straitened bounds of the town show that its territory was cut out of Skirbeck, for that

Fig. 92. Boston; looking SE, June 1950.

parish meets the town ditch on three sides, the river Witham making the fourth. Robert Hall's plan of 1741 shows that the borough territory formed a narrow band about half a mile long on the curving east bank of the river. At its broadest part there was a large triangular market-place with its base alongside the south side of the church, and its apex near the river-bank where the main road, South Street, narrowed to pass under the former St John's Gate, and then followed the river-bank, as it still does, into the fields of Skirbeck, top right. The Bar Ditch, alongside which town walls were placed from 1285, ran parallel to South Street, to which it was joined by a series of short side-streets arranged like the rungs of a long ladder. The northern end of the town was at Bargate on the north-eastern outlet from the market-place (just off the photograph, centre left) and Bargate Green, outside the gate, was again in Skirbeck fields.

On this green and over the fields were planted the booths of the fair which came to be known all over Europe. In 1206 Boston's customs duties were second in the kingdom only to those of London. Its principal export was wool carried to the port by water: Lincolnshire wool from the wide catchment area of the River Witham which, in addition, gathered from the River Trent, via the Foss Dyke, both the wools of the Midlands from the south and the wools of Yorkshire from the north. But there was trade in commodities other than wool. Croyland got its bells here; Bridlington, Bolton and Furness Abbeys their cloth and skins; Henry III's butler bought wine here for the king and rented cellars in Boston to store it.

The town profited by this trading: in 1309 the Norman church was replaced by a larger to which the great tower, the 'Stump', was added in the 1420s. By the end of the Middle Ages there were nineteen religious houses and three friaries but with the decline of wool as an export in favour of manufactured cloth Boston was losing its pre-eminence to the Humber ports, placed nearer to the centres of textile manufacture. In 1607 the corporation pleaded to be reckoned 'a

Fig. 93. Hedon; looking N with the mother village of Preston in the distance, June 1951.

decaied town'. There was some revival in the nineteenth century with the drainage of the surrounding marshland, the coming of the railway and the construction of the Witham docks. Traders' stalls can be seen in the photograph, set out near the market-cross as in the Middle Ages, and alongside the block of permanent buildings which has clearly encroached on the market-place.

Sources

M. R. Lambert and R. Walter, *Boston, Tattershall and Croyland* (1930) and A. M. Cook, *Boston* (1948); *Med. Arch.* II (1958) 200; for river-works at about the time of the foundation: H. E. Hallam, *Settlement and Society* (1965) 41 n. 2 and 219 n. 1.

93. HEDON   Yorkshire, East Riding

Before the end of the twelfth century the lords of Preston in Holderness had seen the potentialities of the stream now known as Hedon Haven. At a site beside the stream, two miles from the wide estuary of the Humber and six miles east of the modern port of Hull, the port of Hedon was planted at the southern tip of Preston parish, and surrounded by a boundary-ditch delineating a rough square. This square, with an additional area to the east which was incorporated before the end of the twelfth century, occupies most of the photograph (fig. 93) below the straight line of the railway. In the distance to the north, beyond the cloud shadow, is the older village of

Preston, a parish whose fields once extended as far as the stream in the foreground of the photograph.

Within the square a town was laid out with streets running north–south. The stream was canalised; from this canal three 'arms' were excavated to enable ships to come right into the town. Two of these long-abandoned 'havens' as they were called, can be distinguished on the photograph. One extends as a narrow finger up the bottom left quadrant; it was being in-filled when the photograph was taken. The other appears near the right margin as a broader, wedge-shaped area fringed by bushes. The church of St Nicholas was built on its left bank but, when the town's prosperity decayed, both this and a second church, St James', fell into disuse. Now there remains only the church of St Augustine, seen in the centre of the town.

Since Hedon was a new settlement in a corner of an old parish, the churches do not ante-date the foundation of the town. St Augustine's was the first; and the other two were built as the houses spread first south and then east. It is likely that the building of St Nicholas' church coincided with the construction of the third haven and the annexation of another strip of land beyond the east ditch of the town. Thus, by the end of the twelfth century the town had three churches and some 850 yards of harbour frontage in three havens. Another sign of the late creation of this community and its complete dependence on commerce and manufactures is that there were never any town fields of Hedon. There is virtually no extramural area and 320 acres of the borough lay within the town ditch; only a small area of commons were to be found in the south-west corner of the borough.

The retreat of prosperity from this inland port began with the success of the rival royal port of Kingston upon Hull and the temporary (although powerful) rivalry of the now-submerged port of Ravenserod on Spurn Head. The silting of the River Hedon aided the eclipse and there is evidence that the burgesses cooperated in efforts to establish a port at Paull Fleet at the mouth of their river by moving the village of Paull from an older site at what is now Paull Holme. Even this enterprise failed to save the borough, and shortly after the church-wardens' accounts of St Nicholas' and St James' come to an end in 1476 these two churches fell into disuse. Since the community had built them, the sites were regarded as common property and the corporation disposed of them; during the life of these churches the unique proprietary relationship of the burgesses had been demonstrated by the election of the church-wardens at burgess meetings.

In the well-known list of English port dues collected in 1203–5 Hedon was eleventh, but by 1280 an inquisition found that 'there are near the aforesaid town two other towns – namely Ravenserod and Hull – with two good ports increasing daily where many wish to remove, for in this town they are every year taxed with tallage'. When Leland visited Hedon in the reign of Henry VIII he wrote 'the sea creeks parting about the said town did insulate it, and ships lay about the town ... it is evident to see that some places where the ships lay be overgrown with flags and reeds, and the Haven is sore decayed'.

The neat, north–south line of the streets still shows in the photograph although only about one-third of the original borough area is now built upon. In Walker Gate, Souter Gate, Fletcher Gate and Baxter Gate the street-names commemorate the craftsmen who lived in them. To the right of the church is a wider street where the Elizabethan markets were held, while the open space which lies to the left of and above the churchyard, Market Hill, was the site of the town hall and of medieval markets and fairs. The borough lost its member of parliament at the Reform Act of 1832 but the engineers who planned the railway had cause in 1854 to remember something of medieval borough-rights. The railway station lies just within the northern tip of the borough boundary, but the unloading shed for waggons was carefully sited a few yards farther north in Preston parish in order to avoid being charged toll for the unloading of goods under Hedon's confirmatory charter of Henry II.

Sources

G. R. Park, *History of Hedon* (1895); J. R. Boyle, *Early History of Hedon* (1895), esp. plan, p. 179, and 1804 map, p. 197; Inq. A.Q.D. 5/16; *Med. Arch.* XVII (1973) 171.

94. LAUNCESTON   Cornwall

The influence determining the site and plan of Launceston is seigniorial. The origin of the town, clustered round the castle and guarded by walls, was described in retrospect by a charter granted to the priory between 1140 and 1176: 'the earl of Mortain transferred the Sunday market from the town of St Stephen at Launceston to a new town by the castle of Dunheved, the canons retaining for themselves and the burgesses all the liberties of the old borough except the market'.

Fig. 94. Launceston; the Norman castle and borough of Dunheved, looking S, April 1966.

This description of the creation of a new borough shortly after the Norman Conquest is confusing until it is realised that the present town of Launceston has suffered a double change of name. The original pre-Conquest borough at St Stephen's, across the valley and 1200 yards north-west of the present castle, was once known as Launceston and the new borough of the Norman earls was first christened Dunheved. With the decay of the old borough and the neglect of its privileges, Dunheved has taken over the name of its predecessor. Confusion is worse confounded by the late development of a third community, also with borough privileges, in the suburb of Newport just outside the north gate of the walled town and between old and new Launceston. From 1529 when it began to return members to parliament, this third borough was called Launceston after the decayed Launceston at St Stephen's. The present Launceston, the walled town, had been sending members to parliament since 1295 under the name of Dunheved. This parliamentary representation followed from the close connection of the boroughs with the Earls of Cornwall, lords of the castle and the town.

In fig. 94 the view is to the south across the castle where two of the three concentric walls of the shell-keep can be seen at the summit of a conical hill. This hill, probably artificial, is *c.* 60 feet high, 210 feet in diameter at the base and 91 feet at the apex. John Leland, visiting Launceston when the walls both of town and castle were still substantial, wrote: 'the large and auncient Castelle of Launstun stondith on the knappe of the hill by south a little from the

221

paroche chirch'. The tower of this church can be seen half-way up the photograph, near the left margin. Apart from the keep, only a few ruins of the castle now remain. The top of the guard-tower is visible beyond the high keep. From the keep and guard-tower the ground falls steeply to the lower court of the castle now laid out with trees and grass. The castle walls encircled this courtyard; the south-west gate can be seen at the farthest end of the castle grounds.

In the Middle Ages the walls of the town and castle were joined, so that the castle occupied the south-west quarter of the town; regarded in another way, the town lay in the outer base-court of the castle. The town walls had three gates, while a fourth, that described above, was shared with the castle. The curve of the house-frontages on the left shows how they accom-modated themselves to the position of the castle ditch, where there is now a narrow street. Very little is left of the town walls and only one gate is standing.

Launceston burgesses, like the burgesses of Totnes, New Buckenham and Hedon, provided themselves with a new and ornate church. Shortly before 1380 a town church replaced a dilapidated chapel attached to the castle. The fourteenth-century church survives only in its tower; the main building was ruinous by the late fifteenth century and a new church was presented to the town in 1511 by Henry Trecarell, of Trecarell, an alderman of the borough and twice its mayor.

Sources

R. and O. B. Peter, *The Histories of Launceston and Dunheved* (1885); A. F. Robbins, *Launceston* (Launceston, 1888); Lysons, *Magna Britannia* III. 186–92; Richard Carew, *Survey of Cornwall* (edn of 1769) 116; Survey of 1607 (imperfect): L.R. 2/207/149.

95. PLESHEY   Essex

In 1174, twenty-five years before the Bishop of London founded Chelmsford, William de Mandeville obtained licence from Henry II to build a castle just off the upper Chelmer valley, seven miles north-west of the future site of Chelmsford. The name of this castle, *Plessis*,[5] was taken for the town that grew up within an earthen wall built out in a loop from the castle. The earthworks of the castle, which were

[5] 'Plessis' means much the same as 'pleached' which describes branches and foliage of trees or bushes which have been interwoven to make a growing wall or enclosure as for an arbour, or a laid hedge. In Norman French *le plessis* or *plessier* was part of a forest enclosed by such a fence.

covered with trees until recent times, appear in fig. 95 as they were not seen for many years.

Pleshey lay in a remote part of High Easter parish and for this reason the bishop allowed a chapel to be built for the town and castle. Its site is now vacant, as are many of the building-plots of the borough. The motte is set partly into the circuit of an oval bailey, centre left, and the earthworks of the town defences make up vir-tually a huge, second bailey, semi-circular rather than oval.

No borough charter has survived but a docu-ment of 1336 mentions burgages. In 1329 there were 118 dwellings. A series of fifteenth- and sixteenth-century surveys show that markets and shops were then still flourishing, with occupied houses in 1623, but the defences had ceased to be relevant to the commercial needs of the town. Indeed, in 1339 a collegiate church was founded outside the walls to replace the chapel as the place of worship for the townspeople. Lack of subsequent development has preserved the lines of the defences almost intact, and the abruptness of the transition to open countryside is as marked as at New Buckenham (fig. 97) or the Welsh towns of the next century (pp. 231–7, below).

Sources

P. A. Rahtz, *Pleshey Castle: first interim report* (1960), esp. figs. 2–3, pls. 1–2; 1336: C. 135/8; other surveys: D.L. 29/42/820; D.L. 29/74/1480; D.L. 43/3/18–19; D.L. 44/1; S.C. 11/197; R.C.H.M. *Essex*, II (1921) 200.

96. CHELMSFORD   Essex

In 1591 John Walker, *architector*, produced his maps of Chelmsford and Moulsham, two adjacent Essex manors. The art of the Elizabethan map-maker has rarely been shown to better advantage, and the full glory of Walker's map can be seen in the coloured fron-tispiece to the Essex Record Office's *Art of the Map-maker in Essex*. The black and white repro-duction (fig. 96A) loses some of its vividness with the colours.

Walker's map was described in the cartouche as 'a trew platt' wherein the user should find 'in the seide platt the Towne in true proportion'. The same might be said of the air photograph (fig. 96B) where the town is seen from the south. Walker would not have much difficulty today in finding his way from the riverside through the old market-place to the parish church beyond. He would notice that the style of buildings had changed, but the frontages which he measured and drew are almost exactly those of the modern

Fig. 95. Pleshey; William de Mandeville's castle and the Norman borough, looking W, June 1961.

shops and houses. The first road on the right above the bridge shows this conservatism of frontage; this is the road from Colchester which comes into Chelmsford across the 'Chellmer or auncient Ryver' of the 1591 map. In that map the two corners where the road joins the High Street do not exactly align: the upper corner projects farther into the High Street. The shop blinds which happen to have been down when the air photograph was taken emphasise that the modern frontages still preserve this difference.

Walker would be most surprised when he came to the market-place. Not only has the market been removed from the old site, but the encroachment of buildings, already begun in 1591, has been carried to completion. A traveller passing through the narrow streets on either side of the central block of shops might be forgiven for not realising that the heart of Chelmsford once lay in a long triangular market-place extending from the churchyard at one end to the river-crossing at the other.

The Tudor plan shows a stage intermediate from the open medieval market-place. The pressure on space had already brought the tol-

eration of encroachments by shops and stalls where drapery, fish, and leather-sellers are listed in Walker's survey. The most considerable change by 1952 is the making of a new road and bridge to the left (west) of the old one. The river frontage has been less affected by change and the buildings adjacent to the old bridge seem to be in the same positions as the Tudor houses. The trees in the photograph give something of the country market-town atmosphere depicted in Walker's green meadows and *backsydes* within a stone's throw of County Hall and the modern car parks. In the mid-1960s yet a third bridge was built farther west to carry a 'relief road' which now cuts through that part of the town in the foreground of this view.

The researches of Miss Hilda Grieve have made it possible to trace back the development of the plan of Chelmsford from Walker's map to Domesday Book. The 'great thorowefare and markett towne' of Walker's day was a small agricultural manor in 1086 (fig. 96c), the property of the Bishop of London. This hamlet was dwarfed by Writtle which adjoined it on the west. Yet the hamlet became the county town.

223

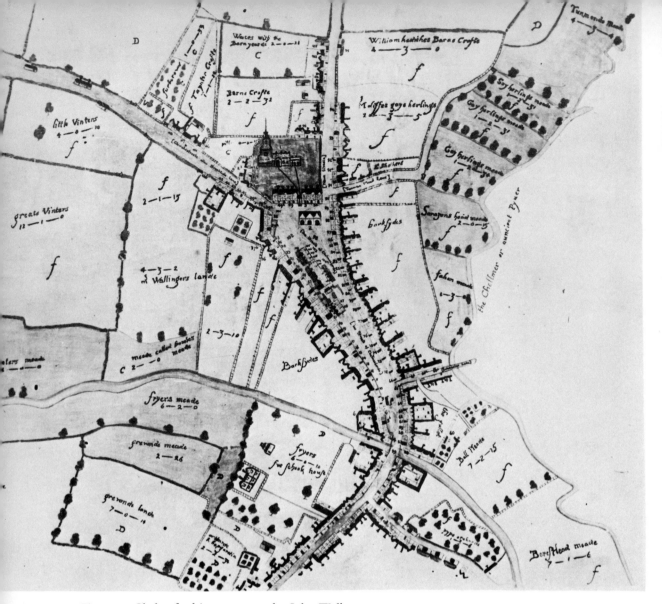

Fig. 96A. Chelmsford in 1591; map by John Walker.

These 'hare-and-tortoise' fortunes can be connected with the building of new bridges by the bishop in the second half of the twelfth century. These bridges enabled the traffic from London to Colchester to avoid the detour previously necessary to cross the River Can near Writtle (fig. 96C). This traffic, now crossing the Can lower down by Chelmsford bridge, passed direct into the lower end of the triangular market-place of Chelmsford, and then turned right (east) to negotiate the Chelmer by a second bridge.

As well as diverting traffic to new routes, the construction of the bridges shifted the whole centre of gravity of Chelmsford. The old manor house, chapel, mill and four villein houses with their swine and sheep lay far from the bridges. The land which the bishop laid out for market-place, church, churchyard and building-plots

was taken from the outer demesnes of the manor much as Hedon was planted on a northern river. With his new bridges the bishop had promoted a new town.

It is not known exactly when this took place. In 1201 Chelmsford bridge had been in existence long enough to be accepted as a boundary-point in a perambulation of the forest. In 1199 the bishop obtained the liberty of private jurisdiction here. The market-charter itself dates from 1199; in a second charter of 1200 the bishop granted parcels of land from his demesne to be held by occupiers with the full privileges of freehold; in 1201 a fair was granted. In the early thirteenth century Chelmsford had become the usual meeting place for the assizes and the county justices. Ordinations were held in the parish church in 1223.

From this evidence it seems clear that the last

Fig. 96B. Chelmsford; looking N, June 1952.

quarter of the twelfth century must have been crucial in the rapid growth of the town. A tradition reported by Camden credited Bishop Maurice (1086–1107) with the bridge-building; the three charters were obtained by Bishop William.

The townsmen never obtained a full borough independence. The court was the court of the bishop's bailiff, and the unpopularity of the seigniorial jurisdiction of the bishop is shown in the burning of the court rolls in the Peasants' Revolt of 1381. Richard II made the town his headquarters for a week of that troubled July. The same year also produced the poll-tax collection from which, despite its evasions, Miss Grieve has been able to compile a virtual directory of the householders who by that time had spread all along the sides of the triangle, making what Walker was to call *the Streete of Chelmesforde*. At least sixty-seven households were placed along its frontage, almost as many as in Walker's plan. An earlier poll tax of 1377 shows 240 persons paying their groat tax. The island in the market-place was coming into existence, first as a row of temporary stalls. Thirty-two stalls were licensed for erection on market-days in 1381 and some shopkeepers owned land in front of their shops as a pitch for stalls. The corn-sellers congregated at the upper end of the street near the churchyard and the market-cross. There were other recognised precincts for sellers of leather, fish, poultry and flesh. An open watercourse ran through the market down the slope to the bridge.

Since the principal roads led into the market-place it was easy to control market-practice and to collect tolls; Bishop Simon of Sudbury attempted to widen the narrow street, only

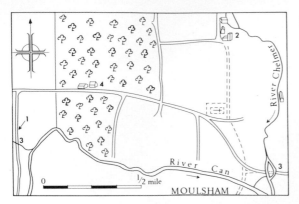

Fig. 96C. The site of Chelmsford; Domesday topography.

1. Road to Writtle, part of main road to London.
2. Manor house and chapel.
3. Fords.
4. Villein settlement of four households.

The dotted lines indicate the results of the Bishop of London's new bridge and the market-place and church of the new town.

twelve paces wide at the bridgehead, to make way for traffic, but he was defeated by the ostlers who kept an inn there. To this day the narrow bridgehead remains intact and now the modern by-pass takes much of the traffic.

To the south of the bridge, Walker's map shows the overspill of houses into Moulsham. This manor was in Chelmsford parish, but it belonged to the Abbot of Westminster and was only brought under the same ownership as Chelmsford when the Mildmays acquired both properties after the Dissolution. It was by the bridge that 'forestallers' like Robert Snell of the *Cock* and *Boar's Head* waited to catch the country-folk with their produce to snap it up before it could reach the stalls. Today the Shire Hall stands at the top of the market-place where formerly stood the bishop's court-house for the trial of such forestallers. The county councillor or justice who steps out of the Hall no longer commands a full view of a crowded market stretching down to the bridge, but if he wishes he can read more history into what he sees than may councillors in many other shire towns.

Sources

Poll tax of 1377: E. 179/107/46; MS. notes by Miss Hilda Grieve who has kindly loaned maps and transcripts; *Med. Arch.* XVII (1973) 167.

97. NEW BUCKENHAM   Norfolk

The lord of Buckenham, William de Albany (d. 1154) wished to build a new castle, being dissatisfied with the site chosen by his predecessors. The parish, fifteen miles south-west of Norwich, covered some 5000 acres, much of it poor quality land, still sparsely settled. The village of (Old) Buckenham lay at the west side of its parish, but the site which de Albany coveted for his new castle was near the south-east corner on the boundary of Banham parish. This site was not part of the manor of Buckenham, and it had to be obtained from the Bishop of Norwich. A new flint castle was built here, and the stone from the old castle was used to build the priory which William founded in Old Buckenham in about 1146.

The new castle was a mile and a half from Old Buckenham and no nearer to any other village: its defences consist of the circular bank and ditch seen in the foreground of the photograph (fig. 97), where they are viewed from the south-west. The site lay on the route from Bury St Edmunds to Norwich, and these two factors may have suggested the creation of a borough adjoining the castle. For this purpose 360 acres were cut out of the parishes of Banham and Carleton Rode. The boundary of Old Buckenham parish runs along the far side of the open space, 220 yards wide, which separates the town from the castle. A chapel just outside the castle ditch, and also outside the borough, served for both townspeople and castle-dwellers, until Sir Robert de Tateshale founded the church of St Martin, the present parish church. The castle chapel decayed and in the eighteenth century was used as a barn.

As at Hedon, the small area of field-land, about 355 acres, would have been insufficient to maintain an agricultural community, but the townspeople acquired supplementary sources of income from their market, for which a charter was obtained in 1285; from the craftsmen and tradesmen ministering to the castle, and from travellers on the Norwich road. In the tax of 1334 New Buckenham was already passing the assessment of Old Buckenham. Indeed, only half the 355 acres of the parish of New Buckenham can ever have been cultivated, the other half being the heath seen in the background of the photograph. The existence of two enclaves of about 180 acres each, protruding into Banham and Carleton parishes, suggests that New Buckenham was simply given two equal areas cut from Banham Heath and Carleton Rode Heath for its field-land and grazing. The eighty head of

Fig. 97. New Buckenham; looking NE, April 1965.

stock permitted on the common of New Buckenham today may be a distant reflection of an
original right of eighty houses in the town. In
1595 a long-standing dispute between Buckenham and its neighbours over the boundaries
on the heath was waged through the county
court, Common Pleas and Exchequer, the rights

of Buckenham eventually being confirmed. In
the course of the evidence witnesses described
the fair of Buckenham 'upon the sayde waste
grounde with their Boothes and Standinges'.

Because the borough was so closely encircled
by rural parishes it was easy for illicit traffic to
poach upon the preserves of the burgesses'

227

Fig. 98. Brackley; looking NE, June 1951.

privileges. There was an interesting case in 1638 when unlicensed tobacco-retailers took money from customers in New Buckenham but gave delivery a stone's throw away in the shadow of the castle ruins and in the free air of Old Buckenham parish.

The field which intervenes between castle and borough bears no signs of former streets or houses. The borough itself formed a neat square about 200 yards in size. This symmetry is upset only by the church and churchyard which lie, on the left, outside the limits of the square. It has already been mentioned that the church was no part of the original foundation but the gift of a later lord of Buckenham. In the lawsuit of 1595 witnesses still referred to the church as 'new erected' and deposed that no tithes were paid.

The fact that the town was planned and not shaped by organic growth can also be seen in the right-angled discipline of the streets. The two

main streets lie parallel, with subsidiary back-lanes and cross-lanes. A market-place was provided in the space between the two main streets at the end of the town farthest from the castle, near the point at which the Norwich road enters from the heath. Although there have been some encroachments, much of the market-square can be seen as an open space with grass and trees.

Sources

Blomefield, *Norfolk* 1. 268; 1334: E. 179/149/11; 1595: E. 134/38 Eliz. Hil. no. 24, E. 123/25/308; tobacco: E. 178/5534.

98. BRACKLEY Northamptonshire

The traveller to Brackley, which lies in the south-western corner of Northamptonshire, is struck by the remoteness of two normal features of a market-town. There is no church to be seen near the long, broad High Street, and the oddly named Central Station lies well outside the northern end of the town. The photograph (fig. 98) shows Brackley from the south-west.

There are historical explanations of the determined isolation of both church and station, but it is only with the church that this account is concerned. The parish church, which can be seen at the top right-hand corner of the plate, is remote because the centre of gravity of the town has moved. Yet even 'Old Town', the group of houses around the church, is itself the result of an earlier move. Brackley lies within the Anglo-Saxon parish of Halse, now a small cluster of farms two and a half miles to the north-west. By the time of Domesday Book there was a daughter settlement of Halse near the present Brackley church, in *Bracca's leah* or clearing. Only a footpath now leads down from Old Town to the mill and ford across the Ouse, a quarter of a mile to the east, but it seems likely that the potentialities of the river-crossing explain the migration from Halse.

In the time of Henry III, a castle was built in a tributary valley, and a new borough laid out upon the slopes beside it. The castle, which has been destroyed, lay outside the lower margin of the photograph. The borough has declined in importance since the thirteenth century, but its plan has been little altered. When Leland visited Brackley in the early sixteenth century he was amazed to see a town so much in decay: you could see the former circuit, he said, and it was every inch of two miles round. He was not far wrong. From the castle to the end of High Street is nearly 1500 yards, and the full width of the borough area (as at the foot of the photograph) is nearly 500 yards.

Brackley had flourished as a market-town for the local wool-clip, and the broad High Street was the sign of its mercantile purpose. The burgesses of Brackley always went to the parish church of St Peter in the Old Town, yet the houses in the lanes near the church were never considered part of the borough. There in the Old Town, the agricultural life continued. The isolation of Old Town was increased by a southward diversion of the main road to Buckingham which now leaves High Street on the right where the market-place narrows at the end of a green. As a result the old route from Halse to Buckingham, which, it is suggested, determined the site of Old Town, has become a footpath.

Like Warkworth (fig. 62), Brackley seems to have had only one back-lane, parallel to High Street and serving the ends of the long, narrow crofts of the burgesses' houses on the left. The

fall of the ground on the right-hand (east) side of High Street made for much shorter crofts there. The large buttressed building between High Street and a playing-field marks the site of St John's Hospital which came into the possession of Magdalen College, Oxford in the fifteenth century. The hospital was used as a retreat for the Fellows when plague visited Oxford, and was later established as Magdalen College School to which the present building belongs.

Sources

Baker, *Northants* I. 560; *P.N. Northants.* (1933) 49; E. R. Forrester, *Magdalen College School* (1950) maps of 1760.

99. BALDOCK   Hertfordshire

There are interesting parallels between the foundation of a new town at Royston (fig. 77) and the almost contemporary foundation of another town only nine miles to the south-west. In each a religious house was responsible for the new community and for the privileges of market and fair which were given to the townsmen. Each site stood in open country where the Icknield Way, following the foot of the chalk hills, intersected a north-bound road from London. The present main road (A1) comes to Baldock through Hatfield, but the alignment of parish boundaries and a partly disused succession of lanes and footpaths suggest that an older route approached Baldock up the Beane from Hertford.

The intersection of the two important roads at Baldock made, as at Royston, a right angle. At Royston the north-bound main road was widened to give room for the market-place. At Baldock the transverse road was widened and at the head of the triangle of open ground a new church was built. The diversion of the Great North Road and the abandonment of the route from Walkern to Baldock may date from the setting out of the market-place along the south-western arm of Baldock crossroads, for it is into this arm that the present route leads.

Like Royston, Baldock lay on the edge of three parishes and not far from the meeting place of five. The 150 acres or so (in the north of the parish of Weston) which made up the town and its fields were granted to the Knights Templars between 1138 and 1148. The king gave charters for a market and fair in 1199, but even in the great survey of Templar possessions in 1185 an active town was in being, and the description of Baldock is very different from that of the men and their holdings in Weston two miles away,

Fig. 99. Baldock; looking ENE along the Icknield Way, June 1954.

where the Templars maintained a demesne on which villeins worked, rendering both rent and labour services. In the town there were no services rendered: the Templars were rent receivers only. The area of field-land, about 100 acres, was too small to maintain the 122 tenants whose names appear in the survey. A typical entry is: 'Ricardus de Herford tenet iii acras de burgagio in villa de baldach', and the surnames of the tenants indicate what alternative occupations there were to work in the fields, and how the Templars found it profitable to relieve such men of their obligation to do agricultural work, tak-

ing only a money rent. There were thirty-one houses, seven shops, a smithy and stalls (*seudas*) in the market-place. The surnames include a blacksmith, an ironmonger, a tailor, a shoe-maker, a tanner, a mason, a cook, a carter, a reeve, a mercer, a weaver, a saddler, a goldsmith, a merchant and a vintner.

That the town was a new and deliberate plantation is certain from the absence of early references and from the words used by the Earl of Pembroke in the early thirteenth century, ratifying the grant of his ancestors: 'confirmavimus ... illas decem libratas terrae ... in eodem man-

230

erio in qua terra ipsi [i.e. the Templars] construxerunt quendam burgum qui dicitur Baudoc'. As a last witness it is not inappropriate to cite the name of the new town itself: 'Baudoc' is Baghdad, a name brought from the east by the Templars, but the reason for this curious choice of name remains unexplained. The Templars' commercial optimism must have been high if they hoped to create a new Baghdad in Hertfordshire.

The photograph (fig. 99) shows Baldock from the west-south-west. The Icknield Way enters the town from the east, at the top of the photograph, and can be seen to widen for the old market-place as it approaches the parish church and the main crossroads in the centre of the town. The island of buildings which now encroaches on the market-place is clearly indicated. To the right of the church is the broad road coming from London which led straight to the centre of the market-place. There traffic was forced to turn on to the line of the Icknield Way, and to traverse the length of the wide street. At the farther, narrower, end a second right-angle turn, this time to the left, enabled traffic to resume its northward course. The modern A1 followed this double turn, and irritated motorists on busy Saturdays must blame the zeal of the town's founders who were anxious that traffic should not ignore their market-place nor fail to pay their dues.

Sources

V.C.H. Herts. III (1912) 66ff; *Cal. Rot. Cart.* (Record Comm.) 2, for charter; B. A. Lees, ed., *The Templars' Inquest of 1185* (1935) cxxxvi and 66; Dugdale, *Monasticon*, VI. 762; *P.N. Herts.* (1938) 120–1.

III. SOME TOWNS OF EDWARD I

The building of towns[6] formed only one aspect of the strenuous achievements of Edward I, and the towns illustrated in this section are but part of the constructional work on castles, town houses, streets and town walls undertaken in England and Wales between 1277 and 1296. His improvements to Berwick were separately illustrated in chapter 8, section III, when walled towns were considered.

Winchelsea and Newton apart, the Edwardian towns of this period are by-products of the campaigns in Wales and Scotland which occupied so much of the king's energies after 1277. The magnitude of the effort represented a heavy drain on royal finances, a considerable effort of organisation and planning, and an impressive assembly of labour and raw materials. Altogether, the towns and castles had no small effect on the English economy in those crowded years. At one time Edward had five castellated boroughs under construction simultaneously as part of the North Wales defences after the victory over Llewelyn in 1282: Caernarvon,

[6] For the work of Edward I as a town-builder see the books and articles cited in the Source-notes, and T. F. Tout, 'Medieval town planning', *Collected Papers* III (1934) 59–92; E. A. Lewis, *The Medieval Boroughs of Snowdonia* (1912); J. G. Edwards, 'Edward I's castle building in Wales', *Proc. British Academy* XXXII (1946) 15–81; G. P. Jones, 'Trading in medieval Caernarvon', *Trans. Caerns. Hist. Soc.* X (1949) 3–12; F. M. Powicke, *The Thirteenth Century* (1953) 429–44; C. Shillaber, 'Edward I, builder of towns', *Speculum* XXII (1947) 297, adds nothing to these. The Exchequer records contain many rentals and surveys from the early years of the Edwardian towns: e.g. Beaumaris, S.C. 11/767; Conway, S.C. 12/17/87–8; Caernarvon, S.C. 12/17/86.

Conway, Criccieth, Bere and Harlech. Five years earlier the end of a period of hostilities had produced the castles and towns of Flint, Aberystwyth and Rhuddlan; Beaumaris and Bala arose after the disorders of 1294. In addition to these new or extended towns and castles the wars with the Welsh princes also produced new Marcher castles such as Builth and the rebuilding of others on modern principles (as at Dinefwr and Llandovery), while the Scottish campaigns caused Berwick to be remodelled and a new circuit of walls to be built around it.

It was for Berwick that Edward summoned his parliament of town-planners to Bury in 1296, towards the end of a lifetime closely associated with the logistics of creating urban communities. The Edwardian towns are usually described as 'new' although the adjective occasionally requires qualifications: a walled borough such as Flint was placed in open country, but the walls of Conway necessitated the prior removal of a Cistercian house and the clearing of the small town gathered outside its gate, while at Winchelsea and Caernarvon there were older settlements on the sites chosen for the new walled towns. At Beaumaris a Welsh settlement had to be removed to Rhosfair, thirteen miles away, where the borough of Newborough (Newport) in Anglesey was created in 1303; at Rhuddlan the town replaced an already existing community settled around the old castle; at Denbigh the new town succeeded the hill-top settlement which had been the centre of a Welsh barony.

The grant of borough status accompanied Edward's town-building whether or not the town was linked to the castle by means of walls. Thus Flint, Conway, Caernarvon, Criccieth, Harlech, Beaumaris, Bere, Rhuddlan (a re-foundation), Aberystwyth, Builth, Caerwys and Newborough acquired borough privileges between 1277 and 1303. In the same period, Welshpool and Llanfyllin were founded by Welsh lords.

The intermingling of garrison and tradesmen, like the juxtaposition of market-place and battlements, is characteristic of these new Welsh towns and also of Berwick-upon-Tweed, a market-centre with a long pre-Edwardian tradition. The market-place and the tradesmen's shops were even more important in the plans for Winchelsea and Newton, while the improvements in and along the approaches to the king's town (Kingston) upon Hull were designed both to defend it against enemies without and to facilitate the approach of goods from its hinterland. In North Wales the rural areas near the new towns were treated strictly as 'catchment areas'; trading *in patria* outside the urban market-place needed specific permission. The urban monopoly of trade within the rural catchment area was more easily imposed in a conquered country, but it was not far from the ambitions of many old-established English towns. The latter, however, were usually set among rivals with privileges which limited or defeated a monopolistic ambition.

Details of the foundation and character of the new towns, as expressed in castle, streets and buildings, are given individually in the commentaries that follow.

100. FLINT   Flintshire

In the late fourteenth century the burgesses of Beaumaris could look back to the origins of the buildings that they saw around them, and say that Edward I, 'for consideration of pacifying Anglesea', had built their castle. They put the emphasis correctly, for neither the topography nor the constitutional position of Edward's Welsh towns can be understood except as the plantation of garrisons in a conquered and potentially rebellious countryside.

The burgesses continued, 'for the munitioning of the said castle he had ordained the town to be set near, whither English folk had come to reside'. The characteristic conjunction of town and castle which is seen at Beaumaris, Caernarvon, Flint and Conway, to take only a few examples, sprang from Edward's keen per-

ception that peaceful opportunities for trade and agriculture would impress themselves on the minds of Welshmen, and make them more tolerant of the military garrisons in their midst. Reciprocally, the towns and their markets would help to ensure the supply of provisions for the garrisons.

The first two Edwardian towns in North Wales were Flint and Rhuddlan. Rhuddlan was completed in four and a half building 'seasons', each from April to November, beginning in August 1277, after the end of the campaign of that year. The principal expenditure there was on the castle, six times as much as on the town.

Flint was begun a month before Rhuddlan and finished in about the same period. Within a year of completion it was involved in a renewed outbreak of hostilities in Dafydd's attack of 1282, when some houses were burned. There is evidence that there had been something like a burghal settlement around the walls of the eleventh-century castle at Rhuddlan but Flint was an entirely new foundation. It was possible, therefore, to lay out a town *de novo* without consideration of any existing lines of streets. The result appears in the symmetrical gridiron plan of the town. The royal surveyors decided on a site for the castle on an outcrop of sandstone by the riverside, about half-way between Rhuddlan and the English headquarters at Chester, and then laid out the walled town on the adjacent open land of two Welsh vills.

Quite apart from masons, to whom a summons to leave their work and build for the king would have been no novelty, there was need for carpenters, tilers and general labourers to dig ditches and make up the mounds which were to form the defences. Among the ditch-diggers (*fossatores*) at Flint and Rhuddlan in the first season of 1277 were 300 men from Holland in Lincolnshire whom the sheriff had sent with three mounted guards in case they deserted (*ne fugerent per viam*). Three hundred Derbyshire carpenters were also cutting and hammering wood in North Wales. In the first week's work at Flint 950 ditch-diggers were employed on the castle and town ditches. Some traces of the double bank and ditch remain, but the most obvious monument to Edward's conception is the castle and the grid of streets of which the central member leads direct to the castle. Both town and castle are seen in the photograph (fig. 100) from the north-east.

The plan of Flint was not symmetrical, as Speed's map of about 1610 shows. The axis of the town, now a broad street leading over a level-crossing, follows the same course as in

Fig. 100. Flint; looking SW, June 1956.

Speed's plan. St Mary's church is on the left of this street, set at an angle to it in order to lie east and west. A three-storeyed gabled building occupies much of the market-place; a market and fair were chartered in 1278. To the right of the main street are three narrower streets. The seventeenth-century plan shows that the

defences lay between the second and third of these. To the left of the main street the position of the ditches and mound is marked by gardens between the third and fourth streets, counted outwards from the axis.

On the seaward side, the town ditch linked with the castle moat, now partly filled up as a

233

result of the silting of the Dee estuary. The photograph was taken at low water, and thus prevents a proper appreciation of the waterside defences.

At Flint the town defences were probably never furnished with a stone wall like those at Conway or Caernarvon. The proportion of stone-masons among the 1685 workmen who received their pay during an average week in the first five weeks' working was one to every three carpenters, and for every three carpenters there were twelve ditch-diggers. The masons would be at work on the castle, and the carpenters on the houses and on the wooden palisade which surmounted the earthen ramparts of the town, in lieu of a stone wall.

Sources

R.C.H.M. *Flintshire* (1912) 25–9, reproducing Speed's plan of *c*. 1610; Department of the Environment, *Guide to Flint Castle*; J. G. Edwards, 'The building of Flint', *Flints. Hist. Soc.* XII (1951) 1–20, and 'Edward I's castle building in Wales', *Proc. British Academy* XXXII (1946) 15–81; J. D. Lloyd, *Flints. Hist. Soc.* VI. 21.

101. CAERNARVON   Caernarvonshire

At Caernarvon the town is more closely integrated with the castle than at Flint. The defences are a massive stone wall and towers, and the town wall guarded one approach to the castle, just as the castle formed a defence for the townspeople. The construction at Caernarvon dates from the suppression of the revolt of 1282, so that Flint was complete before the more westerly town was begun. Just as Flint must be considered as the half-way point in a chain of defences from Chester to Rhuddlan, so Caernarvon is a link between Conway and Harlech, two other castles built after 1282, as well as a key point from which to control the Menai Straits. Caernarvon was not set in open country but on a coastal site already occupied by a Norman castle and not far both from the Roman fort of Segontium, founded in the first century, and from a third-century fort on the cliff above the River Seiont. The photograph (fig. 101) shows the walled town from the east: on the left is the Seiont which flows past the castle to join the waters of the Menai Straits.

The ditch and town wall were completed by 1285, and in subsequent seasons the castle was begun, but not completed until 1322. The junction of the town wall with the castle in the foreground has been destroyed by the cutting of a modern street. The general plan of the enclosed area is symmetrical, with the east gate in the centre of the landward side of the town where the guildhall now straddles the wall. Eight of the half-round bastions set at intervals around the wall can be seen, two of them above the roofs of the houses along the waterside. A west gate gave on to the waterside at a point exactly opposite the landward east gate. There was a gridiron pattern of streets.

Professor J. G. Edwards has calculated that the works at Caernarvon had already cost something in the region of £16000 by 1301, about one-fifth of the total estimated cost of the seven castles or towns which the King had undertaken.

Within the walls the building-plots were made ready for Englishmen. The early rentals show that not all the plots were immediately taken, and it was ordered that only those burgesses who fulfilled their promise to come and occupy plots could remain their lawful owners. Timber for building the new houses was brought from the forests; the King had men at work along the coastal plain clearing trees to permit easier manœuvring by his troops, as well as to provide for his building projects. Some of the unused castle materials were later made available as surplus stores for the burgesses' house-repairs.

The rentals for Caernarvon begin with that of 1298, in which fifty-six burgesses have one burgage plot and six others a half-plot each. The normal rent for a burgage was a shilling a year paid in two instalments. By 1312 there were 124 occupied burgages in Caernarvon and inequality in the size of holdings was beginning to make itself shown; the residence rule was being laxly administered. Similar inequality was shown in the holdings of the field-land outside the walls. By 1410 one burgess held six burgages and 200 acres of field-land; another five burgages and 120 acres. In the first rental of 1298 there was only one burgess with more than a single plot, but the area of field-land varied. The half-burgages had five acres, but a full burgage had anything from five to seventy acres. The size of a burgage plot is not given in this rental, but Professor E. A. Lewis quotes an account in which the plot measured eighty feet by sixty feet. Fourteenth-century deeds registered the transfer of plots which were twenty-one feet wide and twenty-eight feet long, but subdivision could have taken place by that date.

The thirteenth-century burgesses included carpenters, tailors, smiths, butchers and bakers, but the cases in the court rolls examined by Professor G. P. Jones suggest general tradesmen as the normal townsfolk rather than a community made up of specialist craftsmen. Some

Fig. 101. Caernarvon; looking W, July 1948.

port-dues were paid, although in peacetime there is no evidence of any considerable use of the port. In time of war supplies were brought by sea from Chester and the Wirral.

The extramural suburbs developed early in the life of the town. The rental of 1298 standardised the extramural houses to a thirty-foot frontage. One of the town's two watermills stood outside the walls. The houses outside were, of course, highly vulnerable in times of trouble: sixty houses in the suburb beyond the east gate were damaged during the revolt of Owen Glyndwr. In recent centuries the town has outgrown the walls in all the landward directions. The modern market-place with its fountain and parked 'buses is separated from the quayside by a row of shops.

Sources

J. G. Edwards, 'Edward I's castle building in Wales', *Proc. Brit. Academy* XXXII (1946) 15–81; E. A. Lewis, *Medieval Boroughs of Snowdonia* (1912); G. P. Jones, 'Trading in medieval Caernarvon', *Trans. Caerns. Hist. Soc.* X (1949) 3–12; deeds in *Bulletin of Celtic Studies* IX (1938) 242; rental of 1298: S.C. 12/17/86; T. F. Tout, 'Medieval town planning', in *Collected Papers* III (1934) 59–92; Department of the Environment, *Guide to Castle and Town Walls*; for other accounts: M.A. 1170/4, 9, and 14; R.C.H.M. *Caernarvonshire* II (1960).

102. DENBIGH Denbighshire

The brother of Prince Llewelyn, Dafydd ap Gruffyd, had his residence at Denbigh, probably on the hilltop where the castle and walled town now stand. After Dafydd's revolt in 1282 the strong point was captured by Edward I who spent seventeen days there in the autumn of 1282, during which time he granted the district to the Earl of Lincoln so that he could build a castle while the king himself moved away to the coast. A town was planned to lie alongside the castle, gathered within the common protection of the walls encircling the plateau. Of the sixty-six and three-quarter acres assigned in the foundation charter, the town of Denbigh was to occupy fifty-seven and a quarter. The hilltop unity of town and castle is more striking here

235

than at Caernarvon where the coastal terrain is level and the isolation of the citadel from the surrounding countryside less marked.

The charter of 1290 allocated forty-seven burgage plots within the town walls and forty-one burgesses took them up, six burgesses accepting two plots each. Almost all the plots carried with them a curtilage outside the walls and an oxgang of land in the fields. A close connection was established between occupation and garrison obligations, 'each burgess shall find a man armed for each burgage and curtilage which he holds'.

Four years later the town fell again to the Welsh, and after its recovery there seems to have been closer supervision of the completion of the fortifications which the revolt must have found unfinished. The present ruined condition of the castle dates from the end of the Civil War; it had been garrisoned by royalist troops but surrendered in 1646. The virtual disappearance of the town from within the walls of Denbigh and its migration to its present extramural site date from an earlier civil war, that of the Roses. The town began by being a Yorkist stronghold but was captured by the Lancastrians in 1460 and recaptured in 1461. In 1462 Edward IV granted 1500 marks to the rebuilding 'by occasion of brennying of the same Towne violently doon'. If the date given in Richard III's confirmation of the grant in 1483 is correct, the town was captured and burned by Jasper Tudor in 1468 and some traditions date the foundation of the new town from this period. Leland wrote: 'the new towne of Denbigh was close defacid with fier by hostilitie, 1468.' Camden's account of the migration describes no sudden movement but a gradual shift of population after the siege of 1468:

since which time either because the inhabitants disliked the situation of it, for the declivity of the place was in no way convenient, or else because it was not well served with water, they removed thence by degrees: in so much that the old town is now deserted and a new one, much larger, sprung up at the foot of the hill which is now so populous that the church not being large enough for the inhabitants, they have now begun to build a new one where the old town stood.

The isolation of the old town site was described in a survey of about 1530:

near the same castle are a few houses and a fair chapel called the Borough of Denbigh, the same Borough and Castle being walled about with a strong wall standing high, and the way going forth of the said North Gate lieth in the suburbs of Denbigh wherein the great number of the Burgesses and inhabitants of the said town doth inhabit, the same being three quarters of a mile long. And in the High Street is a fair

room where the Market is kept every Wednesday, the same being the shire town.

The castle park began at the south wall of the castle and ran down to the Afon Ystrad.

The castle did not escape the scrutiny of the surveyors in the first few years of Elizabeth's reign; there is a short survey of 1561, another of the parks in 1583 and a fuller survey in 1594, followed by another in the first year of James I's reign. By this time a new building had sprung up within the empty space where the old town had stood. The Earl of Leicester, who possessed the lordship from 1563 to 1588, had already built a town hall in the new market-place (c. 1571). Finding, as Camden described, that the populous town had grown too large for the little church of the old town, the Earl also began to build a spacious church on ground vacated by the migration of the medieval town. The project was never carried through and the shell of the unfinished church partners the ruined castle and the disused chapel of the medieval town.

The photograph (fig. 102), taken from the north, looks across the streets and market-place of the new extramural town to the castle and old town site on the hill. At the far end of the hill stands the castle; its curtain walls are linked to the defences of the town which follow the circuit of the hill. The town wall has intermittent postern-towers. It runs through the woods to the complicated extension of the walled area on the limestone cliff at the centre left. The double line of walls here is caused by an enlargement of the fortified area after the recapture of the town in 1294. Within the base of the Goblin Tower, a high tower running right up the cliff face away from the camera, is a deep well. It would seem that the old castle well had proved insufficient in a siege and that this complicated and expensive salient was added solely to guarantee a water-supply.

From this salient the wall returns across the near slope of the hill. Its thickness is apparent in this sector when it is not obscured by houses. A little farther on, the line can be seen to end in the roofless Burgess Tower, the fortified gateway to the old town. In front of the walled area the ground falls to the centre of the new town whose plan included an elongated triangular market-place of the familiar pattern. The site may be identified on fig. 102 by the row of parked cars that stand along its axis. The large building at the left of the triangle is Leicester's 'market-house', or town hall.

Leicester's unfinished church can be seen, roofless, within the old town. It lies at the near

Fig. 102. Denbigh; looking S, June 1956.

end of the dark wedge of trees which crosses the hill, and trees are actually growing within the area of the building. No signs of houses of the medieval town can be discerned in the cleared space of Castle Green between the wood and the castle gate, although the surface there is very uneven. The tower of the chapel of St Hilary stands at the side of the open area of grass, about half-way between Leicester's church and the castle gate. This was 'the chapel within the walls' of the 1334 survey, a building 120 feet long and forty feet wide, of which the foundations appear as lines of parching in the grass to the left of the tower. It was the church of both castle and borough, and contemporary in foundation with the town. As in some late-founded English towns, the new borough made an island in the parish of Llanfarchell, and when the town moved outside the borough walls it found itself once more in Llanfarchell parish. Possibly this dependence on another parish church in an isolated position a mile away (at SJ 071662) gave

force to the project of Leicester's church. The new extramural town had no church until 1840.

The castle is now in the care of the Department of the Environment and the circuit of the town wall may be made on application to the custodian at the castle.

Sources
Department of the Environment, *Denbigh Castle and Town Walls* (1949); R.C.H.M. *Denbighshire* (1914) 39–46; P. Vinogradoff and F. Morgan, eds., *Survey of the Honour of Denbigh, 1334, Records of the social and economic history of England and Wales*, 1 (Brit. Acad. 1914); J. Williams, *Ancient and Modern Denbigh* (Denbigh, 1856); W. J. Hemp, 'Denbigh Castle', *Y Cymmrodor*, XXXVI (1926); survey of 1561: S.C. 12/27/28; of 1603: E. 178/3413; grant of Richard III and charter of 1290, confirmed in 1587, from Williams, *op. cit.*; L. A. S. Butler, 'Leicester's church, Denbigh', *Jnl Brit. Arch. Assoc.* 3rd ser. XXXVIII (1974) 40–62.

The Edwardian towns of North Wales show that the king was well aware of the necessity to

Fig. 103A. Winchelsea; looking SSE, June 1958.

encourage merchant communities and trading within the walls of the garrison towns. The summons to Berwick had called for men who knew how to lay out a town 'suitable for merchants', and it was on the trading and commercial class that Edward relied to occupy the new burgage plots in the southern foundations which are considered next. At Winchelsea the inflow of burgesses was stimulated by the decay and destruction of Old Winchelsea nearby; at Newtown, Isle of Wight, Edward acquired the town already founded some thirty years before, but the little port could not withstand commercial competition and, as will be seen in the next section, the plantation failed.

103. WINCHELSEA   Sussex

Winchelsea has deservedly received much attention from students of medieval town-planning. It has a well-documented origin, beginning with the floods which swept away Old Winchelsea, and was surveyed in unequalled detail in its very first years. The town has suffered little dis-

turbance by the rebuilding of houses in the last three centuries, and its history as a great Channel-port ends with the final irony that a town which had arisen because of the sea's erosion decayed because of the silting up of the estuary of the Brede.

Old Winchelsea, the predecessor of Edward's town, stood on the east side of the Camber (the *Camera* or *Chambre* formed by the mouths of the Brede). Some marshland on that side of the river is today within the parish of St Thomas in New Winchelsea, which must have retained its rights even after the erosion and the submergence of the old town. The lordship of the town had belonged to a foreign monastery (Fécamp) since a grant by Canute, but it was too valuable a strategic point for the Crown to be comfortable with alien ownership, and in 1247 the gift was revoked and the town became royal demesne once more. The storms of 1244 had already caused serious damage, and erosion seems to have continued. Foreseeing the final loss of the port, Edward I took the first steps to replace it by acquiring the manor of Iham in Icklesham where

Fig. 103B. New Winchelsea; plan based on the rental of 1292.

the church ruins being finally removed in 1810 to make way for the present windmill.

The plateau which had been acquired for this town lent itself by its flatness to a street plan of the simplest kind. The streets (*strata*) were drawn approximately at right angles to each other forming thirty-nine 'Quarters' varying in size from one to three acres, intended for houses. Other areas were allocated to such public uses as churches and market-place. The church of St Thomas, transferred from the old town, was given a central position, set in a churchyard of nearly three acres. Its chancel, chapels and vestry may be seen in the centre of the town, their east–west alignment slightly askew to the line of the streets. The much reduced size of the church may derive from failure to complete the original plan rather than from vandalism in a French raid. A second church, St Giles, which occupied part of Quarter XXI, was pulled down in 1760; a house of the Grey Friars, the only religious house to be moved from the old town, also took four acres. Eighty-seven and a half acres were available for the 611 houses. In addition to the 611 house plots there were also seventy-nine houses on the slopes north and west of the town overlooking Iham marsh. These areas, called *subpendentes montis* in the rentals, were the 'pendanntes of the hylles' of the document of 1544 already cited.

The survey of 1292 takes the form of a rental, street by street, Quarter by Quarter, building-plot by building-plot, and the information could hardly have been more fully expressed had a map been drawn.

Some historians have seen the rental of 1292 as a prospectus rather than a survey; but it is a curious prospectus which gives the names of burgesses and the rent which they are paying. A compotus in the British Library shows that the rents stated in the survey of 1292 were actually being paid between 1297 and 1304; but vacant holdings did begin to appear before the mid-fourteenth century. In 1342, ninety-four holdings were excused rent, and in 1365, 294 tenants in the town and 148 from the *subpendentes* received some rent relief. Some of these were only partial reliefs, and in 1369 there were at least 377 inhabited houses, but there are other signs that all was not well. Apart from the plagues, there were raids from France, and the Exchequer heard frequent petitions from those whose houses had been burned. By 1575, when the retreat of the sea and the silting of the estuary had taken away the mainspring of the town's life, it was said that there were fewer than sixty inhabited houses in the town. The names of the

a plateau, high above the level of the marshes, fronted the River Brede on two sides. In the best traditions of Canute, the merchants were reluctant to leave the old town even after the king had begun to lay out the new site to receive them, but the storms of 1287, probably the same which diverted the Rother and robbed New Romney of its harbour, wrought the final destruction of Old Winchelsea, and its site is now under the sea.

The echoes of the exchange by which Edward I acquired the site were still being heard in the Court of Exchequer as late as 1544 when a local jury testified that it was in 'the ollde scituation of the manor of *Higham* [Iham] whereupon the towne of newe Wynchesle was edified and [on] the pendanntes of the hylles ... on the easte northe and south easte of the said scituation'. As late as 1484 the church of St Leonard, Iham, stood in the north-west corner of Winchelsea and its bounds were beaten annually until 1747,

Fig. 103C. Winchelsea; vertical photograph, August 1967. Scale 1:2700.

Quarters were still used in borough rentals of the eighteenth century and on an excellent plan of the town in 1763 drawn by Charles Stephens. The perquisites of the borough franchise, par-ticularly at times of parliamentary elections, pre-served Winchelsea's identity and set it apart from neighbouring villages which were equally large. The contraction of trade brought about decay of houses, so that twenty-seven of Edward's thirty-nine Quarters are now grass-grown, with some of the former streets marked as hollow-ways in the grass or indicated by lines of hedges breaking the countryside into small squares. *New Gate*, once at the south end of the town, stands in rural isolation. One church is lost and St Thomas's more than half ruined. Foundations of buildings under the turf can be seen here and there in orchards and paddocks, and the local tradition is that the ruined houses of the medieval town were used as a quarry when Henry VIII was building Camber Castle to defend the coast. Thirty or forty of the surviving houses in the northern quarters have the original vaulted cellars of about 1300, although the style of the superstructure is far from medieval.

Another indication of early set-backs experienced by the new town is seen in the history of its defences. Initially, there were no walls, but by 1295 the borough was allowed to levy an extra toll on shipping to help raise funds to build them, and more building took place in 1321–8. It is probable that the full circuit of the wall around the perimeter of the Quarters was never completed, and in 1415 a fresh beginning was made on a less ambitious project to exclude the outer line of Quarters on the western side which had presumably become unoccupied. Even this shorter wall was never completed.

It has seemed best to give a connected account of the growth and decline of the town before commenting on the two photographs (figs. 103 A and C).

The oblique photograph (fig. 103 A) looks southwards; it includes the former estuary in the foreground, below the tree-covered cliffs of the hill chosen for the thirty-nine Quarters (*Quarteria* in 1292) shown in fig. 103 B. The steep road up the cliff to *Strand Gate* can be seen on the extreme left, leading into what the rental of 1292 called Third Street (*Tertia Strata*). First Street runs across the foreground, on the cliff edge, where *Land Gate* still stands. The Quarter with the partly ruined St Thomas's church can be seen between Third and Fourth Streets; on the far side of Fourth Street not all the Quarters are now occupied, and from Fifth Street to Ninth Street we are in open country. Just before the belt of trees at the end of the plateau the modern road can be seen making for the former *New Gate* at the south end of the town. The cross-streets, running up the photograph, had no medieval names; on the right, the course of the longest can be seen, first as a road and then as a tree-line, from the foreground to *New Gate*. In the distance, where the plateau narrows there was

insufficient room to lay out five Quarters along each street as at the near end. Even by *Land Gate*, as the grass field on the right-hand edge of the photograph shows, Quarter IV and its neighbours to the south and west are now empty including those once containing St Giles' and St Leonard's churches. The market-place, two Quarters beyond the church and churchyard of St Thomas, is now tree-covered parkland.

The vertical photograph (fig. 103 C) permits a full appreciation of the ordered lay-out of Edward's officials. As a report on the decayed town informed the Privy Council in 1570: 'xxxix quarters, the most part square, with streats very large and broad, all strayght as the same wear layd with a line'. The 'pendanntes of the hylles' can be recognised by their tree cover, and the four corner-towers of *Strand Gate* are etched in white. Entering Third Street by this gate, the road can be seen passing between Quarters VI and XII (constricted by the shape of the hilltop and smaller than the full-size Quarters VII and XIII next encountered), to reach the unnumbered Quarter assigned to St Thomas's church. In a dry summer parch-marks in the grass reveal the line of former streets and buildings in Quarters now empty, and outside the town, to the west of Quarter XI, the sites of windmills. A standing mill now marks the position of St Leonard's church.

Only a visitor on foot can appreciate the positive quietness, more emphatic than a mere absence of noise, and the streets themselves, wider and straighter than any village, flanked by dignified, almost Dutch, houses. Few shops have found their way into the town. There are the cathedral-like ruins of the church and the windy green pastures overlooking the marsh by the windmill where St Leonard's church stood. *Strand Gate* is a picturesque obstacle to motorists who negotiate it in single file helped by a large mirror. The through traffic passes down *Tertia Strata* on its way to *New Gate*, but Sixth, Seventh and Eighth Streets are crossed without knowing it, since they are now marked by hedges in open country. 'It is', wrote Defoe, 'rather the Skeleton of an Ancient City than a real town.'

Sources

V.C.H. Sussex IX (1937) 62ff; W. D. Cooper, *History of Winchelsea* (1850); Tudor maps: M.P.F. 3 and 212; plan of 1763: *V.C.H.* IX. 64; G. E. Chambers, 'The town plan of Winchelsea', *Arch. Jnl* XCIV (1938) 177; rental of 1292: S.C. 11/673 and 674; Iham in 1544: S.C. 12/25/47; 1370: E. 142/85/2; 1343: S.C. 6/1032/6; 1368–9: S.C. 11/677; rents, 1297–1304: B.L. Add. Ch. 8813; Defoe, *Tour*, ed. G. D. H. Cole, I (1927) 130.

IV. UNSUCCESSFUL PLANTATIONS

The shepherd on the east hill could shout out lambing intelligence to the shepherd on the west hill ... without great inconvenience to his voice, so nearly did the steep pastures encroach upon the burghers' backyards. But the community which had jammed itself in the valley, thus flanked, formed a veritable town, with a real mayor and corporation.

THOMAS HARDY, *Fellow Townsmen*
(*Collected Short Stories* 99)

In our first edition this chapter concluded with Newton, Dorset, an abortive planned town of Edward I. Being abortive, the site was not certainly known; the trees and scrub of the heaths of Poole harbour effectively concealed the ground from aerial observation, and 'Newton' seems in fact to have lain elsewhere, at the southern end of Newton Bay.[7] It appeared best therefore to substitute two indubitable planted boroughs which had modest success at first but which have long been in decline.

104. NEWTOWN (FRANCHEVILLE)
Isle of Wight

The manor of Swainston (Calbourne), in the north-west of the Isle of Wight, formed part of a large estate of the bishops of Winchester given to them by the King of Wessex in 826. In the first half of the thirteenth century successive bishops augmented the economic potential of their scattered estates and their own rent rolls by elevating two villages (Farnham and Witney) to boroughs and by planting six other boroughs on virgin sites, beginning with New Alresford (Hants.) in 1200. Newtown was the last of these projects, initiated in 1256 with the grant of a charter to the 'borough of Swainston', soon to be known as *Francheville* in commendation of its liberties. The exceptionally full episcopal account rolls have allowed the plantation to be studied in detail. Within a year, seventy-three burgage plots were taken up by townsmen. Edward I thought the site important enough to acquire it from the bishop in 1284, the year of the foundation of Caernarvon, and to confirm its charter; and at least seventy plots were occupied at the end of the century. The French raids of the next century did damage to the town and the development of the port was hindered by the close proximity of Yarmouth and Newport in the same quarter

[7] H. C. Bowen and C. C. Taylor, 'The site of Newton', *Med. Arch.* VIII (1964) 223–6 and fig. 77.

of the Island, and by Lymington and Portsmouth across the Solent.

Despite a fresh charter to her tenants by Elizabeth I the town languished, and the little William-and-Mary town hall, now owned by the National Trust, rested more on the economics of a rotten borough than on the silted haven and grassy wharves at the west end of what has long been a ghostly grid of burgage plots. Only eleven houses were assessed for the hearth tax in 1674, and six were relieved of payment on account of their poverty. A plan of 1768 (fig. 104B) shows only fifteen buildings altogether, and at least forty-two vacant plots. St Mary's chapel was then in ruins, but in 1836 it was rebuilt by the lay patron, possibly in thanks for the survival of the petty Corporation after the Municipal Reform Act of 1835, despite acid comments by the Commissioners. It was a far day from 1334 when the borough's tax-assessment was twice that of the island's capital, Newport.

The photograph of Newtown in 1968 (fig. 104A) can be compared with fig. 104B, which is taken from the plan of the borough made in 1768. The land route from the bishop's manor at Swainston entered the low-lying site of the borough by a bridge at the head of the creek, left centre, coming in to a wide green now largely covered with scrub. The town hall is the long building with a light-toned roof standing at the point where this green meets the edge of the long grid of burgage-plots. The present metalled road enters this grid by the *Town Hall* and turns westward taking up the line of the old *High Street*. It does not continue for the whole length which leads to *Key Close* where was once the medieval quay, but turns again into a short but wider cross-street, *Church Street* on the plan, where markets and fairs were once held. Continuing to the north, it turns at a group of sheds on the edge of the marsh, leading eventually to the old salt-pans and quays on the Newtown River. The restored church of St Mary (marked *Ch* on fig. 104B) stands immediately beside the market-green (*Church Street*). The long axis of the town, running east–west, was made up of two streets, *High Street* and *Gold Street*. Only short lengths of these are now metalled but their extension in each direction as grassy tracks can be clearly seen. The twenty or so buildings that make up modern Newtown lie mainly between these two streets; their tree-lined plots can be compared with the boundaries in the plan. Else-

Fig. 104A. Newtown (Francheville); vertical photograph, September 1968. Scale 1:6200.

where, most of the plots are empty, but discontinuous hedge-lines preserve the positions of the old boundaries. (Thinner lines on the figure mark boundaries which are depicted on the map of 1768 but which are not visible on the photograph.)

The grassy remains of the two principal streets can be traced down the photograph, away from the village. Two close-set parallel hedges still mark part of *Marsh Lane* whence a farm-track preserves the way to *Clamerkin Creek*, the loop of water at the right margin of the photograph. The *Bowling Green* (fig. 104B) has the dimensions of the market-green at the other end of the town, and both are equidistant from *Broad Street*, the cross-street near the present town hall. If the

243

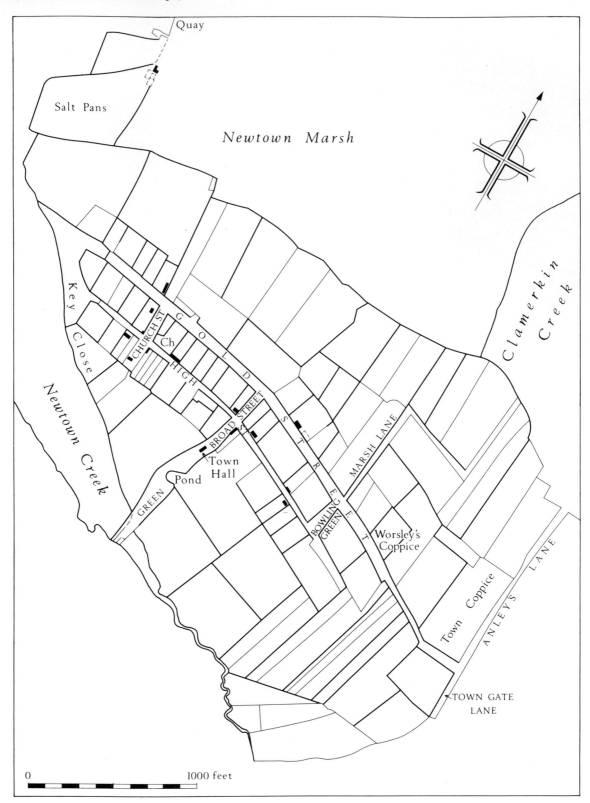

Fig. 104B. Newtown in 1768, after Mallet.

Fig. 105A. New Radnor; looking N, July 1967.

lay-out of the town was as symmetrical as the position of these three cross-streets suggests, the burgage plots were intended to continue still farther east, as outlined in field-boundaries in 1768. Indeed, the hedges marking the former *High Street* and *Gold Street* do continue eastward. The latter has become a lane running into the wood, bottom right, where *Town Gate Lane* and *Anley's Lane* can just be made out amongst the trees. *High Street* seems to end in mid-field exactly where parcels of strips are shown on the 1768 plan; one such parcel may now be distinguished as a belt of trees. Ridge-and-furrow is faintly discernible on the photograph hereabouts.

Sources

M. W. Beresford, 'Six new towns of the bishops of Winchester', *Med. Arch.* III (1959) 187–214; Hants. Record Office, MSS. Eccl. Comm. 2/159292 and 159296; plan of 1768 in A. H. Estcourt, 'The ancient borough of Newtown', *Proceedings of the Hampshire Field Club* II (1890–3) 89–109; plan of 1793: M.R. 489; the plan of 1636 mentioned by Estcourt has not been traced.

105. NEW RADNOR   Radnorshire

The road which takes the traveller through Radnor Forest into the valleys of mid-Wales had been protected since Norman times by a castle at Old Radnor, three and a half miles west-

north-west of Kington, where there are still the earthworks of the castle, and the parish church of the small settlement around it. In the mid-thirteenth century a fortified town was built at New Radnor, two and a half miles farther west than Old Radnor. This town is seen in fig. 105A from the south, the position chosen for John Speed's view in 1611 (fig. 105B).

In the foreground is the Summergil Brook, the upper valley of which offers a convenient route to Llandrindod and Builth. The road which follows its northern bank, crossing the photograph from left to right, was taken for the main street of the new town. For the eastern, or right-hand, boundary an earthen bank was thrown up beyond a stream, the Mutton Brook, the course of which can be seen incised in the hillside above the town. This stream which once provided the town water-supply, is shown on Speed's plan running down the centre of a street; it is now carried in a gutter by the roadside. The line of the south defences may be seen in the foreground just above the brook. Before the left margin of the photograph is reached the bank turns back towards the castle. Speed marks this sector as *The Ruines of the old wall*.

At the upper end of the town the defences are linked with those of the castle. There, advantage was taken of the deep valley of the stream on the east flank, the slopes being steepened. The levelled surface of the hillside gave room for the

245

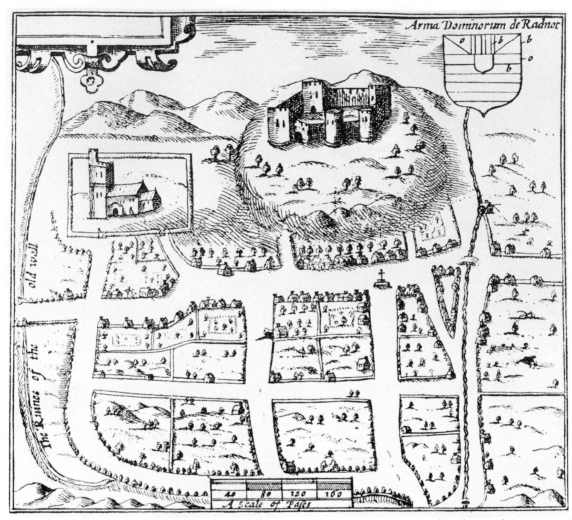

Fig. 105B. New Radnor in the early seventeenth century; map published in Speed's *Theatre of the Empire of Great Britain*, 1611.

castle buildings which stood, as Speed indicates, on the farther edge of an oval platform. This platform has a ditch on its left-hand side, and beyond is a large outer enclosure with a bank round the perimeter, the *Beili Glas* or Green Bailey.

Immediately below this outer bailey was the parish church of the new town, erected in the mid-thirteenth century. The present church, visible among the trees, was built in 1862. The town took the common form of one long main street from gate to gate, set at right angles to shorter streets, here three in number. At the bottom right-hand corner one of these streets left the town by the south gate to Kington and Presteign. The market-cross shown on Speed's plan has been removed but it will be seen that in all essential details the present lay-out of streets follows that delineated in 1611. Thus, the curve

in the road below the church (top left), and the angle of the road on the right of the market-cross, remain in the modern street plan much as Speed showed them. Two sections of road within the town have fallen into disuse. The middle cross-street is now in existence for only two-thirds of its length, while the lower cross-street is also no longer complete; its former course is marked in the grass fields on the left by a hedge-line curving up towards the church.

Source

R.C.H.M. *Radnorshire*, (1913) 129–34 and plan.

In these decayed boroughs the burghal plan and burgage plots have been preserved in the form of hedges and grass lanes. Yet, for centuries after the boroughs had ceased to be places of trade and crafts, there were occasional hours when economic activity returned. At election times money again passed in the streets and the old boundaries of burgage plots acquired a temporary notoriety. House of Commons committees heard the local traditions of ownership in frequent dispute and examined plans to see exactly where the few square yards of vote-bearing soil lay. The plan of Aldborough (fig. 28B) was made for such a purpose; and the 1832 Boundary Commission, in redrawing the limits of boroughs for election purposes, produced a set of borough maps worthy to set alongside those of Speed two centuries earlier.

PART FOUR

INDUSTRIAL AND OTHER FEATURES

10

SOME INDUSTRIAL REMAINS

Surveyor. Divers Lordships yeeld extraordinary commodities, some under the earth, some of the earth: some above the earth.
Landlord. But these are chargeable commodities to get.
Surveyor. So is the Lord of the Manor at no cost in planting plowing setting or sowing them.
Landlord. That is true.
NORDEN, *Surveior's Dialogue,* 70

... tin, lead, copper, coal, stone, marble, freestones, millstones, limestones, grindingstones, marl or chalkpits, slimy or moorish earth fit for soyling of land, potters clay, clay for bricke or tile, fullers earth, sand- or gravel-pits. . . .
LIST OF 'CASUALTIES' TO BE NOTED BY THE CAREFUL SURVEYOR OF A MANOR, *ibid.* 116

I. INTRODUCTORY

One major aspect of medieval 'industry' has already been illustrated. Photographs of villages and fields have shown the productive units of the most wealthy and the most widespread of all medieval industries, that of agriculture. Villages and towns were the scene of exchange of agricultural commodities in periodic markets and fairs; the roads and rivers served for the movement of this produce.

A stricter definition of 'industry' still leads to fields and villages, for the manufacture of cloth was closely connected with the land. Raw wool came from the backs of animals grazing in the fields. The wool was spun in cottages and washed in the village streams; and when, in the later Middle Ages, water-power was harnessed for fulling-mills, it was in the country districts and not the towns that the new mills were to be found. Fuller's earth was dug from pits in the ground and some of the common dyes were extracted from plants grown in the fields. Even an industrial product like Wealden glass used local raw materials: beech and birch trees provided 'billets' for the fires; potash came from the ashes of green bracken; the silica from local sands; pots or crucibles from Sussex clay.

If the term 'industry' embraces any mechanical process, then the watermills of Domesday Book are to be included here, for they show the mechanisation of corn-grinding more than a century before that of fulling; in the last quarter of the twelfth century there are documentary references to a new invention, the windmill. The

windmill stands where it will best catch the wind; if that is in the open fields, as at Great Gidding, then the carts made their way to the mill along the lanes and balks. Towns could scarcely find room for windmills except on their outskirts. The Tudor drawings of Great Yarmouth and Rye show windmills outside the walls.

Watermills, on the other hand, were found in both town and country. Most towns stood on a river to gain the natural advantages that a river brings. Yet the town mills, driven by the constant head of water of a broad river, were principally used for corn-milling; when it came to power for mechanical processes like raising the hammers of the fulling-mill or driving the gig-mill it was the fast-flowing hill-streams which gave the best results. Professor Carus-Wilson has shown how the migration of industry in the later Middle Ages from old town centres to new rural districts depended largely on this search for water-power. Illustrations of the centres of cloth-making in the twelfth century are provided by Beverley, York, Ripon or Lincoln; but in the fifteenth and sixteenth centuries the work had migrated to more hilly country such as the upper Stour valley in Suffolk and Essex, the Aire and Wharfe in Yorkshire, Rossendale in Lancashire or Castle Combe in Wiltshire (fig. 113).

The urban industries were often no more than country crafts writ large; the exceptions lie in the field of luxury goods. Most villages had a baker who was economically third cousin to a master baker in York, Bristol, Norwich or London. Most city brewers, fishmongers, tanners, shoemakers, tailors, smiths or butchers had lesser counterparts in the villages; the smaller the village, the more likely that one man might play several parts, being smith, shoemaker and tailor and the rest.

But the specialist crafts of the semi-luxury and luxury products were not found in villages; no village could expect to have even one goldsmith, but the poll tax of 1381 shows eleven goldsmiths in the city of York, which also had in the same year twelve men making pins, five making rivets, three drawing wire, three making locks, nineteen making girdles and six making saddles. Twelve spicers and three saucemakers served those who rode into the city on the saddles while the alehouses catered for those who walked in to sell their eggs and lambs, or drove in their calves and pigs.

The workshop of the town craftsman does not lend itself to air photography. The nearest approach is at York (fig. 71) where some of the narrow streets perpetuate the medieval street plan, with their tightly packed buildings more medieval in appearance from the air than on the ground. It was the size, the closely packed houses and the narrow streets of cities like York, Norwich, Chester and Salisbury that visibly demonstrated prosperity long before the Tudor or the Hanoverian industrial revolutions.

The larger medieval towns and cities derived numbers and wealth from two occupations which were neither agricultural nor industrial. The first was the service of church and town and the administration of their laws and property, the second that of trade. Within the town walls were the monks, the clergy, the lawyers and the scriveners, while innkeepers and butchers provided for the pilgrim and the litigant. The town masons were a group of men who formed a true craft-guild, with an employer–employee relationship nearer to the modern wage-earner than most medieval workmen. Masons worked on the construction and maintenance of religious buildings, others on town walls and castles. York in 1381 had as many tilers as it had dyers, and as many masons as it had spicers. Alongside the masons were the plasterers, the glaziers, the sawyers, the joiners and the wrights. Their contribution is seen in the photographs as churches, cathedrals, bridges, town walls and some town houses.

For merchants and tradesmen not even a craftsman's workshop was necessary: the counter, the stall, the notebook, the purse, the iron-bound chest, the wharfside and the rivers and seas themselves, these are the tools of the trade and the places where such men worked. The nearest the photograph comes to recalling them is in the sweep of a market-square; for example the two market-places at King's Lynn, one for Saturday and one for Tuesday. Ports like Hedon, Fowey or Winchelsea bear witness to mercantile activity. A merchant's income flowed along channels partly visible. His taxes helped to finance the king's wars, of which only ruined castles survive as tangible and visible evidence. His gifts and taxes helped to build the city guildhalls, the town wool-markets, butter-markets and cheese-markets, or went to assist the making and repair of bridges. His pious bequests might finance the building of a chantry-chapel, a new parish church or a row of almshouses. Occasionally, as at Chipping Campden, his own house remains.

But in the last analysis, most urban activities, whether in manufacture or trading, depended on the countryside for raw materials. Imported goods apart, the craftsman and tradesman bought from the villages and fields. The weaver looked to the countryman for spun yarn, the innkeeper for barley, the tanner for hides, the sawyer and mason for wood and stone.

These raw materials, whether crops, timber, clay or stone, all derived from the ground. The scars of felled woodland or of clay-pits are soon smoothed away, although there are parts of England (such as the south-east corner of the Wirral) where long continued digging of clay and marl has pock-marked the fields with small ponds. Stone quarrying has left deeper scars. From hundreds of small quarries in the stone counties came the stone for medieval churches and manor houses, for seventeenth- and eighteenth-century cottages, for the walls of enclosed fields and for the roads of the Age of Improvement.

Quarries for ornamental stones, like alabaster or Purbeck 'marble', have not all been continuously worked, so that genuinely medieval quarrying can be pointed out in small beds of rock which would have been quickly exhausted by a few generations of exploitation. The woods east of Chellaston, Derbyshire[1] (SK 386304), form a light cover to the scars of alabaster workings which yielded a material once much in vogue for monumental effigies. In the Isle of Purbeck[2] there are not only villages like Corfe

---

[1] The earliest references to quarries here date from 1374: Mrs A. Esdaile, *Jnl Derbys. Arch. and Nat. Hist. Soc.* n.s. XIII (1939) 84; and *ibid.* XXXVIII (1916) 135.
[2] See Corfe, Sources, p. 147.

where the marblers worked (fig. 58) and ports, such as the short-lived Newton, from which the marble was exported, but also hollow-ways worn by the traffic from the quarries to the workshops. Tumbled debris, as at Downshay Farm (SY 980797) and Afflington (SY 970801), marks the very site of the medieval quarries.

Pottery manufacture was another industry depending upon raw materials extracted from the ground. Since so much medieval archaeology hinges on the dating of pottery and the identification of local styles, it is surprising that so little is known of the location of the industry. There are half a dozen English villages with the distinctive 'Potter' in their name, and kilns have been excavated at some of these, but characteristic disturbances marking either kiln-sites or clay-pits have yet to be identified from the air. In view of the uneven distribution of suitable clay, a substantial local trade in pottery might always be expected, but the documentation so far published is very slender. Tiles and bricks depended on the same raw materials and essentially on the same technique of firing, and considerable scars, not all of them in areas of modern clay-pits, should be sought. Here and there, as at Kirby Muxloe, there are suggestions that moats and fishponds of the larger houses were made by digging clay within a few yards of where the finished bricks would be laid. The mining of coal and metallic ores also scars the surface but it is not easy to date such workings as positively medieval.

The archaeology of the Industrial Revolution of the eighteenth and nineteenth centuries is in a more elementary stage; and only when activities of that period are more easily differentiated will it be possible to identify earlier remains. But the case is not desperate, and, in the areas of medieval industry which have not been swamped by the Industrial Revolution, a few remains of early industry have been recovered. No doubt county historians familiar with local traditions and with farmers' reports of old slag-heaps or pits would be able to add considerably to these illustrations. Sometimes industrial activity may be dated directly: thus Dr F. Villy in investigating the slag-heaps of the forges at Harden, near Bingley in Yorkshire (SE 096382), found that Harden Grange built in 1616, stands partly upon them. It can hardly have been built while the slag-heaps were still fresh.[3] Other debris from iron-smelting is frequently found in the Kent and Sussex Weald, but unless there is positive documentation it is only possible to distinguish medieval from later workings when

[3] F. Villy, *Bradford Antiquary* v (1912) 433, and vi (1913) 1.

stratified objects occur in the slag or when the heaps can be seen in relation to some known feature of later date.

No such difficulties, fortunately, arise in the case of the most important manufacture of the later Middle Ages and Tudor period, the cloth industry. The coming of steam-power transformed a cottage craft into a great industry with characteristic new buildings. Just as the retreat of arable makes the deserted village an excellent specimen for dissection, so the retreat of cloth manufacture from the villages of East Anglia and Wiltshire has left some excellently preserved specimens of the industrial village of about 1600–50. The rebuilding which took place during the sixteenth century produced buildings solid and durable enough to outlast the migration of the industry. Thus the house of a clothier like Paycocke survives beside the main road at Coggeshall in Essex, and there is half a village of period houses in the Lavenham of the Spring family.

No photographs of the remains of medieval coal-mines have been included. These are not difficult to identify. The printed cartularies of Fountains, Rievaulx, Guisborough and Whitby, to take only a group of northern religious houses, enable many medieval coal-mines to be located but many are lost amongst large modern workings. The scars of some of the smaller mines, early worked out, are now hidden under a covering of scrub and may only be traced on the ground.

The mining of copper in Elizabethan times in the Lake District along the shores of Derwentwater and in the Newlands valley has produced characteristic and informative earthworks, but conditions do not always allow of flying in mountainous country at an altitude low enough to yield detailed photographs. Good photographs might, indeed, be obtained on the ground from the high summits of the Derwent Fells. It had also been hoped to include some earthworks remaining from the late sixteenth-century alum workings in north-east Yorkshire. The map still carries the names of famous mines like Slape Wath and grass-grown spoil-heaps and shafts have been located on the ground. But it is apparent that some of the mines have been worked as recently as the last century, as have the cliff-face workings between Saltburn and Ravenscar. The inclusion of a photograph of these could no more be justified than could views of a modern Nottinghamshire colliery simply because beneath the pithead buildings lay the disused shaft of one of the Willoughby's Elizabethan mines.

Inland salt-workings have not been examined from the air but superficial inspection does not seem to reveal any medieval remains among the modern salt-works either in Cheshire or at Droitwich. The coastal salterns have left better traces. A low coastline with marsh or near-marsh conditions offered the best opportunity for trapping the incoming tides and gathering the salt water into evaporating pans. Where the sea has retreated a long distance in the last few centuries, salterns may occur as much as fifteen miles inland, like those at Bicker Haven, Lincolnshire. The great circles of former salterns are prominent in otherwise flat fields, and many arable fields show large rings of black charcoal that yield fragments of medieval pottery in each year's ploughing.

English industrial archaeology is still not far from its beginnings and would well repay further study. The remains of medieval agriculture form the commonest class of earthworks visible on the surface of Britain, while every extractive industry has left some scar upon the surface. Even when land has been levelled, infilled pits become visible by crop-effects while scatters of slag or charcoal may be seen as soil marks. The few illustrations in this section may encourage those who are unaware of industrial remains in this green and pleasant land before the period of 'dark Satanic mills' and concentrations of power-driven machinery.[4]

[4] There are now national and local societies for Industrial Archaeology, but much of their work is concerned with post-medieval sites. The student of medieval industry should turn to the appropriate summaries in the journal *Medieval Archaeology* for reports of fieldwork on early sites.

II. QUARRYING

What goods fill the carts which rumble over the medieval tracks? What are the pack-horses carrying? What will the customs-inspector find in that barge when he succeeds in boarding it?

Among the traffic there would certainly be such mundane necessities as millstones and salt. If only the watermills recorded in Domesday Book are considered, the task of quarrying the required number of millstones will be seen in its real proportions; perhaps even more striking is the distance which the quarried stones had to be carried. Outcrops of rock suitable for millstones are far from common, and yet there were watermills in every centre of rural population, and the coming of windmills in the late twelfth century must have increased the demand. The long journeys of the millstones from quarry to mill may sometimes be traced in the carting services which appear among the customary duties of villagers in manorial records. Selby Abbey, for example, drew its millstones from quarries twenty miles away in the West Riding.

Essential commodities such as salt, millstones, or iron found their way into trade early; without them there would have been no salted meat and fish, no mills and no ploughshares. Trade in other commodities may appear at an early date because their purchasers had the incomes or the command over labour to bring them from long distances despite the cost. These were the goods sought after by the crown, the landed nobility and the great monasteries.

One important commodity of this type was building-stone. In the English lowlands there are many areas where durable stone for building does not lie near enough to the surface for quarrying to be possible. Here the peasant houses would perforce be of timber and wattle-and-daub; for wood and clay were usually available even in the absence of stone. The wealthier alone could hope to build in transported stone bought afar off, and in many villages only two buildings had achieved the dignity of stone by the end of the Middle Ages: the manor house and the church. Churches in timber are not unknown, but surviving examples of Norman churches in districts remote from sources of stone show that by that period many villages were bringing stone from a distance. The lords of manors would consider a stone building more attractive than timber, while abbeys and castles were designed on a scale which put timber construction out of the question. Each stone church, tower, bridge, manor house, castle, abbey, palace and town wall presupposes a quarry.[5]

106. BARNACK   Northamptonshire

The two great limestone belts, the Jurassic and the Chalk, which cross the English lowlands, ensured that stone of some kind was available for those who could transport it. Not all the limestone is suitable for building; the Jurassic system yields the most durable stone.

Some of the best-known medieval quarries lay

[5] D. Knoop and G. P. Jones, 'The medieval English quarry', *Econ. Hist. Rev.* IX (1938) 17–37; L. F. Salzman, *Building in England* (1952) 119–39; W. J. Arkell, *Oxford Stone* (1947); F. W. Brooks, 'A medieval brickyard at Hull', *Jnl Brit. Arch. Assoc.* 3rd. ser. IV (1939).

Fig. 106. Barnack. Medieval stone quarries, looking W, July 1970.

at Barnack, three miles south-east of Stamford. In the seventh century King Wulfere used this stone for Peterborough cathedral; Barnack church itself has Saxon work in stone from the local quarry; and abbey after abbey drew its building stone from Barnack. The main quarry, known now as the field of 'hills and holes', nearly sixty acres in extent, lies in the angle between the two roads in the middle of the photograph (fig. 106). The ground in some neighbouring fields has also been worked for stone but the surface is now reconditioned. Barnack stone was practically worked out by the early sixteenth century and some of the abandoned workings have been covered with grass and scrub. Many medieval buildings in Cambridge had come from this quarry and, after the Reformation, Barnack served the new buildings at second hand when stone from the abbeys of Ramsey, Thorney and Barnwell was taken for the colleges of Corpus Christi and King's. The northern abbeys stood in country where stone was easily accessible and cheap, so that their new owners were less tempted to use them as ready-made quarries.

In the time of Edward the Confessor, Ramsey Abbey was licensed by Peterborough for the taking of 'werkstan at Bernak'. Four thousand fenland eels made the journey to Peterborough in simple barter. In the twelfth and thirteenth centuries Ramsey, like Crowland and St Edmund's at Bury, obtained from its Northamptonshire benefactors grants of land including concessions and leases of strips of ground in Barnack quarries. Sawtry Abbey had a special canal made from Whittlesea Mere to bring in Barnack stone, for water transport was best suited to so heavy a commodity. St Edmund's at Bury had a permanent grant of a right of way from Barnack to the wharves at the Welland ferry, over a mile distant. Norwich cathedral took its Barnack stone down the Welland, round the coast and up the Yare in the early fourteenth century. The church at Lavenham in Suffolk, sixty miles away, is built of Barnack stone.

For all this, medieval Barnack was not particularly large. In the poll tax of 1377 there were 122 taxpayers, which makes the village no larger than many of its neighbours. It was, however, a wealthy village with a substantial tax payment.

Sources

V.C.H. Northants. I (1902) 293–5; II (1906) 463; Ramsey Cartulary: *Chronicles and Memorials* no. 79 (1884) I, 166 and 189; *History of Ramsey Abbey* (Rolls Series), II. 334–5; 1334 taxes: E. 179/155/28; 1377: E. 179/155/109.

255

III. IRON-MINING

107. BENTLEY GRANGE, EMLEY
Yorkshire, West Riding

The earthworks shown in this illustration do not appear in any textbook of archaeology. They consist of the waste material from medieval iron-pits disposed around the openings of shallow shafts which led down to the bed of ore. The shafts have now collapsed, but in the hollows left by the subsidence a tree or thorn-bush has found protection. In the area included within the photograph (fig. 107), six and a half miles north-west of Barnsley, the pits are unusually frequent, but for more than a mile up the valley to the north-west, following the bed of Tankersley ironstone, scattered pits of similar shape could be seen until destroyed recently by open-cast workings. Workings of similar appearance, although not necessarily of medieval date, have already been described at Catherton Common, Salop (p. 96, fig. 34); other well-preserved examples of spoil-heaps around bell-pits occur near Tankersley (SK 352987), and near Threshfield (SD 976630), both in the West Riding of Yorkshire.

Both Bentley Grange and Denby, three miles away, were outposts of Byland Abbey which early in its history had acquired land in the locality from an unknown benefactor. A number of charters from the first years of the thirteenth century have survived to show how the monks were using the land. The Bentley charters do not suggest that a village ever stood here. They are principally concerned with rights of way: one (*c.* 1197–1215) gave a grant of a right of way to and from the chapel of St Werbergh in the Grange; another gave a road to the monks' millpond. The Archbishop of York, who held land nearby, gave a right of way 'for them, their men, their beasts and their necessaries through his land from their forge of *Bentleia* as far as *Denebi*'. In 1259 the monks obtained another grant of a way for carts 'through their lands of *Benteley*, going to *Deneby* and returning'. The farm-house to the right of the photograph bears the name of Bentley Grange and incorporates stone-work which may date from before the Dissolution. There is no evidence that the iron was still worked locally after the sixteenth century, and in the Dissolution rentals the assets of the Grange were only enclosed pastures. In the mid-fifteenth century the Denby charters show that Byland had ceased to work iron there and that the land was leased out like any agricultural property.

Byland itself lay forty-six miles from Bentley Grange, but there would have been no need for the ore to make that journey. The district was well wooded, and the 'forge' in the Archbishop's charter could use iron smelted with Bentley charcoal.

There is one other important detail in the photograph. Between the iron-pits the ground carries the marks of ridge-and-furrow, which is seen to extend to the edge of each spoil heap, and to continue in exact alignment beyond. Digging would confirm that the heaps overlie the ploughing ridges, which could not therefore have been formed after the pits had been abandoned, that is after the early sixteenth century. Indeed, since the charters mention furlong names in their grants and delineations of rights of way, this ridge-and-furrow must have been created as part of the arable husbandry of Emley, within which parish Bentley Grange was built, and, as the working of the pits began in the late twelfth century, must be some 800 years old. Other fields have had their ridges levelled by more recent ploughing; the six-foot high mounds of spoil have protected this small area.

The light-coloured field, top right, is restored after open-cast coal-mining which began in 1951. The iron and coal here occur in close association, the ironstone beds being from ten to twenty-five feet above the coal, but no record is known of Cistercian coal-mines at Bentley. A few miles to the north-west, both Fountains and Kirkstall had coal-workings, and there exists a partition of about 1170 which allocated all mineral rights in Emley and eight neighbouring villages between the monks of Byland and Rievaulx.

Sources

D. A. Wray, *The Mining Industry in the Huddersfield District* (1929); Byland Cartulary: B. L. Egerton MSS. 2823, fol. 9 v; Add. Ch. 7432, 7453, 7456, 7459; *Yorkshire Deeds* VI Yorks. Arch. Soc. Rec. Ser. LXXVI (1930) 36–60; Rievaulx Cartulary. Surtees Soc. LXXXIII (1887) 179. National Grid ref. SE 265131.

108. FURNACE POND, COWDEN
Kent and Sussex

Woodland was an important asset in any Tudor survey, whether of a royal park, a dissolved monastery or a private estate. The timber was used for both building and fuel. Even houses in stone or brick required timber in their structure, while town and castle gates needed great beams.

Fig. 107. Bentley Grange, Emley. Medieval iron-pits, looking W, August 1953.

Nearly every mechanical device from the plough to the cart and the loom made use of timber.

Both domestic and industrial consumers of fuel contributed to the destruction of woodland. In the later Middle Ages the expanding iron industry led to the exploitation of timber at a rate that was viewed with alarm by Tudor governments who were worried both by the rising prices of wood and of charcoal and by a possible shortage of best quality oak for ship-building. The ironmaster and the shipbuilder were held to be competitors for the same length of oak, and legislation followed to restrict the cutting of trees in southern England for indus-trial uses.

In his description of the Weald in the *Britannia* (1610 ed.), William Camden looked both back-ward and forward:

Full of iron mines it is in sundry places, where for the making and fining whereof there bee furnaces on every side, and a huge deal of wood is yearly spent, to which purpose divers brookes in many places are brought to runne in one chanell, and sundry meadowes turned into pooles and waters, that they might bee of power sufficient to drive hammer milles,

which beating upon the iron, resound all over the places adjoyning. Howbeit, commodious enough to the iron Maisters who cast much ordinance thereof and other things to their no small gaine: now whether it bee as gainfull and profitable to the common wealth may bee doubted, but the age ensuing will bee better able to tell you.

Norden himself had a long aside in the *Surveior's Dialogue* criticising the loss of timber around the Sussex ironworks and echoing the fears of ship-builders that the oaks might soon all be con-sumed.[6]

Since the charcoal used in iron-smelting was produced from upper and side branches of the trees, which shipbuilders would not use, these fears may have been exaggerated. What may have been happening was indiscriminate pur-chase by ironmasters who took whole trees unnecessarily. Many of the complaints against the rising cost of fuel came from towns and from rival industrial users of charcoal. Defoe, in 1724, found the fears 'groundless'.

The conflict was most acute in the Weald of

[6] *Surveior's Dialogue*, 174–6.

257

Fig. 108. Cowden; looking W up the Kent Water, July 1954. The stream was dammed in the Middle Ages to provide a head of water for the iron foundries.

Kent and Sussex where the iron industry of the later Middle Ages was principally concentrated. The Weald had not been extensively assarted in the course of medieval colonisation, for the soils were unattractive. Its timber, however, was in demand on the London market for fuel and for building, besides being drawn upon by ship-builders and by ironmasters, exploiting the Sussex ironstone, who found it convenient to take their fuel alongside their mines and quarries. Brewing, brick-making, paper-making and glass-making[7] were also using local timber. In a

survey of 1574, one of many made in the deforestation scares, approximately 115 'works' were listed: thirty-eight forges and thirty-two furnaces were located in Sussex. Visible signs of this industrialisation in a now rural region appear in the artificial ponds strung along the narrow valleys of the Weald.

The valley which is the subject of this photograph (fig. 108) forms the boundary of Kent and Sussex, eight and a half miles west of Tunbridge Wells. The view is to the west. The county and parish boundaries followed the original course of the stream even after the building of a great dam had created a thirty-acre pond, and those who wished to beat the bounds on Rogation

[7] For the Wealden glass industry in the Middle Ages, see S. E. Winbolt, *Wealden Glass* (1933).

Days would have had to take to a boat. Although the mill was in Kent the millwheel was in Sussex. The head of water that was available can be judged by the modern houses below the dam with their gardens on the natural level of the valley floor and their roofs only just above the top of the dam, or 'bay', as it was called.

Among the woods in the Weald are many heaps of slag from an older process of smelting; a spongy 'bloom' was produced by firing alternate layers of charcoal and ore on a sandstone hearth in a beehive furnace of brick or clay. Hand- or foot-bellows were inserted at the bottom of the pile. The 'blooms' were then brought to red heat and acquired a normal metallic appearance under the blows of hammers weighing from 1200 to 2500 pounds. From the late fifteenth century onwards, the single process in a simple blast-furnace became the normal method of large-scale producers. This pond, Furnace Pond, is only one of a chain running up the valley west of Cowden. The head of water was sufficient both to work the mechanical bellows which blew into the furnace where the ores were heated, and to drive the great hammers in the forges.

The woods near Furnace Pond which have the significant names of Hammer Wood, Forge Wood and Cinder Hill, cover scarred and pitted hillsides; Mr Straker has calculated that only about 40 per cent of Wealden furnaces had forges on the same site or within a short distance. There were many complaints of the damage done to local lanes by heavy loads, and the Acts of 1581, 1584 and 1597 compelled ironmasters to contribute cinders, ash and gravel for road repairs as well as their quota of carting services. In order to reduce transport costs of such heavy raw materials as the industry needed, the forges and furnaces were set as near to the ores as possible, though at the cost of losing the use of the Weald's largest streams. The smaller streams were insufficient to give a constant supply of water in all seasons, and ponds, often in strings, were constructed to conserve the head of water for dry seasons. Even so, there were many furnaces which had to be considered for winter use only. On the main rivers, power was obtained by running sideleats like an ordinary millrace for a cornmill. The accumulation of silt at the bottom of the Wealden ponds is considerable, and in Kent a number of former ponds will be found in use for hop growing.

In the survey of 1574 the Cowden Furnace was worked by Michael Weston of Lye; by 1664 it had been abandoned for some years. Nearby is a cave from which sandstone for the furnace was quarried. Many cannon balls have been found here, and the gardens are full of slag. About 1860, the famous 'Cowden Gun' was dug up at this mill, a rejected faulty casting, full of air cavities. Half a mile farther up the valley there is the pond of Scarlets (or Scalehurst) with the house (c. 1597) of the ironmasters, the Knight family of Basing Farm. This upper mill was in use after the lower mill was abandoned, but probably not long after the beginning of the eighteenth century. By that time the industry had begun to move westwards and northwards. With the cost of fuel forming three-quarters of the total costs of production, industrialists were sensitive to the expense of timber, and when coke became available the ironmasters moved to the coalfields. In the early nineteenth century the Weald had a few small forges but its furnaces were almost extinguished.

Sources

M. C. Delany, *Historical Geography of the Wealden Iron Industry* (1921); E. Straker, *Wealden Iron* (1931); G. S. Sweeting, 'Wealden iron ore', *Proc. Geol. Assoc.* LV (1944) 1–15; M. A. Lower, *Sussex Archaeological Collections* II (1849) 169–220, XVIII (1866) 10–16; *V.C.H. Sussex* II (1907) 241–9.

IV. LEAD-MINING

109. BONSALL LEAD MINES
Derbyshire

The ground between the rivers Dove and Derwent in central Derbyshire is scarred with old lead-workings wherever the veins of ore approach the surface. Lead has been obtained in the High Peak District since Roman times, but it is not usually possible to disentangle the workings of various periods. In the Middle Ages there was a general right of prospecting on the moors, the royal interest being served by a royalty of one dish in thirteen of the molten metal. By the early sixteenth century the individual prospector–smelter was being supplanted by miners employed by wealthier smelters and merchants, and by the end of the century the pressure on land was bringing conflicts between the interests of prospectors and farmers. In 1553, a regulation in the High Peak provided that derelict mines could be filled in by farmers.

Fig. 109. Bonsall; looking W, July 1958. The ground is scarred by medieval lead mining.

In 1631, the justices of the High Peak, report-ing to the Privy Council on the treatment of the poor, congratulated themselves that the lead-mining parishes were fully employed – 'the leade mynes whereof our hundred of High Peake hath much imployment and almost alltogether sett to worke by them'. Yet the villages of the High Peak were not industrial villages: they had fields and pastures beneath which ran the veins of ore. In 1620 the court of the Duchy of Lancaster heard a long dispute between the copy-holders of Wirksworth and Bonsall and the miners. The farmers complained that their cattle were 'over-thrown and killed' by falling in the 'grove holes and olde pitts'; they found their plots of land broken into by prospectors and disturbed by miners claiming free entrance and egress for the carriage of lead and timber. One such area, a mile west of Bonsall, is seen in the photograph (fig. 109) from the east. The moor, here composed of Carboniferous Limestone, is about 950 feet above sea-level. It has been parcelled out at the enclosure of the moorland, but within the stone-walled fields are heaps of spoil from old workings. Two periods of activity may be dis-tinguished. The more recent is represented by the spoil heaps, recognisable on the photograph by the light colour of the waste rock composing them. The numerous small grass-grown hol-lows and upcast-mounds are older, shallow workings, perhaps of seventeenth-century date, closely spaced in lines following the veins of ore.[8]

Sources

1620: B. L. Add. MSS. 6687 fol. 1; 1631: S.P. 16/193 (5th June); *V.C.H. Derbys.* II (1907) 323ff. National Grid ref. SK 264571.

[8] Miss Nellie Kirkham has kindly given advice about these lead-mines.

Fig. 110. South Tawton; looking S, April 1966. Curving ridges of gravel remain from early tin streaming.

V TIN-MINING

110. SOUTH TAWTON   Devon

English tin-mines were amongst the richest in Europe, and the metal was a prized export throughout the Middle Ages. Physical evidence for the prehistoric or Roman tin-mining in south-west England is now difficult to find, and there is no mention of such mining in Domesday Book. When documentation began in the mid-twelfth century most activity was recorded in Devon rather than in Cornwall, the centres being the rich alluvial deposits in the valleys of some Dartmoor streams, such as that on the northern side of the moor near South Tawton, in fig. 110. Prolonged weathering of the granite which bears the parent lodes has yielded alluvial gravels containing the heavy mineral cassiterite, the common ore of tin. The gravels were worked open-cast, water being used to separate the heavy ore from the rest of the gravel deposit. The surface of the gravel was dug away to expose the lower layers in which the ore was concentrated. As the working face moved forward across the valley floor so curving ridges of gravel waste were left behind, yielding the distinctive pattern in the photograph. The tin-stone was separated from the gravel by running water, often brought to the workings in artificial leats. After separation, the tin-stone was crushed and then smelted. When improved methods of treatment were developed in the thirteenth century, the smelting was concentrated in 'blowing-houses' where use of water-driven bellows to create a blast enabled a sufficient temperature to be reached with charcoal for fuel, or even with peat.

The value of the metal was such that the miners had to take their product to one of a small group of stannary towns where it was weighed and assayed that the correct duty might be levied, and these towns retained a monopoly of sale. In 1198 a new royal official, the Warden, replaced the lord of Lydford manor as supervisor of the stannaries, and from about that time a

261

'stannary parliament' enacted the regulations by which the industry was governed. At Lydford (fig. 82) a castle tower had been built in 1195 as a prison for offenders against stannary laws. The tinners were important enough to the Crown to have undisputed prospecting rights, even on private ground, and control was made easier by the fact that the whole area was deemed a forest in Plantagenet times. In 1328 Dartmoor was divided into four zones, each with a stannary town for its sole vent of tin.

The disturbance to the landscape was not insignificant. In the late thirteenth century some forty to fifty tons of refined tin were presented for assay at the stannary towns of Devon each year, and nearly five times as much in the 1520s, when shaft-mining had begun to augment streaming. These amounts of tin were not obtained without the turning over and stream-ing of many times that bulk of alluvium, and the disturbance of the surface has remained in val-leys such as that at South Tawton. Another con-sequence was the consumption as fuel, first of any timber, yielding charcoal, and then of peat. From the fourteenth century there were repeated complaints of waste sludge coming down the streams in such quantity that ports on the south coast were being choked. The tinners declared in 1532 that their custom was to dump the debris near the mines and let the grass cover it.

Until about 1450 all tin-mining in Devon was by streaming, although the technology of shaft-working was practised for other minerals: at depth for lead and silver, and in shallow shafts for iron and coal (p. 256). But within a century of the peak output recorded at the stannaries in the 1530s, tin-working, as Professor Hoskins writes, 'had ceased to be of much consequence in the Devon economy'. No workings near South Tawton appear in a list of those lately abandoned which Lysons published in 1822.

Sources

John Hatcher, *English Tin Production and Trade before 1500* (1973) esp. table 16; H. P. R. Finberg, *Tavistock Abbey* (1951) ch. 7; Lysons, *Magna Britannia* (1822) vi, cclxxxi; W. G. Hoskins, *Devon* (1954) 130–5; H. French and C. D. Linehan, *Trans. Devon. Assoc.* 95 (1963) 178–9. The site lies at SX 628916.

VI. SALT EXTRACTION

111. MARSH CHAPEL   Lincolnshire

The creeks and marshes of the low-lying Lin-colnshire coasts have been used for salt-making since prehistoric times. Between the coastal vil-lages and the sea lay the marshes, threaded with narrow channels along which high tides brought salt-water within accessible distance. Thus the villages such as Friskney, which stood on islands or peninsulas of firm ground, had salt-marshes on one side and inland marshes and fens on the other.

The salters would establish a workshop or salt-house on suitable ground out in the marshes. The process of salt-making involved the extrac-tion of salt both from sea-water and from salt-impregnated mud. After impurities had been allowed to settle from the solution, the water was driven off by evaporation using the sun's heat either alone or with the assistance of char-coal and turves slowly burning around the pans.

The collecting channels and the heaps of debris, chiefly burnt clay and ash, form the earthworks of salterns studded over the reclaimed marsh and fen. The accumulation of the mud from which salt had been extracted was itself an agent in the reclamation of the marshes, so that the salt-makers were driven farther and farther seawards by the very success of their own efforts. The hump-backed mounds of older debris were soon difficult to distinguish from solid ground as they acquired a grass covering and became fit for pasture.

South of Grimsby a coastal plain often as much as four miles wide extends beyond Skeg-ness to the mouth of the Wash and then along the north side of the Wash itself, some forty-five miles in all. The villages lie along the old coastline; between them and the existing coast are parallel banks marking the steps by which the sea has been permanently excluded from reclaimed marshland.[9] The ground between the 'Old Sea Bank' and the villages is crossed by winding channels no longer flooded at the spring tides, and among them, often rising four or five feet above the general level of the ground, are the earthworks of salterns.

There is a particularly fine concentration of abandoned salterns to the north-east of the vil-lages of Tetney, North Coates, Marsh Chapel and Grainthorpe, seven miles south-east of Grimsby. The local term for reclaimed salterns,

[9] The salterns and salt-pans at Sutton on Sea, Lincolnshire, were exposed by the scouring of the sea and floods in 1953: *Country Life* CXIII (30 April 1953).

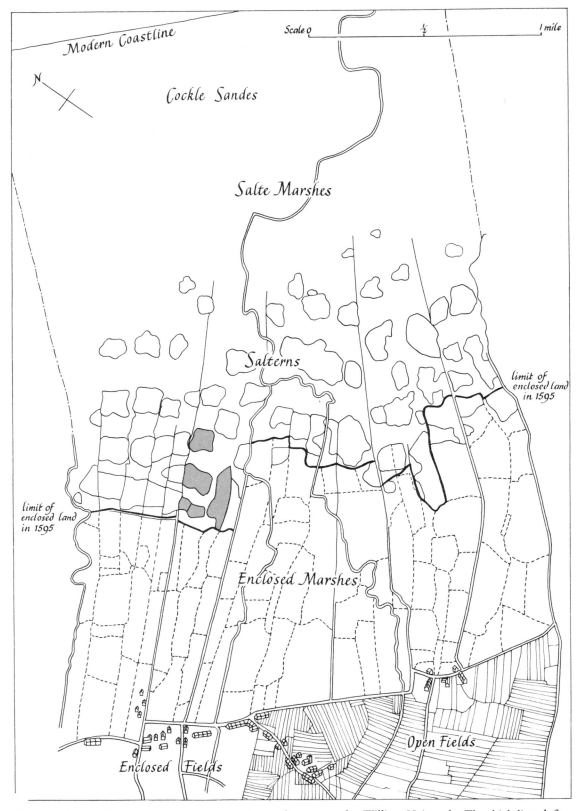

Fig. 11A. Marsh Chapel. Salterns in 1595, redrawn from a map by William Haiwarde. The thick line defines the limit of reclaimed land; the stippled areas are saltern mounds that remain unploughed: see fig. 11B.

Fig. 111B. Marsh Chapel. Saltern mounds near Poplar Grove Farm corresponding to the stippled areas in fig. 111A. Looking NE, March 1955.

the fitties, remains on the Ordnance Map as an element in farm names. It was for one such plot that John Benet of North Coates paid an assart rent in 1481 in order to build upon 'les Fittes unam berchariam vel unam saltcote'.

Salt-making seems to have declined in this area soon after 1600, but the reclamation of land continued and the salterns of the sixteenth century are now 400 to 2000 yards from the coast. Ploughing has since scattered pottery, burnt clay, slag and charcoal over the fields. Other salterns are visible as irregular mounds, conspicuous in country so flat that passing ships seem to tower over the sea-bank. In some of these mounds the circular clay-lined hollows of the pans can still be seen under their thin grass cover.

The whole process is illuminated by a map of 1595 by William Haiwarde (redrawn in a simplified form as fig. 111A) which covers both the marshland and the permanent arable fields of Fulstow and Marsh Chapel. The field-land to the west and south-west of the villages is shown in the normal strips and furlongs of open fields; at Fulstow three fields remained unenclosed until 1819. At Marsh Chapel comparison of the intricate pattern of ridges near the church with the strips and furlongs of the map yields the same precise equivalence as has been described at Ilmington and Padbury (figs. 5A, B and 7A, B above).

East of Marsh Chapel, the map shows the salt-makers' cottages and fields, beginning on the old line of settlement (the present main road) but stretching seawards. The irregular shapes show that the crofts were all originally 'islands' of relatively dry ground which grew and coalesced as mud and spoil from the salterns were deposited around them. At the eastern edge of the map such islands appear still surrounded by creeks, and on the islands Haiwarde drew the salterns and the salt-houses. (These temporary buildings are omitted from fig. 111A.)

Soon after this map was drawn, local salt-

264

making ceased, and the more conventional methods of reclamation by drainage and construction of sea-banks have been assisted by marine deposition. This later reclamation has produced flat, level fields without the characteristic rise and fall of dried-up creeks and mounds where the salterns have been.

In the cartouche of Haiwarde's map the process is explained:

the rounde groundes at the east ende of Marsh Chapell are called *maures,* and are first framed by layinge together a great quantitie of moulde for the makinge of salt. When the *maures* grow greate, the salt-makers remove more easte and come nearer to the sea, and then the former *maures* become in some fewe yeares good pasture grounds. Those *maures* that have the cottages nowe uppon them are at this present use in salt.

At the time of Haiwarde's map, the edge of reclaimed land was already about two-thirds of a mile east of Marsh Chapel. The 'islands' with the salt-houses upon them occupied the next half-mile and then came the *Salte Marshes* and the *Cockle Sandes* before the sea was reached. The sea-wall is now two miles from the village. The photograph (fig. 111B) looks north-east from a point (TF 366998) south of Poplar Grove farm. The hedge at the foot of the photograph marks the limit of the reclaimed land in 1595 (this is shown by a thick line on fig. 111A). In the grass field beyond are the remains of salterns, the shadows indicating the fall in level at the edge of the mounds. The shaded areas in fig. 111A indicate the 'islands' then in existence, and the close correspondence with the present grassy mounds is apparent.

The salterns in adjacent arable fields are in course of being levelled but are visible as crop- or soil-marks in favourable seasons. The sinuous lines in the light-toned field (left centre) mark the edge of a group of salterns much reduced by ploughing. The present shore lies beyond the upper margin of the photograph and the intervening fields have been reclaimed from the Salt Marsh and Cockle Sands of 1595. New channels have been cut for drainage, but some of the winding channels of 1595 are still in use; others can be seen as dried-out hollows in the grass, or as soil patterns.

Sources

Haiwarde's map: B. L. Map Room no. 3365, reproduction of original, *penes* Mr G. R. Walshaw, published in the *Lincolnshire Magazine* II (Sept.–Oct. 1935) 196. Mrs E. H. Rudkin of Willoughton kindly drew attention to the site, and Mr P. M. Tillott gave valuable advice on local salt-working.

VII. CLOTH MANUFACTURE

The two examples in this section show the industrial village characteristic of the English cloth industry before the application of power to spinning and weaving. Kersey, in Suffolk, has retained many half-timbered weavers' cottages which give an antique air to the village. Lavenham, in the same county, was a larger village, and is still as extensive as it was in the sixteenth century; there also, the number of genuine pre-Industrial Revolution cottages and houses is large. These villages have churches commensurate with their medieval and Tudor prosperity.

There is no large industrial building to mark out medieval industry in the way in which a factory chimney indicates a modern mill. The cottages were both home and work-place. As the French herald said in his wordy contest with the English herald (1549) 'your clothiers dwell in great farms abroad in the country where as well they make cloth and keep husbandry as doo graze and feed sheep and cattle'.[10] This was

meant to be disdainful but as an argument for the superiority of town-dwelling French weavers it fell flat.

The fields surrounding the villages illustrated in this section emphasise the combination of husbandry and craftsmanship. A valuation of the demesne arable of the deceased lord of Kersey in 1396 begins with arable, meadow, pasture and woodland but finishes with the income from the fulling-mill. At Castle Combe, however, there was a deliberate segregation of husbandmen and craftsmen. These rural industries had the advantage of being near the wool supply and of having the spinners and weavers in the closest proximity, that of husband and wife, brother and sister. The villages were free of the restrictive influences which by the fifteenth century were characterising the guilds in the older urban centres. They had the benefit of water-power for their fulling-mills, and, later, for their gig-mills. Mechanisation had gone no further. The factors which had encouraged industry in early medieval towns were weakening, and there was as yet none of those different advantages which

[10] Reprinted in R. H. Tawney and E. Power, eds., *Tudor Economic Documents* III (1937) 1–11.

Fig. 112. Kersey; looking S, June 1963.

Fig. 113. Castle Combe; looking NW, June 1952.

were to take weaving back into the urban factories of the nineteenth century.

112. KERSEY   Suffolk

Kersey, which lies two miles north-west of Hadleigh, has retained the air of a late medieval and Tudor village. A high proportion of its houses are half-timbered and the whole range is laid out to view on the two sides of a valley, seen here from the north (fig. 112), with the church in a dominating position at the top of a hill. In a corresponding position at the near end of the village stood Kersey Priory, a house of Augustinian canons. Part of the ruined chancel is attached to the farmhouse of which the roof-ridge is just visible among the trees in the foreground of the photograph.

The distinctive cloths made in this village, narrower and lighter than the traditional English broadcloths, were soon taken over and manufactured in other parts of the country. The Elizabethan customs-men were recording the export of Devonshire kersies from the western

ports, and kersies were also coming off Yorkshire looms. The spread of the manufacture of a cloth of new dimensions and quality involved its makers in a long series of arguments with both the ulnagers and the customs-officers. Taxation based on traditional cloth standards was difficult to apply to the new materials. In a statute of 1464 they were given a standard measurement: kersies were to be eighteen yards long and a yard and a nail's breadth wide. By 1605 the statutory length of a kersey had become twenty-four yards and the weight, twenty-eight pounds.

Sources

V.C.H. Suffolk II (1907) 254–70; Statutes of the Realm: 4 Ed. IV, c. 1; 1 Rich. III, c. 8; 4 & 5 Ph. and Mary, c. 5; 14 Eliz. c. 10; 3 Jas. I, c. 16; surveys: 1359, C. 135/148/19; 1396, C. 136/92; 1429, C. 139/24/5.

113. CASTLE COMBE   Wiltshire

Worstead, Melford, Clare and Lavenham, together with such other important East Anglian clothing centres as Hadleigh, Bildeston, Sudbury and Kersey, drew both upon the local wool supply and upon the output of the East Midlands. Each was a market-village, and well placed to deliver its cloths to the markets of London or the Continent. Our second example of a medieval cloth-workers' village lies far from East Anglia.

The skill in cloth-making of a certain wife of Bath has been favourably compared elsewhere with that of Ypres and Ghent craftsmen. The village of Castle Combe, in a narrow valley ten miles north-east of Bath, is seen in fig. 113 from the south-east. It is not a suburb of Bath and Bristol industry but a child of migration from them.

The village spreads around the castle; down to Nether Combe, and up to Over Combe on the lip of the valley. The prosperity of the village arose from the Combe rather than from the Castle. Few signs remain of the castle on the hill, and by the earliest extant survey of 1340 the lord of the manor was living down in the valley. The successor to his manor house can be seen in a loop of the stream towards the left of the photograph. In the 1340 survey there were four watermills in Combe, one of them a fulling-mill. There had been two watermills in Domesday Book, and it was no doubt the availability of water-power for fulling which enabled the weavers of the village to prosper, and which attracted weavers from outside. Professor Carus-Wilson has shown how the rural industry in centres like Combe flourished while the older urban centres fulminated against the migration of cloth-workers. In the fifteenth and early sixteenth century Combe was at the height of its prosperity as an industrial village, and the surveyor of 1458 noted down the folk-tradition that three men named Tokers (sc. tuckers or fullers) were the first inhabitants to be artificers of wool and cloth here, and that one Roger Young had lived in Combe as a clothier in the late fourteenth century.

Since the number of surviving rentals and surveys is unusually large, information about the size of the village can conveniently be tabulated. The only landowner in Combe was the lord of the manor, and these rentals must comprise all the parishioners. Table 4 shows that for 200 years the number of occupied houses was between forty-seven and sixty-one, and for much of that period there were four mills.

Agriculture survived alongside weaving, with the husbandmen living on the hill in Over Combe and the craftsmen down by the stream. Some of the later rentals have phrases that locate the messuages and cottages. The majority of the cottages were 'by the ford', 'at Woodford', 'by the church', 'at the market-place', but the messuages were occupied by customary tenants with agricultural services and holdings in the two open fields, *North* and *South Field*, which remained 'open' until the second half of the seventeenth century. By 1447 the lord of the manor was levying a poll tax of 2d. each on 'weaver, fuller, dyer and other craftsman'.

The surveyor of 1458 remembered how Sir John Falstof had purchased a hundred pounds' worth of cloth each year from the village crafts-

Table 4

Year	Number of messuages	Cottages	Mills	Poll tax
1340	31	20	3 corn 1 fulling	
1377	33	28	2 corn 1 fulling	138 (national) over age of 14
1447	28	19	1 gig 3 'touking'	53 craftsmen pay a local poll tax
1454	33	24	2 corn 3 fulling 1 gig	
1458	50 houses newly rebuilt		2 mills repaired	
1481				45 ,, ,,
1507	31	29	2 fulling	
1527				21 ,, ,,
1533				17 ,, ,,
1545	29	32	2 fulling 1 grist 1 'mill'	
15— (n.d.)	28 and two shops	33	3 fulling 1 grist	

men: 'in this manner he divided the rents and profits of his manors ... among his tenants and clothiers. ... These were the principal causes of the common wealth of the said town and of the new buildings raised in it.' Among these new buildings was the fifteenth-century church tower with its decorations based on cloth-working implements, while fifty houses had been rebuilt just before 1458. In 1454 the rental included a new cottage at the middle of the town, 'in le market', the triangle of open roadway in the centre of the photograph where the covered market-cross can still be seen. This cottage had been erected by Margery the miller who was leasing all three mills, the cornmill, the fulling-mill and the gig-mill.[11]

When Aubrey wrote (*c.* 1670), the art of cloth-making had departed from the town for other parts of Wiltshire. The local tradition is

[11] In the fulling-mill the cloth was beaten with hammers while immersed in a suspension of fuller's earth in water; in the gig-mill the cloth was 'raised' for shearing.

that the dryness of the brook enforced this migration. It was still a busy place in Aubrey's day whenever 'the most celebrated sheep fair in North Wiltshire' was held: 'whither sheep-masters do come from Northamptonshire'. The farmers in Over Combe and on the downs had come into their own; men then journeyed to Nether Combe to buy and sell stock and not, as in earlier centuries, to trade in wool and cloth.

Sources

G. P. Scrope, *History of Castle Combe* (1852), prints the rentals and surveys of 1340, 1454 and 1458; an extensive series of manorial and other documents in the B.L. includes the following, used in the compilation of table 4: Add. Chs. 18471 (1377); 18480 (1447); 18250 and Add. MSS. 28206 (1481); Add. Chs. 18490 (1507); 18496 (1533); 18497 (1545); 18492 (n.d., sixteenth century). In addition there is a poll tax on servants, 1527, Add. Ch. 18272; and an undated (?fifteenth century) document (Add. Ch. 18495) lists twenty-eight messuages, thirty-four cottages and a fulling-mill.

VIII. TURBARIES

The industries already mentioned, developed long before the age of steam, were voracious consumers of fuel particularly for such processes as smelting and forging. The cloth industry also used fuel in dyeing, and the important pottery industries of which the kilns are hardly to be illustrated in aerial photographs, were wholly dependent on the generation of intense heat. Coal was mined in very limited areas, mainly from surface outcrops, and the cost of transport was high, while its chemical composition rendered it unsuitable for many industrial uses; charcoal, derived from the branches of forest timber, was more generally useful and more widely available. However, the same process that multiplied villages and increased the area of medieval cultivation – that is, assarting – was continually reducing the area of woodland, the lowlands being generally denuded before the uplands. Thus, an alternative fuel came to be intensively exploited, namely peat, the accumulated vegetable debris of the fresh-water fens, which was cut in *turbaria*, or turbaries.

The greatest extent of low-altitude peat-deposits lay in the Lincolnshire and Cambridgeshire Fens, in the Somerset Levels, and in the 'raised bogs' of the Welsh Marches, but perhaps the most remarkable landscape monuments to centuries of turf-delving are the Norfolk Broads. These inland waters, much admired as an enclave of Nature, are now known to be the

product of human activity, the flooded hollows of old peat-workings in shallow river valleys. This identification is due to the researches of Dr Lambert and her collaborators. The combined skills of botanist, geomorphologist, historical geographer and archaeologist were able to demonstrate the origin of the Broads and to suggest how the workings subsequently were flooded. Professor Sir Harry Godwin has summarised the results:

The broads were shown to have steep margins, to be filled with loose muds quite unlike the material of the untouched 'ronds' [of clay], to have rectangular profiles, and, most dramatic of all, to contain balks and islands of uncut peat reaching nearly to present water-level. Equally striking, the balks and straight boundaries were found to correspond with the limits of different properties shewn in old tithe award maps, some strips crossing completely from one side of a broad to the other. Air photography, pollen analysis and contemporary ecology all gave evidence conformative to the new hypothesis, unlikely as it seemed at first glance.

An unpublished study of Inclesmoor, the peat-land near the Humber estuary between the Don and the Trent, shows that it too was worked in turbaries from the villages on the river-banks. They were not flooded until the nineteenth century when the process of *warping* gave them a fertile cover of river silt.

Fig. 114. Barton Broad; looking N, June 1952. Extensive beds of peat in some Norfolk river valleys were dug for fuel mainly before the fifteenth century. These diggings, or 'turbaries', subsequently flooded to become shallow lakes.

114. BARTON BROAD   Norfolk

Fig. 114 looks north over a large broad in the upper reaches of the River Ant. The broad lies in two parishes, Irstead, a village just below the bottom of the photograph, and Barton Turf, now a tiny settlement more than a mile west of the broad.[12] The parish boundary, an important division between the cutting rights of the two village communities, ran across the valley near the centre of the photograph. The lines of semi-submerged vegetation and the narrow peninsulas that jut into the broad indicate narrow balks of uncut peat just below the surface; these are parallel in the Irstead part of the broad but change direction north of the parish boundary.

[12] The significance of *Turf* in the parish name seems to have been missed, but in view of the early documentary evidence of turbary rights in Barton (1153–68), there can be little doubt that it was named from turves of peat. The opinion of E. Ekwall and A. H. Smith that *turf* must be a grass greensward seems to have caused this straightforward interpretation to be overlooked.

Parallel balks of this sort have been found to match boundaries on a number of tithe-award maps for the Broads.

The documentation for Barton set out by Dr C. T. Smith shows that the cutting of turves gave way to the extraction of *mora*, or 'fens', which seems to have referred to wet peat, often a mixture of peat and mud, not cut from peat mosses but dug or dredged from beneath standing water. In many places the peat floor lies little more than six feet below the present level of the broad, so that in an early stage of flooding the floor would not have been difficult to reach from the uncut balks, or from a boat. The *mora* would have had to be shaped into 'bricks' and left to dry out before they could be used as fuel. Evidence for such flooding is provided by the rising costs of extraction, and by the eventual cessation of turbary income in the accounts of manors that, like South Walsham in the 1260s, had been able to produce over 200 000 turves a year. (The kitchens of Norwich Cathedral Priory, it is

Fig. 115. Upwell Fen; looking NW, April 1955. Medieval turbaries filled with river-silt are revealed in light tone contrasting with the dark peat of the fens.

known, were consuming about twice this amount each year in the early fourteenth century.) Places that had once yielded rents for turbaries were now having their fisheries valued instead: fishery income begins in Barton records in 1422, at the very time when *mora* are recorded being dredged from the 'private pond-water of the lord of the manor'.

Explanation of the flooding which produced the Broads is less straightforward. Perhaps it followed the climatic deterioration of the late thirteenth century, the same period when storms overwhelmed Old Winchelsea. A fall in the general level of the land relative to the sea, if indeed this occurred, would have represented no more than a temporary reversal of the land emergence and marine regression which in Saxo-Norman times raised such inland valleys as that of the Ant, so making available the layers of peat that had accumulated centuries before. But when the waters returned to the valleys they had a greater space to fill: Dr Smith has estimated that more

than thirty million cubic yards of peat were taken from the Norfolk Broads.

Source

J. M. Lambert and others, *The Making of the Broads* (*Royal Geographical Society Research Series*, no. 3, 1960) esp. 63–106.

115. UPWELL FEN   Cambridgeshire

This photograph (fig. 115), taken from the south-east, embraces an area of reclaimed fenland to the east of the Sixteen Foot Drain, which appears as a straight line across the background. The Drain was cut in 1651, crossing the Fens east of March and south of Wisbech between the old courses of the Nene and Croft rivers; it is crossed in the middle distance by Bedlam Bridge (TL 469948). The feature of especial interest in the photograph is the group of light-toned soil-marks, forming bold rectangles separated by narrower lines of black, peaty soil. In the distance is another group of rectangles, but on a different alignment; since they are interrupted by the Sixteen Foot Drain, they must be earlier than 1651.

Before the modern drainage of the Fens, beginning in the early seventeenth century, the natural courses of the fenland rivers developed levees, built up by the deposition of silt which came to override the peat, forming low banks on either side of the river. Deposition also occurred within the river-channel and, if extensive flooding or other accident should cause a river to change course, silting continued in the abandoned channel. Many of these old river-channels, now filled with silt, can be traced across the peat fens as meandering banks (roddons), slightly higher than the modern surface of the peat. The depth of the peat has been progressively reduced by draining which causes it to shrink and by wastage from the surface so that the level of that surface is now lower than that of the silts choking the river-channels. Hollows, for example of turbaries cut in this peat, would be liable to silt up in this way, especially if such excavations were connected to a river.

Post-medieval drainage of the Fens has led to the reclamation for agriculture of this area at Upwell where formerly there were extensive turbaries; farther east the map shows 'Turf Fen' at Lakenheath, and there were turbaries in the fen below Chippenham. The broad pale bands on the photograph mark areas of silt where the surface is higher than the surrounding land, as may be judged from the depth of the cuttings for the open field-drains that cross there. In fact they stand up like platforms some four feet higher than the surface of black peat around them. The narrow black bands between the rectangles of silt represent balks of uncut peat between the turbaries. The silt of the platforms is at least six to eight feet thick, but the depth of the original cuttings must have been greater, for today's level of the peat surface is perhaps ten or twelve feet below the estimated level of the natural fenland. The width of the rectangles may be estimated at between 100 and 200 feet, and the total area of the turbaries seen in this photograph amounts to some half a million square yards, about 100 acres. If the average depth be estimated at about twelve feet, this group of turbaries represents a volume of two million cubic yards of cut peat.

The economic value of turbaries to villages on the edge of peat fens has been shown in Norfolk to influence the alignment of parish boundaries, and it will be noted that this part of Upwell Fen, though six miles from Upwell village, is still within the parish.

Source

V.C.H. Cambs. II (1948) 80–1.

11

MISCELLANEOUS FEATURES

And because that it may be some things be omitted which you now instantly call to mind, blush not to declare it here before you be deprived of that you have written. There may be defects in the forme of your answers yet if you have observed the main purpose which is the seeking out and the delivering the truth you have discharged [your] honest parts.

NORDEN, *Surveior's Dialogue*, 144

This short chapter brings together a number of significant features from the historical landscape which could not be conveniently considered in any earlier context.

I. ROADS

The illustrations of earlier chapters show only those comparatively short lengths of medieval roads which form the streets of villages and towns. But just as the labourers spent the greater part of their working day away from the village, so the roads of medieval and Tudor England ran for the greater part of their length amongst fields, heaths, woods and moors.

The alignment and purpose of pre-medieval roads were usually foreign to the immediate needs of early medieval life, for such roads either followed the ridges of higher ground which cross England from north-east to south-west or had formed part of the network of the Roman road-system. It was to be many centuries before Englishmen again wished to travel to London in such numbers that the roads converging there became the most important in the kingdom. The old ridge-roads were even more out of the picture. Their direction was alien both to the very localised life of the fields and to journeying to county or feudal headquarters.

The first need for regular travel beyond a limited horizon came when villagers were involved in wider social and economic relations. If a village were part of an estate of a great land-owning lord, the track leading to his principal demesne or to his local seat would carry more traffic of men and horses than any other. Along this track the carting services of the villeins were performed, taking the produce of the manor to its owner: along the same track the lord's officers would come in their work of inspection and accounting. The long-distance carriage of such elementary essentials as salt, iron and millstones would bring into being other tracks with more than local significance.

First the parochial, and then the episcopal systems, would add other local foci served by roads of more than ordinary importance. The hamlets had their tracks to the mother church of the parish, and even if a dependent chapelry were endowed to save a long walk to ordinary services, the occasions of baptism, marriage and the last rites would usually involve a journey. On rarer occasions there would be a journey to the seat of the bishop or the archdeacon, and church officers used the roads with much the same purpose as the officers of lay lords. For the few – the venturesome, the fortunate, the litigants, and the conscripted – there were journeys of pilgrimage, journeys to seaports, to the universities, to law courts and to the wars.

Journeys to markets, churches and courts are the principal exceptions to the generalisation that most medieval roads were entirely local in purpose with an ambition no higher than to serve the villagers' immediate wants. There was need for lanes to provide access to holdings in the fields; to take loaded waggons to the windmill (see Gidding, fig. 32E) or to the watermill in the meadows; to reach the woodland with its timber, its fruits and its pannage for swine; and to take flocks to the common pastures and heaths. The course of roads with a purpose so limited would be determined only by local needs. They would not necessarily make through connections with similar roads in an adjacent parish. They would tend to radiate from a village like the spokes of a wheel, and would follow as direct a course as natural obstacles permit. They would respect the bounds of land already cleared and incorporated in fields. They would be extended piecemeal as the area of field-land was extended.

This is the type of road which an Elizabethan map (like that of Padbury, fig. 7B) indicates among the furlongs: sometimes broad; sometimes narrow; sometimes accompanied by a stream; sometimes broadening to take in a pond, spring or tract of stream-side grass too damp to be ploughed. These are the field-balks still to be seen at Laxton (fig. 11), now a little constricted after the rearrangement of strips which took place there in 1906–9. These are the broad, unridged arteries which can be seen winding amongst the ridge-and-furrow of the Midlands just as the oxen, ploughs and carts once threaded their way through the furlongs to reach the farthest strips of arable. In many Midland fields watering-pits or marl-pits have been dug at the side of these balks, that is at the furlong-edge. Norden's surveyor described 'many old drie pits aunciently digged in fields ... many of them bearing still the names of Marle Pits'. It is often possible to trace the course of field-balks across the enclosed fields of Northamptonshire and Leicestershire by the line of water-holes. Enclosure also rendered many field-balks superfluous, as will be seen later, but their course sometimes remains as a footpath or right-of-way assigned in the Enclosure Award.

Remains of these field-roads will, of course, only be found in countryside where villages had substantial open-field ground, and where the village houses were clustered together. In the dispersed settlements of the west counties the medieval road-system is much better preserved. The detailed appearance of a modern map is itself very different in these counties from, say, Leicestershire or south Warwickshire.

In the western counties, with so much scattered settlement, there is rarely any obvious centre to which tracks might lead. The tracks ran from house to house, forming a network. The West also has many more modern roads which are simply hedged field-lanes. This high proportion of road length per square mile of fields reflects the different agricultural history of these non-champaign counties. In open-field country the assarted land tended to be incorporated into the open-fields, and the new roads which led to it were extensions of old field-roads and, like them, unfenced. The additions made to the cultivated areas in the more wooded counties

and in the fens were often taken directly into individual ownership, the sign of which was the hedged or banked field. The service roads thus passed between hedged or drained fields and were themselves enclosed with hedges or bounded by drains. The piecemeal nature of enclosure in these counties gave no opportunity for any later and thorough replanning of local field-roads such as came to the enclosure commissioners in the Midlands; so that, except in areas of former moorland, there are very few post-enclosure roads in these districts.

To see if there are objective differences between the 'Midland' and the 'Southwestern' road patterns the length of hedged roads within an area of 120 square kilometres chosen from each of the two districts has been measured. The classification into 'good' and 'bad' roads is that of the Ordnance Survey which colours each class of road distinctively. It will be seen from table 5 below that the Midland roads are rather fewer but that the proportion of 'good' roads, metalled and suitable for traffic, is much higher than in the Cornish area. Only about 6 per cent of the Midland roads were 'bad' by modern classification; in the Cornish sample just over 50 per cent fell into this category.

If the maps of the two areas are compared it will be seen that the Cornish lanes are rarely straight, seldom extend direct from village to village, and serve principally to link isolated farms. The Midland roads are relatively straight and gathered in the form of adjacent webs, the centre of each being a village.

In the early-enclosed counties the older roads are the most deeply sunken, sometimes even giving the effect of a tunnel when the hedge growth is high overhead. These 'tunnels' arise partly from the characteristic high banks on which the hedges grow (see Cholwich, fig. 33), a feature typical of piecemeal enclosure, but partly because the roadway is worn down below the general level of the surrounding fields in contrast to the raised balks of the open-field land. This is due to the ease with which the lighter soils of non-champaign country are eroded by the passage of heavy traffic and by the scouring action of rain. The sands of the Weald, the sands and marls of north-west Warwickshire and central Worcestershire all have their deeply cut roads, often no wider than the tracks which the loaded pack-animals wore into the soft rock.

The very existence of hedges is a second reason why no 'causeway' has been built up. In the open fields the 'causeways' had, immediately on their flank, land which was being ploughed in the same direction between the same boundaries

Table 5

	Length of 'good' road, hedged or fenced	Length of 'bad' road, hedged or fenced	Total length of hedged or fenced road
(1) Sample area, *Midlands*: 120 square kilometres north and west from Churchover, Warwickshire (SP 500800)	155 km (94%)	10 km (6%)	165 km
(2) Sample area, *Cornwall*: 120 square kilometres north and west from Polruan (SX 130500)	90 km (47%)	100 km (53%)	190 km

for centuries. Just as continuous ploughing on slopes may tend to form lynchets, so continuous ploughing away on either side of a field-balk might produce a causeway. In hedged fields, on the other hand, a plough could not approach so near to a road, and the very fact that the field was hedged and individually farmed would mean that ploughing did not necessarily follow the same direction each season. 'Lands' built up could later be cast down, and extra-deep furrows near the boundary could be filled in another year.

Since the purpose of modern roads is very different from that of medieval roads, both additions and subtractions must be made to the system if any air photograph of lowland England is to reflect the road pattern before the sixteenth century. This is as true of local field-lanes as it is of long-distance roads between towns. Roads are always the servants of contemporary purposes, and the transformations in the field-landscape at enclosure, which were described in chapter 6, involved many changes in the local system of roads.

Before enclosure, it was possible for a road to take a much more liberal course through common fields, or common pasture and woods, and, as fig. 116 shows, the area over which traffic might wander in negotiating a steep slope or wet ground was quite considerable. The post-enclosure road was more disciplined, its bounds are relatively narrow and are often limited by both a hedge and a ditch; even if a substantial width has been allowed at enclosure, so that there will still be grass at the side for drovers' herds, the bounds will be parallel and fixed. In the second place, enclosure rendered certain old tracks superfluous. If a series of hedged fields replaced a maze of strips in a particular part of a parish, the number of people interested in access to that part would be much diminished. The roads from the new farms to their fields were very different from the web of pre-enclosure roads from the village to the furlongs (see figs. 5A and 5B, 7A and 7B).

Just as the enclosure-surveyor occasionally took an existing furlong boundary as the limit of a new field, so he sometimes laid out a road along an older track or balk, straightening it when necessary and giving it a uniform width. For this reason, the last few feet of former ploughlands may sometimes be seen as ridge-and-furrow protruding on the verges of existing roads, where there is a wide space between the hedges. Sharp elbow-turns of old balks may be visible in adjoining fields where the road now follows a smoother bend. The apparently erratic course of country lanes with successive right-angle turns is often due to the fact that they are following the boundaries of furlongs in the open fields. In a well-known romantic interpretation of the landscape Chesterton credited the rolling English drunkard with the rolling English road. This is poor history; the real credit should go to the sober English ploughmen who laid out their furrows and furlongs on the assarted acres.

A well-documented instance of an important road following the lines and turns of old headlands is King's Road, Chelsea, which originated as a series of headlands on the route which Charles II took from Westminster to Windsor. The facts are recorded in a petition by Sir Hans Sloane in 1719, and the double bend in the road has been removed within living memory.[1]

Many more changes than the mere subtraction of post-enclosure roads have to be made to the present road system to convert it into that of Elizabethan England. The turnpikes, for example, must be allowed for. However, the often conventionally placed 'roads' on the small-scale county maps just coming into vogue at the end of the sixteenth century give some idea of how the Elizabethans travelled around their England.

Fluctuations in the fortunes of villages and towns have produced corresponding changes in

[1] Dr A. Morley Davies kindly drew our attention to this instance described by Faulkner, *History of Chelsea* I (1829) 43–8.

the fortunes of the roads serving them. If the village street of an abandoned village can degenerate into the sunken, grass-covered depressions of fig. 46, how much more easily could the field-ways of these villages disappear. Important changes in location of industry also created a need for improvement of the road system by making turnpikes, and the building of entirely new roads such as the northern turnpikes. At the same time the roads which once brought the waggons and pack-mules to the ironworks of the Weald and to the quarries of Purbeck were going back to grass, just as the railways were to rob the old drove-roads of their traffic and leave them empty but for the occasional traveller. In sparsely populated country, such as the Pennine Dales, 'green lanes' in very much their Elizabethan condition are still to be seen crossing the moors along the lines once followed by pack-trains carrying lead, fleeces and cloth. In the valleys the old local road system usually provided two tracks parallel to the river, one on either bank. With an eye on economy modern highway authorities have commonly adopted only one of these alternative routes, leaving the other unchanged from its condition in the 1880s, which is often substantially the same as its state three hundred years earlier.[2]

116. TWYFORD DOWN, WINCHESTER   Hampshire

In modern England we are used to roads, even country tracks, having a defined width, but before the days of metalled roads travellers often had to make detours to avoid deep mud or impassable bogs, conditions not improved by long-continued use of the route. There would have been some resistance to such detours from owners and occupiers of cultivated land in the days before enclosure, and the widest spread of alternative tracks occurred on unenclosed wastes. Enclosure brought with it the definition of the bounds of private property as hedges and walls between which highways were confined more narrowly. Fans of divergent tracks occur most where much-frequented roads had to climb slopes across commons of grass and furze. In our first edition we illustrated such tracks at Beacon Hill near Bulford, in Wiltshire. The roads in fig. 116 spread in an even wider fan once they are clear of the enclosed ground in the valley bottom; this area lies immediately to the south-

[2] The improvement of rivers by canalisation, contemporary with the turnpiking of roads, has not been specifically illustrated, as lying wholly outside the period of this volume.

east of Winchester and a little east of the Itchen valley. Part of the circuit of the Iron Age fort on St Catherine's Hill is visible at the top left.

To appreciate the significance of these tracks some knowledge of the topography is necessary. In a vertical photograph taken from about 3000 feet, the country seems almost flat. In fact, the road that appears on this photograph at the centre of the upper margin is there at an altitude of 150 feet, some forty feet above the level of the flood-plain of the Itchen at Winchester. The road approaches a steep slope which leads up 200 feet to Twyford Down comprising all the lower part of the figure, with the summit of Deacon Hill a little farther to the right. The modern road takes the slope in a bold oblique course; the routes of earlier traffic spread out in a broad fan of trackways. The ploughed fields and golf-course in the lower half of the photograph lie on the Chalk Downs which, at Winchester, delimit both sides of the Itchen valley. The route for traffic leaving Winchester for the downland villages to the south-east also entered the area of fig. 116 on the low ground near the centre of the top margin. Once it had left the Itchen there was no main valley to follow, only steep and dry chalk coombs like that south of St Catherine's Hill, or steep slopes to climb like that delimiting the north side of Deacon Hill, at the right-hand margin of fig. 116.

The tracks on this photograph suggest a branching of routes, but close examination will show that one group of tracks that begins by following a course that might lead to the left-hand side of the photograph, soon swings back where the grass and scrub give way to ploughland in which the tracks appear as soil-marks. These tracks are obliterated in the farther half of the field but they reappear in the grass of a golf-course where they cross and recross several times. In contrast, a modern track, enclosed between hedges, comes up the left-hand side of the fan and continues as a cutting at the edge of the golf-course where a footbridge crosses it near a green. In the light-toned field that extends to the left of the photograph, the dark lines running the length of the field are the remains of ploughed-out lynchets.

Medieval traffic to and from Winchester and the downlands was not simply an exchange of city and village products. Winchester was the county town, the place of the assizes; it had well-endowed religious houses; it was the administrative centre of surrounding estates, and in particular those of the bishops. One of the great fairs of medieval England was held outside the east gate of the city on the slope of St Giles

Fig. 116. Twyford Down. Medieval trackways near Winchester; vertical photograph, April 1967. Scale 1:5500.

Hill. The fair-ground had toll-gates on its east, south and west sides, the north side leading into the city itself. Six of the approach roads (from Romsey, Redbridge, Hursley, Crawley, Cheriton and New Alresford) and the road from the city each had their toll-collectors at fair time. Justice at the fairs was dispensed in courts of Pie Powder, or *pieds poudrés*, named after the dusty feet of the itinerant merchants, recalling the conditions of travel in the pre-Macadam era.

Twyford Down was linked with the old ridgeway eastward to the South Downs, which was the bishop's route to his manors of Cheriton, Beauworth, the two Meons and Hambledon as well as to his borough of Fareham and his palace and park at Waltham. The downland ridge to the south-east, for which the multiple tracks in fig. 116 are making, also carries the Roman road from Portchester and the medieval road from Portsmouth after the foundation of that town in 1194.

Sources

V.C.H. Hants. V (1912) 36–44; account roll from St Giles' fair, 1291–2, printed in J. Z. Titow, *English Rural Society 1200–1350* (1969) 191–5.

117. PADBURY   Buckinghamshire

Padbury has been chosen for a detailed examination of the changes which time has brought to the tracks of an open-field parish. The large-scale plan of 1591, among the Hovenden maps at All Souls College, Oxford, has already been referred to in chapter 3 (p. 31). The original is unsuitable for reproduction at a reduced scale and in fig. 117B, which is based upon it, the principal features are indicated conventionally. A modern map of the parish is also shown for comparison (fig. 117C).

In 1591 the village was composed essentially of a nucleus of houses facing each other along a street which ran from the church and manor down to the mill where the 'bury' suggests an older fortified earthwork. At the lower end of the village there had also been development around three sides of a small 'island' -green (*Old End*) upon which the 1591 map shows two houses standing. Apart from the irregularities thus introduced, there was a back-lane on either side of the crofts. At more than one point the back-lane was connected to the main street by an alley.

The principal axis of the modern map, in contrast, is the main road (once a turnpike) from Buckingham to Winslow. This cuts through the north end of the village but came too late to attract any ribbon building. In 1591 there was a *Buckingham Waye* but, as fig. 117B shows, it was an unimportant track, the last part of its course within Padbury parish being only a footpath across open-field strips. The Elizabethan road system, continuing the medieval arrangement, can be seen to be based not on a long-distance thoroughfare but on seven tracks which have the village street as their starting point and the open-field strips and furlongs as their principal objective. Four of these tracks threw off branches shortly after leaving the village and there are eight shorter cross-tracks joining some of these branches and completing the system of access for husbandmen going with their animals from their homes in the village to work in the fields.

Beside the tracks, fig. 117B shows several other unshaded areas where the cartographer in 1591 did not extend his multitude of tiny strips, each with its occupier's name. Near the village were the enclosed crofts attached to each house and some empty plots where houses had probably once stood. There were three pieces of early enclosure: one near the church and manor; one at *Norburye* and the third alongside the *Mylne* and the millrace. In the north, beyond *Hedge Field* were the enclosed *Leaes* (Leys). In the south was the broad finger of *Bradmore Meadowe* projecting into *West Field* while smaller meadows lay near the streams which formed the parish boundary on three sides. Several of the minor roads between the furlongs of the open-field area took advantage of wet land more suited for grass than the plough: *Pinnocke Slade* and *Turninge Slade* are marked in *East Field*.

Apart from the turnpike, only three metalled roads remain in Padbury at the present time now that enclosed fields have replaced the open-field strips, and one of these three is the very short stretch between Norbury and Oxlane Bridge. The metalled road to the north-east follows the line of the former *St Katherine's Waye* and *Stighgate Waye*; from it run the unmetalled tracks giving access to the post-enclosure farmsteads (Hedges Farm, Grange, and Low Farm). Folly Farm and Dunstall Lodge lie on the turnpike and need no access-ways, but the other post-enclosure farms in the former West Field (Padburyhill Farm and Westhill Farm) have bridle roads which follow the new hedges. Many of the field-tracks of the 1591 plan are no longer in being, although the course of several of them may still be seen as a grassy raised causeway among the ridge-and-furrow. One of the medieval tracks, however, has been preserved in the course of a meandering footpath which leads north-eastwards from the church; this was *Whadden Waye* in 1591, but it is unlikely to be much in use today when Whaddon can be reached along firm, metalled roads following a course as direct as the former field-way.

The air photograph (fig. 117A) views the village from the south-west, the church being half-concealed among the trees. The back-lanes have been reduced to footpaths, and the station road and adjacent post-war houses have transformed *Old End*. The straight course of the turnpike can be seen, crossing the upper half of the photograph, with the more sinuous course of *St Katherine's Waye* confined within hedges towards the top margin. The enclosed fields in the foreground were formerly part of *West Field*.

Source

1591 map: Hovenden maps, All Souls College, Oxford.

Fig. 117A. Padbury; looking NE, April 1953.

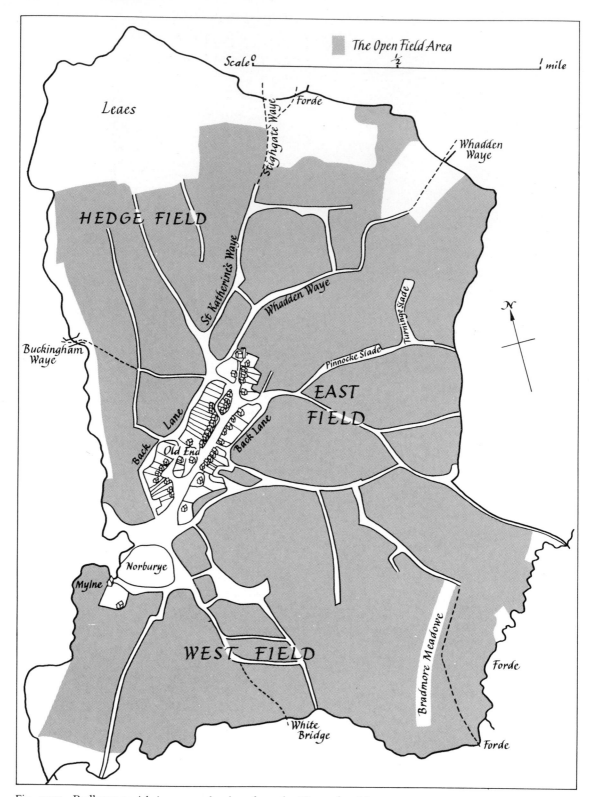

The Open Field Area

Scale 0   ½   1 mile

Leaes

HEDGE FIELD

Forde

Stighgate Waye

Whadden Waye

St Katherine's Waye

Whadden Waye

Buckingham Waye

Turninge Slade

Pinnocke Slade

EAST FIELD

Back Lane

Old End

Back Lane

Norburye

Mylne

N

Bradmore Meadowe

WEST FIELD

White Bridge

Forde

Forde

Fig. 117B. Padbury parish in 1591; plan based on the Hovenden Maps.

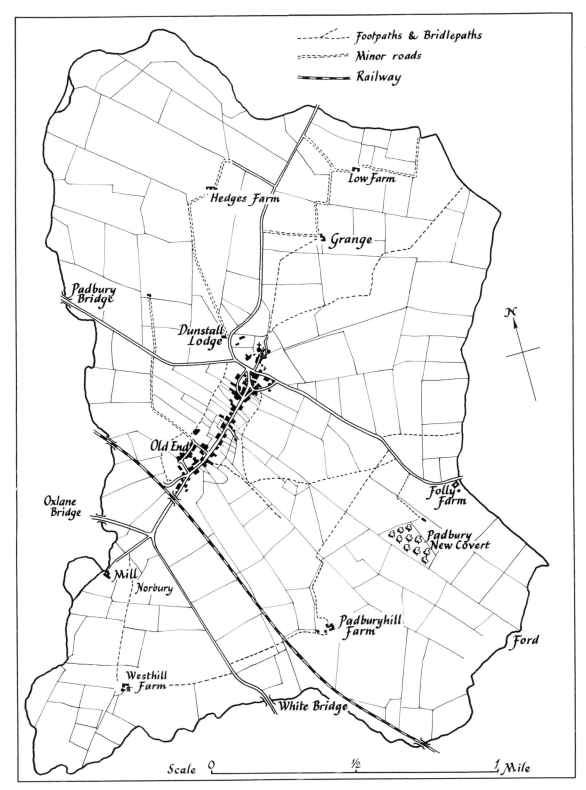

Legend:
- ----- Footpaths & Bridlepaths
- ===== Minor roads
- ▬▬▬ Railway

Low Farm
Hedges Farm
Grange
Padbury Bridge
Dunstall Lodge
N
Old End
Oxlane Bridge
Folly Farm
Padbury New Covert
Mill
Norbury
Padburyhill Farm
Ford
Westhill Farm
White Bridge

Scale 0 —————— ½ —————— 1 Mile

Fig. 117C. Padbury parish in 1955.

II. BRIDGES AND CAUSEWAYS

The medieval bridge is an architectural feature sufficiently common and easy of access to have been well recorded and surveyed long before the coming of air photography, and the important role of bridges in the country's economy is matched by an abundance of references in public records of the Middle Ages and in county records of the mid-sixteenth century onwards. The question nearly always at issue was who should pay for the maintenance of a bridge. Bridges crossed water, and water was often taken as a boundary, whether between parishes, manors, or counties. Thus it was almost inevitable that two parties would be at variance as to where one's responsibility finished and the other's began. The multiplication of traffic in the seventeenth and eighteenth centuries produced 'county' bridges, a charge on the whole county instead of on the immediate locality. A device of respectable medieval antiquity, the toll-bridge, is still occasionally to be found, whereby the cost of maintenance and some reward to the owner is met from the tolls collected from travellers. Grants of *pontage*, licences to collect tolls for a limited period, were frequently made by medieval kings, and the duty to make (and repair) bridges found its way into clause 23 of Magna Carta.

The opportunity of seeing a genuine medieval bridge is in fact rather greater than that of seeing an untouched medieval manor house.[3] In Huntingdonshire, for example, where only three medieval manors are to be found, there are seven or eight medieval bridges.[4] The importance of the bridge, and the bridgehead street, in the plans of St Ives and St Neots has already been indicated, and several other photographs illustrate medieval town and village bridges. At Chelmsford (p. 222) the very existence and development of the Bishop of London's new town hinged solely upon his enterprise in erecting a bridge. The Bishops of Durham provided the bridges for the east and west approaches to their city, as well as for the southern approach from Yorkshire into their county palatine across the Tees at Yarm. The chapels built into the bridges at Wakefield and Huntingdon are a reminder that gifts to endow bridges were a proper object of pious charity.

The actual point of crossing would be deter-

mined by favourable physical conditions, such as a narrow channel and a firm foundation in the river-bed, together with a good approach across solid ground. The same conditions had favoured fords, and many later medieval bridges represent simply the replacement of a ford. Where an old crossing proved inadequate, the construction of a new bridge at a different point soon diverted traffic and seriously challenged the fortunes of any village which had depended upon the old route. Boroughbridge grew up in the fields of Aldborough at the point where the diverted Great North Road crossed the Ure by the new Norman bridge. A small shift in position, when an old bridge has been replaced by an improved structure, is often indicated by a lack of alignment between the medieval street plan and the bridge now in use. Telford's 'Welsh Bridge' at Shrewsbury shows by its position that it appeared on the scene much later than the main medieval streets which lead to a focus elsewhere, while the streets on the south bank of the Tweed at Berwick are clearly aligned to the old bridge there.

Over low-lying ground it was necessary to give a firm foundation for an approach road across water-meadows, especially those liable to floods. The medieval bridge from Godmanchester to Huntingdon is approached by a series of small arches linked to form a causeway, but this is a miniature compared with the long causeways of the neighbouring fenlands, which are in the form of raised embankments for the roads with intermittent bridges to allow the passage of streams, drains and flood water.

118. ALDRETH CAUSEWAY
Cambridgeshire

Need for access to the islands of the Fens led to the construction of causeways for the passage of foot- and wheeled-traffic. The Isle of Ely with its cathedral and market-town was served in the Middle Ages by two landward causeways. On the south-east, Stuntney Causeway led across the Ouse to Soham and the higher ground near Newmarket; while to the south-west a road led out through Haddenham and Aldreth, where a long neck of firm ground protrudes into the fen. The photograph (fig. 118) shows the road from Ely approaching along this neck, dropping slowly down from Haddenham to the village of Aldreth on the fen edge. To reach solid ground near Willingham some two miles of fen and then the River Ouse had to be crossed.

[3] A survey of old English bridges will be found in E. Jervoise, *The Ancient Bridges of ... England*, 3 vols. (1930–2).

[4] R.C.H.M. *Huntingdonshire* (1926): Alconbury, Alconbury Weston, one or possibly two at Huntingdon, St Ives, St Neots, Somersham and Spaldwick.

Fig. 118. Aldreth Causeway; looking NE, June 1951.

The medieval causeway (in the foreground) still carries a modern lane; its direct course can be seen beginning at the near end of the village. Its straightness contrasts with the gentle curve of the ridge-road on the higher ground.

The construction of both these causeways seems to date from the late eleventh or early twelfth century. Stuntney Causeway was built in the time of Bishop Hervey (1109–31), and tradition ascribes the Aldreth Causeway either to that bishop or to William I (1066–87). The first documentary reference, however, is in 1172–3, when a payment appears in the Pipe Roll. At Aldreth there may have been an earlier ferry. In 1169 the Pipe Roll records a 'passage for boats' here. The boats are mentioned again in 1279 when the bridge was reported to have been broken since 1263. The toll was then a halfpenny for a man and horse or one farthing for a man on foot. The upkeep of the causeway was the collective responsibility of certain of the bishop's manors and tenants in the Isle. The manors of Outwell and Upwell, twenty miles away, were responsible for forty-four perches of it. As late as 1361 there were duties of providing an armed man to guard the bridge of Aldreth against the king's enemies if the Isle were attacked. The causeway and the 'High Bridge' over the Ouse at the end of it have only a minor place in modern communications. In the late seventeenth century the present main road to Ely via Stretham (A10) came into use, and within a hundred years had captured the traffic from the Aldreth route.

Sources

V.C.H. Cambs. IV (1953) 141 and references there cited; E. Miller, *The Abbey and Bishopric of Ely* (1951) 158 and 226; *Rot. Hund.* II. 452.

INDEX